Contractor's Guide to the Building Code

by Jack M. Hageman

Based on the 1997 Uniform Building Code™

Craftsman Book Company
6058 Corte del Cedro / P.O. Box 6500
Carlsbad, CA 92018

Acknowledgments

All portions of the **Uniform Building Code**™ are reproduced from the 1997 edition, ©1997, with the permission of the publisher, the International Conference of Building Officials (ICBO), 5360 Workman Mill Road, Whittier, CA 90601.

All portions of the **Uniform Plumbing Code**™ are reproduced from the 1997 edition, ©1997, with the permission of the publishers, the International Association of Plumbing and Mechanical Officials (IAPMO), 20001 Walnut Drive South, Walnut, CA 91789.

All portions of the **Uniform Mechanical Code**™ are reproduced from the 1997 edition, ©1997, with the permission of the publisher, the International Conference of Building Officials.

The author expresses his thanks to ICBO and IAPMO for their assistance and permission to use charts, tables and quotes from their respective books. However, the interpretation, summaries and comments listed herein are solely the responsibility of the author and bear no reflection on the publishers of the Uniform Building Code, the Uniform Plumbing Code, the Uniform Mechanical Code, or the publishers of this book.

Craftsman Book Company acknowledges and thanks the dedicated staff at the International Conference of Building Officials (ICBO) for reviewing portions of the text and providing valuable input and materials to make this a more accurate and useful reference.

Library of Congress Cataloging-in-Publication Data

Hageman, Jack M.
Contractor's guide to the building code / by Jack M. Hageman.
p. cm.
"Based on the 1997 Uniform Building Code."
Includes index.
ISBN 1-57218-058-7
1. Building laws—United States—Popular works. 2. Building-Standards—United States.
3. Construction industry—Standards—United States. I. Title.
KF5701.Z95H34 1998
343.73'07869—DC21   98-6825
                                                 CIP

First edition	©1983 Craftsman Book Company
Second edition	©1990 Craftsman Book Company
Third edition	©1992 Craftsman Book Company
Fourth edition	©1996 Craftsman Book Company
Fifth edition	©1998 Craftsman Book Company

Second printing 1999

Cartoons by John R. Hageman

Contents

Introduction to the Last Guide of the Century

This fifth edition of **Contractor's Guide to the Building Code** will be the last guide to the *Uniform Building Code*. The next will be a guide to the *International Building Code*, which is scheduled for release in April, 2000.

What other changes do we have to look forward to? We'll just have to wait and see. You've probably already noticed the change in the size of the Code. It's now 8½ by 11 inches. And I've been told there may be a change in the way seismic calculations are made.

I've looked at a copy of the "working draft" of the International Building Code, and it looks good — forthright and probably easier to use.

In the 1997 edition of the *UBC*, you'll find that two chapters have been completely revised. In the first, Chapter 10, *Means of Egress*, there are no surprises. What they accomplished was a more orderly presentation. The second, Chapter 23, *Wood*, was reorganized in such a way that you may be scratching your head. And they renumbered all the lumber tables. This might be confusing, especially if you use the tables a lot and are used to certain numbers. I've tried to straighten it out for you.

For years, builders have been frustrated by the index that's in the *UBC*. While a building inspector knows the code and what categories and subcategories to look under, it often proves impossible for a builder who looks under the terms he commonly uses. At the request of my publisher, I sat down with the 1997 edition of the *UBC*, cranked up my trusty computer, and completed a comprehensive index. This one's easy to use, tells you what page to look on, and uses the terms builders use, not the technical legal ones the Code is based on. You can order a copy using the order form at the back of this book. It's also available hole-punched so it fits in the binder with your copy of the *UBC*.

Where I Come From

A lot of what's in the code is either just good sense or what good craftsmanship demands. Maybe that's why most of the building inspectors you meet consider themselves both reasonable people and good judges of craftsmanship. It's part of their job, or should be.

I took woodshop classes in high school and spent a lot of weekends working for a general contractor. To this day I enjoy laying wood shingles. I also did a lot of carpentry in the Civilian Conservation Corps. For my younger readers, the CCC was one of President Roosevelt's make-work programs. It was supposed to get us out of the Great Depression. As it turned out, the CCC didn't do it. World War II did. But the CCC taught me how to be a carpenter.

I don't consider myself a finish carpenter, mostly because I don't have enough patience for that kind of work. But I know a stud from a joist, can drive a straight nail, and enjoy the smell of a newly-framed house. That doesn't really qualify me as a carpenter. But maybe it's enough to make me a retired carpenter.

When I got out of the Army in 1946, I was older that most of the young bucks that were flooding into the construction trades. I thought I was smarter too. So I took on-the-job training as an architectural draftsman. As a draftsman and designer I had to know the code. Of course, it was a lot easier in those days. The entire building code was a slim little book then, not much thicker than my wallet. You could carry it around in your back pocket. Try doing that today.

Eventually I hung out my shingle as a construction contractor. Custom home building, spec building and remodeling can be the fastest legal way I know to get rich with only a few tools, a little capital and no special knowledge. I didn't get rich. But I made a good living and more than a few good friends in the business. And I'm proud of the product I put out: good homes where people can raise families.

No one will ever erect a monument in my memory. That's OK. I don't need it. The homes I built in those days are monument enough. When I drive by one, I still remember having built it. I don't know the people living there and they don't know me. But I had an influence on their lives, for the better, I hope. And when I notice what these homes are selling for now, I wince. Right now I'd be one of the richest people in America if I'd built those homes and never sold one, just rented them out. That's what I should have done. But it never occurred to me at the time.

By 1965 I'd pretty well burned myself out in the contracting business. Basically, it's a young man's game, and I wasn't young anymore. When the job of building inspector opened up in Kennewick, Washington in 1965, I applied. Inspecting was about the only thing I hadn't done in construction. And if knowing the code qualified me for the job, I was qualified.

1

'Cuz it says so in *The Book!*"

Why Do I Need A Permit?

One of the most common complaints I used to hear from architects, engineers and contractors was that there were too many different building codes. It seemed like every city, county and state had its own idea about what was good construction and what was bad construction.

Of course, every city, county and state has the perfect right to make up its own laws, ordinances or regulations — including laws that control building. There was a time when most did. But the result was far too many different codes. What was perfectly acceptable in one community may have been strictly prohibited in the community right next door. That's foolish.

The proliferation of codes made the task of architects, builders and inspectors far more difficult than it had to be. Fortunately, times have changed. Now, most communities have adopted one of the three model codes. The

Uniform Building Code is by far the most used, followed by the National Building Code, and then the Standard Building Code.

Some cities still write their own codes, usually because their first code was adopted before there was a national model code. Inertia keeps some of these cities from replacing their do-it-yourself code with a modern national code. But even some of these cities are switching. Eventually I expect they all will. It's to everyone's advantage to reduce the differences between building codes.

Whatever the code in your city, if you're a builder, you're going to have building code problems. Every contractor has had an inspector hold up his job or delay a permit until some minor discrepancy is handled just the way the code requires. From your standpoint, following the code is usually just an annoying and expensive necessity. You know how to build properly, and don't need a government agency telling you how. But the building department, and probably the owner or architect that set your project in motion, regard the code as a good defense against poor practice that might otherwise plague generations of occupants of the building you erect.

No matter what your viewpoint, the building code is a fact of life that every builder must deal with. Your objective, and mine in writing this book, is to make following the code as simple, painless and inexpensive as possible.

Every construction contract you sign assumes that you will build according to the code. You aren't going to get paid until what you build has passed inspection. It's no defense that your estimate didn't include what the inspector demands. You're assumed to know the code and build every project accordingly.

Unfortunately, knowing the code isn't easy. The building code is a complex law intended to be enforced rather than read and understood. The code book itself doesn't have a good index. Related subjects are covered in widely separated sections (although the latest editions have done much to correct this). Some hard-to-understand sections refer to sections that are even harder to follow. The code seems to grow larger and more complex every time it's revised. There are exceptions, within exceptions, within other exceptions. A lawyer used to handling intricate tax problems would feel right at home with the building code.

But you can't spend a career mastering the building code. At least you shouldn't. Your job is building, not nit-picking. As a builder you need to know only enough to stay out of trouble and avoid expensive mistakes. This book will help. You also need the code itself, of course. The manual you're now reading isn't the code, so don't try to quote from it to any building inspectors. They may not be impressed. Instead, use this manual as your answer book on code problems. Go to the chapter or section in this book that addresses the problem you're having. Read enough so you

have some background on what the code demands. Then go to the code itself, if necessary, to sort out the fine details. Use the index in this manual to direct you to the code sections that apply to your situation. This should save you hours of valuable time and prevent expensive mistakes.

Now a word about the code itself. The code we're talking about is the 1997 edition of the Uniform Building Code, as published by the International Conference of Building Officials in Whittier, California. The ICBO is a non-profit organization founded in 1922. More than 3,300 city and county building departments and state agencies all across the U.S. belong to the ICBO, and participate in drafting and approving the model code. Many other organizations, companies and private individuals participate in the code drafting and revising process. The ICBO also sponsors research in the field of building safety.

Every three years the code or its revisions are republished as a recommendation to the building department members of the ICBO. Each county or city then decides if it will adopt the revisions as a regulation for that community. Most adopt the revisions routinely. The model code the ICBO publishes is a very well-researched and highly persuasive document. But many communities change some sections, delete others or add material they feel is important. So the code in force in your community may not be exactly like the most recent code published by the ICBO.

Be aware that there are two other "model" building codes in the U.S. The Building Officials and Code Administrators International and the Southern Building Code Congress International also offer model codes. These have been adopted by many communities east of the Mississippi. But the ICBO code is the most widely adopted. And the differences between all three major model codes are becoming less significant. After all, what's good building practice west of the Mississippi should also be good practice east of the Mississippi.

You need a copy of the current building code in force in the communities where you do business. Some bookstores sell the UBC. If your local bookstore doesn't have a copy, buy it directly from the ICBO. The address is:

International Conference of Building Officials
5360 Workman Mill Road
Whittier, California 90601-2298
(562) 699-0541

The ICBO will accept phone orders on a charge card. Their order department number is (800) 284-4406, and the fax number is (888) 329-4226. But every building department that really wants to help contractors follow the code should sell it right over the counter at every office. Only your building department has the official version enforced in your community. If the inspector can't supply one, have him refer you to a convenient source. The building department expects you to know and follow the code; expect them to furnish you with a copy at reasonable cost.

No matter how carefully you build and how knowledgeable you are about the code, you're going to have an occasional dispute with an inspector. Let me offer some advice. I've stood on the inspector's side of the counter through many disputes with contractors and have heard most of the arguments. You're not going to win very many direct confrontations with a building department. But there's a lot you *can* do to get them to see your side of the argument.

First, understand that the building department holds all the best cards. They can make any builder's life very unpleasant and cost him a lot of money. They have the full power of government behind them and can use it effectively to compel compliance on your part. But they would usually prefer to have your voluntary cooperation.

Adopt this attitude toward the building department and inspectors you deal with: "You have a job to do. I have a job to do. Together we're going to put up a building that both you and I as professionals in the construction industry will be proud of." The more you think of building officials as implacable adversaries, the more likely they will become just that.

In a dispute with the building department, you have one point in your favor. The inspector didn't make the rules and can't write the code to fit your situation. He can only enforce the code as it's written. An inspector can require anything the code demands. But that's all! He's on very shaky ground if he insists on something that isn't in the code book. That's why you need a copy of the code. If a dispute arises, have the inspector cite the specific section and words involved. Then read those words yourself in your copy of the code. If those words don't support the inspector's position, you're going to win the point.

Of course, inspectors make a living by knowing the code. They probably know it much better than you ever will. But they can be wrong. So don't be afraid to request reference to a specific code section, read that section, and form your own opinion of what is required. If the inspector is wrong and can't be persuaded to change his mind, there's a perfectly good appeal process available to every contractor. More on that later in this chapter.

Inspectors know they can't enforce what the code doesn't require. So the highly-experienced inspectors and plans examiners who wrote the code built some "wiggle room" into the book. That way they can maneuver and negotiate where that may be in the best interest of everyone concerned. Section 104.2.1 says in part:

The building official shall have the power to render interpretations of this code and to adopt and enforce rules and supplemental regulations to clarify the application of its provisions. Such interpretations, rules and regulations shall be in conformance with the intent and purpose of this code.

In simple language this means the building department has a lot of discretion.

Every experienced contractor has heard an inspector say that the code actually requires this or that, "but it will be OK if you handle it this way." No, he's not giving away the store. He's just trying to get the result the code intends while saving you some time, trouble and money.

If an inspector seems to be giving you a favorable interpretation of the code, it's probably because he (or she) wants your cooperation on some point that's not too clear in the code. You're usually better off cooperating when an inspector complains about some minor point that's vague or omitted in the code. If you demand strict interpretation of code sections, you may get exactly that. And the inspector can cite more sections that can be enforced strictly than you ever thought possible. The point is worth emphasizing: Cooperation will save you more money than confrontation will save you.

Sometimes you're going to face a code issue so important that there's no easy way to compromise with the inspector. Then you'll have to take it up with the head of the building department. Before going through the appeal procedure explained in this chapter, request a meeting with one of the senior inspectors or the "building official." Offer to meet early in the morning before the inspectors start their field work. Be sure both the inspector involved and his supervisor can be at this meeting. Prepare your case very carefully. Show that the code doesn't really require what you are being asked to do, or point out an alternative that will save money and is just as good. Above all, show that you're a conscientious, professional, cooperative contractor interested in quality construction. Invite a negotiated settlement on the issue in dispute. More than likely you'll get one if any legitimate compromise is possible.

But don't expect any inspector to waive a clear code requirement just to save you money or trouble, especially if you're asking for special treatment other contractors don't receive. Code protection is too valuable to waive on a whim. If you've traveled in other countries where no codes exist or where codes aren't enforced, you know how important our building codes are. And be aware that cities and counties are liable for the mistakes their building departments make. Owners of defective buildings have recovered substantial sums from municipal governments that didn't enforce the building code they adopted. All building officials know the importance of the code they administer — and that they can be held liable.

Purpose of the Code

Several points are worth mentioning before we begin careful examination of code sections. One of these is the purpose of the code. Section 101.2 makes it clear that health, safety and protecting property are the primary aims of the code:

The purpose of this code is to provide minimum standards to safeguard life or limb, health, property and public welfare by regulating and controlling the design, construction, quality of materials, use and occupancy, location and maintenance of all buildings and structures within this jurisdiction and certain equipment specifically regulated herein.

The purpose of this code is not to create or otherwise establish or designate any particular class or group of persons who will or should be especially protected or benefited by the terms of this code.

Notice the words "minimum standards" in the first sentence. You can build to higher standards. Nearly every building you put up will include far more than the code requires. But it must also include everything in the code.

There's an important point in Section 101.2 if you ever have to dispute some code interpretation. Argue that what you want to do protects health, safety and property as well as, or better than, what the code requires.

Can I Use That Material?

The building code doesn't demand that you use only the methods and materials it lists. Section 104.2.8 states the following:

The provisions of this code are not intended to prevent the use of any material, alternate design or method of construction not specifically prescribed by this code, provided any alternate has been approved and its use authorized by the building official.

"Building official" is the title of the senior person in the building department office. He (or she) may require proof that the method or material conforms to the intent of the code. If you're thinking about using a new method or material, something that hasn't had much use in your area, check with the building official *beforehand*.

For example, earth-sheltered structures are being built in some areas. Many inspectors throw up their hands at inspecting earth-sheltered buildings. Why? Because they're not adequately covered in the code. This is an area where you have to look at the intent of the code and not the literal meaning.

Unfortunately, many inspectors don't have the experience or the time to do much evaluation. And there are some who feel that the only way they can prove they're doing their job is to find something wrong with every project. They forget that the purpose of the code is to make construction safe, not to impede progress.

Because it's a law, the building code is written in "legalese." To either enforce the code or comply with it, you have to first understand it. As I said, that's not always easy. And, to make matters worse, the code is written to give (or even require) the inspector a chance to use good common sense. That takes both knowledge and experience. Fortunately, most inspectors have the knowledge and experience required of professionals in their field.

When an inspector sees something that isn't covered in the code, a good inspector will always start doing some homework. Some less-experienced inspectors might see the same thing, look up wide-eyed and say: "I can't find it in the book, so you can't use that material or do it that way." Fortunately, that isn't what the code says. Section 104.2.8 allows use of any material or method that is approved by the building department in your community, even if it isn't approved specifically in the code itself.

The Appeal Process

"That's fine," you say. "But how can I get approval for what I want to do?" Section 105.1 is titled *Board of Appeals*. This section says that you have the right to appeal any inspector's decision.

105.1 General. In order to hear and decide appeals of orders, decisions or determinations made by the building official relative to the application and interpretation of this code, there shall be and is hereby created a board of appeals consisting of members who are qualified by experience and training to pass on matters pertaining to building construction and who are not employees of the jurisdiction. The building official shall be an ex officio member and shall act as secretary to said board but shall have no vote on any matter before the board. The board of appeals shall be appointed by the governing body and shall hold office at its pleasure. The board shall adopt rules of procedure for conducting its business and shall render all decisions and findings in writing to the appellant with a duplicate copy to the building official.

105.2 Limitations of Authority. The board of appeals shall have no authority relative to interpretation of the administrative provisions of this code nor shall the board be empowered to waive requirements of this code.

A key phrase here is that the board members "are qualified by experience and training . . . ." So even if the inspector lacks construction knowledge, the people you are appealing to should have it. And if what you're trying to do with your material is controversial, the inspector may want you to appeal just to get the opinion of other experts.

Notice also that Section 105.2 clearly states that the board can't waive any provisions of the code. That means you can't slip anything past the board just because you asked.

When Is a Permit Needed?

Section 106.1 tells you when you'll need a permit:

106.1 Permits Required. *Except as specified in Section 106.2, no building or structure regulated by this code shall be erected, constructed, enlarged, altered, repaired, moved, improved, removed, converted or demolished unless a separate permit for each building or structure has first been obtained from the building official.*

That's pretty broad language. Almost any type of construction, no matter how minor, needs a building permit. Section 106.2 exempts certain types of work. Most important in these exemptions are small out-buildings such as playhouses, small walls and fences, and finish work like painting and paperhanging. Everything else needs a permit.

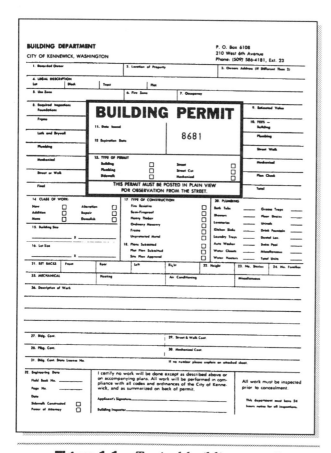

Figure 1-1 *Typical building permit*

Figure 1-1 shows a typical building permit. Permit fees are set by the county or city. They're calculated to pay most of the costs of the building department. (That way, tax money doesn't support your building department.) Those who use the services pay for them. Figure 1-2 shows the permit fee schedule recommended by the Uniform Building Code. This fee schedule was probably used when the code was adopted in your community. But check with your local department to be sure.

Demolition of Buildings

You need a permit to remove or demolish a building too. This usually requires a small fee which covers the cost of issuing the permit. A copy of every permit issued goes to the tax assessor. This is the assessor's cue to do some checking. Someone is about to have their tax rate changed.

Many cities and counties now have ordinances that control unsafe or dilapidated buildings. Even if the city requires that a building be demolished, you'll still need a demolition permit.

Posting the Permit

Always post the building permit and inspection record card on the site. In some jurisdictions, you only have to post the inspection card. There must be someplace the inspector can sign that a required inspection has been made. This is your guarantee that he has been there and approved the job to that point. If your job doesn't pass the inspection, the inspector will leave a Notice of Non-Compliance or a Correction Notice explaining what you have to correct before you can proceed. (See Figure 1-3.)

Many people think that work inside a building doesn't require a permit. If you're doing work exempted by the code, such as replacing kitchen cabinets, that assumption is correct. But any remodeling or renovation that isn't exempt will require a permit.

TABLE 1-A—BUILDING PERMIT FEES

TOTAL VALUATION	FEE
$1.00 to $500.00	$23.50
$501.00 to $2,000.00	$23.50 for the first $500.00 plus $3.05 for each additional $100.00, or fraction thereof, to and including $2,000.00
$2,001.00 to $25,000.00	$69.25 for the first $2,000.00 plus $14.00 for each additional $1,000.00, or fraction thereof, to and including $25,000.00
$25,001.00 to $50,000.00	$391.75 for the first $25,000.00 plus $10.10 for each additional $1,000.00, or fraction thereof, to and including $50,000.00
$50,001.00 to $100,000.00	$643.75 for the first $50,000.00 plus $7.00 for each additional $1,000.00, or fraction thereof, to and including $100,000.00
$100,001.00 to $500,000.00	$993.75 for the first $100,000.00 plus $5.60 for each additional $1,000.00, or fraction thereof, to and including $500,000.00
$500,001.00 to $1,000,000.00	$3,233.75 for the first $500,000.00 plus $4.75 for each additional $1,000.00, or fraction thereof, to and including $1,000,000.00
$1,000,001.00 and up	$5,608.75 for the first $1,000,000.00 plus $3.65 for each additional $1,000.00, or fraction thereof

Other Inspections and Fees:
1. Inspections outside of normal business hours .... $47.00 per hour[1]
   (minimum charge—two hours)
2. Reinspection fees assessed under provisions of Section 305.8 .... $47.00 per hour[1]
3. Inspections for which no fee is specifically indicated .... $47.00 per hour[1]
   (minimum charge—one-half hour)
4. Additional plan review required by changes, additions or revisions to plans .... $47.00 per hour[1]
   (minimum charge—one-half hour)
5. For use of outside consultants for plan checking and inspections, or both .... Actual costs[2]

[1]Or the total hourly cost to the jurisdiction, whichever is the greatest. This cost shall include supervision, overhead, equipment, hourly wages and fringe benefits of the employees involved.
[2]Actual costs include administrative and overhead costs.

From the Uniform Building Code, ©1997, ICBO

Figure 1-2 *Building permit fees*

This brings up a point. I used to be a building inspector. As I traveled around my city, I would notice construction materials or rubble piled near a back door, in a driveway or under a carport. This almost always meant that work of some kind was going on inside. I usually checked with our office to see if there was a permit for work at that address. If not, I would have a little talk with the occupant. I tried not to be heavy-handed. And a little tact usually paid off. They usually wanted to know who squealed on them, never realizing that they squealed on themselves. A pile of rubble is a dead giveaway every time.

Right of Entry

Section 104.2.3 gives the building official the authority to make any necessary inspections:

Right of entry. When it is necessary to make an inspection to enforce the provisions of this code, or when the building official has reasonable cause to believe that there exists in a building or upon a premises a condition that is contrary to or in violation of this code that makes the building or premises unsafe, dangerous or hazardous, the building official may enter the building or premises at reasonable times to inspect or to perform the duties imposed by this code, provided that if such building or premises be occupied that credentials be presented to the occupant and entry requested. If such building or premises be unoccupied, the building official shall first make a reasonable effort to locate the owner or other person having charge or control of the building or premises and request entry. If entry is refused, the building official shall have recourse to the remedies provided by law to secure entry.

CITY OF KENNEWICK

INSPECTION DEPARTMENT

CORRECTION NOTICE

IMPORTANT: Call for re-inspection when items are completed.
DO NOT cover until approved.

PROJECT ADDRESS 4321 Anny Place

COMMENTS _____

1) Footing insufficient depth must be

below frostline

2) Backfill under footing not adequate settled

FINAL INSPECTION REQUIRED ON ALL
BUILDINGS BEFORE OCCUPANCY

DATE 11-18-95 ____ SIGNED *I.M.Segman*

DO NOT REMOVE

Figure 1-3 *Correction notice*

This right of entry is seldom needed. And it isn't nearly as ferocious as it sounds. Most people are cooperative, and most building inspectors use this right judiciously.

Required Inspections

A permit always requires some sort of inspection. The inspection depends on the scope of the job. It can be a simple drive-by to see if the obvious has been completed, such as in the case of a re-roof. Or there may be twelve to sixteen highly technical inspections. For most residential and small commercial work, there are five required inspections, set forth in Section 108:

1) *108.5.2 Foundation inspection.* This is made after the trenches have been exca-

vated, the forms erected, and all the materials for the foundation delivered. Concrete supplied by the transit mix truck doesn't have to be on the site during inspection.

2) *108.5.3 Concrete slab or under-floor inspection.* This is made after all in-slab or under-floor building service equipment, conduit, piping accessories and their ancillary equipment items are in place, but before any concrete is poured or floor sheathing installed, including the subfloor.

3) *108.5.4 Frame inspection.* This is made after the roof, all framing, fire blocking and bracing are in place; chimneys and vents are complete; and after the rough electrical, plumbing and heating wires, pipes and ducts are approved.

4) *108.5.5 Lath or gypsum board inspection.* This is made after all lathing and gypsum board, interior and exterior, are in place, but before any plastering is applied or before gypsum board joints and fasteners are taped and finished.

5) *108.5.6 Final inspection.* This is made after finish grading, when the building has been completed and is ready for occupancy.

In addition to these, there are a number of special inspections that may be required by the building code. The inspections required depend on the scope of the project. For example, the code may require special inspections or tests of concrete, reinforcing steel and prestressing steel, welding, high-strength bolting, structural masonry, reinforced gypsum concrete, insulating concrete fill, spray-applied fireproofing, piling, drilled piers and caissons, special grading, excavation, or backfill. And of course, the building official can add any other tests or inspections that he feels are needed.

If an inspection shows that the project is not acceptable, a correction notice is issued and another inspection scheduled. The project can't continue until the project passes on reinspection. Usually there will be a fee for each reinspection. Larger projects, such as major shopping malls and multi-story buildings, often require a full-time inspector on the job. This inspector's salary is paid by the owner, either directly or through his contractor. In most cities and counties, new construction requires a Certificate of Occupancy before anyone can occupy the building and before utility companies can begin serving the building. This certificate is issued when the inspector signs off on the final inspection.

The Inspector Doesn't Like the Way You Did It

Occasionally, an inspector finds a job that could be done better using a different method. He may offer advice, and probably will. But his advice isn't binding unless it's supported by either the code or a local ordinance. He can stop the job for safety reasons, but only if the code backs him up. If something isn't in the code, he can't enforce it. You have the right to ask what section of the code is being invoked. And you always have the right to appeal the inspector's decision.

Some building inspectors are pretty good craftsmen themselves. It may be to your advantage to heed their advice. But an inspector isn't really inspecting the craftsmanship of your building unless craftsmanship is required by ordinance. It seldom is. Craftsmanship is a matter of judgment, nothing more. Your opinion is just as good as his, maybe better. But if poor craftsmanship weakens a building or makes it unsafe, the inspector will probably cite some code sections that back up his opinion. Figure

Figure 1-4 *This chimney is legal, but . . .*

1-4 shows some questionable workmanship, but it meets the code. You decide if that's the kind of work you want to be known for.

I've often used a little charm to get shoddy work improved. I once visited a house where the trim around a split entry stairway had been butted in square, without mitering. I mentioned this to the contractor and he jumped on me about exceeding my authority. "Besides," he added, "who'll ever know?"

"Everyone will," I assured him with charm, "because I'm the biggest tattletale in town and I can hardly wait to start telling everyone you do this kind of work." When I came back later, all the corners had been neatly mitered.

Who Drew These Stupid Plans?

For many years I was a building inspector and plans examiner. What I did most was find mistakes made by architects, designers and contractors. That put me on the hot seat. No one likes to be told they made a mistake, especially a dumb mistake. But that was my job. So I tried to do it without ruffling any more feathers or crushing any more inflated egos than necessary.

Sometimes I couldn't settle a dispute without a squawk. Architects hate to admit they blew it. The truth is, though, that most architects don't have more than a basic knowledge of building codes. Architecture schools teach good design, not code compliance. Very few offer classes on the building code. And I don't know any that require a test on the code before graduating. Maybe that's a mistake.

I'd like to claim that all building inspectors and plans examiners are code experts. Like architects, they should be. But many aren't. That's too bad. Plan checking is an important part of what should happen in every building department. If both the architect and the plans examiner miss something, the owner's going to have to live (or die) with the mistake.

Since the first edition of this book was published in 1982, I've talked to lots of building inspectors. Nearly all claim to run a tight ship. But I also talk to the contractors they deal with. From them I get a different story. One contractor I talked to says his local building department sends *all* plans out to a plan checking company for review and approval. Doesn't anyone at the building department know enough about the code to approve plans? I think that adds to the cost and delays the job. But maybe I'm old fashioned. You be the judge.

So what kind of mistakes do you find on plans for a home or small commercial building? Nothing serious, usually. I do recall one time, however, when I found a room that had no door. I'm serious! No way in or out. I used to draw plans - back in the days when I was a contractor. I can guess what happened. The owner asked the designer to move a door from one wall to another. The draftsman erased the old door, filled in the wall section, took a coffee break, and then forgot to add the new opening. No one caught it.

My point is that construction is too expensive and too permanent to be careless about design and code compliance And, unfortunately, the code is written so that only the careful and determined will understand it completely.

I recall a hospital addition I checked. According to the code, one area had to be contained by latched fire doors. Another section of the code said those doors had to be instantly operable. What would you do?

I'd drop that one like a hot potato.

2

"His Nibs will see you now."

Getting Your Permit

If you're just replacing some worn-out shingles, getting a permit is simply a matter of paying the fee down at the building department. The plans examiner can check your plan (or sketch) right at the counter and issue a permit immediately. But if you're building anything more complex, there's a lot more involved.

Usually the plans examiner will need a week or so to study your plans and find the discrepancies. He or she will then return the plans and ask you to make the changes needed. Your architect or designer then makes the revisions and you resubmit the plans for approval. If the revised set meets the plans examiner's approval, your permit should be granted a week or so later. If more changes are needed, you'll have to make those changes and submit the plans again.

How long will it take to get your plans approved? That depends on the size and com-plexity of the project, the backlog in the plans examiner's office, and how good your plans are. As a rule of thumb, allow about a month for a custom home or a small store. Of course, it can go faster — and it can take much longer.

What Plans Are Needed?

The plans and specifications don't have to be drawn by an architect or engineer. Here's what UBC Section 106.3.2 says:

Submittal documents. Plans, specifications, engineering calculations, diagrams, soil investigation reports, special inspection and structural observation programs and other data shall constitute the submittal documents and shall be submitted in one or more sets with each application for a permit. When such plans are not prepared by an architect or engineer, the building official may require the applicant submitting such plans or other data to demonstrate that state law does not require that the plans be prepared by a licensed architect or engineer. The building official may require plans, computations and specifications to be prepared and designed by an engineer or architect licensed by the state to practice as such even if not required by law.

EXCEPTION: *The building official may waive the submission of plans, calculations, construction inspection requirements and other data if it is found that the nature of the work applied for is such that reviewing of plans is not necessary to obtain compliance with this code.*

The code allows exceptions and these vary from place to place. Find out what the requirements are in your area.

Not many building departments have an engineer on staff. In most cases no one in the office is qualified to judge if walls and headers and joists and supports are strong enough. But they do have many charts and tables at their disposal. And of course, everyone knows that 2 x 4s 16 inches on center will hold up the roof. No problem getting plan approval there. But if your project includes anything that might not be strong enough to support the intended load, expect the building department to require review of the plans by a licensed engineer.

The plans examiner will almost certainly accept the opinion of any state-licensed engineer you select. The engineer only has to certify that the plans meet accepted engineering standards. He or she will stamp the plans with a seal, certifying that the design meets accepted standards.

Many building departments request plans for remodeling work. Usually this is to make sure you've really thought carefully about the work that's going to be done. If you rip out a wall, is the ceiling going to collapse? Believe me, it happens. Check with your inspector to find out what plans are needed for your remodeling project.

But what about new construction? To get a permit for new construction you'll need three items:

1) Plans

2) Specifications

3) Engineering data and notes to back up items shown on the plans or the accompanying specifications

Plans vs. Specifications

Plans (also known as working drawings, or blueprints) are a graphic representation of what's being built, and how. Specifications provide details not shown on the plans. For example, the plans may show only an exterior door and a 3'0" x 6'8" opening. The specifications may describe the door as solid core, exterior grade, two-lite, left-hand swing. There is only room for so much detail on the drawings. What won't fit on the plans goes in the specifications. On a small job the specifications may be just one page. But I've seen specs that are several hundred pages long. You don't want to sit in the waiting room while *those* are being approved.

What happens when the specs and plans are in conflict? For example, suppose the specs describe a 3'6"-wide door and the plans show a 3-foot-wide opening. What then? I'll leave that question to the lawyers. For our purposes, we'll consider the plans and specs equally important. Whether something is in the plans or specs doesn't matter to the inspector. No part of the plans or specs takes precedence over any other part. The building code considers all documents a part of the whole.

Most plans for new construction will include the following:

1) Plot plan

2) Foundation plan

3) Floor plan

4) Roof plan

5) Elevations

6) Any sections or details needed to show what's being built and how it's being built

For larger projects, the plan sheets will usually be divided into the following categories:

1) Architectural plans

2) Structural plans

3) Electrical plans

4) Plumbing plans

5) Mechanical plans (heating, cooling and ventilation)

For smaller projects, like homes, information on structural, electrical and mechanical parts of the building may be included with the architectural drawings.

The Plot Plan

The plot plan shows a bird's eye view of the lot and where the proposed building will be on that lot. It also shows parking areas and yard improvements. The plans examiner will check the plot plan carefully to be sure the proposed building complies with any zoning ordinance in effect.

Zoning ordinances aren't building codes and I won't spend much time on them in this book. But you should know what the local zoning ordinance requires before applying for a permit. Can you build a duplex on this lot? What are the setbacks from the street and the property lines? How much of the lot area can be covered with building? Are there any height restrictions? The building department won't issue a permit until they're sure your plot plan complies with the zoning ordinance.

Zoning Laws

Zoning ordinances usually establish four broad categories of land use:

1) Residential — Where we live

2) Commercial — Stores and offices

3) Industrial — Where goods are produced

4) Agricultural —Where food is produced

Usually there are several sub-categories within each category. For example, R-1 is usually single-family residences. R-4 might be high-density residential with up to twenty living units or more per acre. You should know what zones have been established in your community and what is permitted in each zone. Usually the local planning department administers zoning ordinances.

You can't always tell from looking at a neighborhood exactly how it's zoned. Just because there's a commercial building next door is no guarantee that your client can put up a store on his lot. The dividing line between R-1 and C-1 (commercial) might run right down the property line.

You can usually build "down" but you can't build "up." Residential is the highest use, followed by commercial and industrial. Agricultural is the lowest use. So you can probably build a house in a commercial zone, industrial zone or agricultural zone. But you can't put up a store in a residential zone. Check with your planning department for details.

This rule of building down but not up also applies within zones. Suppose there are three residential zones: R-1 (single-family), R-2 (duplex) and R-3 (multi-family). You can usually build a single-family home in an R-2 or R-3 zone. Just don't try putting an apartment house in an R-1 zone.

The building inspector or the planning department can tell you what's allowed and what isn't. Of course, zoning can be changed, but changing it takes time, money and effort. Usually it's easier and cheaper to buy property zoned for the use you intend than it is to change zoning for the property you have.

Other Approvals

Even if you've satisfied local zoning ordinances and have met requirements in the building code, there may be other hurdles. For example, your local fire department and health department probably regulate certain types of businesses. The building department may forward a set of your plans to these or other municipal offices to get their approval. If they find discrepancies, your permit will be held up until changes are made.

A land covenant may also affect your plans. Most communities permit land owners to agree that land will be used only for certain purposes or that only certain types of buildings will be constructed on the land. These agreements between landowners are called covenants, conditions and restrictions (CC&Rs) and run with the land from one owner to the next. If you buy land in the covenant, you probably have to comply with this agreement.

Many CC&Rs require landowners to submit plans to an architectural review board before beginning construction. Your local building department won't enforce the CC&Rs, but other landowners may through the courts. Be aware of any CC&Rs that apply before you begin drawing plans. And understand that CC&Rs may conflict with the zoning. For instance, you could buy a plot in a zone that allows duplexes, but the property agreement prohibits them. By all means make sure you have checked the environmental aspects of this construction. Actually, this should have been done before the plans were drawn but it is wise to make certain.

What the Inspector Looks At

Near the front of the UBC is a simple outline inspectors often use for plan checking. It's reproduced here as Figure 2-1. We'll be considering each of these points in the next few chapters. Let's start with item 1-A on the inspector's checklist, occupancy group.

Types of Occupancy

Occupancy refers to the use or type of activity intended for the proposed building. Occupant load refers to the number of people who will be occupying the space. We'll cover occupancy in this chapter, and occupancy load in the next chapter. These two terms may look somewhat alike, but their definitions are very different.

There are ten major occupancy categories: *A* (assembly), *B* (business, such as offices), *E* (educational), *F* (factory and industrial), *H* (hazardous), *I* (institutional, such as hospitals), *M* (mercantile, such as stores), *R* (residential), *S* (storage) and *U* (utility). Most categories are broken down into divisions. More about this later.

This classification system assumes normal use of the building. That means the number of people and things in the building and what they're doing there is about what you would expect. That's normal occupancy. But it's also possible to have abnormal occupancies that create special hazards. Paint booths in a car repair shop are abnormal, for example. In that case, expect the building department to impose special requirements beyond what would be required for normal occupancy.

Occupancy Is Based on Degree of Hazard

Generally, occupancies are grouped by type of hazard. For example, buildings intended for meetings (such as theaters) have special design requirements. In an emergency, everyone wants out at the same time. People will rush to the exit, fighting and climbing over each other. It takes longer to evacuate a mob of panic-stricken people than it does to evacuate an organized group the same size. Obviously, the code has to set the minimum number of exits per occupant. In addition, the building should be able to resist structural failure for a longer time.

So that you understand the thinking that went into occupancy groups, I'll review the hazards we all face in buildings.

The most important consideration in setting up occupancy groups is the hazard to human life. Property hazards are considered secondary. Let's take a look at these risks to human life.

Common hazards — People are the greatest hazard to other people. Man is his own worst enemy. He smokes, works, gathers in groups, uses flammable liquids, and fills rooms with

EFFECTIVE USE OF THE
UNIFORM BUILDING CODE

The following procedure may be helpful in using the *Uniform Building Code:*

1. Classify the building:

   A. **OCCUPANCY CLASSIFICATION:** Compute the floor area and occupant load of the building or portion thereof. See Sections 207 and 1002 and Table 10-A. Determine the occupancy group which the use of the building or portion thereof most nearly resembles. See Sections 301, 303.1.1, 304.1, 305.1, 306.1, 307.1, 308.1, 309.1, 310.1, 311.1 and 312.1. See Section 302 for buildings with mixed occupancies.

   B. **TYPE OF CONSTRUCTION:** Determine the type of construction of the building by the building materials used and the fire resistance of the parts of the building. See Chapter 6.

   C. **LOCATION ON PROPERTY:** Determine the location of the building on the site and clearances to property lines and other buildings from the plot plan. See Table 5-A and Sections 602.3, 603.3, 604.3, 605.3 and 606.3 for fire resistance of exterior walls and wall opening requirements based on proximity to property lines. See Section 503.

   D. **ALLOWABLE FLOOR AREA:** Determine the allowable floor area of the building. See Table 5-B for basic allowable floor area based on occupancy group and type of construction. See Section 505 for allowable increases based on location on property and installation of an approved automatic fire sprinkler system. See Section 504.2 for allowable floor area of multistory buildings.

   E. **HEIGHT AND NUMBER OF STORIES:** Compute the height of the building, Section 209, and determine the number of stories, Section 220. See Table 5-B for the maximum height and number of stories permitted based on occupancy group and type of construction. See Section 506 for allowable story increase based on the installation of an approved automatic fire-sprinkler system.

2. Review the building for conformity with the occupancy requirements in Sections 303 through 312.

3. Review the building for conformity with the type of construction requirements in Chapter 6.

4. Review the building for conformity with the exiting requirements in Chapter 10.

5. Review the building for other detailed code regulations in Chapters 4, 7 through 11, 14, 15, 24 through 26, and 30 through 33, and the appendix.

6. Review the building for conformity with structural engineering regulations and requirements for materials of construction. See Chapters 16 through 23.

From the Uniform Building Code, ©1997, ICBO

Figure 2-1 *Sample outline for plan checking*

highly-combustible materials. In short, man creates most of his own hazards. And, when something bad happens, he panics and creates additional hazards.

Day and night occupancies — There are two broad categories: where people work and where they sleep. Where you work (day occupancy) is usually more hazardous, depending on the type of work involved, the size of work groups, and the materials and equipment used.

Night occupancies are where you rest or sleep. These include hotels, dormitories and apartment houses, but exclude one- and two-family homes. They're included under dwelling occupancies, below. Of course, a night occupancy can be hazardous. A fire may burn out of control longer when there's no one awake to discover it.

Dwelling occupancies — Dwelling occupancies include one- and two-family homes. More deaths occur each year in one- and two-family dwellings than in any other type of occupancy. But most of these deaths are caused by fires, involve only one or two casualties, and probably couldn't be prevented by changes in the building code. That may be why the code considers homes much less hazardous than other types of buildings.

Commercial and industrial hazards — This is a broad category and includes many different types of uses. Generally, the hazard varies with what's happening in the building. For example, storing or using highly combustible materials creates special risks.

Hazards are lower when a building has a relatively small number of people per square foot of floor and when the occupants are familiar with potential hazards and the location of exits. For example, employees in a plant can be expected to know what to do in case of fire. Shoppers in a store might not even know where the exits are. Code requirements are based on reasonable assumptions about who will be present and what they can be expected to know.

The type of occupancy determines the minimum fire and safety precautions required, the protective devices needed, and the arrangement, area, and height of rooms. The code tries to strike a balance between safety and economy by setting requirements appropriate for each type of hazard.

Height and area hazards — How do height and area pose hazards? Hazards to life increase as building heights increase, especially on floors too high for fire fighters to reach from the street. And think about basement fires. Many basements don't have direct access from the street and may be hard to get out of in an emergency. Fire fighters approach basement fires with extra caution.

Area means the space on a single level which is entirely separate and enclosed by a fire-resisting barrier. If there are no fire barriers, area is the entire floor space on each level. The greater the area, the greater the risk of material and human loss and the harder it may be to reach the center of the fire.

Hazards in General

What are the dangers the code is trying to reduce? Let's review some of the obvious hazards found in buildings.

- Hazards based on the nature of the occupancy

- Height and area hazards

- Spread of fire due to air currents, dirt and lint, combustible decorations and draperies, combustible finishes, trim, and the structure itself

- Toxic and heated gases

- Unprotected openings

- Lack of adequate separation between areas

- Exposure, or lack of separation between buildings

These are the main hazards in buildings. But there's one more consideration. It's one that we've talked about before. And when mixed with any of those listed above, you have the makings of a catastrophe. That hazard is large groups of people. In any decision on hazards, the building official will consider the number of people that will usually be in a building.

Occupancy Groups

The 1997 Uniform Building Code consists of ten major occupancy groups with 32 divisions. Let's take a look at these groups and divisions.

A — Assembly (See Section 303.1.1)
B — Business (See Section 304.1)
E — Educational (See Section 305.1)
F — Factory and Industrial (See Section 306.1)
H — Hazardous (See Section 307.1)
I — Institutional (See Section 308.1)
M — Mercantile (See Section 309.1)
R — Residential (See Section 310.1)
S — Storage (See Section 311.1)
U — Utility (See Section 312.1)

Under the code, every building in town gets squeezed into one of these ten groups. Of course, UBC divisions make the classification a little easier. Let's examine these groups and divisions one at a time and see what the requirements are. UBC Table 3-A (Figure 2-2) describes each type of occupancy.

Group A Occupancies

Where people assemble in large numbers for entertainment, deliberation, worship, to wait for transportation, or to eat, the hazards are considered to be great. Group A is further broken down into five divisions, determined first by occupant load and second by the activity. The first division is the most hazardous to human life. The last division is the least hazardous.

TABLE 3-A—DESCRIPTION OF OCCUPANCIES BY GROUP AND DIVISION[1]

GROUP AND DIVISION	SECTION	DESCRIPTION OF OCCUPANCY
A-1	303.1.1	A building or portion of a building having an assembly room with an occupant load of 1,000 or more and a legitimate stage.
A-2		A building or portion of a building having an assembly room with an occupant load of less than 1,000 and a legitimate stage.
A-2.1		A building or portion of a building having an assembly room with an occupant load of 300 or more without a legitimate stage, including such buildings used for educational purposes and not classed as a Group E or Group B Occupancy.
A-3		Any building or portion of a building having an assembly room with an occupant load of less than 300 without a legitimate stage, including such buildings used for educational purposes and not classed as a Group E or Group B Occupancy.
A-4		Stadiums, reviewing stands and amusement park structures not included within other Group A Occupancies.
B	304.1	A building or structure, or a portion thereof, for office, professional or service-type transactions, including storage of records and accounts; eating and drinking establishments with an occupant load of less than 50.
E-1	305.1	Any building used for educational purposes through the 12th grade by 50 or more persons for more than 12 hours per week or four hours in any one day.
E-2		Any building used for educational purposes through the 12th grade by less than 50 persons for more than 12 hours per week or four hours in any one day.
E-3		Any building or portion thereof used for day-care purposes for more than six persons.
F-1	306.1	Moderate-hazard factory and industrial occupancies include factory and industrial uses not classified as Group F, Division 2 Occupancies.
F-2		Low-hazard factory and industrial occupancies include facilities producing noncombustible or nonexplosive materials that during finishing, packing or processing do not involve a significant fire hazard.
H-1	307.1	Occupancies with a quantity of material in the building in excess of those listed in Table 3-D that present a high explosion hazard as listed in Section 307.1.1.
H-2		Occupancies with a quantity of material in the building in excess of those listed in Table 3-D that present a moderate explosion hazard or a hazard from accelerated burning as listed in Section 307.1.1.
H-3		Occupancies with a quantity of material in the building in excess of those listed in Table 3-D that present a high fire or physical hazard as listed in Section 307.1.1.
H-4		Repair garages not classified as Group S, Division 3 Occupancies.
H-5		Aircraft repair hangars not classified as Group S, Division 5 Occupancies and heliports.
H-6	307.1 and 307.11	Semiconductor fabrication facilities and comparable research and development areas when the facilities in which hazardous production materials are used, and the aggregate quantity of material is in excess of those listed in Table 3-D or 3-E.
H-7	307.1	Occupancies having quantities of materials in excess of those listed in Table 3-E that are health hazards as listed in Section 307.1.1.
I-1.1	308.1	Nurseries for the full-time care of children under the age of six (each accommodating more than five children), hospitals, sanitariums, nursing homes with nonambulatory patients and similar buildings (each accommodating more than five patients).
I-1.2		Health-care centers for ambulatory patients receiving outpatient medical care which may render the patient incapable of unassisted self-preservation (each tenant space accommodating more than five such patients).
I-2		Nursing homes for ambulatory patients, homes for children six years of age or over (each accommodating more than five persons).
I-3		Mental hospitals, mental sanitariums, jails, prisons, reformatories and buildings where personal liberties of inmates are similarly restrained.
M	309.1	A building or structure, or a portion thereof, for the display and sale of merchandise, and involving stocks of goods, wares or merchandise, incidental to such purposes and accessible to the public.
R-1	310.1	Hotels and apartment houses, congregate residences (each accommodating more than 10 persons).
R-3		Dwellings, lodging houses, congregate residences (each accommodating 10 or fewer persons).
S-1	311.1	Moderate hazard storage occupancies including buildings or portions of buildings used for storage of combustible materials not classified as Group S, Division 2 or Group H Occupancies.
S-2		Low-hazard storage occupancies including buildings or portions of buildings used for storage of noncombustible materials.
S-3		Repair garages where work is limited to exchange of parts and maintenance not requiring open flame or welding, and parking garages not classified as Group S, Division 4 Occupancies.
S-4		Open parking garages.
S-5		Aircraft hangars and helistops.
U-1	312.1	Private garages, carports, sheds and agricultural buildings.
U-2		Fences over 6 feet (1829 mm) high, tanks and towers.

[1]For detailed descriptions, see the occupancy definitions in the noted sections.

From the Uniform Building Code, ©1997, ICBO

Figure 2-2 *Categories of occupancy*

Remember, the higher the human load, the higher the hazard.

People assemble for meetings and classes in offices and schools. Why are educational and office buildings excluded from Group A? Think about what I said about familiarity with surroundings. Most Group A buildings will be occupied by people not completely familiar with the building layout. Office workers and students are usually in the same building day after day. They're probably much more familiar with the buildings where they meet. They probably know what to do in case of fire or emergency.

Note in UBC Table 3-A that buildings with "legitimate" stages have the highest hazards. That's probably because so many people have been killed in theater fires. Legitimate stage, by the way, means live theater as opposed to movie theaters.

Theaters have changed a lot in the last few decades. You won't find fly galleries in drive-in theaters or most new movie theaters, nor will you find a proscenium wall. What's a fly gallery? It's a narrow platform at the side of the theater stage. Stagehands stand in the fly gallery while pulling lines that control suspended scenery. A proscenium wall is an arch that frames the stage and separates it from the rest of the auditorium.

Group A-4 covers stadiums, reviewing stands and amusement park buildings not included within other Group A Occupancies.

Group B Occupancies

Group B Occupancies include only one division. The code defines it as:

304.1 Group B Occupancies Defined. Group B Occupancies shall include buildings, structures, or portions thereof, for office, professional or service-type transactions, which are not classified as Group H Occupancies. Such occupancies include occupancies for the storage of records and accounts, and eating and drinking establishments with an occupant load of less than 50. Business occupancies shall include, but not be limited to the following:

At this point the code lists 21 different uses including animal hospitals, banks, barber and beauty shops, fire stations, police stations and telephone exchanges. Generally, this seems to be pretty much a catchall for those hard-to-place items that are not covered elsewhere in the code.

Group E Occupancies

Group E occupancies are day-use educational buildings. Here, the three divisions are concerned more with type of occupants.

Section 305.2.2.1 lists three atmospheric conditions that must be taken into consideration in school design. This is undoubtedly due to the sedentary and restricted use by the students. They are as follows:

Common Atmosphere. A common atmosphere exists between rooms, spaces or areas within a building which are not separated by an approved smoke- and draft-stop barrier.

Separate Atmosphere. A separate atmosphere exists between rooms, spaces or areas that are separated by an approved smoke barrier.

Smoke Barrier. A smoke barrier consists of walls, partitions, floors and openings therein as will prevent the transmission of smoke or gases through the construction. See Section 905.

One other item of interest is the fact that rooms used for kindergarten, first- or second-grade pupils shall not be located above or below the first floor.

Group F Occupancies

306.1 Group F Occupancies Defined. Group F Occupancies shall include the use of a building or structure, or a portion thereof, for assembling, disassembling, fabricating, finishing, manufacturing, packaging, repair or processing operations that are not classified as Group H Occupancies. Factory and industrial occupancies shall include the following:

It then lists 42 types of businesses that are allowed in Division l and seven in Division 2. There's also a disclaimer that says they're not limited to those uses listed.

Group H Occupancies

H stands for hazardous. Many of the occupancies are based on risk to humans and on human loads. Most of the divisions under Group H have a relatively low human load.

H-4 is for repair garages and H-5 is for aircraft repair hangars. Why should aircraft repair be rated less hazardous than automotive repair? Think about it for a moment. Repair garages are usually smaller and have more flammable or combustible material stored closer together. Hangars are larger, with fewer people and better opportunity to control a fire.

H-6 is used for semiconductor fabrication facilities and semiconductor research buildings. Buildings where computer chips are made didn't fit very well into any other category.

Group I Occupancies

Group I buildings usually house people under close supervision. The four divisions are based on the degree of supervision.

The big items here are the first two divisions. I-1 covers children under the age of six and patients in hospitals or nursing homes who can't walk. These people couldn't respond to directions in an emergency.

But people in I-1 buildings can come and go somewhat at will. Why are prisoners in jail (Group I-3) considered less at risk? In a fire, they couldn't get out without help even if they tried. The answer is probably in the type of construction. Escape-proof buildings are naturally fire resistant.

Group M Occupancies

Group M has only one division and includes uses described as mercantile, such as drug stores, department stores, shopping centers and other mercantile types.

Group R Occupancies

Group R includes hotels, motels, apartments, condominiums and private residences. There are only two divisions here, multi-family structures and dwellings (single-family houses).

Notice that there isn't any R-2 category. That's space reserved for future use. If the building officials decide to create an intermediate group between R-1 and R-3, there's a place for it without renumbering everything.

Remember the night and dwelling occupancies we talked about earlier? Typical night occupancy buildings include hotels, dormitories and large multiple dwellings (Group R-1). Single-family residences are under Group R-3, along with lodging houses.

But why are lodging houses listed under residences and not under hotels? It's a matter of definition. In Chapter 2 of the UBC we'll find that a *hotel* is any building with six or more guest rooms. A *lodging house* can have up to five guest rooms. Again we can see that the degree of hazard is determined by the number of occupants.

Group S Occupancies

Group S consists of buildings or structures used for storage of materials not classified as hazardous. Division 1, a moderate hazard group, is for the storage of combustible materials that are not included in Division 2. Division 2 lists 23 low-hazard storage occupancies which include beer or wine storage, cold storage and creameries, frozen foods and appliance warehouses. Before you ask, I haven't the remotest idea why whiskey and other liquors aren't included with beer and wine.

There are a total of five subdivisions in this category, all containing low or moderate hazard uses. Under Division 5 (Section 311.9.2.1) there is an attempt to categorize the major types of parking facilities as follows:

Mechanical-Access Open Parking Garages *are open parking garages employing parking machines, lifts, elevators, or other mechanical devices for vehi-*

cles moving from and to street level and in which public occupancy is prohibited above the street level.

Open Parking Garage is a structure of Type I or II construction with the openings as described in Section 311.9.2.2 on two or more sides and which is used exclusively for parking or storage of private or pleasure-type vehicles.

Ramp-Access Open Parking Garages are open parking garages employing a series of continuously rising floors or a series of interconnecting ramps between floors permitting the movement of vehicles under their own power from and to the street level.

Group U Occupancies

This group consists of two subdivisions. The first division is for private parking garages, carports, sheds and agricultural buildings. The last subdivision is for fences over 6 feet (182.9 mm) high, tanks, and towers.

Are You Confused?

Some of the occupancy classifications we've discussed in this chapter probably seem to overlap. Other types of buildings probably don't seem to be covered very well. If you're confused, don't worry. It's impossible to fit every building ever constructed into one of ten neat categories. There's lots of room for interpretation and doubt. But most buildings fit more or less into one of the ten categories. Your task is to figure out which group is most like the building you plan to construct.

If there's any doubt, get some help from the building department early in the planning process. The building department will usually favor the more restrictive classification and you'll almost certainly argue for the more permissive application. The outcome of that discussion can have a major effect on the cost of your building. But it's always more expensive to make changes later than it is to do it right the first time. Get a decision on occupancy group as early as possible.

Most disagreements on occupancy classes boil down to the way some term is defined and used in the code. Hotels and motels are a good example. In the building code there's no difference between the two. But most planners and zoning officials would insist that there is a difference. Motels have room access directly to the exterior. Hotels don't. But for building code purposes, a motel is always a hotel. That's just the way it is.

Now that we've determined the occupancy group for your building, let's look at occupant load and how we determine it.

Sidewalks Anyone?

Everybody knows how much kids love a good sidewalk. We know how curbs and sidewalks reduce dust and debris in a neighborhood. Well, one day about 15 years ago, the city engineer and I sat down to make life better and easier for the kids and housekeepers and homeowners in Kennewick who didn't live in neighborhoods with curbs and sidewalks. We decided to revise our public works ordinance. Anyone who built a new house or did very much remodeling had to have a sidewalk in front of their home. If they didn't already have one, they had to build one. The city council went along with us and our draft became law.

That created quite a sir. Contractors were against it. Some homeowners were against it. But the city council stood by their guns.

About a year later I had a contractor breeze into my office insisting he built the best houses around. And he also insisted that a sidewalk wasn't needed in front of the new house he was going to build. It would be the only house on the block with a sidewalk and a curb. That seemed ridiculous to him. I issued him a permit for a new residence . . . and a sidewalk to go with it.

He built the house and I did the final inspection, including a check of his curb and sidewalk forms. It was a corner lot, so he had a lot of frontage. His forms checked out perfectly, so I signed off the inspection and left for the next job.

About an hour later, I had a thought: I forgot to make the final plumbing inspection for this contractor. I drove back to his job just in time to find him filling in part of the sidewalk forms with gravel. I guess he was still mad about spending those extra bucks for curb and sidewalk. Anyhow, he turned apologetic and started digging out the forms again.

"I'm curious," I said. "About how much concrete did you expect to save by filling in the forms."

"Oh, maybe ten or fifteen dollars worth."

"What do you figure your time is worth?"

He stared at me for almost a minute. Then started to grin. "Wasn't going to save much, was I?"

"Guess not," I agreed. "Let's see how long it takes you to dig out all that extra gravel. I'll sit right here and time you while you're digging. Then, when you get ready to pour, I'll be back to keep track of your time on that too." And that's exactly what I did.

I passed by that home a few months ago. Sidewalks and curbs run all the way up and down both sides of street now. The city had to complete the last few stretches where sidewalks hadn't been installed. But my ordinance (and a little arm twisting) did the job. I'm sure the kids appreciate growing up in a neighborhood with good sidewalks. I wish I had the same advantage. And, judging by the asking prices for homes on that street, my sidewalks didn't do the homeowners any harm, either. Funny thing, I don't hear contractors complaining about my sidewalk ordinance any more. I guess people get comfortable with code changes eventually. Anyhow, they've got some newer changes to complain about.

3

Occupancy Loads and Occupancy Groups

I talked a lot about hazards in the last chapter. But we've only scratched the surface of this important subject. Hazard is going to follow us through every chapter of this book. That's because the primary concern of the building code is risk to human life. If all buildings were perfectly safe, we wouldn't need building codes. Unfortunately, there's no such thing as a risk-free building. But we're a lot closer now than we were years ago before the first model codes were adopted.

In the last chapter we saw how all buildings were classified into one of ten code categories. Each category (occupancy group) has buildings with similar hazards. Later, you'll see how code requirements vary for each category. But even within occupancy divisions the hazard can vary with the occupancy load. As the number of people in a building (the occupancy load) increases, the hazard to the people there also increases. That's why we've got to determine occupancy loads for the buildings we plan.

Computing Occupancy Loads

Figuring the occupancy load isn't a simple matter of calculating how many people can squeeze into a given area. The code is more concerned with the number of people who can use the space *safely* and for its *designed purpose*.

There are two people who have a stake in this number. First, of course, is the owner, the person who will be using the property and who has to know how many people can use the restaurant, factory, shop or whatever. The other interested party is the building inspector.

How many people will occupy a site? What's their normal activity? Once we answer these questions, we can determine the type of occupancy and, in many cases, the type of construction needed for the building.

An important reference is UBC Table 10-A, *Minimum Egress Requirements*, reproduced here as Figure 3-1. Mark this spot well in your copy of the code. Of all the charts and tables in the UBC, this table will be among the most useful. It's the table the inspector normally uses to determine the number of people who will assemble in an area. Column 1 describes the use. Column 2 describes the number of occupants for which two or more exits are required. Column 3, the one we'll probably use most, lists the number of square feet assumed per person for each type of use. In this chapter we'll be dealing mainly with Columns 1 and 3.

I've been told that Table 10-A shouldn't be used as a design tool. According to what I've heard, designers shouldn't start with the number of occupants expected and then use Table 10-A to figure out how much space is required. But I don't see any reason why they can't use Table 10-A that way. Sure, Table 10-A is a tool designed for the inspector or fire marshal. But why design anything the inspector or fire marshal won't approve? My advice: When you're planning for the occupant load, go ahead and use Table 10-A.

Footage Often Indicates Activity

The square footage per occupant in Column 3 varies from a minimum of 3 square feet to a maximum of 500 square feet. The assumed number of people per square foot varies with the type of activity. For example, the first item on the list is *aircraft hangars (no repair)*. Most hangars are big buildings with relatively few people per square foot of floor. The code assumes that you'll have one person in the hangar for each 500 square feet of floor. So if you have a 5,000 square foot hangar, your assumed occupant load would be ten people.

Now compare this with *auction rooms*, the second item in the table. People usually stand shoulder to shoulder at an auction. Here, the assumed space is 7 square feet per occupant. If your auction room has 700 square feet of floor, the assumed occupant load is 100 people.

How did the authors of the code arrive at this figure of *7 square feet* per occupant? Seven square feet is accepted as the normal amount of space a standing person needs to move and act normally. For example, if you were to stand in a closet 2 feet wide by 3½ feet long (7 square feet), you probably wouldn't be too uncomfortable. You'd have room to turn around and stretch out a little. For a few hours at a time you could probably tolerate it pretty well.

Of course, there's more to the 7-square-foot space standard than that. Part of that space — 2 feet by 3½ feet — is usually used for aisles or hallways or furniture or machines.

Notice that there are two types of assembly areas in UBC Table 10-A. One is for *concentrated use* and the other is for *less-concentrated use*. The major difference is that concentrated use refers primarily to occupancies with a large seating area. Less-concentrated use refers to areas with tables and chairs.

Computing the Size of Your Building

The plans examiner will use Table 10-A to compute the assumed occupant load when you submit plans. But you can use the same space standards to design your building. If you know how many people will be using a building, let UBC Table 10-A help you compute the square footage needed. Multiply the number of occupants by the square footage per person in Figure 3-1. This will give you the total number of square feet of floor required.

The figure in the book is the *minimum size* for that occupancy. You may build larger than the minimum — as large as the owner's wallet will allow — but you may not build smaller.

Take a few minutes to study these figures. The building inspector is going to use them when computing the number of people permitted in the building — the number listed on the sign showing room capacity.

TABLE 10-A—MINIMUM EGRESS REQUIREMENTS[1]

USE[2]	MINIMUM OF TWO MEANS OF EGRESS ARE REQUIRED WHERE NUMBER OF OCCUPANTS IS AT LEAST	OCCUPANT LOAD FACTOR[3] (square feet) × 0.0929 for m²
1. Aircraft hangars (no repair)	10	500
2. Auction rooms	30	7
3. Assembly areas, concentrated use (without fixed seats) Auditoriums Churches and chapels Dance floors Lobby accessory to assembly occupancy Lodge rooms Reviewing stands Stadiums Waiting area	50 50	7 3
4. Assembly areas, less-concentrated use Conference rooms Dining rooms Drinking establishments Exhibit rooms Gymnasiums Lounges Stages Gaming: keno, slot machine and live games area	50 50	15 11
5. Bowling alley (assume no occupant load for bowling lanes)	50	4
6. Children's homes and homes for the aged	6	80
7. Classrooms	50	20
8. Congregate residences	10	200
9. Courtrooms	50	40
10. Dormitories	10	50
11. Dwellings	10	300
12. Exercising rooms	50	50
13. Garage, parking	30	200
14. Health care facilities— Sleeping rooms Treatment rooms	8 10	120 240
15. Hotels and apartments	10	200
16. Kitchen—commercial	30	200
17. Library— Reading rooms Stack areas	50 30	50 100
18. Locker rooms	30	50
19. Malls (see Chapter 4)	—	—
20. Manufacturing areas	30	200
21. Mechanical equipment room	30	300
22. Nurseries for children (day care)	7	35
23. Offices	30	100
24. School shops and vocational rooms	50	50
25. Skating rinks	50	50 on the skating area; 15 on the deck
26. Storage and stock rooms	30	300
27. Stores—retail sales rooms Basements and ground floor Upper floors	50 50	30 60
28. Swimming pools	50	50 for the pool area; 15 on the deck
29. Warehouses[5]	30	500
30. All others	50	100

[1]Access to, and egress from, buildings for persons with disabilities shall be provided as specified in Chapter 11.

[2]For additional provisions on number of exits from Groups H and I Occupancies and from rooms containing fuel-fired equipment or cellulose nitrate, see Sections 1018, 1019 and 1020, respectively.

[3]This table shall not be used to determine working space requirements per person.

[4]Occupant load based on five persons for each alley, including 15 feet (4572 mm) of runway.

[5]Occupant load for warehouses containing approved high rack storage systems designed for mechanical handling may be based on the floor area exclusive of the rack area rather than the gross floor area.

From the Uniform Building Code, ©1997, ICBO

Figure 3-1 *Minimum egress requirements*

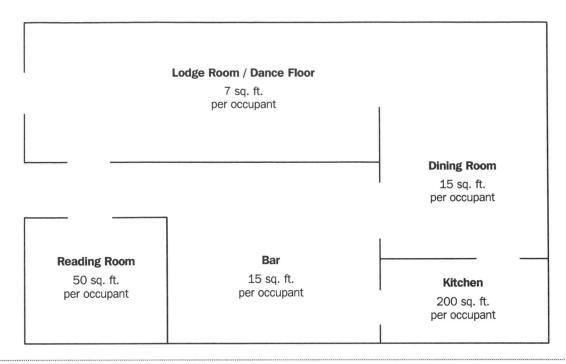

Figure 3-2 *Sketch of lodge*

Computing Building Size for Mixed Occupancies

Many buildings house different occupancy groups. If you're designing a mixed building, go through the same steps as for a single-occupancy building, only you'll have to repeat them several times. Schools are a good example, since they have auditoriums, gymnasiums, vocational shops, libraries and administrative offices in addition to classrooms. Each has its own requirements, as shown in UBC Table 10-A.

Let's take an example. Suppose the design is for a building to house a lodge with a membership of 250 people. On dance night there may be as many as 400 people in the building. They want a dining room to accommodate 150 persons at a time and a bar that will hold another 100. They'll have a kitchen staff of four. The library, or reading room, will be open to the members and normally will serve about ten people at a time.

How much space should you provide? For the moment, let's assume that other problems such as fire resistance and type of construction have been solved. What we're after now is simply the amount of space the building will require.

Find *lodge rooms* in UBC Table 10-A (Figure 3-1). The table tells us that lodge rooms require 7 square feet per occupant. With a membership of 250 multiplied by 7, we find that the main lodge room must be no smaller than 1,750 square feet. That's a room about 35 feet wide by 50 feet long.

Look at Figure 3-2. Here's how to calculate the other areas:

Dance floor: 400 people x 7 square feet
= 2,800 square feet

Dining room: 150 people x 15 square feet
= 2,250 square feet

Bar: 100 people x 15 square feet
= 1,500 square feet

Reading room: 10 people x 50 square feet
= 500 square feet

Kitchen: 4 people x 200 square feet
= 800 square feet

As you can see, the building will have an occupant load of 664 based on 9,600 square feet of floor area.

So what happens if this is more space than the lodge feels they can afford? Do a little juggling. Have the design changed a bit. By making minor adjustments, you can still give your clients the space they need at a price they can afford.

You could combine the lodge hall with the dance floor, for instance. That eliminates 1,750 square feet. If you do that, the lodge couldn't hold a lodge meeting and a dance at the same time. That's not a big drawback. If this is an "adults only" dining room, state liquor law may permit you to combine the bar and the dining room. You could even omit the reading room. But don't tamper with the kitchen space.

In fact, I doubt that a kitchen staff of four could operate in only 800 square feet, considering all the sophisticated kitchen equipment in use today. But I'd be inclined to go along with the recommendations of any kitchen consultants involved in designing the kitchen, so long as they provide at least 200 square feet per person.

If the membership figures are correct and the estimates of dining and dancing are also correct, the figures we've come up with should be OK. If we need more space, a second or even a third story may be required. Of course, that will change exit requirements.

Occupancy or Occupant Load?

What we've just done was determine the occupant load for one building use. *Do not confuse this with establishing occupancy.* We did that in the last chapter. *Occupancy* is the type of business or operation being conducted. *Occupant load* is the number of people that can

be expected to use the building while it's open for business.

Mixed Occupancy and Different Ownerships

Suppose we have a building with several uses, like the lodge building, but also with several different tenants. Our approach has to be a little different. We'll begin by identifying each of the tenants and establishing them as separate uses.

Let's say the second floor is designed as a meeting hall for the Loyal Order of Hose Handlers. Part of the first floor is a ballroom to be leased by the Rompers and Stompers. The rest of the ground floor will be used by the Greasy Spoon Restaurant and Taphouse.

The lodge room would be an assembly room, probably without a stage, although it could easily have one. From the floor area, we know the occupant load will be less than 300 people. UBC Table 3-A (look back to Chapter 2, Figure 2-2) tells us that this is either Group A-2.1 or A-3 occupancy. But beware! There's a trap here. Group A-2.1 has "an occupant load of 300 or more without a stage." Group A-3 can have "an occupant load of less than 300 without a stage."

It doesn't seem like much of a difference until you consider the type of construction allowed. UBC Table 5-B (Figure 3-3) permits you to use Type II-N, III-N or V-N construction for Group A-3, but not for Group A-2.1. This difference can really add to construction costs. (We'll discuss types of construction in detail in the next chapter.)

Using the magic number of 300 as an occupant load may be the key to saving money. You may be better off reducing the floor area by a few square feet to get an occupant load of 299. On a building 30 feet wide, the reduction needed may be only a few inches.

Now, assume the dance hall has a legitimate stage. Since it will have over 300 occupants, the hall will be in an A-1 group. The

TABLE 5-B—BASIC ALLOWABLE BUILDING HEIGHTS AND BASIC ALLOWABLE FLOOR AREA FOR BUILDINGS ONE STORY IN HEIGHT[1]

TYPE OF CONSTRUCTION		TYPES OF CONSTRUCTION								
		I	II			III		IV	V	
		F.R.	F.R.	One-hour	N	One-hour	N	H.T.	One-hour	N
		Maximum Height (feet)								
		UL	160 (48 768 mm)	65 (19 812 mm)	55 (16 764 mm)	65 (19 812 mm)	55 (16 764 mm)	65 (19 812 mm)	50 (15 240 mm)	40 (12 192 mm)
Use Group	Height/Area	Maximum Height (stories) and Maximum Area (sq. ft.) (× 0.0929 for m[2])								
A-1	H	UL	4	Not Permitted						
	A	UL	29,900							
A-2, 2.1[2]	H	UL	4	2	NP	2	NP	2	2	NP
	A	UL	29,900	13,500	NP	13,500	NP	13,500	10,500	NP
A-3, 4[2]	H	UL	12	2	1	2	1	2	2	1
	A	UL	29,900	13,500	9,100	13,500	9,100	13,500	10,500	6,000
B, F-1, M, S-1, S-3, S-5	H	UL	12	4	2	4	2	4	3	2
	A	UL	39,900	18,000	12,000	18,000	12,000	18,000	14,000	8,000
E-1, 2, 3[4]	H	UL	4	2	1	2	1	2	2	1
	A	UL	45,200	20,200	13,500	20,200	13,500	20,200	15,700	9,100
F-2, S-2	H	UL	12	4	2	4	2	4	3	2
	A	UL	59,900	27,000	18,000	27,000	18,000	27,000	21,000	12,000
H-1[5]	H	1	1	1	1	Not Permitted				
	A	15,000	12,400	5,600	3,700					
H-2[5]	H	UL	2	1	1	1	1	1	1	1
	A	15,000	12,400	5,600	3,700	5,600	3,700	5,600	4,400	2,500
H-3, 4, 5[5]	H	UL	5	2	1	2	1	2	2	1
	A	UL	24,800	11,200	7,500	11,200	7,500	11,200	8,800	5,100
H-6, 7	H	3	3	3	2	3	2	3	3	1
	A	UL	39,900	18,000	12,000	18,000	12,000	18,000	14,000	8,000
I-1.1, 1.2[6,10]	H	UL	3	1	NP	1	NP	1	1	NP
	A	UL	15,100	6,800	NP	6,800	NP	6,800	5,200	NP
I-2	H	UL	3	2	NP	2	NP	2	2	NP
	A	UL	15,100	6,800	NP	6,800	NP	6,800	5,200	NP
I-3	H	UL	2	Not Permitted[7]						
	A	UL	15,100							
R-1	H	UL	12	4	2[9]	4	2[9]	4	3	2[9]
	A	UL	29,900	13,500	9,100[9]	13,500	9,100[9]	13,500	10,500	6,000[9]
R-3	H	UL	3	3	3	3	3	3	3	3
	A	Unlimited								
S-4[3]	H	See Table 3-H								
	A									
U[8]	H	See Chapter 3								
	A									

A—Building area in square feet.
H—Building height in number of stories.
H.T.—Heavy timber.
NP—Not permitted.

N—No requirements for fire resistance.
F.R.—Fire resistive.
UL—Unlimited.

[1]For multistory buildings, see Section 504.2.

[2]For limitations and exceptions, see Section 303.2.

[3]For open parking garages, see Section 311.9.

[4]See Section 305.2.3.

[5]See Section 307.

[6]See Section 308.2.1 for exception to the allowable area and number of stories in hospitals, nursing homes and health-care centers.

[7]See Section 308.2.2.2.

[8]For agricultural buildings, see also Appendix Chapter 3.

[9]For limitations and exceptions, see Section 310.2.

[10]For Type II F.R., the maximum height of Group I, Division 1.1 Occupancies is limited to 75 feet (22 860 mm). For Type II, One-hour construction, the maximum height of Group I, Division 1.1 Occupancies is limited to 45 feet (13 716 mm).

From the Uniform Building Code, ©1997, ICBO

Figure 3-3 *Allowable building heights and floor areas*

TABLE 3-B—REQUIRED SEPARATION IN BUILDINGS OF MIXED OCCUPANCY[1] (HOURS)

	A-1	A-2	A-2.1	A-3	A-4	B	E	F-1	F-2	H-2	H-3	H-4,5	H-6,7[2]	I	M	R-1	R-3	S-1	S-2	S-3	S-5	U-1[3]
A-1		N	N	N	N	3	N	3	3	4	4	4	4	3	3	1	1	3	3	4	3	1
A-2			N	N	N	1	N	1	1	4	4	4	4	3	1	1	1	1	1	3	1	1
A-2.1				N	N	1	N	1	1	4	4	4	4	3	1	1	1	1	1	3	1	1
A-3					N	N	N	N	N	4	4	4	3	2	N	1	1	N	N	3	1	1
A-4						1	N	1	1	4	4	4	4	3	1	1	1	1	1	3	1	1
B							1	N[5]	N	2	1	1	1	2	N	1	1	N	N	1	1	1
E								1	1	4	4	4	3	1	1	1	1	1	1	3	1	1
F-1									1	2	1	1	1	3	N[5]	1	1	N	N	1	1	1
F-2										2	1	1	1	2	1	1	1	N	N	1	1	1
H-1	NOT PERMITTED IN MIXED OCCUPANCIES. SEE SECTION 307.2.9																					
H-2											1	1	2	4	2	4	4	2	2	2	2	1
H-3												1	1	4	1	3	3	1	1	1	1	1
H-4,5													1	4	1	3	3	1	1	1	1	1
H-6,7[2]														4	1	4	4	1	1	1	1	3
I															2	1	1	2	2	4	3	1
M																1	1	1[4]	1[4]	1	1	1
R-1																	N	3	1	3	1	1
R-3																		1	1	1	1	1
S-1																			1	1	1	1
S-2																				1	1	N
S-3																					1	1
S-4	OPEN PARKING GARAGES ARE EXCLUDED EXCEPT AS PROVIDED IN SECTION 311.2																					
S-5																						N

N—No requirements for fire resistance.

[1]For detailed requirements and exceptions, see Section 302.4.

[2]For special provisions on highly toxic materials, see the Fire Code.

[3]For agricultural buildings, see also Appendix Chapter 3.

[4]See Section 309.2.2 for exception.

[5]For Group F, Division 1 woodworking establishments with more than 2,500 square feet (232.3 m²), the occupancy separation shall be one hour.

From the Uniform Building Code, ©1997, ICBO

Figure 3-4 *Required separation in buildings of mixed occupancy*

bar/restaurant with less than 300 occupants is back in the A-3 grouping.

Because you have an A-1 grouping (the dance hall) in your building, you must have Type I or II-F.R. construction throughout the entire building. This is an important consideration when mixing occupancies, If you left out the dance hall, you could go to a less expensive type of construction.

Occupancy Separation

Occupancy separations are like fire breaks. They help retard the spread of fire between rooms. Installing occupancy separations lets you design part of an area for a high hazard occupancy and the remainder of an area for a lower hazard. Without the occupancy separation, you'd have to design the entire area to meet the higher hazard.

Occupancy separations are usually defined in terms of hours of fire protection. A one-hour fire wall means that an adjacent area will be protected from fire for at least one hour.

Will we need an occupancy separation in our two-story lodge/ballroom/restaurant building? UBC Table 3-B says no, but let's take a closer look. See Figure 3-4. For mixed occupancies within Group A, no separation is needed except the usual partitions to divide the space and to support the building. This depends on the location, area, and height of the building, and on a few other considerations, but not occupancy.

Access Between Occupancies

Related to occupancy separation is *access between occupancies*. Could you provide access from one occupancy to another without having to go out to the street and come back through another door?

In most cases you can if you provide a complying fire door between the two uses. Depending upon the required rating of the separation wall, the door might need to be labeled as one-hour, 90-minutes or 3-hours. The access provided between different occupancies must also meet the exiting requirements that we'll discuss later.

Sometimes a hallway or corridor can be considered as a buffer between two imcompatible uses. Many times it's still necessary to construct a fire-resistive separation somewhere between the different occupancies. Building the hallway wall as a fire wall provides the needed separation.

Since we're on the subject of aisles, halls, and access, it's a good time to bring up *vomitories*. Vomitories have been around a long time — and they're not what you may think. You may have one in your church, theater, auditorium or gymnasium. The dictionary says it's an entrance piercing the banks of aisles of a theater or auditorium. In practice, it's an interior court into which several hallways might enter. Examples are a hallway in a shopping mall or a cluster of businesses opening into a central court.

Occupancy — Restrictive Requirements

Now, what about some of the more restrictive requirements of the different occupancy groups we've discussed? These requirements can alter the shape, size and capacity of a proposed building. In some cases there may be

trade-offs. (If you do this, then you can enlarge that, for instance.)

Up to this point we've been dealing mostly in generalities. Now it's time to get a little more specific.

Buildings or parts of buildings classed in Group A-1 must be Type I or Type II-FR construction. I'll explain types of construction shortly. They can't exceed the area and height limits specified in Section 504, 505, or 506. These sections and UBC Table 5-B govern the gross floor area and the heights of buildings for this group. They also allow increases in the limits if you install certain safety items, like automatic sprinkler systems.

Is this good or bad? That depends on what you want to do. Let's take a closer look. You'll find UBC Table 5-B in Figure 3-3.

Group A-1, you'll recall, is *any assembly building with a legitimate stage and an occupant load of 1,000 or more in the building.* Remember that we're working with gross floor area and that most of the occupants will be seated. At 15 square feet per occupant for 1,000 occupants, we have a gross floor area of 15,000 square feet. This isn't exceptional for a grand ballroom in some of the larger hotels. Even a skating rink could be larger than that (using nominal figures, about 100 feet times 150 feet). Type I construction is about the most fire resistive the code calls for. It's also expensive to build. Will it be worth the cost? Would a slightly smaller building (less than 15,000 square feet) be nearly as good? Of course, that's up to you, the owner, and the owner's banker.

The code also says that if the main floor slopes, the slope can't exceed 1 in 8. Also, the building must front directly on or have access to a public street at least 20 feet wide. The code also requires you to furnish light and ventilation by windows or skylights. They must have an area at least one-tenth the total floor area, one-half of which must be openable. (You can provide mechanical ventilation and artificial light instead of windows.)

Recent events have created a need for detailing required separations in hospitals and

Water Closets		Urinals	Lavatories
Males	Females		
3: 201-400	11: 201-400	4: 401-600	3: 401-750
Over 400, add 1 fixture for each additional 500 males and 1 for each 125 females		Over 600, add 1 for each additional 300 males	Over 750, add 1 for each additional 500 persons

From the Uniform Plumbing Code® with permission of the International Association of Plumbing and Mechanical Officials ©1997

Figure 3-5 *Plumbing requirements*

nursing homes. You will find that Group I, Division 1.1 now requires separations as shown in Table 3-C.

Plumbing Requirements

Plumbing requirements of the UBC aren't too restrictive for the general public, but they're more specific for the disabled. In general, you must provide, in an approved location, at least one lavatory for each two water closets for each sex and at least one drinking fountain for each floor level. This is a rather strange requirement because the UBC doesn't cover water closets in Group A occupancies. For this you must consult your plumbing code. Figure 3-5 shows the Uniform Plumbing Code requirements.

Before anyone yells "Foul!" because of the difference in the two codes, I'll explain the discrepancies. In the first place, the Uniform Building Code and the Uniform Plumbing Code are written by different groups. If you're in an area that uses only the UBC and not the UPC, go by the requirements of the UBC. Otherwise, the more restrictive of the two would apply. Although the UBC says you need only half as many lavatories as water closets, the UPC clearly states that for 1,000 occupants you need five water closets for men and 16 for women. The men would also have urinals. Likewise, you would need four lavatories for each sex, even though the building code only calls for three for men and three for women.

You'll find other code requirements covering plumbing fixtures in UBC Chapter 29.

Sprinklers and Exits

We'll take a close look at sprinklers and exiting in later chapters. Section 904 covers fire-extinguishing systems and standpipes. Chapter 10 of the UBC covers exiting systems, now called means of egress.

Type of Construction vs. Occupancy

Group A occupancies, you will remember, have five major divisions. You can't have Division 2 and 2.1 occupancies in buildings without at least one-hour fire-resistive protection. This is spelled out in UBC Table 5-B (Figure 3-3). Let's take a look at this table and discuss how it could affect your building plans.

UBC Table 5-B shows the type of construction allowed in various occupancies and the allowable square footage. The column at the left of the chart gives the occupancy. The other columns give the square footage of floor area allowed for any of these occupancies for the type of construction shown. We'll look more closely at these in the next chapter. But for now, all you need to know is that there are five main types of construction. Type I is the most fire-resistive; Type V is the least.

Building Height vs. Type of Construction

Take a look at UBC Table 5-B (Figure 3-3). This shows how the type of construction governs the height of a building. In effect, it says: If you want to build this high, this is what you have to do for this particular occupancy.

Type I construction, which is about as noncombustible as you can get, has no height limitations. Type II construction may go to 160 feet with *fire-resistive (FR)* construction. All lesser types range between 40 and 65 feet high. To further confuse you, note that below the height limitation in feet is *maximum height in stories*. Also notice that in some instances there are certain occupancies that are not allowed in some types of construction regardless of height or area. This is very important to remember.

The use of "N" in these charts means there are *no requirements* for fire resistance. Unless otherwise noted, this "N" description applies to any of the UBC charts.

Allowable Area Increases

UBC Table 5-B may seem very restrictive. Well, maybe it is. But relief is available. For instance, there are several ways to increase the basic allowable floor area. One is to use a higher type of construction. If that's too expensive, there's another alternative. I call it *spatial separation*. It refers to allowing more space around your building as a barrier against fires that start in adjacent buildings. And conversely, it protects adjacent buildings from fires that start in *your* building.

Another good way to increase allowable floor area is to install automatic sprinkler systems. But this option is limited to certain occupancies and certain conditions. Although it's expensive, an increasing number of jurisdictions are requiring them, regardless of floor area.

There are several ways to get more floor space without turning to more expensive types of construction. Which method you choose is a matter of balancing the cost against the benefit. Let's see what the UBC permits:

505.1 General. *The floor areas specified in Section 504 (referring to Table 5-B) may be increased by employing one of the provisions of this section:*

505.1.1 Separation on two sides. *Where public ways or yards more than 20 feet (6096 mm) in width extend along and adjoin two sides of the building, floor areas may be increased at a rate of 1¼ percent for each foot (305 mm) by which the minimum width exceeds 20 feet (6096 mm), but the increase shall not exceed 50 percent.*

505.1.2 Separation on three sides. *Where public ways or yards more than 20 feet (6096 mm) in width extend along and adjoin three sides of the building, floor areas may be increased at a rate of 2½ percent for each foot (305 mm) by which the minimum width exceeds 20 feet (6096 mm), but the increase shall not exceed 100 percent.*

505.1.3 Separation on all sides. *Where public ways or yards more than 20 feet (6096 mm) in width extend on all sides of a building and adjoin the entire perimeter, floor areas may be increased at a rate of 5 percent for each foot (305 mm) by which the minimum width exceeds 20 feet (6096 mm). Such increases shall not exceed 100 percent, except that greater increases shall be permitted for the following occupancies:*

1. *Group S, Division 5 aircraft storage hangars not exceeding one story in height.*

2. *Group S, Division 2 or Group F, Division 2 Occupancies not exceeding two stories in height.*

3. *Group H, Division 5 aircraft repair hangars not exceeding one story in height. Area increases shall not exceed 500 percent for aircraft repair hangars except as provided in Section 505.2.*

Section 505.3 and Section 506 allow the maximum floor and height limitations to be compounded by the use of automatic sprinkler systems throughout. This almost becomes a moot point because so many jurisdictions are now requiring fire sprinkling systems in so many different buildings. There is even a nationwide push on now to require them in all Group R occupancies.

Personally, I have some problems with this for a number of reasons, especially the availability (or unavailability) of water. However, in the long run I still favor their use.

Compounding Area Computation

I explained earlier that you could increase the area in your building if it's surrounded by yards and streets — what I call *spatial separation*. Let's go back to that 10,500-square-foot building. By providing sprinklers we found that you could increase that footage to 31,500, provided it was all on one story. Now let's assume that this building has a 50-foot-wide street on two sides. Going back to Section 505.1 you'll find that the area can be increased again at the rate of 1¼ percent for each foot the minimum width exceeds 20 feet. For our 50-foot street, the excess is 30 feet. The total increase can't exceed 50 percent.

This amounts to a substantial increase in the size of your building. Let's figure it out:

10,500 x 1¼% x 30' x 3 (for sprinklers)
= 11,812 square feet

Which should you figure first, the percent increase gained by the separation, or the tripling for the sprinklers? Let's try it this way:

10,500 x (30' x 1¼%) x 3 = 11,812 square feet

It works either way. Now add 11,812 to 31,500 square feet. The building can be 43,312 square feet.

Let's go over this once more. This time let's assume that instead of a separation on just two sides, there will be a separation on all sides. Remember, the code says that we use a 5 per-cent increase for each foot of side yard by which the minimum width exceeds 20 feet. For our purposes we'll assume that the yards are all 50 feet wide.

10,500 x (30' x 5%) x 3 = 47,250 square feet

However, the maximum increase permitted is 100 percent, so we've got to redo our calculation:

10,500 x 100% x 3 = 31,500 square feet

When we add this number to our original 31,500 square feet, we see the building can now be up to 63,000 square feet in floor area. By either installing a fire sprinkler system or providing open space around a building, or both, we see how the maximum permitted size of the building can be increased.

Maximum Height of Buildings and Increases

Adding sprinklers to a building increases its allowable height. The maximum height and number of stories of every building depend on its occupancy and construction. Limits are in UBC Table 5-B.

If completely sprinklered, a building may be increased in height by one story. But this increase is *not* allowed if you've already computed the increase in floor area based on the sprinklers. Sorry about that.

If erected as part of the building and as long as they aren't used for habitation or storage, towers, spires and steeples made of non-combustible material are limited in height only by structural design. If they're made of combustible material, they can't exceed 20 feet above the height limitations in UBC Table 5-B.

Elevators and High-Rise Buildings

While we're discussing building height and area, I'd like to mention several hazards posed by elevators in high-rise buildings.

In 1972, following the earthquake in Sylmar, California, a study was done on elevator problems in multi-story buildings damaged by the earthquake. All that shaking caused the cables and counterweights to bang around in the elevator shafts, putting the elevators out of service even though there was little structural damage. In a five- to ten-story building this might be little more than a nuisance. But can you imagine what it would be like in a 30-story building?

If there's a fire in a high-rise building, automatic elevators can be a hazard. Most modern elevators have automatic controls. Unfortunately, the automatic controls respond to heat. The automatic control summons all elevators directly to the floor of the fire and opens the doors automatically. Any fire fighters riding in those cars would be exposed to a sudden burst of heat or flame as the door opens. And if the fire is close enough to the elevator, heat may stop the car — also an unpleasant situation for any riders. So fire fighters have to haul their equipment up many flights of stairs to get to the fire.

Most jurisdictions now require signs forbidding the use of elevators during fires.

Groups M and S Area Requirements

Generally, Groups M and S area requirements are quite lenient. And since most buildings outside the downtown area are surrounded by parking areas and streets, you can usually get increases. Allowable heights are also generous. UBC Table 5-B allows an S-1 or M occupancy in a Type V-N building (frame, with no fire-resistive construction) of 8,000 square feet. But Section 311.2.3.2 limits service stations (S-3) to noncombustible or one-hour fire-resistive construction. Storage garages must have floors protected against saturation.

In Group M occupancies, you must separate storage areas larger than 1,000 square feet in wholesale and retail stores from the sales area with one-hour occupancy separation walls unless the building has sprinklers. Then the allowable area may be increased.

Attic Separations

Section 708.3.1.2 usually requires attics exceeding 3,000 square feet to be divided by area separations if they're built with combustible materials. However, if the attic will have sprinklers, the allowable area may be increased. Draft stops are also included in this section and the reason is very simple — to prevent the spread of fire. That is also the reason that if automatic sprinklers are installed in an attic space the area may be increased to 9,000 square feet.

These separations are very important. Two serious motel fires in 1980 were aggravated by openings cut in the area separations by plumbers and electricians and not made fire-safe.

These separations must be made of gypsum wallboard (sheetrock) at least ½-inch-thick, 1-inch-thick tight-fitting wood, ⅜-inch-thick plywood, or other approved noncombustible material with adequate support. Protect any openings in attic separations by installing self-closing doors. And be sure to protect all wiring, plumbing and ductwork.

Exits

The code requires that all store exit doors swing in the direction of egress (the way out) when the occupant load exceeds 50 people. These doors can't swing over the public right of way. That means most exit doors in commercial buildings built to the property line must be recessed. Many property owners are reluctant to do that because it robs them of space inside the store. On new construction this problem can be addressed in the design. But what about replacing doors in existing buildings? This is something the inspector will take a hard look at.

There's another related problem: exiting from basements in Group M occupancies. All basements in Group M occupancies need two exits, one of which must open to the outside. But many older buildings aren't designed this way. And many owners of new buildings are reluctant to meet this requirement.

It's possible to get around this by having the basement stairs end near the rear door to provide easy exit. But check with the building inspector. He or she will be the one granting final approval.

How Much Remodeling Is Acceptable?

Some builders are surprised by code compliance problems when they start remodeling a home or store. One of the first questions the inspector may ask is why you intend to remodel. If you're just upgrading the property with no change in occupancy, there shouldn't be many problems. But if there'll be a new tenant with a different type of business, that's a different story. A changed occupancy may require basic changes in the building that weren't anticipated. You'd have to go all the way back to the basic question of occupancy group determination. For our purposes, let's assume you're only upgrading the premises.

If your city adopted the UBC without amendment, the following sections would apply:

3403.1 General. Buildings and structures to which additions, alterations or repairs are made shall comply with all requirements of this code for new facilities except as specifically provided in this section. See Section 310.9 for provisions requiring installation of smoke detectors in existing Group R, Division 3 Occupancies.

3403.2 When Allowed. Additions, alteration or repairs may be made to any building or structure without requiring the existing building or structure to comply with all the requirements of this code, provided the addition, alteration or repair conforms to that required for a new building or structure.

The code then goes on to say that the modifications shall not create an unsafe condition in any part of the structure. This happens all too often, particularly with homeowners doing their own work. The unsafe conditions include hazards or obstructions and also fire danger. The section continues:

Additions or alterations shall not be made to an existing building or structure that will cause the existing building or structure to be in violation of any of the provisions of this code and such additions or alterations shall not cause the existing building or structure to become unsafe.

Finally, we get down to Section 3403.5, which considers the conditions of historic buildings. Because this is both a local and federal situation, I'll refer you to your local building official for a final decision.

Incidentally, moved buildings must conform to these sections on alterations as well as any intended change of use. This is found in Sections 3404 and 3405, respectively.

If the owner is just trying to bring the building up to current code standards or making changes to qualify for more favorable insurance rates, no problem. But I suggest that you invite the building inspector to go through the place with you, pointing out all areas of non-compliance. You don't have to renovate the whole building, of course. But the inspector may require some changes that involve key hazards. It's better to find out about those early in the project.

Group E Occupancies

This group covers schools. The trend today is toward larger, consolidated schools. Usually larger contracting firms (or groups of smaller firms) get these jobs.

Normally, plans for new schools are examined very thoroughly for code compliance well before construction begins. State (and maybe federal) authorities go over the plans with a fine-tooth comb. The local building department will give them another review. All the general contractor has to do is follow the plans. But many smaller construction firms do remodeling work in public schools and build smaller private schools. In that case, some code problems may have to be worked out as you go.

Group E occupancies (the educational group) may be any type of construction. Of course, they're still governed by UBC Table 5-B (Figure 3-3). Both area and height dictate the type of construction.

Notice that all areas for kindergarten, first and second grades must be located on the first floor, not above or below. Keep this in mind when you're asked to convert a basement in an existing home into a day-care center. Consult the local building inspector or fire marshal before going too far with your plans.

The building code rarely specifies a definite number of water closets, urinals and lavatories, except in Group E occupancies. Section 2902.4 states:

Water closets shall be provided on the basis of the following ratio of water closets to the number of students:

	Boys/Girls
Elementary schools	*1:100/1:35*
Secondary schools	*1:100/1:45*

In addition, urinals shall be provided for boys on the basis of 1:30 in elementary and secondary schools.

There shall be provided at least one lavatory for each two water closets or urinals, and at least one drinking fountain on each floor for elementary and secondary schools.

Group E Exits and Corridors

All exit doors serving areas of more than 50 occupants must swing outward and have panic hardware. It's a good idea to have all exit doors swing outward, even where it's not required.

This is a good place to bring up the requirements for school corridors. Section 1007.3.5

requires that a hallway or corridor in a Group E, Division 1 occupancy must be the width required by Section 1003.2.3 plus 2 feet, but not less than 6 feet. There's one exception. If it serves less than 100 occupants, the hallway or corridor can be 44 inches wide.

To determine the width of the exits, Section 1003.2.3.2 states:

Minimum width. The width, in inches (mm), of any component in the means of egress system shall not be less than the product determined by multiplying the total occupant load served by such component by the applicable factor set forth in Table 10-B. In no case shall the width of an individual means of egress component be less than the minimum required for such component as specified elsewhere in this chapter.

Where more than one exit or exit-access doorway serves a building or portion thereof, such calculated width may be divided approximately equally among the means of egress components serving as exits or exit-access doorways for that area.

Can the hallway or corridor be reduced by so-called "natural" barriers? Yes, but very little. Section 1004.3.4.2 states:

Width. The width of corridors shall be determined as specified in Section 1003.2.3, but such width shall not be less than 44 inches (1118 mm), except as specified herein. Corridors serving an occupant load of less than 50 shall not be less than 36 inches (914 mm) in width.

The required width of corridors shall be unobstructed.

Exception: Doors, when fully opened, and handrails shall not reduce the required width by more than 7 inches (178 mm). Doors in any position shall not reduce the required width by more than one half. Other nonstructural projections such as trim and similar decorative features may project into the required width 1½ inches (38 mm) from each side

Later in this book I'll explain in detail how exit widths are determined. But there's one other requirement I'd like to mention here. The maximum distance from any point in the school building to the nearest exit must not exceed 150 feet for unsprinklered buildings and 225 feet for sprinklered buildings.

Group F Occupancies

Most of the "Factory and Industrial" uses have been accumulated into Group F Occupancies. Division 1 includes 42 moderate hazard industrial uses, while Division 2 contains seven in the low hazard group. There is one thing that concerns me and that is the long list of items in Division 1 and the short list under Division 2. No, my concern isn't in the uses themselves but in the fact they've tried to cover all bases. Somewhere, someone is going to come up with a use that's not listed. Also, what if a company wants to produce something in both divisions? There is a small disclaimer in the Division 2 list which states " . . . including, but not limited to, the following."

Group H Occupancies

Group H includes seven divisions. In general, the most hazardous uses are in the first divisions, followed by reduced hazards in the lower divisions.

Group H (hazardous) occupancies include areas where highly flammable materials are stored, processed or used, or where highly combustible manufacturing is done. See UBC Table 3-D (Figure 3-6), *Exempt amounts of hazardous materials presenting a physical hazard.* Table 3-F (Figure 3-7) lists the distance from property lines and wall openings for storage of explosive materials. At first glance one would suspect this was a large-city problem. However, after looking at the number of uses contained in Group H occupancies, it's easy to see they could be used anywhere. Here's another place where you have to consider environmental concerns.

There are a number of special regulations that apply only to this category. Floors must be of noncombustible, liquid-tight construction. Spill control, such as the use of curbs and secondary containment, is often required in order to prevent the flow of hazardous liquids to adjoining areas. Sometimes a standby power system or an emergency power system is necessary to ensure continued electrical power.

Group H occupancies are also much more limited in height and floor area than other types of uses. For example, UBC Table 5-B (Figure 3-3) restricts most of the high hazard uses to buildings of one or two stories. While a Type II-N warehouse (S-1) could normally be up to 12,000 square feet in area, when it contains hazardous materials (H-3), it's limited to 7,500 square feet.

If highly flammable or combustible liquids are stored, the building department may require a detailed report by an expert to identify methods of protection.

The concept of open space around a building strikes fear into the hearts of many developers. But space required by the UBC usually isn't a major problem. I mentioned that a street 60 feet wide would serve as part of the open space. Most buildings have a city street at least that wide on one side. Plus most zoning ordinances require a certain amount of off-street parking for commercial buildings. That usually provides plenty of space on a second side.

Exhaust Ventilation

Exhaust ventilation is strictly controlled in Group H occupancies. The Fire Code and Mechanical Code contain requirements for exhausting explosive, corrosive, combustible, flammable or highly toxic fumes and vapors. Ducts conveying such products must extend directly to the exterior and not pass through plenum areas.

Good ventilation is just as important in your own garage if you plan to run a car engine there. But you don't need to install an exhaust system. Opening the garage door is much more effective.

TABLE 3-D—EXEMPT AMOUNTS OF HAZARDOUS MATERIALS PRESENTING A PHYSICAL HAZARD
MAXIMUM QUANTITIES PER CONTROL AREA[1]
When two units are given, values within parentheses are in cubic feet (cu. ft.) or pounds (lbs.)

CONDITION		STORAGE[2]			USE[2]—CLOSED SYSTEMS			USE[2]—OPEN SYSTEMS	
Material	Class	Solid Lbs.[3] (Cu. Ft.) $\times 0.4536$ for kg $\times 0.0283$ for m³	Liquid Gallons[3] (Lbs.) $\times 3.785$ for L $\times 0.4536$ for kg	Gas Cu. Ft. $\times 0.0283$ for m³	Solid Lbs. (Cu. Ft.) $\times 0.4536$ for kg $\times 0.0283$ for m³	Liquid Gallons (Lbs.) $\times 3.785$ for L $\times 0.4536$ for kg	Gas Cu. Ft. $\times 0.0283$ for m³	Solid Lbs. (Cu. Ft.) $\times 0.4536$ for kg $\times 0.0283$ for m³	Liquid Gallons (Lbs.) $\times 3.785$ for L $\times 0.4536$ for kg
1.1 Combustible liquid[4,5,6,7,8,9]	II	N.A.	120[10]	N.A.	N.A.	120	N.A.	N.A.	30
	III-A	N.A.	330[10]	N.A.	N.A.	330	N.A.	N.A.	80
	III-B	N.A.	13,200[10,11]	N.A.	N.A.	13,200[11]	N.A.	N.A.	3,300[11]
1.2 Combustible fiber (loose)		(100)	N.A.	N.A.	(100)	N.A.	N.A.	(20)	N.A.
(baled)		(1,000)	N.A.	N.A.	(1,000)	N.A.	N.A.	(200)	N.A.
1.3 Cryogenic, flammable or oxidizing		N.A.	45	N.A.	N.A.	45	N.A.	N.A.	10
2.1 Explosives		1[10,13]	(1)[10,13]	N.A.	1/4[12]	(1/4)[12]	N.A.	1/4[12]	(1/4)[12]
3.1 Flammable solid		125[6,10]	N.A.	N.A.	[14]	N.A.	N.A.	[14]	N.A.
3.2 Flammable gas (gaseous)		N.A.	N.A.	750[6,10]	N.A.	N.A.	750[6,10]	N.A.	N.A.
(liquefied)		N.A.	15[6,10]	N.A.	N.A.	15[6,10]	N.A.	N.A.	N.A.
3.3 Flammable liquid[4,5,6,7,8,9]	I-A	N.A.	30[10]	N.A.	N.A.	30	N.A.	N.A.	10
	I-B	N.A.	60[10]	N.A.	N.A.	60	N.A.	N.A.	15
	I-C	N.A.	90[10]	N.A.	N.A.	90	N.A.	N.A.	20
Combination I-A, I-B, I-C[15]		N.A.	120[10]	N.A.	N.A.	120	N.A.	N.A.	30
4.1 Organic peroxide, unclassified detonatable		1[10,12]	(1)[10,12]	N.A.	1/4[12]	(1/4)[12]	N.A.	1/4[12]	(1/4)[12]
4.2 Organic peroxide	I	5[6,10]	(5)[6,10]	N.A.	1[6]	(1)[6]	N.A.	1[6]	(1)[6]
	II	50[6,10]	(50)[6,10]	N.A.	50[6]	(50)[6]	N.A.	10[6]	(10)[6]
	III	125[6,10]	(125)[6,10]	N.A.	125[6]	(125)[6]	N.A.	25[6]	(25)[6]
	IV	500[6,10]	(500)[6,10]	N.A.	500[6]	(500)[6]	N.A.	100[6]	(100)[6]
	V	N.L.	N.L.	N.A.	N.L.	N.L.	N.A.	N.L.	N.L.
4.3 Oxidizer	4	1[10,12]	(1)[10,12]	N.A.	1/4[12]	(1/4)[12]	N.A.	1/4[12]	(1/4)[12]
	3[16]	10[6,10]	(10)[6,10]	N.A.	2[6]	(2)[6]	N.A.	2[6]	(2)[6]
	2	250[6,10]	(250)[6,10]	N.A.	250[6]	(250)[6]	N.A.	50[6]	(50)[6]
	1	4,000[6,10]	(4,000)[6,10]	N.A.	4,000[6]	(4,000)[6]	N.A.	1,000[6]	(1,000)[6]
4.4 Oxidizer—gas (gaseous)[6,10]		N.A.	N.A.	1,500	N.A.	N.A.	1,500	N.A.	N.A.
(liquefied)[6,10]		N.A.	15	N.A.	N.A.	15	N.A.	N.A.	N.A.
5.1 Pyrophoric		4[10,12]	(4)[10,12]	50[10,12]	1[12]	(1)[12]	10[10,12]	0	0
6.1 Unstable (reactive)	4	1[10,12]	(1)[10,12]	10[10,12]	1/4[12]	(1/4)[12]	2[10,12]	1/4[12]	(1/4)[12]
	3	5[6,10]	(5)[6,10]	50[6,10]	1[6]	(1)[6]	10[6,10]	1[6]	(1)[6]
	2	50[6,10]	(50)[6,10]	250[6,10]	50[6]	(50)[6]	250[6,10]	10[6]	(10)[6]
	1	N.L.	N.L.	750[6,10]	N.L.	N.L.	N.L.	N.L.	N.L.
7.1 Water reactive	3	5[6,10]	(5)[6,10]	N.A.	5[6]	(5)[6]	N.A.	1[6]	(1)[6]
	2	50[6,10]	(50)[6,10]	N.A.	50[6]	(50)[6]	N.A.	10[6]	(10)[6]
	1	125[10,11]	(125)[10,11]	N.A.	125[11]	(125)[11]	N.A.	25[11]	(25)[11]

N.A.—Not applicable.   N.L.—Not limited.

[1]Control areas shall be separated from each other by not less than a one-hour fire-resistive occupancy separation. The number of control areas within a building used for retail or wholesale sales shall not exceed two. The number of control areas in buildings with other uses shall not exceed four. See Section 204.

[2]The aggregate quantity in use and storage shall not exceed the quantity listed for storage.

[3]The aggregate quantity of nonflammable solid and nonflammable or noncombustible liquid hazardous materials within a single control area of Group M Occupancies used for retail sales may exceed the exempt amounts when such areas are in compliance with the Fire Code.

[4]The quantities of alcoholic beverages in retail sales uses are unlimited provided the liquids are packaged in individual containers not exceeding 4 liters.
    The quantities of medicines, foodstuffs and cosmetics containing not more than 50 percent of volume of water-miscible liquids and with the remainder of the solutions not being flammable in retail sales or storage occupancies are unlimited when packaged in individual containers not exceeding 4 liters.

[5]For aerosols, see the Fire Code.

[6]Quantities may be increased 100 percent in sprinklered buildings. When Footnote 10 also applies, the increase for both footnotes may be applied.

[7]For storage and use of flammable and combustible liquids in Groups A, B, E, F, H, I, M, R, S and U Occupancies, see Sections 303.8, 304.8, 305.8, 306.8, 307.1.3 through 307.1.5, 308.8, 309.8, 310.12, 311.8 and 312.4.

[8]For wholesale and retail sales use, also see the Fire Code.

[9]Spray application of any quantity of flammable or combustible liquids shall be conducted as set forth in the Fire Code.

[10]Quantities may be increased 100 percent when stored in approved storage cabinets, gas cabinets or exhausted enclosures as specified in the Fire Code. When Footnote 6 also applies, the increase for both footnotes may be applied.

[11]The quantities permitted in a sprinklered building are not limited.

[12]Permitted in sprinklered buildings only. None is allowed in unsprinklered buildings.

[13]One pound of black sporting powder and 20 pounds (9 kg) of smokeless powder are permitted in sprinklered or unsprinklered buildings.

[14]See definitions of Divisions 2 and 3 in Section 307.1.

[15]Containing not more than the exempt amounts of Class I-A, Class I-B or Class I-C flammable liquids.

[16]A maximum quantity of 200 pounds (90.7 kg) of solid or 20 gallons (75.7 L) of liquid Class 3 oxidizers may be permitted when such materials are necessary for maintenance purposes or operation of equipment as set forth in the Fire Code.

From the Uniform Building Code, ©1997, ICBO

Figure 3-6 *Exempt amounts of hazardous materials*

TABLE 3-F—MINIMUM DISTANCES FOR BUILDINGS CONTAINING EXPLOSIVE MATERIALS

QUANTITY OF EXPLOSIVE MATERIAL[1]		MINIMUM DISTANCE (feet)		
		×304.8 for mm		
Pounds Over	Pounds Not Over	Property Lines[2] and Inhabited Buildings[3]		Separation of Magazines[4,5,6]
×0.4536 for kg		Barricaded[4]	Unbarricaded	
2	5	70	140	12
5	10	90	180	16
10	20	110	220	20
20	30	125	250	22
30	40	140	280	24
40	50	150	300	28
50	75	170	340	30
75	100	190	380	32
100	125	200	400	36
125	150	215	430	38
150	200	235	470	42
200	250	255	510	46
250	300	270	540	48
300	400	295	590	54
400	500	320	640	58
500	600	340	680	62
600	700	355	710	64
700	800	375	750	66
800	900	390	780	70
900	1,000	400	800	72
1,000	1,200	425	850	78
1,200	1,400	450	900	82
1,400	1,600	470	940	86
1,600	1,800	490	980	88
1,800	2,000	505	1,010	90
2,000	2,500	545	1,090	98
2,500	3,000	580	1,160	104
3,000	4,000	635	1,270	116
4,000	5,000	685	1,370	122
5,000	6,000	730	1,460	130
6,000	7,000	770	1,540	136
7,000	8,000	800	1,600	144
8,000	9,000	835	1,670	150
9,000	10,000	865	1,730	156
10,000	12,000	875	1,750	164
12,000	14,000	885	1,770	174
14,000	16,000	900	1,800	180
16,000	18,000	940	1,880	188
18,000	20,000	975	1,950	196
20,000	25,000	1,055	2,000	210
25,000	30,000	1,130	2,000	224
30,000	35,000	1,205	2,000	238
35,000	40,000	1,275	2,000	248
40,000	45,000	1,340	2,000	258
45,000	50,000	1,400	2,000	270
50,000	55,000	1,460	2,000	280
55,000	60,000	1,515	2,000	290
60,000	65,000	1,565	2,000	300
65,000	70,000	1,610	2,000	310
70,000	75,000	1,655	2,000	320
75,000	80,000	1,695	2,000	330
80,000	85,000	1,730	2,000	340
85,000	90,000	1,760	2,000	350
90,000	95,000	1,790	2,000	360
95,000	100,000	1,815	2,000	370

(Continued)

From the Uniform Building Code, ©1997, ICBO

Figure 3-7 *Minimum distances for explosive materials*

TABLE 3-F—MINIMUM DISTANCES FOR BUILDINGS CONTAINING EXPLOSIVE MATERIALS—(Continued)

QUANTITY OF EXPLOSIVE MATERIAL[1]		MINIMUM DISTANCE (feet)		
		× 304.8 for mm		
Pounds Over	Pounds Not Over	Property Lines[2] and Inhabited Buildings[3]		Separation of Magazines[4,5,6]
× 0.4536 for kg		Barricaded[4]	Unbarricaded	
100,000	110,000	1,835	2,000	390
110,000	120,000	1,855	2,000	410
120,000	130,000	1,875	2,000	430
130,000	140,000	1,890	2,000	450
140,000	150,000	1,900	2,000	470
150,000	160,000	1,935	2,000	490
160,000	170,000	1,965	2,000	510
170,000	180,000	1,990	2,000	530
180,000	190,000	2,010	2,010	550
190,000	200,000	2,030	2,030	570
200,000	210,000	2,055	2,055	590
210,000	230,000	2,100	2,100	630
230,000	250,000	2,155	2,155	670
250,000	275,000	2,215	2,215	720
275,000	300,000	2,275	2,275	770

[1]The number of pounds (kg) of explosives listed is the number of pounds of trinitrotoluene (TNT) or the equivalent pounds (kg) of other explosive.

[2]The distance listed is the distance to property line, including property lines at public ways.

[3]Inhabited building is any building on the same property that is regularly occupied by human beings. When two or more buildings containing explosives or magazines are located on the same property, each building or magazine shall comply with the minimum distances specified from inhabited buildings, and, in addition, they shall be separated from each other by not less than the distances shown for "Separation of Magazines," except that the quantity of explosive materials contained in detonator buildings or magazines shall govern in regard to the spacing of said detonator buildings or magazines from buildings or magazines containing other explosive materials. If any two or more buildings or magazines are separated from each other by less than the specified "Separation of Magazines" distances, then such two or more buildings or magazines, as a group, shall be considered as one building or magazine, and the total quantity of explosive materials stored in such group shall be treated as if the explosive were in a single building or magazine located on the site of any building or magazine of the group, and shall comply with the minimum distance specified from other magazines or inhibited buildings.

[4]Barricades shall effectively screen the building containing explosives from other buildings, public ways or magazines. When mounds or revetted walls of earth are used for barricades, they shall not be less than 3 feet (914 mm) in thickness. A straight line from the top of any side wall of the building containing explosive materials to the eave line of any other building, magazine or a point 12 feet (3658 mm) above the center line of a public way shall pass through the barricades.

[5]Magazine is a building or structure approved for storage of explosive materials. In addition to the requirements of this code, magazines shall comply with the Fire Code.

[6]The distance listed may be reduced by 50 percent when approved natural or artificial barriers are provided in accordance with the requirements in Footnote 4.

Figure 3-7 *Minimum distances for explosive materials (Continued)*

Heliports and Helistops

Helistops are now controlled under Group S, Division 5 and heliports are under the stricter Group H, Division 5. In spite of the fact that they're generally outdoors, requirements regarding their operation are more stringent.

Even if you live in a small town, you may be called on to build a helistop or even the more sophisticated heliport. The local hospital might need one. And many crop dusters are now using helicopters in their business.

It's important to understand the difference between a heliport and a helistop, or landing pad. According to the definition section of the UBC, a heli*port* is any area where helicopters can be completely serviced, while a heli*stop* is only for taking on or discharging passengers. A heliport is subject to far more restrictions because there will be flammable materials present.

The landing pad, or helistop, beside the local hospital would have very few restrictions. But if the pad were on the roof of the hospital, you'd have to include the weight of the helicopter in the anticipated roof load. However, they wouldn't be able to add fuel or do any service work up there. A simple concrete pad with adequate clearance makes the best helistop.

Group I Occupancies

Group I occupancies are considered as institutional uses. Division 1 includes hospitals and nursing homes where the residents can't get out without assistance. Full-time nurseries for small children also fall into this group. Division 2 covers nursing homes with residents who have the ability to evacuate the building under their own power.

Mental hospitals, prisons, jails and similar structures that are built to restrain the occupants are considered Division 3.

Due to the limitations of the occupants' ability to independently and quickly exit a building in case of fire or other emergency, construction restrictions are much more severe. Stringent egress, height, floor area, and type of construction requirements are mandated for all institutional occupancies.

Group M Occupancies

Group M includes the "mercantile" uses and there's only one division. This lists uses normally found in shopping areas, whether in a downtown setting or a shopping center. There are seven uses listed: department stores, drug stores, markets, paint stores without bulk handling, shopping centers, sales rooms, and wholesale and retail stores.

Group R — The Residential Occupancy

Most of the work you do will be either Group R (residential) or Group B (business and commercial). Group R-1 includes hotels, motels, apartment houses, convents and monasteries. Until you get into large occupant loads, the usual construction restrictions are quite liberal.

Under the UBC, hotels and motels are the same. They're both classified as hotels, maybe because hotels have been around for a long time. Motels are motor hotels and first began to appear when cars became common.

Here's the definition of a hotel under the UBC:

Any building containing six or more guest rooms intended or designed to be used, or which are used, rented or hired out to be occupied, or which are occupied for sleeping purposes by guests.

A little further along in the definitions we find that the word motel:

. . . shall mean hotel as defined in this code.

In apartments, every sleeping room below the fourth floor must have an openable window or exterior door to permit emergency exit or rescue. The window must be at least 24 inches high and 20 inches wide, with a minimum of 5.7 square feet of openable area. The sill must be no more than 44 inches above the floor.

There are two main reason for this. First, floors above the fourth are excluded because that's as high as the ladders of most fire trucks can reach. There's not much point jumping out the window from the fifth floor to save yourself. Second, the code requires either Type I or Type II-F.R. construction above the fourth floor. Using more fire-restrictive type of construction reduces the fire danger considerably.

A few other restrictions are noteworthy. Corridors serving 10 or more people, as determined by UBC Table 10-A (Figure 3-1), must be fire-resistive for one hour. All doors leading into this corridor must be fire-rated for 20 minutes; there can be no louvers, grilles or transoms unless they're protected by a fire and smoke damper. The corridor can't have a dead-end length over 20 feet long.

Group S Occupancies

Group S Occupancies has picked up items from several groups of the previous codes. There are five divisions in this group and they're concerned with storage areas not classified as hazardous occupancies. Division 1 is a moderate hazard category used for storage of combustible materials that aren't listed in Division 2.

Division 2 lists 23 items that are considered low hazard. They range from the storage of beer or wine, cement in bags, cold storage and creameries on down to stoves and washers.

Division 3 includes repair garages involved in the exchange of parts and maintenance but no welding or open flames.

Division 4 is for open parking garages and Division 5 is aircraft hangars where maintenance and exchange of repair parts is made.

Group U Occupancies

Group U Occupancies include private garages, carports, sheds, and agricultural buildings in Division 1. Division 2 is for fences over 6 feet in height, tanks and towers.

Leaping from Second Stories

Fire is the major cause of death and injury in buildings. That's why the building code takes fire safety so seriously. But authors of the code can't do much about the weird things people do when there's a fire. You've probably heard about people jumping to their death from tall hotel buildings when a fire broke out many stories below. It happens. Usually you're much safer to stay in the room and keep the door closed.

But jumping from the second story isn't much of a risk compared to exiting through a burning corridor. That's why the code sets minimum window sizes and heights. But I wouldn't recommend *jumping*. A far better alternative is *dropping* from the second floor. Figure 3-8 makes my point. If you're standing on a second floor balcony, your eye level is about 16 feet above the first floor (and probably the exterior grade level). The balcony railing is about 13 feet above grade. If you were hanging by your hands from the balcony railing, your feet would be only about 6 feet above grade — a relatively short and much safer drop to the ground. Even an old building inspector like me could handle that in a pinch.

Dwelling Requirements

Group R-3 occupancies (dwellings) are probably the least restricted of all occupied buildings. Most of the requirements are just common sense. For example, living, dining and

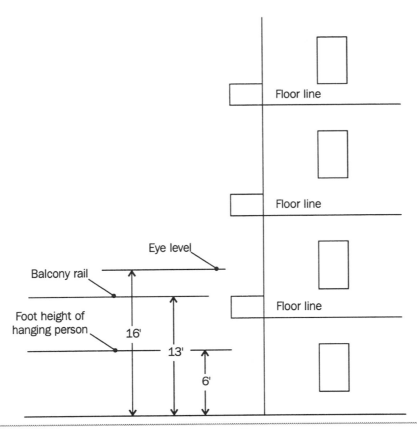

Figure 3-8 *Panic leaping from second story*

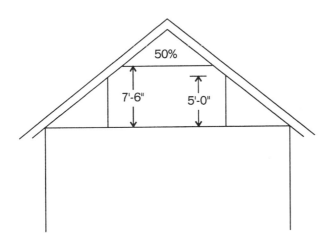

50% of ceiling area of a room must be at least 7½ feet above the floor. No portion measuring less than 5 feet high can be included in minimum size.

Figure 3-9 *Relative ceiling heights*

sleeping rooms are required to have windows. These windows must open directly to the outside, but they can open to a roofed porch if it has a ceiling height of at least 7 feet and is 65 percent open on the longer side. It, too, must open directly to the outside.

Required windows must have a total area of at least 10 percent of the floor area of the room or at least 10 square feet. Bathrooms must have windows at least 3 square feet in area, half of which must be openable. Baths without windows must have mechanical ventilation direct to the exterior.

A room with a toilet must be separated from food preparation or storage rooms by a tight-fitting door. The code used to say that the door *couldn't* open into such an area at all. This restriction has been relaxed, but I still think it's a good idea to avoid this situation where possible.

I grew up on a farm where the toilet was out beyond the woodshed and the bathtub was brought into the kitchen on Saturday night. It seemed fine to me. But now, under modern codes, every dwelling unit must have a water closet, lavatory, and either a bathtub or shower, and the kitchen must have a sink. These fixtures must be provided with hot and cold running water.

The code gives standard height and area requirements. Your ceiling can't be less than 7'6" for at least 50 percent of its area, and no part can be less than 5 feet. See Figure 3-9. One room must have at least 120 square feet of area; bedrooms must be at least 70 square feet. No room (except a kitchen) may be less than 7 feet at any dimension. A water closet compartment must be at least 30 inches wide and have a space at least 24 inches in front of the water closet.

Attached Garages

An attached garage must have a modified one-hour fire-resistive separation between it and the house. And door openings into the house must be solid core or fire-resistive, with a self-closing device. No garage can open directly into a sleeping room.

The separation requirement between the garage and the residence may seem a little ridiculous. A recent survey disclosed that four out of five fires began, not in the garage as often suspected, but in the house. That brings up an interesting question: What are they trying to protect — the car or the house?

The requirement for a self-closing, solid-core door deserves a comment or two. This is intended to protect people inside the house from carbon monoxide coming from an auto idling in the garage. Consider what might happen on a cold day. You open the garage door and start your car. The rest of the family is asleep and you're not aware that the wind is blowing gas fumes into your house. This could be fatal. That's why you must have a door with a self-closing device.

Don't blame the building inspector for this requirement. It's in the code and it's a good regulation. The code has many worthwhile rules. The problem is that there's no provision for follow-up. The inspector can make you install protective devices, but he can't require you to maintain them.

Smoke alarms are required by code in residential units. Many states have laws requiring them in all new residential units. But there's no law requiring regular maintenance. That's up to the occupants.

We Didn't Build Them Like That

I've been in and around construction for over 40 years. And I've seen a lot of changes in those years. Not too long ago I was talking with a retired carpenter friend about changes in the construction industry since we were apprentices. My friend complained to me about the way things are being done today. "They don't build 'em like we used to," he said.

He's right. And maybe it's a good thing. If you compare the quality of workmanship, I think today's tradesmen stand up pretty well against tradesmen 40 or 50 years ago. I've seen a lot of those houses from the good ol' days in various stages of reconstruction or remodeling. What we build today is different, and the workmanship may be better.

But we've seen more changes in materials and techniques than in workmanship. When I first got into the industry, sheathing was diagonal shiplap nailed to toe studding.

All of the openings were hand sawed after the walls were sheathed. Then the wall was covered with building paper and siding. We called it double-wall construction and used it on nearly every home.

That ended in the late 1940s when plywood became popular. Nothing has been the same since. "What happened to double-wall construction?" my old friend asked. "That don't look safe to me." Well, I'm always polite to the old-timers. I'm one myself, now. But I believe the plywood walls we build today are much stronger than the old diagonal shiplap. Authors of the building codes seem to agree. And plywood sheathing sure goes up faster than diagonal sheathing.

There's been one more change in construction in the last 50 years. I think it's the biggest change of all. Maybe you can guess what I'm talking about. It's building codes. There weren't any in most cities and counties in the 1930s. Even the codes we had weren't very good by today's standards. And sometimes they weren't enforced.

I'm not going to claim that houses built in the 1930s aren't safe and durable. They are. Most are still in use today. But most also show their age. Plumbing, heating and electrical systems are unreliable or inadequate. They're more expensive to heat and cool. Floors squeak and sag. Windows stick. And they're drafty.

Don't misunderstand what I'm saying. To me, many older homes have a charm that newer homes can't touch. But you've got to make allowances if you like living in an antique. Most people want all the conveniences, not the inconveniences. It's for those people that building codes are written.

4

Types of Construction and Fire Resistance

In the last two chapters we discussed occupancy groups and occupancy loads. I mentioned several times that each occupancy group requires a different type of construction. In this chapter we'll begin to look at the construction required for each of those occupancy groups.

UBC Table 6-A (Figure 4-1) shows the fire-resistive requirements for each construction type.

Buildings Classified by Construction

Usually the *entire* building (or an entire portion of a building within an area separation wall) must conform to the type of construction specified to meet the minimum requirements for that classification. But note that we're speaking of minimums here, not maximums. The code only requires that a building conform to the minimum requirements for occupancy, height, and area. You can always provide a higher classification of construction. It might even be to your advantage. For example, going to a higher classification might reduce insurance premiums enough to repay the higher construction cost.

You can divide a building by fire walls so that each area is a different classification. But these area separations must be complete from the foundation to the roof, and they must meet minimum standards in the code for fire walls.

The UBC Chapter 6 describes the general code restrictions that apply to all types of

TABLE 6-A—TYPES OF CONSTRUCTION—FIRE-RESISTIVE REQUIREMENTS (In Hours)
For details, see occupancy section in Chapter 3, type of construction sections in this chapter and sections referenced in this table.

BUILDING ELEMENT	TYPE I	TYPE II			TYPE III		TYPE IV	TYPE V	
	Noncombustible	Noncombustible			Combustible		Combustible		
	Fire-resistive	Fire-resistive	1-Hr.	N	1-Hr.	N	H.T.	1-Hr.	N
1. Bearing walls—exterior	4 Sec. 602.3.1	4 Sec. 603.3.1	1	N	4 Sec. 604.3.1	4 Sec. 604.3.1	4 Sec. 605.3.1	1	N
2. Bearing walls—interior	3	2	1	N	1	N	1	1	N
3. Nonbearing walls—exterior	4 Sec. 602.3.1	4 Sec. 603.3.1	1 Sec. 603.3.1	N	4 Sec. 604.3.1	4 Sec. 604.3.1	4 Sec. 605.3.1	1	N
4. Structural frame[1]	3	2	1	N	1	N	1 or H.T.	1	N
5. Partitions—permanent	1[2]	1[2]	1[2]	N	1	N	1 or H.T.	1	N
6. Shaft enclosures[3]	2	2	1	1	1	1	1	1	1
7. Floors and floor-ceilings	2	2	1	N	1	N	H.T.	1	N
8. Roofs and roof-ceilings	2 Sec. 602.5	1 Sec. 603.5	1 Sec. 603.5	N	1	N	H.T.	1	N
9. Exterior doors and windows	Sec. 602.3.2	Sec. 603.3.2	Sec. 603.3.2	Sec. 603.3.2	Sec. 604.3.2	Sec. 604.3.2	Sec. 605.3.2	Sec. 606.3	Sec. 606.3
10. Stairway construction	Sec. 602.4	Sec. 603.4	Sec. 603.4	Sec. 603.4	Sec. 604.4	Sec. 604.4	Sec. 605.4	Sec. 606.4	Sec. 606.4

N—No general requirements for fire resistance.
H.T.—Heavy timber.

[1]Structural frame elements in an exterior wall that is located where openings are not permitted, or where protection of openings is required, shall be protected against external fire exposure as required for exterior-bearing walls or the structural frame, whichever is greater.
[2]Fire-retardant-treated wood (see Section 207) may be used in the assembly, provided fire-resistance requirements are maintained. See Sections 602 and 603.
[3]For special provisions, see Sections 304.6, 306.6 and 711.

Figure 4-1 *Fire-resistive requirements*

construction. Specific restrictions for each building type are listed in the following chapters of the UBC:

Section 602 — Type I fire-resistive buildings

Section 603 — Type II buildings

Section 604 — Type III buildings

Section 605 — Type IV buildings

Section 606 — Type V buildings

In many cases, a broad rule is established for all occupancy groups, and then exceptions are made for certain occupancy groups. For instance, consider Section 712 — Usable Space Under Floors:

Usable space under the first story shall be enclosed, and such enclosure, when constructed of metal or wood, shall be protected on the side of the usable space as required for one-hour fire-resistive construction. Doors shall be self-closing, tight-fitting of solid-wood construction 1³⁄₈ inches (35 mm) in thickness or self-closing, tight fitting doors acceptable as a part of an assembly having a fire-protection rating of not less than 20 minutes when tested in accordance with Part II of UBC Standard 7-2.

Exceptions:

1. Group R, Division 3 and Group U Occupancies.

2. *Basements in single-story Group S, Division 3 repair garages when 10 percent or more of the area of the floor-ceiling is open to the first floor.*

3. *Under-floor spaces protected by an automatic sprinkler system.*

Fire Resistance Determines Type of Construction

Notice that in UBC Table 6-A the fire resistance of certain building elements determines the type of construction you can use. These elements are the exterior and interior bearing walls, exterior nonbearing walls, structural frame, permanent partitions, shaft enclosures, floors, roofs, exterior doors and windows.

Table 6-A is kind of sneaky. It lists everything you must do to build a certain fire resistiveness into a building and establishes the type of construction. But what if you slack up on one little item? Let's say, for instance, that you're building a 15-story apartment building. Checking the UBC Table 5-B (shown in Chapter 3, Figure 3-3) you find that a Type II building is limited to 12 stories for an apartment building. So you'll have to use Type I construction.

Maybe by reducing the roof from a two-hour fire-resistive construction to one-hour you could save a few bucks. After all, a one-hour roof is pretty safe. So you draw up your specifications and then find the plans examiner shaking his head. What went wrong?

The inspector has noted that if one segment or element of Table 6-A is reduced, you've automatically reduced the whole structure one grade. Although you have a fine building, if you insist on going with the one-hour roof, you can only build a 12-story apartment building.

You have to make a choice. Are you going to build a two-hour roof, or are you going to reduce your building to 12 stories? The cost of installing that two-hour roof is very small compared to losing three floors of apartments. Evaluate all the alternatives before deciding. But remember, whenever you reduce one element of the building, the whole building will be classified in a lower grade.

It's possible to have a four-hour exterior bearing wall, a three-hour structural frame, and two-hour floors — all elements of a Type I building — and still wind up with a Type V building because the rest of the elements didn't measure up to the requirements of UBC Table 6-A.

Roof Structures

This is another item that can be tricky. Generally, you'll find that skylights, penthouses, and roof structures must have the same construction as the rest of the building and be the same distance from the property lines. And any roof structure used for housing anything except mechanical equipment is counted as an additional story.

We'll cover the construction details in later chapters. But the type of construction you wish to use will always dictate the construction methods. In other words, if you're building a frame building of Type V construction, the skylight must be of at least Type V construction.

Fire-Retardant Materials

You can use fire-retardant-treated wood in nonbearing partitions — but this brings up some questions. There are two types of fire-retardant-treated wood. One is wood that has been impregnated under pressure with fire retardant. The other is wood with the retardant sprayed or painted on. Both are acceptable, and this is where the problem arises.

What does "acceptable" mean? To the inspector, it means that the material is applied according to the manufacturer's recommendations. It doesn't mean that the users apply the material the way they think it should be applied. There's a vast difference between the two.

For too many builders, it's a matter of economics and what they think they can get away with. If the manufacturer recommends applying a certain retardant material in four coats at eight-hour intervals, there's probably a good reason for it. It's disappointing to hear a subcontractor say that two coats applied at two-hour intervals will do just as well. "After all, the manufacturer is just trying to sell more material." Now of course, the manufacturer is in business for profit. They want to sell lots of that material — but they want their material used properly. They put a lot of money into testing, and the reputation of their product is at stake. If they believe it takes four coats at eight-hour intervals to do the job, then I'm inclined to go along with them.

What about the subcontractor? By skimping on installation methods they can underbid their more conscientious competitor. Someone has to monitor the quality of work. It shouldn't have to be the building inspector. But the inspector will do it if no one else will.

Will Retardant-Treated Material Burn?

Yes, fire-retardant-treated material will burn, but only as long as there's an applied flame. If you throw a piece of fire-retardant wood in the fireplace, eventually it will turn to ashes.

Given enough time, nearly all materials are affected by flame and intense heat. What the retardant does is slow down combustion. That helps keep a structure intact and upright as long as possible so people can get out and fire fighters can get in.

Evaluation Reports

With so many building materials on the market today, how does the building inspector know if a product is acceptable? No, it's not all stored in a big computer somewhere. What the inspector does have is the ICBO Evaluation Reports.

Every other month, the International Conference of Building Officials Evaluation Services (ICBO ES) publishes a report on each material it recognizes for construction. All members of the ICBO receive these material updates. When a manufacturer presents a material for recognition, it must be accompanied by a report from an acceptable testing laboratory or agency. The material and report are reviewed by the staff and members of a review committee. If the committee grants recognition, the ICBO ES publishes the Evaluation Report.

This report lists the product, the manufacturer's name and address, what the product is and what it does, and how it should be used. It also refers to the relevant section of the UBC. Some of these are brief; others are quite lengthy. But they *do* give the inspector the information he or she needs to make a decision.

To be acceptable to the inspector, you've got to use the product or material according to the manufacturer's specification as amended by the testing lab. You can't use any other method unless you're prepared to prove to the inspector that your way is superior. Proving that may be more expensive than just doing it right in the first place.

Following the Code Saves Money

Following the code can save money. Consider nonbearing partitions, for example. In several occupancy categories, partitions don't have to meet any fire rating ("N" in UBC Table 6-A, Figure 4-1 in this book). So you could use plain wood panels in the nonbearing partitions, since plain wood can be used in all types of construction under certain conditions.

But be careful. What seems to be the most economical way to build something could end up costing more in the long run. Many builders use $3/16$ inch wood panels with photoengraved grain over a shoddy backing. You can put your fist right through it. I always recommend backing it with sheetrock. True, this will add to the cost, but it also adds strength and some fire-resistance. If you can put your fist through the panel, think of what a carelessly-placed piece of furniture could do.

In nearly any type of construction, wood veneer can be used over noncombustible surfaces. Wood trim and unprotected wood doors may be used where unprotected openings are permitted.

But what are unprotected openings? And how do you know if they're permitted?

Unprotected Openings

Let's go back to UBC Table 5-A (in the Appendix on page 295). One of the columns is headed *Openings*. This explains how close the building can be to the property line and still have unprotected openings. This is to help prevent the spread of fire from one property to another.

What about buildings downtown that are built right to the property line, facing on a street or alley? This requires a little detective work. Let's backtrack to Section 503.1:

For the purpose of this section, the center line of an adjoining public way shall be considered an adjacent property line.

Not too much help, is it? That depends a lot on how wide the streets are in your town. Let's go to Section 505.1.1:

Separation on two sides. Where public ways or yards more than 20 feet (6096 mm) in width extend along and adjoin two sides of the building. . .

Remember this one? We mentioned it in Chapter 3 in the section about area increases. We established that a 20-foot street was the line of demarcation. But Section 601.5.4 states:

Regardless of fire-resistive requirements for exterior walls, certain elements of the walls fronting on streets or yards having a width of 40 feet (12 192 mm) may be constructed as follows. . .

Isn't that curious? The only difference is in our second and third definitions. One indicates 20 feet to the center line while the other refers to a street 40 feet wide. It appears to be the same thing, doesn't it? On this basis, I would have to assume that 20 feet is the magic number.

That takes care of the separation on the street side. Section 505.1.1 covers the doubtful areas. However, UBC Table 5-A is much more specific for side lot lines for the various occupancies.

Figure 4-2 *A good example of double-wall construction*

Double Walls?

Construction practices are always changing. But I doubt they'll change any more in the next forty years than they have in the last forty. We still don't know for sure how energy conservation will affect the style of our houses or construction techniques in the future. We do know, however, that many changes have taken place and more will come.

When I learned home building, the framing was nailed together as it lay on the subfloor. Then it was erected and braced. Most sheathing was either shiplap or plain 1-inch stock placed horizontally or diagonally on plain studs. Next came a layer of building paper and the siding. Now, with plywood sheathing and siding, entire wall sections are assembled on the floor and lifted into place, complete (in some cases) with windows and paint. This diaphragm wall is more air-tight and may even be stronger structurally.

Some old-timers like me have their doubts about single-wall construction. Yes, the code permits it. But I still prefer double-wall construction, as shown in Figure 4-2.

TABLE 23-II-A-1—EXPOSED PLYWOOD PANEL SIDING

MINIMUM THICKNESS[1] (inch)	MINIMUM NUMBER OF PLIES	STUD SPACING (inches) PLYWOOD SIDING APPLIED DIRECTLY TO STUDS OR OVER SHEATHING
× 25.4 for mm		× 25.4 for mm
$3/8$	3	16[2]
$1/2$	4	24

[1]Thickness of grooved panels is measured at bottom of grooves.
[2]May be 24 inches (610 mm) if plywood siding applied with face grain perpendicular to studs or over one of the following: (1) 1-inch (25 mm) board sheathing, (2) $7/16$-inch (11 mm) wood structural panel sheathing or (3) $3/8$-inch (9.5 mm) wood structural panel sheathing with strength axis (which is the long direction of the panel unless otherwise marked) of sheathing perpendicular to studs.

From the Uniform Building Code, ©1997, ICBO

Figure 4-3 *Exposed plywood panel siding*

Section 1402.1 states that building paper must be applied over studs or sheathing of exterior walls. The paper may be omitted when the exterior wall covering consists of weather-proof panels. Exterior plywood of almost any thickness will satisfy this requirement.

Minimum Plywood Thickness

Section 2310.3 sets the minimum thickness of plywood used for exterior wall covering:

2310.3 Plywood. When plywood is used for covering the exterior of outside walls, it shall be of the exterior type not less than $3/8$ inch (9.5 mm) thick. Plywood panel siding shall be installed in accordance with Table 23-II-A-1. Unless applied over 1-inch (25 mm) wood sheathing or $15/32$ inch (12 mm) wood structural panel sheathing or $1/2$-inch (13 mm) particleboard sheathing, joints shall occur over framing members and shall be protected with a continuous wood batten, approved caulking, flashing, vertical or horizontal shiplaps; or joints shall be lapped horizontally or otherwise made waterproof.

Table 23-II-A-1 is shown in Figure 4-3. Exterior grade $3/8$ inch plywood meets code requirements. But most builders use a $1/2$ inch thick panel unless it's backed by a sheathing panel. That's a better choice, in my opinion. It doesn't cost much more and is just good insurance.

Masonry and Parapet Walls

Wood members aren't allowed to support concrete or masonry. Anything that supports concrete or masonry in buildings over one story high must either be protected with one-hour rating fire protection or meet the fire rating requirements of the wall itself, whichever is greater. You don't need to protect the underside of lintels, shelf angles, or plates that aren't part of the structural frame.

Where required, parapet walls must have the same fire-resistive rating as the walls. Parapets must be at least 30 inches above the point where the roof surface and the wall meet. They can never be less than 30 inches high. If the slope of a roof toward a parapet is greater than 2 in 12, the parapet must be as high as any portion of the roof within the distance where protection of wall openings would be required. Check back to UBC Table 5-A (page 295 in the Appendix). Figure 4-4 illustrates these requirements.

There's one further requirement. The side adjacent to a roof needs noncombustible faces for the top 18 inches, including all counter-flashing and coping materials.

General Items in UBC Chapter 6

You can use unprotected, noncombustible material for eaves, cornices and overhangs on all types of buildings. Type III, Type IV and Type V buildings may include combustible material.

Folding, portable, or movable partitions are acceptable if they meet these requirements:

1) They don't establish exit corridors or block required exits.

2) They're set in permanent tracks or guides.

3) The flame spread classification is not less than that for the rest of the room.

Except in residences, rubbish and linen chutes must terminate in rooms separated from the rest of the building by one-hour fire-resistive construction. The chutes may not open into exit corridors or stairways. See Sections 711.5 and 711.6.

You'll find that code regulations for these shaft enclosures are strict — and rigidly enforced. That's because these shafts have a way of turning into chimneys during a fire, spreading the flames throughout the building in no time.

Water closet compartments are also closely regulated in most public and semi-public buildings, which is nearly all buildings except private dwellings. These are stringent because many of the regulations involve accessibility. Disabled access is found in Chapter 19.

Bathroom floors must be made of nonabsorbent materials, such as cement or ceramic tile. These materials must extend up the walls to a height of 5 inches (48 inches in water closet and urinal areas, 70 inches in shower stalls). Glass or glazing around showers and tubs, even in private residences, must be fully tempered, laminated safety glass or approved plastic. See Section 807.1.

All weather-exposed surfaces must have a weather-resistive barrier to protect the interior wall covering. Building paper and felt must be free of holes and breaks other than those created by fasteners or attachments. They must be applied weatherboard fashion, lapped at least 2 inches at horizontal joints and 6 inches at vertical joints. Balconies, landings, exterior stairways, and similar surfaces exposed to the weather and sealed underneath must be waterproofed. See Section 1402.1.

All openings in floors, roofs, balconies or porches that are more than 30 inches above grade must have guardrails at least 42 inches high. The only exceptions are on the loading side of loading docks and private residences (36 inches is high enough). See Section 509.

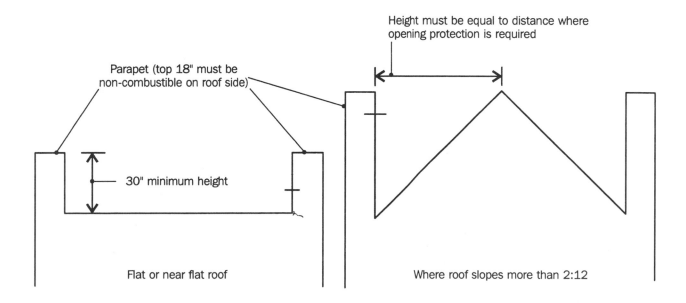

Figure 4-4 *Requirements for parapet walls*

Code sections on foam plastic insulation were revised for the 1988 edition and again for the 1991 edition. Now foam plastic insulation must have a flame spread rating of not more than 25 (exterior walls) or 75 (doors) and a smoke-developed rating of not more than 450. All packages and containers must bear the label of an approved agency showing the manufacturer's name. It must also indicate that the end use will comply with the code. See Section 2602.

The specific requirements in Chapter 26 cover installation of foam plastic insulation in masonry, attics or crawl spaces, cold storage, metal clad buildings, roofing, doors, and siding backer boards. All foam plastics must now be labeled and show the ingredients.

Helistops

In the last chapter I explained the main differences between heliports and helistops. The number of regulations regarding their construction is growing rapidly. Helistops may be built on buildings or other locations if constructed according to Section 311.10. Generally, this requires the following:

■ If the helicopter weighs less than 3,500 pounds, the touchdown area must be at least 20 feet by 20 feet and surrounded on all sides by a clear area with a minimum average width at roof level of 15 feet. No width can be less than 5 feet.

■ The landing area and supports on the roof of a building must be of noncombustible construction. Also, the area must be designed to confine any inflammable liquid spillage and to drain it away from any exit or stairway.

■ Exits and stairways must comply with provisions in Chapter 10 of the UBC, except that all landing areas on buildings or structures must have two or more exits. If the roof area is less than 60 feet long or less than 2000 square feet, the second exit may be a fire escape or a ladder leading to the floor below.

■ Approval must be obtained from the Federal Aviation Administration before operating helicopters from any helistop.

Type I Fire-Resistive Buildings

So far in this chapter I've discussed requirements that apply to nearly all buildings. Now it's time to get a little more specific, covering each building type. I'll start with the highest or most fire-resistive buildings, Type I.

The height of Type I buildings is unlimited by the code. The area is limited only in Groups H-1 and H-2 occupancies. But just because a building is fire-resistant doesn't mean that it's fireproof. Some of the worst fires in history have been in so-called fireproof buildings. In fact, Type I buildings — the most fire-resistant — have been called "concrete coffins." While the building itself doesn't burn, its contents do.

Building codes can't regulate the amount of combustible goods in a building. Hospitals, for example, are usually fire-resistive buildings filled with highly combustible materials. In this country, people are seldom burned to death in building fires. Usually, smoke and toxic fumes cause the greatest loss of life.

Remember the Chicago school fire some years back? One room contained over 30 bodies, yet papers on the desks weren't even singed. A fire-resistive building gives the occupants a better chance of escaping from the building — *if* the toxic fumes from burning material haven't done them in first.

The structural frame of a Type I building must be iron, steel, reinforced concrete, or reinforced masonry and have a three-hour fire rating. If members of the structural frame are in the outside wall, they must be protected the same as the outside wall, or for four hours.

Type I buildings must have four-hour fire-resistive exterior walls. But nonbearing walls that front yards at least 40 feet wide may be of unprotected, noncombustible construction. In some occupancies, nonbearing walls may have a one-hour rating where unprotected openings are permitted, and two-hour rating where protected openings are permitted.

UBC Table 6-A (Figure 4-1) summarizes the main requirements for all types of buildings. For miscellaneous items for each type of construction, refer to Sections 602 through 606 of the UBC. In Section 507 you'll find that a mezzanine floor can't cover more than one-third of the floor area of a room. Also, you can't have more than two mezzanine floors in any room. Mezzanine floors must be of one-hour noncombustible construction.

Stairs and stair platforms must be reinforced concrete, iron or steel. You can only use brick, marble, tile or other noncombustible materials for the finish of treads and risers in the stair enclosures.

Group B office buildings and Group R, Division 1 buildings with floors used for human occupancy located more than 75 feet above the lowest level of fire department access must have an approved automatic sprinkler system. This regulation has been in effect for some time. Newer provisions cover smoke detection systems, alarm and communication systems, smoke control and emergency power and light systems. You must provide mechanical ventilation for smoke removal.

Type II Construction

This category is broken down into three categories. Look at UBC Table 6-A. These are Type II-FR, Type II one-hour, and Type II-N. Fire-resistive requirements are shown in UBC Table 6-A. Allowable height and area are shown in Table 5-B (Figure 3-3, back in Chapter 3).

Maximum height depends on the occupancy and varies from one story for Group H-1 to twelve stories in apartment houses and most business buildings.

There's a fine line between the construction of Type II-FR and one-hour and N. The first must be of steel, iron, masonry or concrete. In the last two types, one-hour and N, the structural elements must only be noncombustible.

The basic difference is in some of the lesser elements. For instance, Type II-FR requires protected noncombustible construction throughout. But permanent nonbearing partitions may be made of fire-retardant-treated wood. In Type II one-hour construction, all elements need be rated for only one-hour fire resistance. In Type II-N there are no fire-resistive ratings on any elements except the shaft enclosures.

The big difference is in area and height allowance. UBC Table 5-B make this clear. For instance, you can have Group A-1 occupancy only in Type II-FR buildings. The area is restricted to 29,900 square feet and limited to four stories. Otherwise, Group A-1 occupancy is not allowed in anything but Type I construction. Type II-FR construction is probably the most common type of commercial and industrial construction except in tall or extra large buildings.

Type II-N Construction

Most people think of Type II-N buildings as stock steel buildings such as service stations, Butler buildings, or even the little metal sheds put out by Wards and Sears. Actually, any building that is entirely noncombustible could be a Type II-N building.

You don't have to protect a Type II-N building, but it must be of noncombustible material. The area and height of a Type II-N building is limited.

I mentioned that stock steel buildings are in this category. Even though the building itself is rated as noncombustible, the skin of the building on the side opposite the fire can get red hot, and will ignite anything touching it. Therefore, allow plenty of setback room for metal buildings, both from the property line and from adjacent buildings.

What can you do to make a Type II-N building into a Type II one-hour building? Add a layer of ¾ inch sheetrock to the wall and ceiling surfaces. If the buildings are for miscellaneous storage, install sheetrock on the outside of the frame and attach the skin directly over it.

This also reduces the possibility of damage to the sheetrock. When sheetrock is broken, the one-hour fire-resistive rating vanishes.

Type III Construction

Buildings with Type III construction must have four-hour fire-resistive exterior walls. But the other elements need only have a one-hour rating (Type III one-hour) or no rating (Type III-N). We used to call this construction "masonry walls and wood guts."

One item is of special interest in the Type III category: the height is limited to 65 feet (one-hour) and 55 feet (N). Generally, the number of stories is limited to two in most occupancy groups. But have you ever seen a 65-foot-high, two-story building? I haven't.

Type IV Construction

Underfloor areas in Type IV buildings must be ventilated. That's because the floors are constructed of wood. The three higher types usually are built on slabs or over basements. Underfloor ventilation requirements will be discussed in detail in Chapter 9.

Type IV-HT (heavy timber) is the "mill type" construction found in many older industrial buildings, particularly on the West Coast. Warehouses and shipping docks are usually Type IV-HT construction, which uses massive beams and joists.

Columns must be at least 8 inches x 8 inches to be classed as heavy timber. Framed timber trusses or glue-laminated arches that support floors must be at least 6 inches x 8 inches. Glue-laminated beams on roofs must be at least 4 inches x 6 inches. Beams or girders that support floors must be at least 6 inches x 10 inches, but on roofs they need only be 6 inches x 8 inches. Framed timber trusses for roofs that do not support floors must be 4 inches thick. Roofs must be at least 2 inches thick.

These measurements are nominal lumber sizes. This means that a 4 x 8 is only about 3½ x 7½ inches, finished on four sides.

Why is something so combustible as a heavy timber building given a Type IV rating? Fire safety doesn't require a noncombustible frame. The issue is how long the building will stand after it begins burning. The bigger the timber, the longer it will take to burn to the point of failure or collapse. Mill buildings burn for quite a while before they collapse completely.

Type V Construction

Type V buildings are wood frame or a combination of wood frame and any other material if the exterior walls aren't required to be noncombustible. In the Type V one-hour, however, all elements must be protected for at least one hour. Type V-N buildings are usually single- and multi-family dwellings. In V-N construction, multi-family dwellings are restricted to two stories, while single-family dwellings may be three stories. Most higher types of construction could easily fall to Type V if the builder hasn't fulfilled all the requirements of UBC Table 6-A.

That's the end of this summary of building types. In the next chapter, we'll take a closer look at what makes a building resist fire.

In the Line of Duty

Most cities have zoning ordinances that limit the accumulation of junk in residential zones. That's a good idea. Piles of junk are unsightly, unsanitary and hazardous. Most cities aren't very aggressive at enforcing these ordinances until someone complains. Then they have to send someone from the building, fire, police or health department out to investigate.

In my city this chore always fell to the building department. After making a few of these calls, I began to wish that I had help from other departments. Making house calls to settle disputes between neighbors isn't my favorite way to spend an afternoon.

I even went to the city manager once with a proposal, a compromise. My department could go in rotation with the other departments. We'd handle the first call. After that the departments would go in alphabetical order: fire, health and the police. Wasn't that fair?

"Well, Jack," the city manager said, "sure, I could divide responsibility. But what will people think when a policeman, fireman or the health department pulls up to the door? They'll think there's some kind of emergency. The way I see it, your building department has exactly the low profile we need for this problem. Anyhow, nobody's better at gentle arm twisting than you are.

Right Jack? You see, it isn't really a matter of fair or unfair. It's who can get the job done best - what's best for our city. That's why we thought you'd be happy to do it."

Funny I didn't see it that way until the city manager explained it to me. I guess that's why he's the city manager and I'm the building inspector.

A little after that I had to make one of these "junk" calls. The homeowner had closed a second-hand furniture store and moved the entire inventory to his backyard. The yard was jammed with plywood shacks, every one bulging with junk. That was mistake number one. Number two was that too much of the lot area was covered with these shacks. No-no number three was that I had no permit on file for any of these buildings. It looked like an open-and-shut case to me.

Before I could knock on the door, the door was flung open and I was looking at the business end of the biggest, ugliest gun barrel I ever saw. "What do you want?" said a voice somewhere behind the gun.

"I'm the building inspector and . . ."

"I don't care if you're Jesus Christ. *Get off my property!*"

Now, if there's anything I try to avoid, it's antagonizing the citizens of our town. And what I had here was one very, very unhappy citizen. No use making things worse, I thought, as I advanced, as the Marines would say, rapidly to the rear.

Anyhow, nobody gives medals for heroism to building inspectors, even a building inspector with a wife and eight kids to support.

Obviously, there was something the city manager had overlooked. They'd sent a boy to do a man's work.

But my friend with the gun had solved the problem.

Yes sir!

This was no job for the building inspector. This was a job for the City Attorney!

5

Fire Resistance in Buildings

The primary purpose of the Uniform Building Code, like all building codes, is to promote public safety. Since fire usually poses the greatest risk to building occupants, fire safety is a recurring theme in the code. In the last chapter we looked at how the code uses fire resistance to classify structures. In this chapter we'll explore the rating system the code uses to classify building materials.

Materials such as steel, concrete, glass and most mineral compounds are considered to be noncombustible. They don't burn. But they aren't immune to the effects of fire. So the code has to consider what happens to those materials when they're exposed to the temperatures that occur in a building fire.

Noncombustible Is Not Nondestructible

The Chicago Coliseum was considered noncombustible when it was built. But it caught fire and was completely destroyed. The fire couldn't have done more damage if the Coliseum had been made of matchsticks and tissue paper.

The designers failed to consider two possibilities. First, the building was filled with paper, cloth and all types of combustibles that made a great fire. Second, the fire started so quickly and grew so fast that firefighters had no chance of controlling it. What happened to the noncombustible building? Well, it didn't burn. It simply melted into a mass of twisted, warped iron and steel. The planners placed complete faith in the alarm system and ignored important fire prevention issues.

This is what I try to explain when someone insists that their metal building is completely "noncombustible." Sure, steel buildings don't burn. But the contents will. And when that happens, the steel frame melts like butter on a slice of hot toast. To prevent that, even steel-frame buildings need fire-resistiveness built in.

Fire Resistiveness — How Do We Get It?

After a major fire, the news media reports what happened and then tries to find someone to blame. There's nothing wrong with that, I suppose. It's news. We're all curious about the accidental death of innocent people. But what they don't report is that laws that aren't being enforced and tight construction budgets are the most frequent causes. Owners and contractors are always trying to find ways to cut costs. Frequently, fire safety is ignored or postponed.

True, the number of people who die as the result of burns in structural fires is remarkably low. And the number of people who die from being trapped in a burning building is even lower. But this doesn't mean that fire-resistiveness is unimportant.

Most death by fire in buildings results from asphyxiation from smoke or toxic fumes. Fire-resistiveness in a structure doesn't stop fires and doesn't prevent asphyxiation. But fire-resistiveness can slow the rate of combustion and keep a building from collapsing long enough so everyone can get out or be brought out.

Noncombustible Materials

Nothing is completely fireproof. Some building materials are noncombustible. Others are fire-resistive. But every building material I know of will fail if it gets hot enough.

Noncombustible materials don't burn, but they transmit enough heat to maintain and even spread combustion. Most fire-resistive materials will burn when flame is applied. Some continue burning even when the flame is removed.

The easiest way to understand the term noncombustible as used in the code is to examine the definition in Chapter 2 of the UBC:

*215. **Noncombustible** as applied to building construction material means a material which, in the form in which it is used, is either one of the following:*

1. Material of which no part will ignite and burn when subjected to fire. Any material conforming to UBC Standard No. 2-1 shall be considered noncombustible within the meaning of this section.

2. Material having a structural base of noncombustible material as defined in Item (1) above, with a surfacing material not over $1/8$-inch thick which has a flame-spread rating of 50 or less.

"Noncombustible" does not apply to surface finish materials. Material required to be noncombustible for reduced clearances to flues, heating appliances, or other sources of high temperature shall refer to material conforming to Item 1. No material shall be classed as noncombustible which is subject to increase in combustibility or flame-spread rating, beyond the limits herein established, through the effects of age, moisture or other atmospheric condition.

Flame-spread rating as used herein refers to rating obtained according to tests conducted as specified in UBC Standard No. 8-1.

What Is Flame-Spread?

Structural members in some types of buildings have to be fire-resistant. Walls and ceilings in some types of buildings have to have a fire-resistive rating. And the finish materials used in some walls and ceilings must have a flame-spread classification based on occupancy. This flame-spread classification, however, doesn't apply to the Group U occupancy.

What, exactly, does fire-resistive mean? This term appears again and again throughout this book. But to understand this term you must first understand flame-spread.

Flame-spread is classified in UBC Table 8-A (Figure 5-1) as I, II, or III, although in some codes you may find it listed as Class A, B, or C. UBC Table 8-B (Figure 5-1) shows the maximum flame-spread classification for the vari-

TABLE 8-A—FLAME-SPREAD CLASSIFICATION

MATERIAL QUALIFIED BY:	
Class	Flame-spread Index
I	0-25
II	26-75
III	76-200

TABLE 8-B—MAXIMUM FLAME-SPREAD CLASS[1]

OCCUPANCY GROUP	ENCLOSED VERTICAL EXITWAYS	OTHER EXITWAYS[2]	ROOMS OR AREAS
A	I	II	II[3]
B	I	II	III
E	I	II	III
F	II	III	III
H	I	II	III[4]
I-1.1, I-1.2, I-2	I	I[5]	II[6]
I-3	I	I[5]	I[6]
M	I	II	III
R-1	I	II	III
R-3	III	III	III[7]
S-1, S-2	II	II	III
S-3, S-4, S-5	I	II	III
U	NO RESTRICTIONS		

[1]Foam plastics shall comply with the requirements specified in Section 2602. Carpeting on ceilings and textile wall coverings shall comply with the requirements specified in Sections 804.2 and 805, respectively.

[2]Finish classification is not applicable to interior walls and ceilings of exterior exit-access balconies.

[3]In Group A, Divisions 3 and 4 Occupancies, Class III may be used.

[4]Over two stories shall be of Class II.

[5]In Group I, Divisions 2 and 3 Occupancies, Class II may be used.

[6]Class III may be used in administrative spaces.

[7]Flame-spread provisions are not applicable to kitchens and bathrooms of Group R, Division 3 Occupancies.

From the Uniform Building Code, ©1997, ICBO

Figure 5-1 *Flame-spread classification*

ous occupancies. These finish requirements, however, don't apply to doors and windows or their frames and trim. Material which is less than $1/28$-inch thick and cemented to the surface of walls and ceilings is also exempt if its flame-spread characteristics are less than paper under the same circumstances. If there's an automatic fire-extinguishing system, the flame-spread classification may be reduced.

Determining flame-spread — A flame-spread rating isn't a fire-resistive rating. The flame-spread rating compares the time it takes flame to spread on the surface of the tested material with the time it takes the same flame to spread on untreated oak. Red oak has an arbitrary rating of 100 and cement asbestos board has a rating of 0.

It's easy to see why cement asbestos board is used for the 0 rating, but what's so special about red oak? Red oak was chosen because of its uniform density and uniform burning rate, not because of its resistance to flames. Also, the smoke developed by burning red oak is more uniform than that of most woods.

The actual spread of flames isn't the only item measured in the flame-spread rating. It also considers the smoke density produced and the amount of fuel the fire consumes. Red oak and asbestos board are also the standards by which other materials are compared.

Tunnel test — Materials are tested for flame-spread in a tunnel test developed by the Underwriter's Laboratory. The code, however, will recognize any independent testing lab equipped to make the same test. At present, to

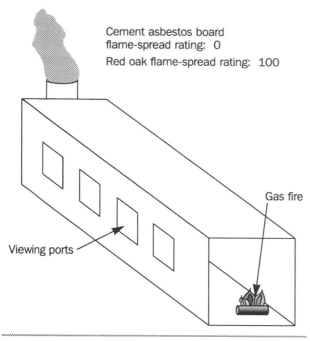

Cement asbestos board
flame-spread rating: 0

Red oak flame-spread rating: 100

Gas fire

Viewing ports

Figure 5-2 *Tunnel test for flame-spread and smoke density*

my knowledge, only UL and one company in Texas have tunnel testing apparatus. Figure 5-2 shows the tunnel test setup.

Building Code Standard 8-1 describes the testing equipment and the method of testing for flame-spread. Here's how it describes the fire test chamber:

The fire test chamber supplied with gas fuel of uniform quality shall be employed for this test method.

The fire test chamber is to consist of a horizontal duct having an inside width of 17½ inches plus or minus ½ inch, a depth of 12 inches plus or minus ½ inch measured from the bottom of the test chamber to the ledge of the inner walls on which the specimen is supported, and a length of 25 feet. The sides and base of the duct are to be lined with insulated masonry. One side is to be provided with draft-tight observation windows so that the entire length of the test sample may be observed from outside the fire test chamber.

The top is to consist of a removable non-combustible insulated structure of a size necessary to cover completely the fire test chamber and to accommodate the test samples. The top is to be designed so that it can be sealed against the leakage of air into the fire test chamber during the test, and it is to be designed to permit the attachment of test samples when necessary.

One end of the test chamber, designated as the "fire end," is to be provided with two gas burners delivering flames upward against the surface of the test sample, and 7½ inches plus or minus ½ inch below the under surface of the test sample. The burners are to be positioned transversely approximately 4 inches on each side of the center line of the furnace so that the flame is evenly distributed over the cross section of the furnace . . . .

This standard sets the type and number of controls, the amount of gas metered in, the air allowed, and other test criteria. The room in which the test is made must have a free inflow of air during the test to ensure that the room is kept at atmospheric pressure. The test chamber is calibrated so flame will spread 19.5 feet in 5½ minutes on red oak flooring. Photoelectric cells determine the smoke density.

Computing flame-spread — The tester watches the progress of the flame, and notes the time it takes to travel 19.5 feet. This is compared to the red oak by one of the following formulas:

■ If the time is 5.5 minutes or less, the formula is 100 times 5.5 divided by 19.5.

■ When it takes more than 5.5 minutes, but less than 10 minutes, the formula is 100 times 5.5 divided by the time it took the flame to spread 19.5 feet plus ½ the difference between the result and 100.

■ If it takes more than 10 minutes, the formula is 100 times the distance in feet that it traveled divided by 19.5.

It's a little confusing, I know. But you don't have to perform the test. Just understand that there is a test of flame-spread that's been used for many years and is accepted as a standard for classifying building materials.

Table 8-A, Flame-Spread Classification (Figure 5-1), shows that Class I material has a flame-spread rating of 0 to 25, or about one-fourth that of red oak. Class II material has a flame spread rating of 26 to 75, or about three-fourths that of red oak. Class III material has a flame-spread rating of 76 to 200. On that basis, red oak at 100 has a Class III rating.

UBC Table 8-B gives flame-spread requirements for finish material in various occupancies for stairs, corridors and rooms. Generally, you'll find that most wood products fall in the Class III category.

Determining Fire Resistance

The test for fire resistance of materials and assemblies is similar to the flame-spread test. A flame is applied to one side of the sample in a test chamber. Thermocouples measure the temperature on the opposite side. If the temperature doesn't exceed 250 degrees F on the exposed side for the time tested, the sample is rated as fire-resistive regardless of its condition. If the sample is a loadbearing member, it's placed under load during that test and must support the load for the time required.

When a door or window is tested for fire resistance, the entire assembly is tested, including the frame and hardware and everything else that will be part of the assembly in actual service. If any part of the assembly fails, the assembly is rated at the time of that failure. A door assembly that failed after 59 minutes would have a ¾ hour rating, not a one-hour rating.

Wall covering materials such as sheetrock must pass the fire test and then a hose stream test. This test is made on duplicate samples after half the fire exposure time rating. Immediately after the fire is shut off, a hose stream is directed against the sample. The method of applying the stream, the size of the nozzle, the distance from the sample, and the water pressure are spelled out in the test procedures.

These test methods and procedures are found in the Uniform Building Code Standards, referred to very frequently in the UBC. The book of standards is a companion to the UBC, but I doubt that most contractors will ever need to refer to it.

Openings in Fire Assemblies

So far we've concentrated on fire-resistive assemblies and coverings. But very little has been said about openings in these assemblies. Sooner or later most fire-resistive assemblies will have to be pierced for things such as plumbing, wiring, or doors. If you have a room that requires a certain amount of fire-resistiveness, what are you going to do about the doors? What about heat ducts and lighting fixtures? And what if changes are made after a structure is completed? Will the plumber or electrician create problems by cutting through your fire-rated wall?

Let's start with ductwork. Fire dampers must sometimes be installed wherever ductwork passes through a wall, ceiling or floor that's part of a fire-resistive assembly. Dampers can be installed in the duct itself or in a collar fastened to the wall or ceiling. But they must be capable of operating even if the duct is damaged. Dampers must close at a temperature 50 degrees F above the normal operating temperature. Dampers in ducts must be at least 16-gauge steel in ducts up to 18 inches in diameter, 12-gauge in ducts up to 36 inches in diameter, and 7-gauge in ducts over 36 inches in diameter.

Openings in area-separation walls must be protected according to the time requirements of the separation. If a four-hour separation is required, any openings would have to be protected for three hours. These assemblies are usually operated by a fusible link on each side of the wall.

A smoke detection device may be required for the fire and smoke assembly. Let me add a word of caution here: Don't paint over smoke detectors and fire safety equipment! It isn't unusual to find fusible links that have been

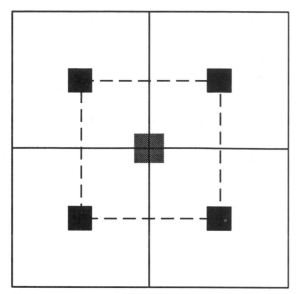

Each square with a solid line equals
100 square feet.

Solid squares indicate acceptable openings.

Broken lines indicate 100 square feet in which four
groups of openings might erroneously be placed.

Figure 5-3 *Allowable openings*

completely painted over several times. Although the paint isn't very thick, it may keep the link from melting when it's supposed to. The first five minutes of a fire are the most critical.

Structural members such as beams, trusses, floor joists, and rafters may be individually protected or protected by a fire-resistive ceiling of the correct rating. Sometimes one method is more practical than another. If one-hour protection is sufficient, steel members may be painted with approved fire-retardant paint, provided they aren't exposed to the weather. If the members are protected by a ceiling, the ceiling must be noncombustible and the assembly must be rated.

Allowable Openings

You can have small openings in the wall or ceiling for pipe, duct, and electric boxes of ferrous metal. The opening can be up to 100 square inches in any 100 square feet of ceiling. Suppose you have a client who wants to group four 100-inch openings at the center of a 400-square-foot ceiling. That's exactly 100 square inches for each 100 square feet of ceiling. Does that comply with the code?

Not in my opinion. It doesn't meet the intent of the code. The code says "100 square inches in any 100 square feet." Your client better find some other way of arranging the openings. See Figure 5-3. It's better to get an inspector's interpretation on a question like this before starting the work. Failing to do so can be expensive.

Textile wall and ceiling coverings make an attractive finish and aid in sound deadening. They must have a Class I flame-spread rating and be protected by automatic sprinklers. This applies to all textiles, whether napped, tufted, looped, non-woven or woven.

Fire-Rated Assemblies

The UBC defines fire-resistive like this:

Fire Code is the Uniform Fire Code promulgated by the International Fire Code Institute, as adopted by this jurisdiction.

Fire Resistance / Fire-resistive Construction is construction to resist the spread of fire, details of which are specified in this code.

Fire-retardant Treated Wood is any wood product impregnated with chemicals by a pressure process or other means during manufacture, and which, when tested in accordance with UBC Standard No. 8-1 for a period of 30 minutes, shall have a flame-spread of not over 25 and show no evidence of progressive combustion. In addition, the flame front shall not progress more than 10½ feet beyond the center line of the burner at any time during the test. Materials which may be exposed to the weather shall pass the accelerated weathering test and be identified as Exterior type, in accordance with UBC Standard No.

23-4. *Where material is not directly exposed to rainfall but exposed to high humidity conditions, it shall be subjected to the hygroscopic test and identified as Interior Type A in accordance with UBC Standard No. 23-4.*

All materials shall bear identification showing the fire performance rating thereof. Such identifications shall be issued by an approved agency having a service for inspection of materials at the factory.

These are from the definitions section of the UBC. Section 713.2 has the following definition:

Fire Assembly *is the assembly of a fire door, fire windows, or fire damper, including all required hardware, anchorage, frames and sills.*

How do you know what materials are fire-resistive? Many combinations of materials qualify as fire-resistive. See more information on this in UBC Chapter 7.

UBC Tables 7-A, 7-B and 7-C are especially helpful if you need this design data.

Fire-Resistive Construction

UBC Table 7-A, *Minimum Protection of Structural Parts Based on Time Periods for Various Noncombustible Insulating Materials*, applies to the structural frame. A note of caution about UBC tables: Check all footnotes. They often specify certain conditions that may apply to your project.

Let's see how the building inspector uses Table 7-A. Suppose the inspector notices on your plans a 6 inch by 6 inch steel column encased in Grade A concrete (not including sandstone, granite or siliceous gravels). The concrete will be a minimum of 2½ inches thick around all portions of the steel column. The inspector will turn to UBC Table 7-A and find that it just happens to be the first item listed. Reading across, you see that 2½ inches of concrete provides a maximum of four-hour protec-

tion. That's good enough for a Type I construction.

Will the concrete be able to insulate the column from fire failure for at least four hours? The inspector consults your specs and determines that the concrete complies. Your structural frame qualifies for Type I construction.

Of course, this shouldn't have happened by accident. Your architect knows code requirements and wrote specs that meet code requirements. If the architect made a mistake, the inspector will probably return your plans for modification. Another option would be to downgrade the type of construction. That might severely restrict how the building can be used, as I explained in Chapter 4.

Fire Resistance for Walls and Partitions

UBC Table 7-B, *Rated Fire-Resistive Periods for Various Walls and Partitions*, will do for your walls and partitions what Table 7-A did for the structural frame. The process of determining the fire rating is exactly the same. If you're designing the building, which one would you elect to use? That depends on a number of things.

First, determine the fire-resistive rating you need. Then select the combinations of construction that will give you that rating. From there it's a matter of selecting materials that will meet code and owner requirements at the lowest cost. But remember, the code only requires the minimum rating. How far you go above that is up to you and your client.

UBC Table 7-B shows the fire-resistive ratings for different wall assemblies. You can't make any substitutions in these assemblies and keep the rating unless it's shown elsewhere in the table. Only the exact construction defined carries that particular rating. In one-hour construction, ceilings may be omitted over unusable space, and floors may be omitted under unusable space.

Calculating the rating is the same as for Table 7-A. Select the hour rating you want. Then look for the components that will give you that rating.

Fire Resistance for Floors and Roofs

UBC Table 7-C, *Minimum Protection for Floor and Roof Systems*, does for floors and roofs exactly what the other two tables did for the structural frame and the walls and ceilings. The table also works the same way as the other two.

But watch out for floor and roof penetrations. All openings for mechanical and electrical equipment must be enclosed as specified in Section 711.1 or protected with a penetration firestop system.

There are two exceptions. First, some pipes may be installed within or through fire-resistive floors if they don't reduce the required fire resistance of the assembly. Second, the provisions of Section 711.1 don't apply when openings comply with results of tests made under provisions of Section 703.2. The result of these two exceptions, of course, is that you must prove your point to the inspector. It may be faster and cheaper to figure out another solution.

Protective Covering

Now that we've examined the method of determining flame-spread and some of the fire-resistive standards, let's take a look at the little things that can cause trouble.

Let's start with protective covering. The thickness of protective covering can't be less than shown in UBC Table 7-A, except as modified in Chapter 7. This pertains to all products, from fire-resistive paint to concrete. The figures shown must be the *net thickness* of the protecting materials. It doesn't include any hollow space in back of the protection.

You may be required to embed metal ties in transverse joints of unit masonry to protect steel columns. These ties must meet the requirements of UBC Table 7-A. Unit masonry, of course, is brick, block or any combination of the two.

You can't embed conduit and pipes in required fire protective coatings or in structural members. If the fire-resistive covering on columns might be damaged when the building is occupied, it must be protected.

Fire Doors

Fire doors must have automatic or self-closing hardware. Automatic closing devices must be equipped with heat-actuated devices on each side of the wall at the top of the opening. If the ceiling is more than 3 feet above the opening, the code requires a fusible link located at the ceiling on each side of the wall.

Glazed openings of 100 square inches are permitted, provided the door has a one-hour or 90-minute fire rating. Doors of ¾ hour rating may have 84 square feet of area. That means you could have a delivery door approximately 8 feet by 10.5 feet.

Exterior windows required to have a ¾ hour fire-resistive rating can't be larger than 84 square feet, and neither the width nor the height can exceed 12 feet.

One more note about fire doors. If the Fire Marshall inspects your plans, he'll probably insist that all fire doors be marked "Fire Door — Do Not Obstruct."

In the next chapter, we'll take a look at a related subject — fire safety.

Fireplaces Are for Friendly Fires

Fireplaces have been warming humans for thousands of years. And they've been causing accidental fires for at least as long. Most of these fires are preventable. Building inspectors don't have much control over the way fireplaces are used. The best I can do is make sure that a fireplace used correctly will give safe, reliable service for many years. That's what I try to do.

Before building codes were written, fireplaces were built of nearly every kind of material imaginable. That doesn't happen any more. But even so, it takes real skill and craftsmanship to build a fireplace out of masonry, mortar and reinforcing alone. Not every mason can build a good fireplace. Even fewer designers can draw plans for a good fireplace. Most don't even try any more. Modern fireplace materials have greatly simplified fireplace construction. The first major improvement was the metal hood that contained the smoke shelf, damper and beginning of the flue. These hoods made it unnecessary to construct a smoke shelf. The second major improvement was the "zero clearance" all-metal fireplace. The third was the double-walled metal flue.

Modern materials make it easy to inspect a fireplace. I have to make sure that all masonry is either separated from wood framing or that the masonry is thick enough so that the wood framing won't ignite when the fireplace gets as hot as it's going to get. Metal hoods have to be properly sealed into the masonry. That isn't always easy to determine after a fireplace is built.

The area where the hood and the front of the fireplace meet always seems to cause trouble. All too often I found this area filled with fiberglass. Now we all know that fiberglass is fireproof, right? True, fiberglass won't burn, but it can melt, letting fire and smoke escape. It took a long time to educate some builders about this. Filler between the hood and the front of the fireplace *has to be masonry*.

But even when filled correctly, modern fireplaces aren't foolproof. For example, one day I went to inspect a fireplace on a small job. It looked great. I even complimented the mason on the design. Then out of the corner of my eye I saw a slight movement in the corner of the firebox. I looked again. Sure enough, it moved. In fact, it winked. I've inspected a lot of fireplaces, but this is the first that ever winked at me. In a moment the eye was gone. I stuck my pencil through the hole. Someone grabbed my pencil and pulled it through!

There was actually a hole through the back of the fireplace into the adjoining garage. I wondered if a winking fireplace would be safe. Probably not. The mason had some more work to do.

Fire Safety

Despite the heroic efforts of firefighters (and lots of insistent pestering of building inspectors), people are going to die in fires. No building is entirely fire safe; some can even be called fire traps. And even in safe buildings, the occupants can make the building dangerous by misusing flammable materials. It's impossible to prevent all fires.

The best any building code can do is to reduce the risk to life and property when a fire does break out. The code does that by requiring contractors and designers to build fire safety into every construction project. Of course, fire safety comes at a price. Fire-safe buildings always cost more. But they shouldn't cost too much more. At least, that's the goal of the code.

Fire Detection and Control Systems

Many types of fire detection and control systems are available. They include simple res-

idential smoke detectors, multiple interconnected smoke detectors placed throughout a building, automatic sprinklers, and wet and dry standpipes. Some businesses even have their own fire suppression teams.

Of course, no system is 100 percent effective. Smoke detectors or alarms detect smoke and signal the occupants. But unless they also signal a fire station, these devices can't put out a fire. They're almost useless where the occupants are severely disabled or incapacitated.

Automatic sprinklers have heat sensors that trigger the system into action. To be truly effective they should be wired to a fire station. But automatic sprinklers are subject to false alarms and can cause a great deal of water damage. It may be a toss-up which costs more to repair, the fire damage or the water damage.

Standpipes provide a source of water for fighting a fire. But they can't put one out on their own. And in-house fire-suppression teams, while effective if properly trained, are expensive to maintain.

These are just some of the considerations when you're thinking about a fire detection and control system. There are many others. If your smoke detectors are electrically operated, what will happen if the power source is cut off? Will the battery backup operate the system? What would happen to your automatic sprinklers if a fire broke out while the city had shut off the water to repair a line? Are backup systems available?

Automatic Sprinkler Systems

The code doesn't require fire sprinklers in Group R-3 (single-family residential) and Group U (miscellaneous and agricultural) occupancies. But other occupancies (with a few exceptions) may need automatic sprinklers. According to Chapter 9 of the UBC, a building of 1,500 square feet or more may need an automatic sprinkler system. First, let's take a look at the code's general requirements.

Section 904.2.2 states that automatic sprinkler systems must be installed:

1. *In every story or basement of all buildings when the floor area exceeds 1,500 square feet (139.4 m²) and there is not provided at least 20 square feet (1.86 m²) of opening entirely above the adjoining ground level in each 50 lineal feet (15 240 mm) or fraction thereof of exterior wall in the story or basement on at least one side of the building. Openings shall have a minimum dimension of not less than 30 inches (762 mm). Such openings shall be accessible to the fire department from the exterior and shall not be obstructed in a manner that firefighting or rescue cannot be accomplished from the exterior.*

When openings in a story are provided on only one side and the opposite wall of such story is more than 75 feet (22 860 mm) from such openings, the story shall be provided with an approved automatic sprinkler system, or openings as specified above shall be provided on at least two sides of an exterior wall of the story.

If any portion of a basement is located more than 75 feet (22 860 mm) from openings required in this section, the basement shall be provided with an approved automatic sprinkler system.

It goes on to define specific areas where sprinklers are required and offer some exceptions. For instance, in buildings where temperatures can be expected to drop below zero, you need a dry fire sprinkler system. Otherwise you'll probably have frozen pipes in cold weather. A dry system doesn't have water in the distribution pipes until water is needed. Flow to the sprinkler heads is controlled by a fusible link that melts if it gets too hot. That opens a pressure-controlled switch which floods the pipes, delivering water to the head where it's needed.

Sometimes antifreeze can be used in cold areas to prime the lines, as set forth in the UBC Standards. But this always needs to be done carefully. Spraying antifreeze could do more damage than the fire it's supposed to put out.

Sprinklers are intended to knock down the fire before it gets started and give the occupants time to get out. That's why the need for sprinklers decreases as the occupancy load decreases. In most cases, automatic sprinklers are all that's needed to put out the fire. The fire's usually out before fire fighters arrive. But what about a flash fire (like an explosion) or a smoldering fire that doesn't create enough heat to set off sprinklers but fills the room with deadly fumes?

In a flash fire, sprinklers work — but do they work in time? Refer to your type of occupancy and area separations to keep the high-danger areas remote from the areas of high human loads.

In certain occupancies smoke detectors are required in addition to the automatic sprinklers because of the possibility of smoldering fires. In some cases they must be photo-eye controlled. All Group R-3 occupancies are now required to have small detectors in sleeping areas.

Sprinklers aren't the only fire suppression system, but they're usually the least expensive.

There are also many chemical systems on the market. Requirements vary. So check with your inspector to see what's allowed in your area.

As I stated previously, there's a move afoot to require sprinklers in all structures, including Group R-3. In fact, I believe that some parts of southern California now require sprinklers in all new residential construction. I still have reservations about this until they can assure me that the sprinkler heads won't accidentally go off during periods when there's no one around to monitor them.

Part of this concern may be covered in Section 904.3.1. It states:

Valve monitoring and water-flow alarm and trouble signals shall be distinctly different and shall be automatically transmitted to an approved central station, remote station or proprietary monitoring station as defined by national standards, or, when approved by the building official with the concurrence of the chief of the fire department, sound an audible signal at a constantly attended location.

This will suffice in an urban situation but might be a bit difficult and expensive in a rural or isolated area.

Automatic Sprinklers for Special Circumstances

There are some areas where sprinklers can be reduced or omitted completely — like a communication center or a power house. Can you imagine what would happen if a sprinkler system went off over a bank of telephone relays? But that doesn't mean that fire alarms or controls aren't required.

Section 904.4 lists the various locations where automatic fire sprinklers may be omitted. Included in the list are such locations as:

■ Where they're undesirable because of contents

■ Where application of water may create a health hazard such as chemical storage

■ Where records are stored that could be damaged by water

■ Where communication equipment rooms are located

■ Other areas where automatic fire-extinguishing systems are installed for special hazards

These omissions can only be used with the approval of the building official and/or the chief of the fire department.

The UBC has a section that covers areas where people are drinking. Section 904.2.3.1 states:

An automatic sprinkler system shall be installed in rooms used by the occupants for the consumption of alcoholic beverages and unseparated accessory uses where the total area of such unseparated rooms and assembly uses exceeds 5,000 square feet. For uses to be considered as separated, the separation shall be not less than as required for a one-hour occupancy separation. The area of other uses shall be included unless separated by at least a one-hour occupancy separation.

Standpipes

Not many homes have standpipes for connecting fire hoses. But most large apartment and office buildings do. UBC Table 9-A (Figure 6-1) defines the types and locations of standpipes. Section 903 tells you what they are and how they're used:

Standpipe System is a wet or dry system of piping, valves, outlets, and related equipment designed to provide water at specified pressures and installed exclusively for the fighting of fires including the following:

Class I is a standpipe system equipped with 2½ inch outlets.

Class II is a wet standpipe system directly connected to a water supply and equipped with 1½ inch outlets and hose.

TABLE 9-A—STANDPIPE REQUIREMENTS

OCCUPANCY × 304.8 for mm × 0.0929 for m²	NONSPRINKLERED BUILDING[1]		SPRINKLERED BUILDING[2,3]	
	Standpipe Class	**Hose Requirement**	**Standpipe Class**	**Hose Requirement**
1. Occupancies exceeding 150 feet in height and more than one story	III	Yes	I	No
2. Occupancies four stories or more but less than 150 feet in height, except Group R, Division 3[6]	[I and II[4]] (or III)	[5] Yes	I	No
3. Group A Occupancies with occupant load exceeding 1,000[7]	II	Yes	No requirement	No
4. Group A, Division 2.1 Occupancies over 5,000 square feet in area used for exhibition	II	Yes	II	Yes
5. Groups I; H; B; S; M; F, Division 1 Occupancies less than four stories in height but greater than 20,000 square feet per floor[6]	II[4]	Yes	No requirement	No
6. Stages more than 1,000 square feet in area	II	No	III	No

[1]Except as otherwise specified in Item 4 of this table, Class II standpipes need not be provided in basements having an automatic fire-extinguishing system throughout.

[2]The standpipe system may be combined with the automatic sprinkler system.

[3]Portions of otherwise sprinklered buildings that are not protected by automatic sprinklers shall have Class II standpipes installed as required for the unsprinklered portions.

[4] In open structures where Class II standpipes may be damaged by freezing, the building official may authorize the use of Class I standpipes that are located as required for Class II standpipes.

[5]Hose is required for Class II standpipes only.

[6]For the purposes of this table, occupied roofs of parking structures shall be considered an additional story. In parking structures, a tier is a story.

[7]Class II standpipes need not be provided in assembly areas used solely for worship.

Figure 6-1 *Standpipe requirements*

Class III *is a standpipe system directly connected to a water supply and equipped with 2½ inch outlets or 2½ inch and 1½ inch outlets when a 1½ inch hose is required. Hose connections for Class III systems may be made through 2½ inch hose valves with easily removable 2½ inch by 1½ inch reducers.*

It's one thing to know what standpipes are — and another to know how to place them. UBC Table 9-A will help you with that. Figure 6-2 shows a typical standpipe location.

According to the UBC, every building with four stories or more must have at least one Class I standpipe for use during construction. This standpipe must be in place before the building is more than 35 feet above grade. If the standpipe isn't connected to a water main, there must be accessible locations for fire department inlet connections.

There's one problem with standpipes. Occupants sometimes try to use them to extinguish a fire before calling the fire department. That's foolish. The first few moments of a fire are critical. In any fire, the best thing to do is call the fire department — then do as much as you can.

Of course, it's different if your building or company is organized to fight fire — and many industrial plants are. In that case, it makes sense to call the local department only if they're really needed.

Fire Safety Includes Construction and Exits

The primary goal of any fire control or fire safety system is to save lives. The secondary goal is to reduce property damage. Almost all structural materials and building components will either burn or melt. A fire-resistive structure can delay progress of the fire long enough for the occupants to get out and for the fire crews and equipment to arrive.

That's why the building code covers construction and exits. All exits must be designed to get people outdoors to safety by the quickest and most direct route. The code doesn't assume that all occupants know where exits are or that they know what to do in an emergency. Buildings should be designed so people can get out easily and quickly. Chapter 12 covers exits in detail.

Exit Size

According to Chapter 10 of the UBC, a required exit door must be at least 3'0" by 6'8". That figures out to be 20 square feet for a standard exit doorway.

But it's not always simple to find the "minimum dimension" of other openings above ground level. Section 1003.3.1.3 states that such openings shall have a minimum dimension of not less than 36 inches (914 mm). However, going back to Section 310.4 we find that:

Escape or rescue windows shall have a minimum net clear openable area of 5.7 square feet. The minimum net clear openable height dimension shall be 24 inches. The minimum net clear openable width dimension shall be 20 inches. When windows are provided as a means of escape or rescue, they shall have a finished sill height not more than 44 inches above the floor.

Why the difference? Maybe we're comparing apples and oranges. Section 310.4 refers to secondary escape paths from sleeping rooms. Section 1003.3.1.3 applies to exit doorways in all types of buildings.

Let's go back to Section 310.4 for a moment. In many parts of the country it appears to be necessary to put bars or grillework on first story windows. That can make the home a deathtrap in the event of fire. Notice that Section 310.4 has this to say:

Figure 6-2 *Typical standpipe location*

Bars, grilles, grates or similar devices may be installed on emergency escape or rescue windows, doors, or window wells, provided:

1. *The devices are equipped with approved release mechanisms that are openable from the inside without the use of a key or special knowledge or effort; and*

2. *The building is equipped with smoke detectors installed in accordance with Section 310.9.*

Will the Opening Be Large Enough?

When a fireman puts a ladder up to a window, the ladder must fit into the window far enough so it can't slip sideways. The average fire ladder is between 16 and 20 inches wide, so it'll probably fit easily into the opening.

Let's say that the window is 44 inches above the floor, the maximum allowable distance. A healthy, able-bodied person shouldn't have too much trouble getting out the window and onto the ladder. But suppose there are four people in the room. One is the firefighter with a bulky air pack on his back. The others are a pregnant woman, a woman who's obese and in poor health, and an elderly man riddled with arthritis. Will they all be able to escape? It makes you wonder, doesn't it? Maybe you should make those windows a little larger and lower.

What Should Be Done?

Here's how one wag defined a really safe building: It's made of reinforced concrete, has no doors or windows, is completely sprinklered, has smoke detectors, has nothing stored in it, and has no occupants. Now of course that would be a safe building, but it sure wouldn't be very economical or practical. We have to balance economy, practicality, and fire safety.

City officials, primarily the fire marshal and the building official, must take a good look at their city and ask themselves some questions:

- Does the city have enough water to make fire sprinklers effective in case of a major catastrophe?

- Does the city have a fire and police communication system that can handle all the calls likely if there's a real emergency?

- Has the city experienced many fires over the years?

- How many lives have been lost in the last three years due to fire? How many lives is that per 100,000 residents?

- Will more stringent rules reduce this figure?

- Will savings in lives and property be worth the cost?

- Are most of the buildings in town relatively new? If so, they may be fairly fire-resistant.

Fire extinguishing systems are expensive. To be effective they must be installed properly. And there's another big problem. If you're building anything except a residential building, you can't be sure of what it will be used for a few years from now. The system installed today may be inadequate in ten years.

Let's say your building is a borderline size, according to the code, with a low-hazard occupancy. Should you install sprinklers now or wait until the occupancy needs of the building require it?

Automatic sprinkler systems usually pay for themselves in from five to ten years. Insurance rates are much lower on sprinklered buildings. In fact, savings on insurance during the first seven years will usually pay for most fire protection systems. Still, many owners don't want to install fire sprinklers. Spec builders trying to make as much as possible on the smallest possible investment usually try to avoid installing sprinklers. But someone is going to use those buildings for many years and the code is written to protect those who do. Many communities have adopted ordinances requiring automatic sprinklers in all structures. It's not yet in the code, so check with your building inspector.

There's a limit to what the building code can do. The best fire suppression system isn't nearly as good as fire prevention. Good construction, clean working areas, reduced fire hazards and informed occupants are your best bet for controlling fire danger.

Who Are You Going to Trust?

I think an inspector should always be willing to answer questions about the code. When a contractor asks for advice, the inspector should do his or her best to help. This isn't a guessing game we're playing: I have the answer and you have to guess what it is. It's everyone doing what they can to put up safe, practical, attractive buildings at reasonable cost.

Of course, I know inspectors who would rather hang by their thumbs than give a contractor free advice. I think that's wrong. But I can understand why they do it. They're afraid of getting sued. If you give bad advice and somebody follows it, you're at fault.

I had a city manager one time who accused me of being too friendly with contractors. Others have said that, too. But so what? I enjoy working with the contractors I know. I hope every building inspector does. And I think knowing something about the people who apply for permits is part of an inspector's job. The code is written in black ink on white paper. But the answer to every code question isn't a matter of black and white.

Here's an example. I've had a lot of people apply for permits with little more than a rough sketch. No plans. Just an idea, a few notes and a line of chatter. What should I do? Well, first, I listened. If the project was a small carport or something simple and they knew what they were doing. I could usually send them off with a permit. That saved days or weeks of construction time and probably some money too. If an applicant obviously didn't understand the project, I'd suggest he or she prepare plans. Maybe that's discriminatory. Maybe it wouldn't work in a larger office handling hundreds of contractors and hundreds of projects a week. But it worked for me.

A lawyer once came in my office for a permit on a small office building. He had sketched the plans himself on scratch paper. I looked them over and turned him down, suggesting he hire an architect. He wasn't willing to take "no" for an answer. So I asked him a few questions: "I've got this pain in my wrist. Right here. Do you think I should give up tennis?"

"I'm a lawyer. Not a doctor. How should I know?" he answered.

"True, you're not a doctor. And you're not an architect either. I'll find a doctor for my wrist and you find a architect for your building."

Like I said, he wouldn't take "no" for an answer. He found a way to outsmart me. Back then our county hadn't adopted the UBC. Outside the city he didn't need a permit. So he built his office just outside the city limits. The basement was O.K. But then work stopped completely. I heard through the grapevine he couldn't get any subcontractors to bid from his sketches.

7

Engineering and Design Requirements

Engineering is a complex subject that most of us would rather leave to trained engineers. Unfortunately, that isn't always possible. Eventually most contractors and tradesmen have to confront engineering and design sections in the code. Fortunately, you don't have to understand how the formulas were developed to follow the code. With a little study, nearly anyone can understand many of the code sections that involve engineering principles. That's what I'm going to emphasize. The rest you can leave to the experts.

What I'm going to cover are the essential formulas — what you need to get a good basic understanding of engineering requirements. Professional engineers who need more details will have to look elsewhere for more guidance.

Engineering is first mentioned in the UBC in Chapter 16:

1601 — Scope. This chapter prescribes general design requirements applicable to all structures regulated by this code.

Loads and Loading

Section 1602 jumps right to the heart of the matter: loads and loading. This includes two items which we'll take in the order they're defined in the UBC:

***Dead Loads** consist of the weight of all materials and fixed equipment incorporated into the building or other structure.*

Live Loads are those loads produced by the use and occupancy of the building or other structure and do not include dead load, construction load, or environmental loads such as wind load, snow load, rain load, earthquake load or floor load.

Another load implied by the definition of live load is the *unit live load*. This is a load localized in one area rather than spread evenly over a larger area. Unit live loads are usually heavier in a given area than the more common distributed loads in a building, such as furniture. Loads for various uses and occupancies are shown in UBC Tables 16-A and 16-B (Figures 7-1 and 7-2).

Unit Live Loads

Designers use the unit live loads shown in UBC Table 16-A to plan floors and foundations that will hold up under both uniform (well distributed) and concentrated loads. If you're designing a factory or shop building that doesn't have isolated pieces of heavy equipment, use the column headed *Uniform Load* for the whole floor. If you're planning for some very heavy equipment or machinery that's different from the rest of the equipment in the building, use the column headed *Concentrated Load* for those areas.

Table 16-B covers special situations that have to be treated individually. Here's an example. Say the floor of your building is a concrete slab 4 inches thick with wire mesh reinforcing. Suppose heavy machinery is expected. Look at Table 16-B. You'll have to beef up the area under your machine by increasing the floor thickness to 6 inches and adding ½-inch rebar reinforcing, for instance.

Another example is a private garage where the load is imposed on four points — one under each wheel of a car. Because cars move into and out of a garage, these points become paths. Each path has to support 2,000 pounds, plus the normal live load. According to Section 1607.3.3, each load-bearing area must be able to carry 40 percent of the gross weight of the heaviest vehicle stored. The standard 4-inch slab will support most autos, but if you're planning to store a motor home, take another

look at the thickness of the slab. This applies to your driveway as well.

When I started out in the business of building inspection, few buildings had automatic fire sprinklers. Regulations were quite lax and many exceptions were allowed. But many experts insist that fire sprinklers are more than worth the cost. In the few communities that require fire sprinklers in nearly all buildings, the fire department can almost be disbanded. That's probably why the BOCA's National Building Code requires residential sprinklers for virtually all new apartments and motels. The UBC doesn't require that. But it does recognize the load that fire sprinklers put on a building. Since 1985 the UBC has included *Fire Sprinkler Structural Support* as a special load in Table 16-B (Figure 7-2).

Design Methods

Section 1605 makes it clear that buildings have to be designed to support the loads assumed in the code.

1605.1 General. *Buildings and other structures and all portions thereof shall be designed and constructed to sustain, within the limitations specified in this code, all loads set forth in Chapter 16 and elsewhere in this code, combined in accordance with Section 1612. Design shall be in accordance with Strength Design, Load and Resistance Factor Design or Allowable Stress Design methods, as permitted by the applicable materials chapters.*

Exception: *Unless otherwise required by the building official, buildings or portions thereof that are constructed in accordance with the conventional light-framing requirements specified in Chapter 23 of this code shall be deemed to meet the requirements of this section.*

Section 1605.1 is the heart of the matter. The rest of this chapter fills in the details.

TABLE 16-A—UNIFORM AND CONCENTRATED LOADS

USE OR OCCUPANCY		UNIFORM LOAD[1] (psf)	CONCENTRATED LOAD (pounds)
Category	Description	× 0.0479 for kN/m²	× 0.004 48 for kN
1. Access floor systems	Office use	50	2,000[2]
	Computer use	100	2,000[2]
2. Armories		150	0
3. Assembly areas[3] and auditoriums and balconies therewith	Fixed seating areas	50	0
	Movable seating and other areas	100	0
	Stage areas and enclosed platforms	125	0
4. Cornices and marquees		60[4]	0
5. Exit facilities[5]		100	0[6]
6. Garages	General storage and/or repair	100	7
	Private or pleasure-type motor vehicle storage	50	7
7. Hospitals	Wards and rooms	40	1,000[2]
8. Libraries	Reading rooms	60	1,000[2]
	Stack rooms	125	1,500[2]
9. Manufacturing	Light	75	2,000[2]
	Heavy	125	3,000[2]
10. Offices		50	2,000[2]
11. Printing plants	Press rooms	150	2,500[2]
	Composing and linotype rooms	100	2,000[2]
12. Residential[8]	Basic floor area	40	0[6]
	Exterior balconies	60[4]	0
	Decks	40[4]	0
	Storage	40	0
13. Restrooms[9]			
14. Reviewing stands, grandstands, bleachers, and folding and telescoping seating		100	0
15. Roof decks	Same as area served or for the type of occupancy accommodated		
16. Schools	Classrooms	40	1,000[2]
17. Sidewalks and driveways	Public access	250	7
18. Storage	Light	125	
	Heavy	250	
19. Stores		100	3,000[2]
20. Pedestrian bridges and walkways		100	

[1]See Section 1607 for live load reductions.
[2]See Section 1607.3.3, first paragraph, for area of load application.
[3]Assembly areas include such occupancies as dance halls, drill rooms, gymnasiums, playgrounds, plazas, terraces and similar occupancies that are generally accessible to the public.
[4]When snow loads occur that are in excess of the design conditions, the structure shall be designed to support the loads due to the increased loads caused by drift buildup or a greater snow design as determined by the building official. See Section 1614. For special-purpose roofs, see Section 1607.4.4.
[5]Exit facilities shall include such uses as corridors serving an occupant load of 10 or more persons, exterior exit balconies, stairways, fire escapes and similar uses.
[6]Individual stair treads shall be designed to support a 300-pound (1.33 kN) concentrated load placed in a position that would cause maximum stress. Stair stringers may be designed for the uniform load set forth in the table.
[7]See Section 1607.3.3, second paragraph, for concentrated loads. See Table 16-B for vehicle barriers.
[8]Residential occupancies include private dwellings, apartments and hotel guest rooms.
[9]Restroom loads shall not be less than the load for the occupancy with which they are associated, but need not exceed 50 pounds per square foot (2.4 kN/m²).

Figure 7-1 *Uniform and concentrated loads*

TABLE 16-B—SPECIAL LOADS[1]

USE		VERTICAL LOAD	LATERAL LOAD
Category	Description	(pounds per square foot unless otherwise noted)	
		× 0.0479 for kN/m²	
1. Construction, public access at site (live load)	Walkway, see Section 3303.6	150	
	Canopy, see Section 3303.7	150	
2. Grandstands, reviewing stands, bleachers, and folding and telescoping seating (live load)	Seats and footboards	120[2]	See Footnote 3
3. Stage accessories (live load)	Catwalks	40	
	Followspot, projection and control rooms	50	
4. Ceiling framing (live load)	Over stages	20	
	All uses except over stages	10[4]	
5. Partitions and interior walls, see Sec. 1611.5 (live load)			5
6. Elevators and dumbwaiters (dead and live loads)		2 × total loads[5]	
7. Mechanical and electrical equipment (dead load)		Total loads	
8. Cranes (dead and live loads)	Total load including impact increase	1.25 × total load[6]	0.10 × total load[7]
9. Balcony railings and guardrails	Exit facilities serving an occupant load greater than 50		50[8]
	Other than exit facilities		20[8]
	Components		25[9]
10. Vehicle barriers	See Section 311.2.3.5		6,000[10]
11. Handrails		See Footnote 11	See Footnote 11
12. Storage racks	Over 8 feet (2438 mm) high	Total loads[12]	See Table 16-O
13. Fire sprinkler structural support		250 pounds (1112 N) plus weight of water-filled pipe[13]	See Table 16-O
14. Explosion exposure	Hazardous occupancies, see Section 307.10		

[1]The tabulated loads are minimum loads. Where other vertical loads required by this code or required by the design would cause greater stresses, they shall be used.

[2]Pounds per lineal foot (× 14.6 for N/m).

[3]Lateral sway bracing loads of 24 pounds per foot (350 N/m) parallel and 10 pounds per foot (145.9 N/m) perpendicular to seat and footboards.

[4]Does not apply to ceilings that have sufficient total access from below, such that access is not required within the space above the ceiling. Does not apply to ceilings if the attic areas above the ceiling are not provided with access. This live load need not be considered as acting simultaneously with other live loads imposed upon the ceiling framing or its supporting structure.

[5]Where Appendix Chapter 30 has been adopted, see reference standard cited therein for additional design requirements.

[6]The impact factors included are for cranes with steel wheels riding on steel rails. They may be modified if substantiating technical data acceptable to the building official is submitted. Live loads on crane support girders and their connections shall be taken as the maximum crane wheel loads. For pendant-operated traveling crane support girders and their connections, the impact factors shall be 1.10.

[7]This applies in the direction parallel to the runway rails (longitudinal). The factor for forces perpendicular to the rail is 0.20 × the transverse traveling loads (trolley, cab, hooks and lifted loads). Forces shall be applied at top of rail and may be distributed among rails of multiple rail cranes and shall be distributed with due regard for lateral stiffness of the structures supporting these rails.

[8]A load per lineal foot (× 14.6 for N/m) to be applied horizontally at right angles to the top rail.

[9]Intermediate rails, panel fillers and their connections shall be capable of withstanding a load of 25 pounds per square foot (1.2 kN/m²) applied horizontally at right angles over the entire tributary area, including openings and spaces between rails. Reactions due to this loading need not be combined with those of Footnote 8.

[10]A horizontal load in pounds (N) applied at right angles to the vehicle barrier at a height of 18 inches (457 mm) above the parking surface. The force may be distributed over a 1-foot-square (304.8-millimeter-square) area.

[11]The mounting of handrails shall be such that the completed handrail and supporting structure are capable of withstanding a load of at least 200 pounds (890 N) applied in any direction at any point on the rail. These loads shall not be assumed to act cumulatively with Item 9.

[12]Vertical members of storage racks shall be protected from impact forces of operating equipment, or racks shall be designed so that failure of one vertical member will not cause collapse of more than the bay or bays directly supported by that member.

[13]The 250-pound (1.11 kN) load is to be applied to any single fire sprinkler support point but not simultaneously to all support joints.

Figure 7-2 *Special loads*

Roof Loads and Design

Most people are more concerned with the loading inside a building than with the roof load. They're more worried about the floor collapsing under the weight of a piano than the weight of 2 feet of snow on the roof. Maybe that's a mistake. You can usually anticipate the load on the floor. Roofs, on the other hand, are subjected to loads that are often temporary and totally unpredictable.

Wind Loads

Two important loads affect the building exterior: wind loads and snow loads. The UBC gets pretty technical on this issue and for a very good reason. These two loads are zero most of the time — but not always. Builders in Los Angeles aren't particularly concerned about snow loads, but the Santa Ana winds common to Southern California can present a serious problem.

Because snow and wind loads can vary so greatly, you may need good advice from an engineer when designing a roof. Your building official will be able to explain local practice to you. Of course, Chapter 16 in the UBC explains the requirements. But you need a background in engineering to understand some of the formulas. Here's some plain English from the Code:

1615 General. Every building or structure and every portion thereof shall be designed and constructed to resist the wind effects determined in accordance with the requirements of this division. Wind shall be assumed to come from any horizontal direction. No reduction in wind pressure shall be taken for the shielding effect of adjacent structures.

Generally, wind and snow loads are not a problem for residences and small commercial structures. Most wood-frame and masonry buildings have the strength to withstand whatever Mother Nature can deliver. But in some areas special precautions are needed. You probably know if you live in an area that has unusually high snow or wind loads. Sometimes homes adjacent to natural land features have wind patterns worse than other homes nearby.

Figure 16-1 in the 1997 edition of Volume 2 of the UBC (Figure 7-3 in this manual) is a wind speed map of the United States. This map represents the fastest wind speeds at 33 feet above the ground for Exposure Category C.

The wind load formula — Even if most mathematical formulas throw you into a panic, you can handle this one. The wind load, or design wind pressure, is calculated by the following formula:

$$P = C_e C_q q_s I_w$$

Where:

P = Design wind pressure

C_e = Combined height, exposure and gust factor coefficient as given in Table 16-G (see Figure 7-4)

C_q = Pressure coefficient for the structure or portion of structure under consideration as given in Table 16-H (see Figure 7-5)

q_s = Wind stagnation pressure at the standard height of 33 feet as set forth in Table 16-F (see Figure 7-6)

I_w = Importance factor as set forth in Table 16-K (Figure 7-7). This pertains to a factor of 1.15 if you're building a hospital, fire or police station, disaster operations or communications center, or a similar structure required for emergency response. On all other buildings a factor of 1.0 is adequate.

With that in mind, let's see what the design wind pressure would be for a residential roof with a 4 in 12 pitch in Kennewick, Washington. The wind speed map shows this area to be in the 70 miles per hour speed zone, which still gives us a q_s factor of 12.6 from UBC Table 16-F (Figure 7-6). Notice in UBC Table 16-H (Figure 7-5) that a roof element on an enclosed structure with a 4 in 12 pitch would have a C_q factor of 1.3.

Now go to UBC Table 16-G (Figure 7-4). You should see the problem right away: Will our structure have Exposure B or Exposure C? A

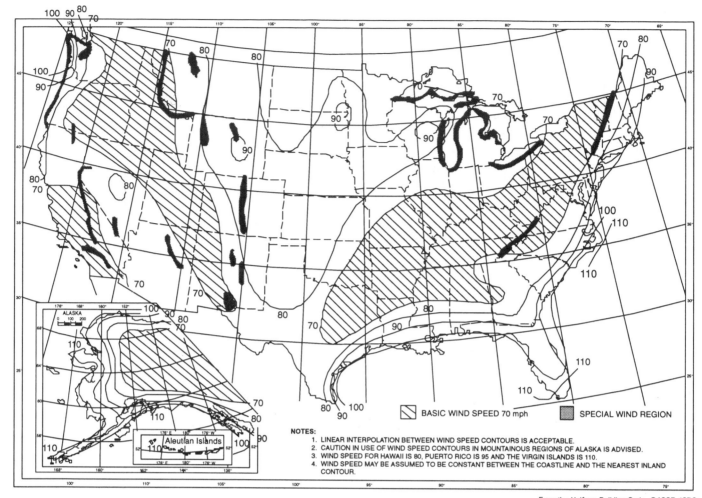

From the Uniform Building Code, ©1997, ICBO

Figure 7-3 *Basic wind speeds*

TABLE 16-G—COMBINED HEIGHT, EXPOSURE AND GUST FACTOR COEFFICIENT (C_e)[1]

HEIGHT ABOVE AVERAGE LEVEL OF ADJOINING GROUND (feet) × 304.8 for mm	EXPOSURE D	EXPOSURE C	EXPOSURE B
0-15	1.39	1.06	0.62
20	1.45	1.13	0.67
25	1.50	1.19	0.72
30	1.54	1.23	0.76
40	1.62	1.31	0.84
60	1.73	1.43	0.95
80	1.81	1.53	1.04
100	1.88	1.61	1.13
120	1.93	1.67	1.20
160	2.02	1.79	1.31
200	2.10	1.87	1.42
300	2.23	2.05	1.63
400	2.34	2.19	1.80

[1]Values for intermediate heights above 15 feet (4572 mm) may be interpolated.

From the Uniform Building Code, ©1997, ICBO

Figure 7-4 *Combined height, exposure and gust factor coefficient*

TABLE 16-H—PRESSURE COEFFICIENTS (C_q)

STRUCTURE OR PART THEREOF	DESCRIPTION	C_q FACTOR

1. Primary frames and systems	**Method 1** (Normal force method)
	Walls:
	   Windward wall
	   Leeward wall
	Roofs[1]:
	   Wind perpendicular to ridge
	   Leeward roof or flat roof
	   Windward roof
	     less than 2:12 (16.7%)
	     Slope 2:12 (16.7%) to less than 9:12 (75%)
	     Slope 9:12 (75%) to 12:12 (100%)
	     Slope > 12:12 (100%)
	   Wind parallel to ridge and flat roofs
		
		0.8 inward
		0.5 outward
		
		0.7 outward
		
		0.7 outward
		0.9 outward or 0.3 inward
		0.4 inward
		0.7 inward
		0.7 outward

	Method 2 (Projected area method)
	On vertical projected area
	   Structures 40 feet (12 192 mm) or less in height
	   Structures over 40 feet (12 192 mm) in height
	On horizontal projected area[1]
		
		1.3 horizontal any direction
		1.4 horizontal any direction
		0.7 upward

2. Elements and components not in areas of discontinuity[2]	Wall elements
	   All structures
	   Enclosed and unenclosed structures
	   Partially enclosed structures
	   Parapets walls
		
		1.2 inward
		1.2 outward
		1.6 outward
		1.3 inward or outward

	Roof elements[3]
	   Enclosed and unenclosed structures
	     Slope < 7:12 (58.3%)
	     Slope 7:12 (58.3%) to 12:12 (100%)
	
	   Partially enclosed structures
	     Slope < 2:12 (16.7%)
	     Slope 2:12 (16.7%) to 7:12 (58.3%)
	     Slope > 7:12 (58.3%) to 12:12 (100%)
		
		1.3 outward
		1.3 outward or inward
		
		1.7 outward
		1.6 outward or 0.8 inward
		1.7 outward or inward

3. Elements and components in areas of discontinuities[2,4,5]	Wall corners[6]
	
	Roof eaves, rakes or ridges without
	   overhangs[6]
	     Slope < 2:12 (16.7%)
	     Slope 2:12 (16.7%) to 7:12 (58.3%)
	     Slope > 7:12 (58.3%) to 12:12 (100%)
	For slopes less than 2:12 (16.7%)
	   Overhangs at roof eaves, rakes or ridges, and
	     canopies
		1.5 outward or 1.2 inward
		
		2.3 upward
		2.6 outward
		1.6 outward
		0.5 added to values above

4. Chimneys, tanks and solid towers	Square or rectangular Hexagonal or octagonal Round or elliptical	1.4 any direction 1.1 any direction 0.8 any direction

5. Open-frame towers[7,8]	Square and rectangular
	   Diagonal
	   Normal
	Triangular
		
		4.0
		3.6
		3.2

6. Tower accessories (such as ladders, conduit, lights and elevators)	Cylindrical members
	   2 inches (51 mm) or less in diameter
	   Over 2 inches (51 mm) in diameter
	Flat or angular members
		
		1.0
		0.8
		1.3

7. Signs, flagpoles, lightpoles, minor structures[8]		1.4 any direction

[1]For one story or the top story of multistory partially enclosed structures, an additional value of 0.5 shall be added to the outward C_q. The most critical combination shall be used for design. For definition of partially enclosed structures, see Section 1616.

[2]C_q values listed are for 10-square-foot (0.93 m²) tributary areas. For tributary areas of 100 square feet (9.29 m²), the value of 0.3 may be subtracted from C_q, except for areas at discontinuities with slopes less than 7 units vertical in 12 units horizontal (58.3% slope) where the value of 0.8 may be subtracted from C_q. Interpolation may be used for tributary areas between 10 and 100 square feet (0.93 m² and 9.29 m²). For tributary areas greater than 1,000 square feet (92.9 m²), use primary frame values.

[3]For slopes greater than 12 units vertical in 12 units horizontal (100% slope), use wall element values.

[4]Local pressures shall apply over a distance from the discontinuity of 10 feet (3048 mm) or 0.1 times the least width of the structure, whichever is smaller.

[5]Discontinuities at wall corners or roof ridges are defined as discontinuous breaks in the surface where the included interior angle measures 170 degrees or less.

[6]Load is to be applied on either side of discontinuity but not simultaneously on both sides.

[7]Wind pressures shall be applied to the total normal projected area of all elements on one face. The forces shall be assumed to act parallel to the wind direction.

[8]Factors for cylindrical elements are two thirds of those for flat or angular elements.

Figure 7-5 *Pressure coefficients*

TABLE 16-F—WIND STAGNATION PRESSURE (q_s) AT STANDARD HEIGHT OF 33 FEET (10 058 mm)

Basic wind speed (mph)[1] ($\times$ 1.61 for km/h)	70	80	90	100	110	120	130
Pressure q_s (psf) ($\times$ 0.0479 for kN/m^2)	12.6	16.4	20.8	25.6	31.0	36.9	43.3

[1]Wind speed from Section 1618.

Figure 7-6 *Wind stagnation pressure*

TABLE 16-K—OCCUPANCY CATEGORY

OCCUPANCY CATEGORY	OCCUPANCY OR FUNCTIONS OF STRUCTURE	SEISMIC IMPORTANCE FACTOR, I	SEISMIC IMPORTANCE[1] FACTOR, I_p	WIND IMPORTANCE FACTOR, I_w
1. Essential facilities[2]	Group I, Division 1 Occupancies having surgery and emergency treatment areas Fire and police stations Garages and shelters for emergency vehicles and emergency aircraft Structures and shelters in emergency-preparedness centers Aviation control towers Structures and equipment in government communication centers and other facilities required for emergency response Standby power-generating equipment for Category 1 facilities Tanks or other structures containing housing or supporting water or other fire-suppression material or equipment required for the protection of Category 1, 2 or 3 structures	1.25	1.50	1.15
2. Hazardous facilities	Group H, Divisions 1, 2, 6 and 7 Occupancies and structures therein housing or supporting toxic or explosive chemicals or substances Nonbuilding structures housing, supporting or containing quantities of toxic or explosive substances that, if contained within a building, would cause that building to be classified as a Group H, Division 1, 2 or 7 Occupancy	1.25	1.50	1.15
3. Special occupancy structures[3]	Group A, Divisions 1, 2 and 2.1 Occupancies Buildings housing Group E, Divisions 1 and 3 Occupancies with a capacity greater than 300 students Buildings housing Group B Occupancies used for college or adult education with a capacity greater than 500 students Group I, Divisions 1 and 2 Occupancies with 50 or more resident incapacitated patients, but not included in Category 1 Group I, Division 3 Occupancies All structures with an occupancy greater than 5,000 persons Structures and equipment in power-generating stations, and other public utility facilities not included in Category 1 or Category 2 above, and required for continued operation	1.00	1.00	1.00
4. Standard occupancy structures[3]	All structures housing occupancies or having functions not listed in Category 1, 2 or 3 and Group U Occupancy towers	1.00	1.00	1.00
5. Miscellaneous structures	Group U Occupancies except for towers	1.00	1.00	1.00

[1]The limitation of I_p for panel connections in Section 1633.2.4 shall be 1.0 for the entire connector.
[2]Structural observation requirements are given in Section 1702.
[3]For anchorage of machinery and equipment required for life-safety systems, the value of I_p shall be taken as 1.5.

Figure 7-7 *Occupancy category*

structure less than 20 feet above the average adjoining ground carries a factor of 1.13 in Exposure C. But it's only 0.67 in Exposure B. So which is right in our case?

Section 1616 (Volume 2) tells us that Exposure C represents the most severe exposure — the terrain is flat and generally open, extending one-half mile or more from the site. Exposure B has terrain with buildings, forest or surface irregularities 20 feet or more in height covering at least 20 percent of the area extending one mile or more from the site. That makes sense. You'll get the full force of the wind if your building is the only obstruction around. In this case we're in a city and can use the factor for Exposure B.

Now our formula, converted to numbers, looks like this:

Multiply 0.67 times 1.3 times 12.6 times 1 to get the design wind pressure of 10.97 pounds per square foot.

But don't stop here. This isn't the end. Suppose that our Exposure Coefficient comes under Exposure C, and that we're building on a knoll which extends considerably above the surrounding terrain. Do you think it would be wise to use the minimum height of 20 feet for a residential structure? I wouldn't recommend it. Instead, add the height of the knoll to the height of your building.

For example, your house will be in Exposure C (flat terrain, generally open for a half mile) but you have chosen to place it on a knoll 50 feet above the height of the surrounding countryside. (The house is 20 feet high and the knoll is 50 feet high). Table 16-G has values for building heights of 60 and 80 feet. Since our building is now 70 feet, use the 80-foot values. Now our formula will look like this:

Multiply 1.53 times 1.3 times 12.6 times 1 to get the design wind pressure of 25.06 pounds per square foot.

That difference might have some effect on the type of roof you choose and the method of installing it.

Just a minute, though. This is only a recommendation, not a requirement. It's not in the book and it's not based on engineering

data. It's based on pure and simple common sense. Normally, a little added strength in your calculation won't be that expensive, especially in a home.

That's all there is to wind loads. But don't try to build that roof for a wind load of 10.01 pounds per square foot. It turns out that the expected wind loads are less than the expected live loads. UBC Table 16-C (Figure 7-8 in this book) gives the minimum roof live loads. These are the minimum figures to use, no matter what the wind load calculations suggest.

Don't stop reading the UBC when you think you have the answer. Take time to read the next paragraph.

Snow Loads

According to Section 1614 of the UBC:

Buildings and other structures and all portions thereof that are subject to snow loading shall be designed to resist the snow loads, as determined by the building official, in accordance with the load combinations set forth in Section 1612.2 or 1612.3

It seems that snow can create some unusual conditions on a roof. For instance, the shady part of a roof is the last part to thaw. Before it finally does, you can expect some strange results. The snow melts a little and then freezes, melts a little and then freezes, causing snow and ice to pile up on the roof. While the shady side is thawing and freezing, the exposed side may be completely bare after a few days. This creates what is known as an unbalanced load. Figures A-16-4, A-16-5, A-16-6, A-16-7, A-16-8 from the UBC Appendix Chapter 16 (our Figure 7-9) show this very well. Figures A-16-11 and A-16-12 (our Figure 7-10) indicate the increased load area in roof valleys.

Even though it's temporary, somewhat like the wind load, snow load still must be calculated into the overall roof load. This is referred to in Section 1614 in Volume 2, UBC:

Potential unbalanced accumulation of snow at valleys, parapets, roof structures and offsets in roofs of uneven configuration

TABLE 16-C—MINIMUM ROOF LIVE LOADS[1]

ROOF SLOPE	METHOD 1			METHOD 2		
	Tributary Loaded Area in Square Feet for Any Structural Member					
	× 0.0929 for m²					
	0 to 200	201 to 600	Over 600	Uniform Load[2] (psf)	Rate of Reduction *r* (percentage)	Maximum Reduction *R* (percentage)
	Uniform Load (psf)					
	× 0.0479 for kN/m²					
1. Flat[3] or rise less than 4 units vertical in 12 units horizontal (33.3% slope). Arch or dome with rise less than one eighth of span	20	16	12	20	.08	40
2. Rise 4 units vertical to less than 12 units vertical in 12 units horizontal (33% to less than 100% slope). Arch or dome with rise one eighth of span to less than three eighths of span	16	14	12	16	.06	25
3. Rise 12 units vertical in 12 units horizontal (100% slope) and greater. Arch or dome with rise three eighths of span or greater	12	12	12	12	No reductions permitted	
4. Awnings except cloth covered[4]	5	5	5	5		
5. Greenhouses, lath houses and agricultural buildings[5]	10	10	10	10		

[1]Where snow loads occur, the roof structure shall be designed for such loads as determined by the building official. See Section 1614. For special-purpose roofs, see Section 1607.4.4.

[2]See Sections 1607.5 and 1607.6 for live load reductions. The rate of reduction *r* in Section 1607.5 Formula (7-1) shall be as indicated in the table. The maximum reduction *R* shall not exceed the value indicated in the table.

[3]A flat roof is any roof with a slope of less than $^{1}/_{4}$ unit vertical in 12 units horizontal (2% slope). The live load for flat roofs is in addition to the ponding load required by Section 1611.7.

[4]As defined in Section 3206.

[5]See Section 1607.4.4 for concentrated load requirements for greenhouse roof members.

Figure 7-8 *Minimum roof live loads*

shall be considered. Where snow loads occur, the snow loads shall be determined by the building official.

The snow load formula — Calculate your snow load reduction by the following formula:

$$R_s = \frac{S}{40} - \frac{1}{2}$$

Where:

R_s = Snow load reduction in pounds per square foot per degree of pitch over 20 degrees

S = Total snow load in pounds per square foot

Do you know what the snow loading is in your community? If you have a lot of snow, you may. But if your work is spread over a larger area, snow loads may vary from one job to the next. For example, my home is in Washington State. Counties vary in elevation from sea level to over 8,000 feet. At sea level, snowfall seldom exceeds a few inches and lasts just a few hours or days, often with little or no freezing. But in the mountains of Washington, snow can reach 15 feet deep or more and stay on the ground in some places from October to June. Is the entire county considered a snow area? Of course. But how do we determine snow loads for each community in the county? Where do you draw the line? At what point do you have a 30-pound

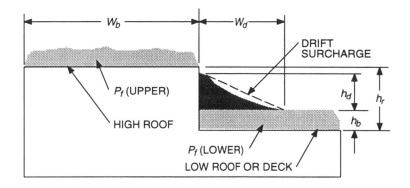

FIGURE A-16-4—DRIFTING SNOW ON LOW ROOFS AND DECKS

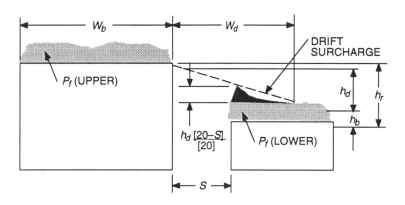

For **SI:** $h_d\left[\dfrac{6.1-S}{6.1}\right]$.

FIGURE A-16-5—DRIFTING SNOW ONTO ADJACENT LOW STRUCTURES

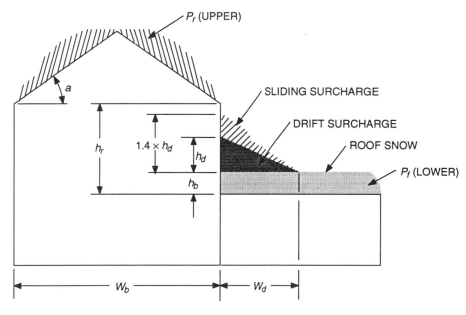

FIGURE A-16-6—ADDITIONAL SURCHARGE DUE TO SLIDING SNOW

From the Uniform Building Code, ©1997, ICBO

Figure 7-9 *Drifting snow creates unbalanced loads*

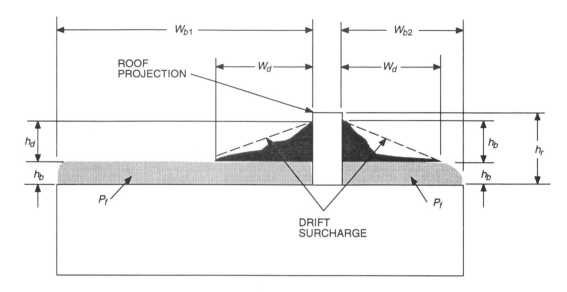

FIGURE A-16-7—SNOW DRIFTING AT ROOF PROJECTIONS

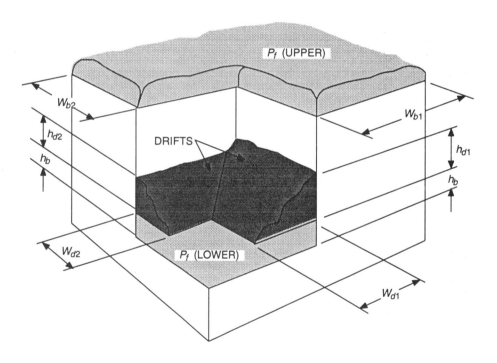

FIGURE A-16-8—INTERSECTING SNOW DRIFTS

NOTE:

$$h_{d1} = 0.43 \sqrt[3]{W_{b1}} \sqrt[4]{P_g + 10} - 1.5$$

For **SI:** 1 foot = 304.8 mm.

P_f is evaluated on the basis of upper roof.

$$h_{d2} = 0.43 \sqrt[3]{W_{b2}} \sqrt[4]{P_g + 10} - 1.5$$

Figure 7-9 *Drifting snow creates unbalanced loads (Continued)*

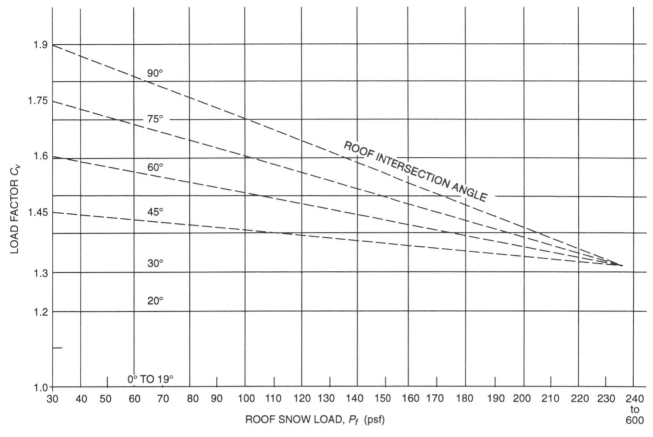

For **SI:** 1 psf = 47.8 N/m^2.

FIGURE A-16-11—VALLEY COEFFICIENT, C_v

Figure 7-10 *Increased load in valley areas*

load, a 40-pound load or a 50-pound load? You can't always depend on elevation because snowfall varies, even at the same elevation. So, too, will freezing and thawing conditions. Obviously, this is another case where it's wise to consult your local building official before going too far.

I once asked the Snohomish County building official about this. Here's what he told me: "In Snohomish County it only snows back of the section line. On one side of the section line you get one rating, on the other side it's something completely different."

This opinion was based on years of experience and observation in his county. Lacking

official reference data, the inspector's opinion may be the best guidance available. If it's based on experience and good judgment, it's probably fair. If you don't agree, then it's up to you to prove that your opinion is better.

Uplift Loads

Ever hear of uplift load? If you haven't, don't worry. Nearly everyone thinks of loads as being caused by gravity pulling everything toward the center of the earth.

Roofs have uplift loads, just like the wing of an airplane. A roof with a parapet wall is especially vulnerable. Winds cause a vortex which creates a vacuum (negative pressure) on the

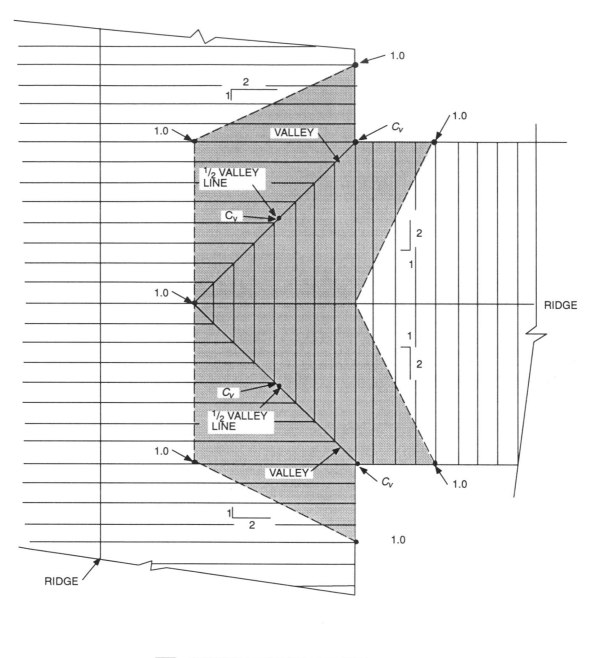

DENOTES INCREASED LOAD AREA:
1. Load is constant on lines connecting points noted 1.0.
2. Load is constant on lines connecting points noted C_v.
3. Load varies linearly between 1.0 and C_v.

FIGURE A-16-12—VALLEY DESIGN COEFFICIENTS, C_v

From the Uniform Building Code, ©1997, ICBO

Figure 7-10 *Increased load in valley areas (Continued)*

roof. Large sections of roofing have been literally sucked off by uplift loads. High-rise buildings with large glass areas can have large negative loads. The only defense is a design that considers negative wind loads.

Gable roofs are also affected. Winds blowing over the roof create negative pressure on the lee side (side away from the wind) of the roof and can send shingles flying. If your chimney is too short or improperly placed, the same force can cause draft problems.

Although we understand the effect of wind, conditions vary considerably from place to place. The problem is compounded by trees and other buildings in the area. Be aware of any conditions that may create uplift loads on your building. Don't rely on trees or other buildings in the neighborhood to reduce the wind load. They may disappear in the next windstorm — leaving your building exposed.

Roofs of unenclosed buildings, roof overhangs, architectural projections, eaves, canopies, cornices, marquees and the like have to be built to withstand upward pressures. In other words, when the inspector tells you to bolt your patio or carport cover to the concrete, he's just trying to keep it out of the neighbor's yard.

In the next chapter we'll discuss subterranean water. It's a problem in many areas. Besides damp basements, groundwater causes another problem. It's known officially as hydrostatic uplift.

1611.8 Hydrostatic Uplift. All foundations, slabs and other footings subjected to water pressure shall be designed to resist a uniformly distributed uplift load, F, equal to the full hydrostatic pressure.

Earthquake Loads

Earthquakes, like fires, are totally unpredictable. The 1997 edition of the UBC (Volume 2) now includes about 14 pages of formulas and regulations designed to protect against damage from earthquakes. The 1982 edition of the code had only six pages. But stay tuned. Our understanding of earthquake damage is changing very quickly. What's in the code today probably isn't the last word on design for earthquake safety. Your inspector may have special regulations if you live in a seismic zone.

Figure 7-11 (UBC Figure 16-2) shows an earthquake probability map. This map divides the country into seismic zones 0 through 4. Zone 0 is where earthquakes are least likely; Zone 4 is where they're most probable.

When you hear that an area is practically earthquake-free, just remember that there have been disastrous earthquakes in areas where none had occurred before. In the 16th century, Lisbon, Portugal had a severe earthquake that almost leveled the city. Loss of life was enormous. This was the only major earthquake in western Europe during recorded history. Portugal hasn't had a serious earthquake since. Reelfoot Lake in Tennessee was formed in the early 19th century when an earthquake caused land to settle in a large depression. There had never been an earthquake in the area before. There have been a few tremors in that area since but no major earthquakes.

Use the earthquake probability map when planning any building. Many structural requirements in the UBC are based on the seismic zones shown in the earthquake map.

There's no such thing as an earthquake-proof building, especially buildings erected near a fault line. Everyone knows that, including the authors of the code. That's why the code doesn't require the impossible. It isn't practical to design buildings to resist every possible earthquake. If the code required that, very few projects would ever be planned. Few people could afford to build. But the code tries to strike a balance between risk to life and property and the cost of construction. You're free to decide if the code is doing the job intended.

Reductions in Live Loads

Live loads are the weight of people and things that will be in the building. The code

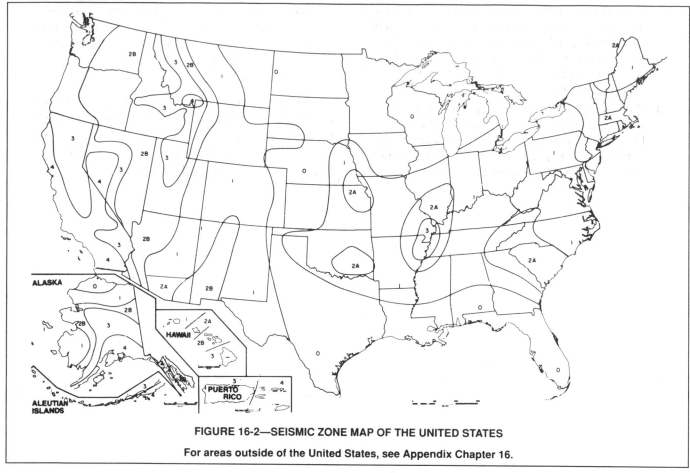

FIGURE 16-2—SEISMIC ZONE MAP OF THE UNITED STATES

For areas outside of the United States, see Appendix Chapter 16.

From the Uniform Building Code, ©1997, ICBO

Figure 7-11 *Earthquake probability map*

establishes live loads you have to design for in each type of building. Some reductions in live loads are permitted under certain circumstances. Formulas in the code show how and when these reductions apply. I'll spare you a discussion of those formulas. Engineers and architects usually work them out, anyway. If you're working on a large building, the designer should check his or her live load figures against the reductions permitted. This also applies to the deflection allowed in structural members.

Special Purpose Loads

Here are special loads which are usually grouped under the title *Miscellaneous:*

■ You must design greenhouse roof bars, purlins, and rafters to support a 100-pound minimum concentrated load in addition to the live load.

■ Roofs must have enough slope or camber to ensure adequate drainage even if the roof sags. You must design the roof to support maximum loads, including possible ponding of water caused by deflection.

■ Properly anchor the roof to walls and columns, and the walls and columns to the foundation to resist overturning, uplift and sliding.

■ Fences less than 12 feet high, greenhouses, lath houses, and all agricultural buildings must be designed to meet the horizontal wind pressures in UBC Table 16-H (Figure

7-5). If the height of the structure is 20 feet or less, you only have to use two-thirds of the first line of listed values. Design the structures to withstand an uplift wind pressure equal to three-fourths the horizontal pressure.

■ To determine stresses, consider that all vertical design loads except the roof live load and crane loads act simultaneously with the wind pressure. Snow loading is the only exception. You normally consider only 50 percent of the snow load in addition to the wind load. But the building official may require you to consider a greater percentage of snow load, depending on local conditions.

That about covers all the design and engineering you need to know to follow the code. It's time to start looking at the building itself. In the next chapter, we'll look at the code requirements for foundations.

Misplaced Stake, Misplaced House

Most lots and plats have been surveyed, mapped, and staked at least once before the contractor arrives. Surveyors set stakes for streets and walks, sewers, water lines, underground power and phone lines. Stakes for these site improvements are usually uprooted, replanted, and generally kicked around while the sitework is being done. Not only that. Kids have a natural attraction for survey stakes. They make lovely swords.

By the time you get to the site, no telling where the survey stakes have wandered. That's why I always recommended a fresh survey when I issued a permit for a new building. A new survey won't cost much, usually less than $200. That's cheap insurance.

I once issued a permit with the usual warning about surveys and such. "Yeah, yeah," the contractor said. I figured he would ignore my suggestion. And he did. When I inspected the foundation, something looked wrong to me. I called the contractor and suggested he get a survey before doing my more work. He finally hired a surveyor. The foundation not only violated the setback requirements, but part of it was on the neighbor's lot!

It was a simple but costly mistake. The lot was on a curve. The contractor took the PT stake (point of tangency) for his base point (lot corner). It was the contractor's error and his loss. The contractor could have asked the owner to get a survey before starting work. I bet he did on every job after that.

8

Concrete

When building homes, apartments or small commercial buildings, you don't need to know very much about concrete. After all, it arrives at the site already mixed and ready to use. But for larger jobs, the requirements are more demanding and there's more you have to know. The last thing you want to have to do is break out a freshly poured foundation.

What Is Concrete?

What's the difference between *concrete* and *cement?* Generally, cement is the powdered limestone used to make concrete. Chapter 19 of the UBC (Volume 2) covers concrete construction — including this definition of concrete:

Concrete is a mixture of portland cement or any other hydraulic cement, fine aggre-gate, coarse aggregate and water, with or without admixtures.

Section 1902 includes about 45 other definitions. Most of them only concern design, and you'll probably never need to know them. I'll just list a few of the most common items in general use.

Admixture is material other than water, aggregate, or hydraulic cement used as an ingredient of concrete and added to concrete before or during its mixing to modify its properties.

Aggregate is granular material, such as sand, gravel, crushed stone and iron blast-furnace slag, and when used with a cementing medium forms a hydraulic cement concrete or mortar.

Deformed Reinforcement is deformed reinforcing bars, bar and rod mats, deformed wire, welded smooth wire fabric and welded deformed wire fabric.

Embedment Length is the length of embedded reinforcement provided beyond a critical section (the length of rebar to embed on either side of a stress point).

Plain Concrete is structural concrete with no reinforcement or with less reinforcement than the minimum amount specified for reinforced concrete.

Precast Concrete is a structural concrete element cast in other than its final position in the structure.

Prestressed Concrete is reinforced concrete in which internal stresses have been introduced to reduce potential tensile stresses in concrete resulting from loads.

Reinforced Concrete is structural concrete reinforced with no less than the minimum amounts of prestressing tendons or nonprestressed reinforcement specified in this code.

Structural Concrete is all concrete used for structural purposes, including plain and reinforced concrete.

Of all construction materials, concrete is probably one of the most abused. It's mismatched, mismixed, and watered down. Products are added to slow or speed hardening. Yet in spite of all this, it's one of the most reliable building products we have.

Weather will erode it, in time, but it won't rust or rot. Even the poorest mixes will last long after the framing, wiring, and other components of a building have deteriorated.

Concrete block is another durable and versatile building material that's adaptable to nearly any design or building application. And it will support greater loads than most other products.

Testing Concrete

With a few exceptions, concrete is hard to inspect properly. That's why the inspector has the right to call for any tests he thinks are necessary. Many of these tests are spelled out in the job specs, so you know in advance what's expected. But if the inspector thinks the specified tests are inadequate, he can call for more sophisticated tests. Fortunately, most on-site concrete tests are easily performed. Two of the most common are the slump and the compression or compressive fracture test.

Slump Test

The slump test is probably the simplest of all concrete tests. It uses a cone-shaped device made of 16 gauge galvanized sheet metal. The cone is about 12 inches high with a base about 8 inches in diameter and a top about 4 inches in diameter. See Figure 8-1. To conduct the test, place it on a board or other flat surface and fill it with concrete. Settle the concrete by pushing a steel rod into it a prescribed number of times, in this case, 27 times. Then measure the height of the settled concrete and remove the cone. Let it settle for several minutes, then measure again. The difference between the first measurement and the second is the amount of slump in that batch.

You'll usually do three slump tests and average the results. The inspector will compare this average with the slump allowed by the specs. If they don't agree within allowed percentages, the inspector can disallow the batch of concrete.

Compressive Fracture Test

The compression test is a little more complicated. Unless a fracturing machine is taken to the job site, the test begins in the field but ends in a laboratory. A cylinder is cast in a round form that can vary from 2 inches in diameter by 4 inches long to 10 inches in diameter and 18 inches long. If the aggregate isn't more than 2 inches in diameter, the form is usually 6 inches by 12 inches. Unless required by the project specifications, don't use cylinders smaller than that.

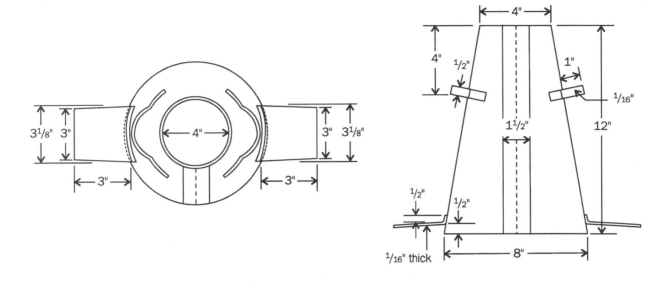

Figure 8-1 *Details of cone used for slump test*

Place the cylinder on a flat surface where it won't be exposed to vibrations or other disturbances, and fill it with concrete. Then rod it the prescribed number of times for even distribution. You'll find the rodding requirements in UBC Tables 26-10-A and 26-10-B in the 1991 edition (Figure 8-2). These tables were apparently omitted from the 1994 and 1997 editions of the UBC, but I feel they should be repeated here. The cylinders must be left undisturbed for the initial setup, or hardening. After that, keep movement to a minimum for the next few hours. The cylinders must be protected from unusually hot or cold weather.

The cylinders are then placed in a compression or breaking press that can apply set amounts of pressure to the cylinder. Several cylinders are tested, one at a time, at specified intervals — normally 24 hours, 7 days, and 28 days. The results are checked against the specs.

Most transit-mix companies run compressive tests on the concrete they sell. The plant may botch an occasional batch, but most problems begin after the mix arrives at the job site.

Mixing the Batch

The cement must meet the requirements and specifications for the particular job at hand. UBC Standard No. 19.101 lists eight types of concrete most commonly used in construction:

Type I *— For use in general concrete construction when the special properties specified for Types II, III, IV, and V are not required.*

Type IA *— Same use as Type I where air entrainment is desired.*

Type II *— For use in general concrete construction exposed to moderate sulfate action, or where moderated heat of hydration is desired.*

Type IIA *— Same use as Type II where air entrainment is desired.*

Type III *— For use when high early strength is desired.*

TABLE NO. 26-10-A — NUMBER OF LAYERS REQUIRED FOR SPECIMENS

Specimen Type and Size, as Depth, in.	Mode of Compaction	Number of layers	Approximate Depth of Layer, in.
Cylinders:			
up to 12	rodding	3 equal	
over 12	rodding	as required	4
up to 18	vibration	2 equal	
over 18	vibration	3 or more	8 as near as practicable
Prisms and horizontal creep cylinders:			
up to 8	rodding	2 equal	
over 8	rodding	3 or more	4
up to 8	vibration	1	
over 8	vibration	2 or more	8 as near as practicable

TABLE NO. 26-10-B — DIAMETER OF ROD AND NUMBER OF RODDINGS TO BE USED IN MOLDING TEST SPECIMENS

Cylinders		
Diameter of Cylinder, in.	Diameter of Rod, in.	Number of Strokes/Layer
2 to <6	3/8	25
6	5/8	25
8	5/8	50
10	5/8	75

Beams and Prisms		
Top Surface Area of Specimen, in.	Diameter of Rod, in.	Number of Roddings/Layer
25 or less	3/8	25
26 to 49	3/8	one for each 1 in.² of surface
50 or more	5/8	one for each 2 in.² of surface

Horizontal Creep Cylinders		
Diameter of Cylinder, in.	Diameter of Rod, in.	Number of Roddings/Layer
6	5/8	50 total, 25 along both sides of axis

Figure 8-2 *Number of layers and rodding required for concrete specimens*

Type IIIA — *Same use as Type III where air entrainment is desired.*

Type IV — *For use when a low heat of hydration is required.*

Type V — *For use when high sulfate resistance is required.*

Unless your specs call for a specific concrete type, check with your supplier for recommendations. The engineer designing the job will make the final determination. Then you'll need to know the right proportions for the job at hand. This should also be spelled out in the specs, probably in three figures, such as 1-3-5. This means "1 sack cement, 3 cubic feet of sand, 5 cubic feet of stone." Finally, you'll add the amount of water necessary to get the slump required by the specs.

The aggregate must be clean and free of pollutants such as ash, dirt, grease, oil or wood chips. The nominal maximum size of the aggregate shouldn't be larger than one-fifth the narrowest dimension between the sides of the form, one-third the depth of the slab, or three-fourths the minimum clear spacing between reinforcing steel. Check the workability of the mix and the methods of consolidation so the finished concrete won't contain honeycombs or voids. It should still be plastic, not too runny or crumbly.

Use water free of oil, acids, alkalis, or organic materials that may affect either the concrete or the reinforcing steel. Generally speaking, if you wouldn't drink the water, you shouldn't use it for concrete.

Spacing the Reinforcement

For reinforcement, choose material that meets job specs and place it according to the plans. UBC Figure 19-1 (Figure 8-3) shows the

Concrete

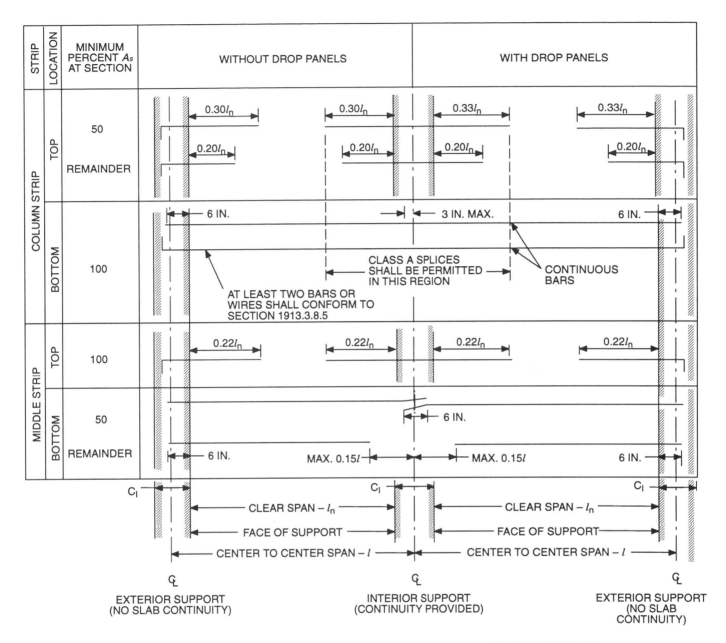

FIGURE 19-1—MINIMUM EXTENSIONS FOR REINFORCEMENT IN SLABS WITHOUT BEAMS
(See Section 1912.11.1 for reinforcement extension into supports.)

From the Uniform Building Code, ©1997, ICBO

Figure 8-3 *Minimum extensions for reinforcement in slabs without beams*

TABLE 19-B—MINIMUM DIAMETERS OF BEND

BAR SIZE	MINIMUM DIAMETER
Nos. 3 through 8	$6d_b$
Nos. 9, 10 and 11	$8d_b$
Nos. 14 and 18	$10d_b$

From the Uniform Building Code, ©1997, ICBO

Figure 8-4 *Minimum diameters of bend*

minimum bend point locations for rebar. UBC Table 19-B (Figure 8-4) shows the minimum diameters of bends.

The clear distance between parallel reinforcing bars in a layer should be at least the same as the nominal diameter of the bars, but not less than 1 inch. This code requirement doesn't apply to splices or to bundles designed as part of an overall reinforcement plan. Figure 10-2, ahead in Chapter 10, shows how to make splices. Don't use lap splices on bars larger than No. 11 except where larger bars are used as dowels in footings.

You may use welded splices. A full welded splice has bars which are butted and welded to develop a bond of at least 125 percent of the specified yield strength of the bar.

Be sure to support all reinforcement. On vertical work, secure reinforcement so it won't touch the sides of the forms or other reinforcement, unless it's planned in the construction of the bundles or mats. In flatwork, such as slabs for floors or roofs, place reinforcement on

chairs to keep it from touching the ground or form below. A chair is a metal device usually constructed of a heavy gauge wire. Figure 8-5 shows typical styles.

Some concrete workers will lay reinforcing bars or mats on the ground when they're pouring slabs. After the pour, the finisher hooks the steel and pulls it up into the concrete. *This isn't acceptable.* Most of the steel won't be centered in the slab. Don't let your workers or subs get by with this shortcut.

Placing Concrete

You can't place concrete without knowing how to build forms. Forms have to hold concrete in the shape shown on the plans until the concrete is hardened. And they have to be strong enough to hold the weight and moisture in the concrete without collapsing or leaking. I've worked on several jobs where the forms weren't braced right. I can assure you that it's

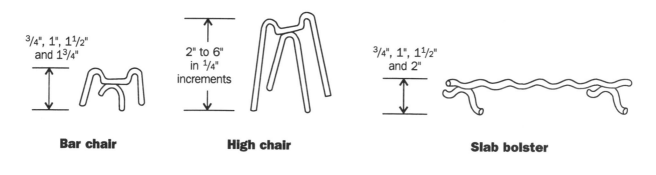

Bar chair $^3/_4$", 1", $1^1/_2$" and $1^3/_4$"

High chair 2" to 6" in $^1/_4$" increments

Slab bolster $^3/_4$", 1", $1^1/_2$" and 2"

Figure 8-5 *Chairs for supporting reinforcing steel*

a frustrating experience to see concrete seeping out where it shouldn't be.

Figure 8-6 shows a formed foundation wall with metal clips on the top of the form to keep the boards from spreading. Forms for pre-stressed members must allow for any movement of the member without causing damage to the form.

Also consider whether your forms are accessible to the ready-mix truck. If they are, the truck can pour the concrete directly into the forms. If not, you'll have to transport the concrete to the forms by wheelbarrow, pump, or even by bucket and crane.

Regardless of the method used, don't let the concrete fall more than 48 inches from the chute to the form. If this distance exceeds 48 inches, use an extension chute. Prefabricated metal chute extensions are available, but you can make your own from scrap wood at the job site. Just be careful to keep the mix from separating while you pour.

When you're ready to remove the forms, be careful not to damage the green concrete. The only load allowed on unshored portions during construction is the concrete itself. No construction can be supported by the new work until the concrete reaches adequate strength. This usually takes from 3 to 28 days. Generally, form removal can begin after 24 hours.

Settling or Consolidating the Concrete

The amount of settling, or consolidating, depends largely on the amount of slump in a mix. A high slump mix requires little consolidation. There are two methods of consolidating — hand spading or vibration. Mechanical vibrators do the work of settling much easier than hand-spading, and they allow for the placement of stiffer mixes. But don't use vibrators if the mix can be hand-spaded. There's always the possibility of the material separating too much. That's why you shouldn't use vibrators to move concrete horizontally.

Figure 8-6 *Foundation wall ready for stripping the forms*

Curing

Time is always important when you're pouring concrete. Of course, concrete additives can delay or increase the curing time, but generally it's just a matter of waiting. In about the first 24 hours, the concrete will acquire over half its strength. By the end of seven days you should have approximately 90 percent of the design strength. Concrete usually doesn't reach full strength until 28 days after pouring.

If you've just poured a basement or foundation wall for a simple structure, you can probably work around the area for a day or two while the concrete hardens. But this doesn't mean you can move a house onto a newly-poured foundation. I doubt the inspector would allow it.

To increase concrete strength, the code recommends that concrete be maintained above 50 degrees F and in a moist environment for at least the first seven days. If you were using a high early-strength concrete, this time can be reduced to about three days. But what happens in the fall and winter, when temperatures fall below 50 degrees F?

Simply covering the concrete will help. The chemical reaction in the concrete itself — the interaction of the water, cement and other chemicals in the mix — creates a great deal of heat. If it's going to be really cold, spread a layer of straw, sawdust, or even polyethylene film to keep the heat in.

Increased Temperatures and Curing Time

Section 1905.11.3 approves certain methods for shortening the curing time:

Section 1905.11.3.1 Curing by high-pressure steam, steam at atmospheric pressure, heat and moisture or other accepted processes, may be employed to accelerate strength gain and reduce time of curing.

Section 1905.11.3.2 Accelerated curing shall provide a compressive strength of the concrete at the load stage considered at least equal to required design strength at that load stage.

Section 1905.11.3.3 Curing process shall be such as to produce concrete with a durability at least equivalent to the curing method of Section 1905.11.1 or 1905.11.2.

How do you know when the concrete has reached proper strength? Remember those test cylinders I mentioned earlier? These cylinders were from the same batch of concrete. When the samples are strong enough, the concrete used in the work should be at the right strength also.

Hot Weather

Section 1905.13. During hot weather, proper attention shall be given to ingredients, production methods, handling, placing, protection, and curing to prevent excessive concrete temperatures or water evaporation that may impair required strength or serviceability of the member or structure.

That's what Section 1905.13 of the code says about hot weather, but it doesn't say how hot. That varies with the humidity and wind conditions. The key is to prevent the rapid evaporation of water from the fresh concrete.

Speed of evaporation will vary with the humidity. If you're in a humid part of the country, you'll have one set of values. In an arid climate you'll have another. The Portland Cement Association reports that if the relative humidity decreases from 90 percent to 50 percent, the rate of evaporation increases five times. If the humidity falls another 10 percent, the rate of evaporation increases nine times.

When it's windy, you'll find the same changes in the rate of evaporation. When the wind changes from 0 to 10 mph, the rate of evaporation increases four times; it's nine times greater when wind velocity increases to 25 mph.

Using cool materials and protecting the work from direct sunlight helps reduce evaporation. Spraying the concrete with a fine mist raises the relative humidity and helps slow evaporation.

Interrupting the Pour

Avoid interrupting the pour if you can, although the code does allow it. The requirements for joining the old pour with the new are in Section 1906.4:

Section 1906.4.1 Surface of concrete construction joints shall be cleaned and laitance removed.

Section 1906.4.2 Immediately before new concrete is placed, all construction joints shall be wetted and standing water removed.

Section 1906.4.3 Construction joints shall be so made and located as not to impair the strength of the structure. Provision shall be made for transfer of shear and other forces through construction joints. See Section 1911.7.9.

If you've ever tried to place a thin concrete slab over an existing one — raising the height of steps or a sidewalk, for example — you're probably aware of how difficult it is to get a good seal or bond between the old and new concrete.

The code calls for a "neat cement grout." That can be a mixture of water and cement spread over the surface. Several other products do this job very well. The point is that you just can't pour new concrete over old without preparing the existing surface first. Ask your concrete supplier about the materials you'll need and how to use them.

The UBC section requires you to remove all standing water and laitance. When standing water collects on the top of settled concrete, it brings with it a mixture of dust, impurities, small amounts of cement and other foreign matter. When the water evaporates, it leaves a dusty, grayish-brown film on the surface of the concrete. That's laitance.

On flat slabs where the surface is worked down and smoothed as part of the finishing process, laitance is insignificant. Much of it is worked off when the slab is prefinished. The rest is worked back into the concrete. On form-work, however, laitance can be a real problem. It prevents bonding. If a pour is interrupted, the laitance must be removed before the job can proceed. This is usually done with sand-blasting equipment.

Have I Got a Deal for You?

I guess I'm a little old fashioned. I get worried when I hear about some great new construction material. There are fads and fashions in construction just like in the garment industry. Comes along a new material and everyone wants to try it. Pretty soon everyone's an expert, either at applying it or selling it or both. Never underestimate the enthusiasm of America's entrepreneurs. If there's a buck to be made, someone's trying to make it.

Roof coatings are an example. A roofing truck pulls up in front of the house. Here's the spiel the homeowner gets: "Sir, I was just driving down the street and noticed that your roof isn't looking so good. I've been resurfacing roofs in this neighborhood and have enough extra time and material to resurface yours tomorrow afternoon. We use a new aerobic silicon polyester coating, the same stuff used to protect the skin of the space shuttle. It adds years to the life of your roof and costs pennies compared to a new roof."

The victim is probably a senior citizen on a limited income or someone worried about leaks in the next rain. This sales pitch is a bolt from the blue. So they sign up. Next day the roofer applies a shiny aluminized coating and it really looks good. Only the first time it rains, the coating does a meltdown. And the roof leaks the same as before. What happened?

Don't bother to look for that high-tech roofer. He's miles away by now. What he did was coat the roof with an aluminum-colored distillate. It costs about $5.00 a gallon and a gallon goes a long way. True, he charged less than the cost of a new roof. But all the homeowner got was a roof shine. Maybe if the homeowner had called the building inspector first . . . .

Remember that the next time you decide to try a new building material. Building inspectors like to be asked about new materials *before you install them* — and they have good ways to identify claims that may not stand up.

Foundations

We've explored occupancies, types of construction related to occupancies, the fire-resistiveness of materials, design and engineering, and the fine points of concrete. It's finally time to look at the building itself — beginning with the foundation. But first, let's consider the building site.

Site Consideration

Here are some of the things you'll want to check for at the site:

- Do you have a water problem (too much or too little)?

- Does the land slope excessively?

- Will you need to move dirt to place the building on the property?

- What are you going to do with any cut banks that remain?

- What about excess dirt remaining after backfilling is complete?

Answering each of these questions may require an understanding of the building code.

Let's say you have a high water table on site. How does that involve the building code? Probably the first thing the inspector will ask is how much water you have and what your plans are for dealing with it. Are you planning to use a sump pump or a drainage system to carry the water to a lower portion of land, or do you have some other method in mind? Perhaps you've considered dumping it into a sanitary sewer (prohibited in most cities). Or you were planning to leave it there and waterproof the basement? Maybe the building doesn't have a basement. In that case, will your building sit on piles or on a fill? Will you have a post and beam floor or a slab on grade?

These are some of the first questions you should consider. You can bet they're some of the first questions the building inspector is going to ask.

Make sure you know exactly where the property lines are, that the corners are properly staked, and that a surveyor has set the stakes for your house. Yes, this will cost a little more. But I've seen houses that encroached on the legal setback area and several that even went over the property line. I even met a contractor who built on the wrong lot! Funny? You bet — unless you're the one caught in the net. It's not only embarrassing but awfully expensive. Hiring a surveyor is your cheapest insurance against problems like that.

Excavation and Fill

Chapter 18 of the UBC covers the quality and design of structural materials used in excavations and foundations. This chapter is backed up by Chapter 33 in the Appendix of the UBC, which regulates grading on private property. The purpose is to safeguard health, property and public welfare. It also lists the conditions for permits and permit fees. (See UBC Tables A-33-A and A-33-B, Figure 9-1 in this manual.)

Section 3306.2 of the UBC states that a permit is required for certain types of excavation and landfill. You don't need a permit, however, for this *exempted work*:

1) *When approved by the building official, grading in an isolated, self-contained area if there is no danger to private or public property.*

2) *An excavation below finished grade for basements and footings of a building, retaining wall or other structure authorized by a valid building permit. This shall not exempt any fill made with the material from such excavation or exempt any excavation having an unsupported height greater than 5 feet (1524 mm) after the completion of such structure.*

3) *Cemetery graves.*

4) *Refuse disposal sites controlled by other regulations.*

5) *Excavations for wells, tunnels or utilities.*

6) *Mining, quarrying, excavating, processing, stockpiling of rock, sand, gravel, aggregate or clay where established and provided for by law, provided such operations do not affect the lateral support or increase the stresses in or pressure upon any adjacent or contiguous property.*

7) *Exploratory excavations under the direction of soil engineers or engineering geologists.*

8) *An excavation that (1) is less than 2 feet (610 mm) in depth or (2) does not create a cut slope greater than 5 feet (1524 mm) in height or steeper than 1 unit vertical in 1½ units horizontal (66.7% slope).*

9) *A fill less than 1 foot (305 mm) in depth and placed on natural terrain with a slope flatter than 1 unit vertical in 5 units horizontal (20% slope), or less than 3 feet (914 mm) in depth, not intended to support structures, that does not exceed 50 cubic yards (38.3 m³) on any one lot and does not obstruct a drainage course.*

Exemption from the permit requirements of this chapter shall not be deemed to grant authorization for any work to be done in any manner in violation of the provisions of this chapter or any other laws or ordinances of this jurisdiction.

As you can see, unless you're working on steep slopes, few operations actually require a permit. So I won't spend a great deal of time on it. But we do need to spend some time on backfilling.

TABLE A-33-A—GRADING PLAN REVIEW FEES

50 cubic yards (38.2 m³) or less . . . . No fee
51 to 100 cubic yards (40 m³ to 76.5 m³) $23.50
101 to 1,000 cubic yards (77.2 m³ to 764.6 m³) 37.00
1,001 to 10,000 cubic yards (765.3 m³ to 7645.5 m³) 49.25
10,001 to 100,000 cubic yards (7646.3 m³ to 76 455 m³)—$49.25 for the first 10,000 cubic yards (7645.5 m³), plus $24.50 for each additional 10,000 yards (7645.5 m³) or fraction thereof.
100,001 to 200,000 cubic yards (76 456 m³ to 152 911 m³)—$269.75 for the first 100,000 cubic yards (76 455 m³), plus $13.25 for each additional 10,000 cubic yards (7645.5 m³) or fraction thereof.
200,001 cubic yards (152 912 m³) or more—$402.25 for the first 200,000 cubic yards (152 911 m³), plus $7.25 for each additional 10,000 cubic yards (7645.5 m³) or fraction thereof.
Other Fees: Additional plan review required by changes, additions or revisions to approved plans . . . . $50.50 per hour* (minimum charge—one-half hour)

*Or the total hourly cost to the jurisdiction, whichever is the greatest. This cost shall include supervision, overhead, equipment, hourly wages and fringe benefits of the employees involved.

TABLE A-33-B—GRADING PERMIT FEES[1]

50 cubic yards (38.2 m³) or less $23.50
51 to 100 cubic yards (40 m³ to 76.5 m³) 37.00
101 to 1,000 cubic yards (77.2 m³ to 764.6 m³)—$37.00 for the first 100 cubic yards (76.5 m³) plus $17.50 for each additional 100 cubic yards (76.5 m³) or fraction thereof.
1,001 to 10,000 cubic yards (765.3 m³ to 7645.5 m³)—$194.50 for the first 1,000 cubic yards (764.6 m³), plus $14.50 for each additional 1,000 cubic yards (764.6 m³) or fraction thereof.
10,001 to 100,000 cubic yards (7646.3 m³ to 76 455 m³)—$325.00 for the first 10,000 cubic yards (7645.5 m³), plus $66.00 for each additional 10,000 cubic yards (7645.5 m³) or fraction thereof.
100,001 cubic yards (76 456 m³) or more—$919.00 for the first 100,000 cubic yards (76 455 m³), plus $36.50 for each additional 10,000 cubic yards (7645.5 m³) or fraction thereof.

Other Inspections and Fees:
1. Inspections outside of normal business
   hours . . . . $50.50 per hour[2]
   (minimum charge—two hours)
2. Reinspection fees assessed under provisions of
   Section 108.8 . . . . $50.50 per hour[2]
3. Inspections for which no fee is specifically
   indicated . . . . $50.50 per hour[2]
   (minimum charge—one-half hour)

[1]The fee for a grading permit authorizing additional work to that under a valid permit shall be the difference between the fee paid for the original permit and the fee shown for the entire project.

[2]Or the total hourly cost to the jurisdiction, whichever is the greatest. This cost shall include supervision, overhead, equipment, hourly wages and fringe benefits of the employees involved.

Figure 9-1 *Grading plan review and grading permit fees*

Backfilling and Compaction

Too few contractors know all they should about proper backfilling. This is unfortunate because sloppy backfill destroys good construction — every time.

You've probably seen homes in your area where the steps have pulled away from the house or where shrubbery around the house has sunk. Usually this is because the area around the basement backfill wasn't properly compacted. If backfilling is done without proper supervision, only a density test can determine if it was done correctly.

The UBC calls for 90 percent compaction. But in dry climates it's hard to get 90 percent. Dry soil packs loosely. When a tractor passes over soil — the usual form of compaction — only the top several inches gets compacted. Unless the backfill is placed in the trench in

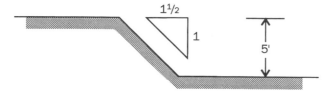

A permit is not required if cut is not deeper than 5 feet or has a cut slope not steeper than one and one-half to one.

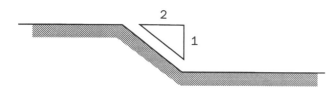

Cut slopes for any permanent excavation shall not be steeper than two to one. Slopes for permanent fills to be the same.

Figure 9-2 *Cut slope dimensions for excavations*

layers, only the top 6 to 10 inches of dirt is compacted.

Water settling is a very effective way to compact most soil. Saturate the fill, wait until it dries, add more fill and saturate again. Because this takes longer, few builders do it. So eventually, Mother Nature does the compaction by settling. This can happen either gradually or all at once. Either way, the home owner finds his shrubbery in a hole that wasn't there before and steps separated from the house.

For proper compaction, you have to place the fill in layers not over 12 inches deep and compact each layer. A little water will help if the soil is dry. The deeper the excavation, the more layers and the more compaction needed. Compacting a 3-foot trench for a water line won't take as long as a 7-foot sewer trench. For a larger job, use a hand held wacker-tamper powered by a small gasoline engine.

Excavation Cut Slopes

According to the code, you can't make the cut slopes for permanent excavation steeper than two horizontal units of measure to one vertical. The same applies to slopes for permanent fill. See Figure 9-2. Whether your unit measure is feet, inches or yards, the proportion is the same.

Don't place fill next to any building or structure unless the building can withstand the additional loads caused by the fill. The usual curing time for concrete in basement walls is about seven days. That's the minimum time to wait. I recommend waiting another week whenever possible.

Cut-Slope Setbacks

In steep, hilly country the code may require that the building be set back from the top of a cut or the toe of a fill. Chapter 33 of the UBC has several illustrations of this. See Figure 9-3 (UBC Figure A-33-1). These setbacks are minimums. In some areas the inspector, acting on the recommendations of soils engineers or his own knowledge of the area, will require a greater setback than shown in Figure 9-3.

A retaining wall can usually be used to reduce the setback requirement. But unless the cut or fill is shallow, the wall should be designed by a registered engineer.

Fill Must Be Stable

When are inspections of fill required? The code says that any time you need a grading permit, an inspection is mandatory. The intensity of the inspection will depend on the scope of the work or whether the grading is designated regular or engineered grading. How do you know how your grading is designated? Section 3309.3 uses 5,000 cubic yards as the dividing line. Under 5,000 cubic yards is considered regular grading and over 5,000 is engineered grading. Regular grading usually requires only minimal inspection. Engineered grading may need all sorts of soils tests. At this point it can get complicated. Ask the building official about local requirements.

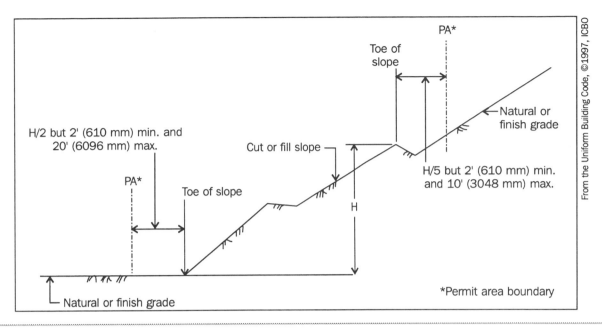

Figure 9-3 *Required setbacks*

The quality, material, and compaction are just as critical for fills as they are for excavations. The code says that fills used to support the foundation of any building or structure must be placed according to acceptable engineering practice. This means you have to treat them like backfill and layer them. Roller compaction will be needed to get the proper density.

On large commercial buildings, specifications provided by the owner or architect may call for compaction testing of backfills on trenches and foundations. Compaction tests are seldom required for single residences unless the home is built on a large fill in a new area. But tests may be required for subdivisions in hilly areas where deep cuts and fills were necessary.

Few building departments are equipped to make compaction tests. That's one reason why compaction is frequently overlooked by many inspectors. But if the inspector is on his toes and suspects there's a problem, he can order that tests be made, at the expense of the owner. This can be difficult and expensive because many communities don't have a soil testing company nearby.

If the fill has been in place for at least a year or two without any problems, it's probably stable.

Soils Classification and Geology

It's not always the fill material or its placement or compaction that causes problems. Sometimes it's what's under the fill that creates trouble. Here's what Section 1803 in the UBC has to say about soil:

1803.1 General. *For the purposes of this chapter, the definition and classification of soil materials for use in Table 18-I-A shall be according to UBC Standard 18.1.*

1803.2 Expansive Soil. *When the expansive characteristics of a soil are to be determined, the procedures shall be in accordance with UBC Standard 18-2 and the soil shall be classified according to Table 18-I-B. Foundations for structures resting on soils with an expansion index greater than 20, as determined by UBC Standard 18-2, shall require special design consideration.*

TABLE 18-I-A—ALLOWABLE FOUNDATION AND LATERAL PRESSURE

CLASS OF MATERIALS[1]	ALLOWABLE FOUNDATION PRESSURE (psf)[2] × 0.0479 for kPa	LATERAL BEARING LBS./SQ./FT./FT. OF DEPTH BELOW NATURAL GRADE[3] × 0.157 for kPa per meter	LATERAL SLIDING[4] Coefficient[5]	LATERAL SLIDING[4] Resistance (psf)[6] × 0.0479 for kPa
1. Massive crystalline bedrock	4,000	1,200	0.70	
2. Sedimentary and foliated rock	2,000	400	0.35	
3. Sandy gravel and/or gravel (GW and GP)	2,000	200	0.35	
4. Sand, silty sand, clayey sand, silty gravel and clayey gravel (SW, SP, SM, SC, GM and GC)	1,500	150	0.25	
5. Clay, sandy clay, silty clay and clayey silt (CL, ML, MH and CH)	1,000[7]	100		130

[1]For soil classifications OL, OH and PT (i.e., organic clays and peat), a foundation investigation shall be required.
[2]All values of allowable foundation pressure are for footings having a minimum width of 12 inches (305 mm) and a minimum depth of 12 inches (305 mm) into natural grade. Except as in Footnote 7, an increase of 20 percent shall be allowed for each additional foot (305 mm) of width or depth to a maximum value of three times the designated value. Additionally, an increase of one third shall be permitted when considering load combinations, including wind or earthquake loads, as permitted by Section 1612.3.2.
[3]May be increased the amount of the designated value for each additional foot (305 mm) of depth to a maximum of 15 times the designated value. Isolated poles for uses such as flagpoles or signs and poles used to support buildings that are not adversely affected by a $1/2$-inch (12.7 mm) motion at ground surface due to short-term lateral loads may be designed using lateral bearing values equal to two times the tabulated values.
[4]Lateral bearing and lateral sliding resistance may be combined.
[5]Coefficient to be multiplied by the dead load.
[6]Lateral sliding resistance value to be multiplied by the contact area. In no case shall the lateral sliding resistance exceed one half the dead load.
[7]No increase for width is allowed.

Figure 9-4 *Allowable foundation and lateral pressure*

TABLE 18-I-B—CLASSIFICATION OF EXPANSIVE SOIL

EXPANSION INDEX	POTENTIAL EXPANSION
0-20	Very low
21-50	Low
51-90	Medium
91-130	High
Above 130	Very high

Figure 9-5 *Expansive soil classification*

If the soil expansion index varies with depth, the variation is to be included in the engineering analysis of the expansive soil effect upon the structure.

UBC Table 18-I-A is Figure 9-4. Figure 9-5 includes UBC Tables 18-I-B and 18-I-C. If the inspector requires this information, you'll need to hire a soils geologist. The geologist will take core samples or run tests on the aggregate. This is expensive. But it's seldom required except on large jobs or where soil conditions are marginal.

Foundations and the Frost Line

Now let's take a look at the foundation itself. Requirements for foundations vary considerably around the country. The code requires that footings (footers) be placed below frost grade or as shown in UBC Table 18-I-C (Figure 9-6).

Frost grade varies with climate. In my home of Kennewick, Washington, the frost depth is figured at 24 inches for building purposes. All footings and water lines must be at least that

TABLE 18-I-C—FOUNDATIONS FOR STUD BEARING WALLS—MINIMUM REQUIREMENTS[1,2,3,4]

NUMBER OF FLOORS SUPPORTED BY THE FOUNDATION[5]	THICKNESS OF FOUNDATION WALL (inches) × 25.4 for mm		WIDTH OF FOOTING (inches)	THICKNESS OF FOOTING (inches)	DEPTH BELOW UNDISTURBED GROUND SURFACE (inches)
	Concrete	Unit Masonry	× 25.4 for mm		
1	6	6	12	6	12
2	8	8	15	7	18
3	10	10	18	8	24

[1]Where unusual conditions or frost conditions are found, footings and foundations shall be as required in Section 1806.1.
[2]The ground under the floor may be excavated to the elevation of the top of the footing.
[3]Interior stud bearing walls may be supported by isolated footings. The footing width and length shall be twice the width shown in this table and the footings shall be spaced not more than 6 feet (1829 mm) on center.
[4]In Seismic Zone 4, continuous footings shall be provided with a minimum of one No. 4 bar top and bottom.
[5]Foundations may support a roof in addition to the stipulated number of floors. Foundations supporting roofs only shall be as required for supporting one floor.

From the Uniform Building Code, ©1997, ICBO

Figure 9-6 *Foundations for stud bearing walls*

deep. But the city requires that water lines run at 36 inches below ground level. This way the water lines come in below the foundation if there is no basement.

It isn't always necessary to excavate for footings. If your lot is in a low area and you plan to fill after the house is constructed, form the footings on the surface, excavating only enough so that the footing will be level. However, when the house is completed and the fill material brought in, the footings must be at or below the frost line. This, of course, is the bottom of the footing pad — not the bottom of the foundation wall. Figure 9-7 shows this measurement and other footing and foundation requirements. Typical footings and foundation walls are shown in Figure 9-8.

Excavation for the foundation must remove all stumps and roots and must go down at least 12 inches below the surface of the ground under your building. Also, when you're finished with the building, there shouldn't be any form material or wood scraps under the house or buried in the backfill. Don't provide breeding grounds for termites.

When you dig footings down to the frost line, make sure you leave 18 inches of crawl space below the joists. This is shown in Figure 9-7.

If you're going to install an underfloor furnace, you'll need to furnish some additional space, plus a crawl hole large enough to allow the heating plant to be removed or serviced

without dismantling. Pipes and ducts must not interfere with access to or access within any crawl space.

All accessible underfloor space must have an entry hole at least 18 inches by 24 inches. Note the word accessible. That's just what it means. You can't hide it in a closet or under a rug.

Underfloor Ventilation

Whenever you have an underfloor crawl space that's not a basement or a usable space, you must provide adequate ventilation. One way is to cut vent holes in the foundation walls or provide mechanical ventilation such as a

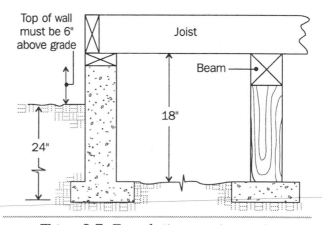

Figure 9-7 *Foundation requirements*

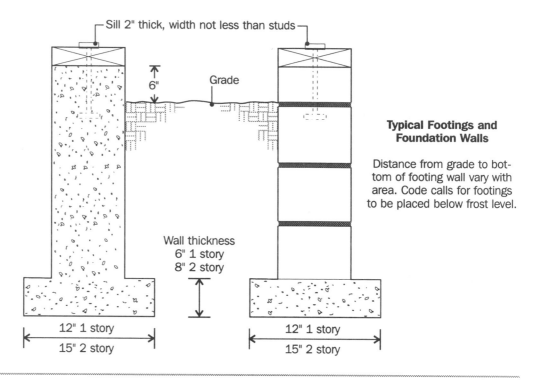

Sill 2" thick, width not less than studs

6"

Grade

Typical Footings and Foundation Walls

Distance from grade to bottom of footing wall vary with area. Code calls for footings to be placed below frost level.

Wall thickness
6" 1 story
8" 2 story

12" 1 story
15" 2 story

12" 1 story
15" 2 story

Figure 9-8 *Residential foundations*

fan. Size the foundation vent holes according to Section 2306.7. To reduce dry rot in the foundation, arrange the vents to give cross-ventilation to all areas of the unused space.

Vent holes must be covered with corrosion-resistant wire mesh not less than ¼ inch or more than ½ inch in any dimension. This keeps

Figure 9-9 *Prefabricated wall vent cast in wall at time of pouring*

your crawl space from becoming a maternity ward for cats.

Prefabricated vents, like those shown in Figure 9-9, are available from your building material dealer. They're made of plastic or galvanized metal, complete with screen, louvered cover, and a hinged flap. Many people think they have to cover their vents to have warm floors in winter. This isn't necessarily so, but hinged flaps are available and allowable. The only drawback is that the homeowners often forget to open them in the spring, which can lead to dry rot and other problems.

Foundation Plates

On the top of the foundation wall is a wooden member called a plate. This is required whether the foundation wall surrounds a crawl space or a basement. But it's not required if the rest of the structure is masonry.

The plate is normally a 2 x 6 laid flat and fastened to the foundation wall with anchor

Figure 9-10 *Foundation bolts cast in place*

bolts cast into the wet concrete. Although using a 2 x 6 is customary, the code doesn't specify what it has to be. Section 2306.4 states that all plates, sills, and sleepers must be treated wood or Foundation grade redwood or cedar. This reduces the hazard of termites. If you don't have a termite problem, use any wood approved by the inspector.

Figures 9-10 and 9-11 and the sketch in Figure 9-8 show the proper installation of anchor bolts and plates. You'll need ½-inch steel bolts set 7 inches deep in concrete or masonry foundations to bolt the plate to the foundation wall. Place bolts at least every 6 feet. There must be at least two bolts in each piece of plate material and neither may be more than 12 inches from the end. That means an 8-foot plate would need two anchor bolts, but a 9-foot piece would require three.

Bolts that are set wrong can be a major problem. Suppose bolts are set assuming a continuous 26-foot piece of plate material. But the framers splice the plate, using one piece 14 feet long and one piece 12 feet long. Now the anchor bolts don't meet code. Some builders keep extra plate material on hand for the framing subcontractors.

Anchor bolts are supposed to keep the house anchored to the foundation. But I have some doubt about their effectiveness. I have several photos of what used to be homes in earthquake and tornado zones. The anchor bolts and plates are still in place — it's the homes that are missing. But I don't know of any alternative to anchor bolts.

You'll find information about foundation plates and sills in Sections 1806.1 and 3302. UBC Table 18-I-C (Figure 9-6) lists the size of the footing and foundation wall for one-, two- and three-story buildings. Notice the column called *Depth Below Undisturbed Ground Surface*. Remember, your foundation must go down to the frost line. If you're in a frost-free area, however, these are the code minimums for foundation depth.

Post and Beam Foundation

Many houses are built of posts and beams and without concrete or masonry foundations. The code doesn't prohibit this. It simply ignores it. What it does say is in Section 1806.3:

> **Bearing Walls.** *Bearing walls shall be supported on masonry or concrete foundations or piles or other approved foundation system that shall be of sufficient size to support all loads. Where a design is not*

Figure 9-11 *Foundation plates installed*

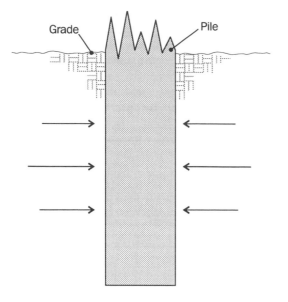

Arrows indicate lateral pressure

Figure 9-12 *Direction of lateral pressure*

provided, the minimum foundation require-ments for stud bearing walls shall be as set forth in Table 18-I-C, unless expansive soils of a severity to cause differential movement are known to exist.

Exceptions: *1. A one-story wood- or metal-frame building not used for human occu-pancy and not over 400 square feet (37.2 m²) in floor area may be constructed with walls supported on a wood foundation plate when approved by the building offi-cial.*

2. The support of buildings by posts embedded in earth shall be designed as specified in Section 1806.8. Wood posts or poles embedded in earth shall be pressure treated with an approved preservative. Steel posts or poles shall be protected as specified in Section 1807.9.

Confusing, isn't it? If you want to use a post and beam foundation, the building inspector will have to approve your plans. This means that if the inspector is inexperienced, is not an engineer, or just doesn't like post and beam construction, you may run into difficulty.

In high seismic risk areas you might run into design problems. My suggestion is that you be knowledgeable about post and beam construc-tion and be very persuasive with the building official.

Pole Buildings

These are generally agricultural or light industrial buildings. They're referred to in the second exception to Section 1806.3 mentioned above.

Section 1805 describes how to calculate the depth of embedment to get the required lateral constraint to support your load. This lateral force is illustrated in Figure 9-12.

To calculate these pressures you must know what the loading will be on your building. We discussed loads and loading in the last chapter. I suggest you hire a structural engi-neer to figure the load values. If you're con-structing an engineered building, these calcu-lations will be done as part of preparing the building plans and specifications.

Different Types of Foundations

Many types of foundations can be used to overcome problems associated with multi-story buildings, unusual soil types and extreme cli-matic conditions. Foundation piles can include:

- Round wood piles
- Uncased cast-in-place concrete piles
- Metal-cased concrete piles
- Precast concrete piles
- Precast, prestressed concrete piles
- Structural steel piles
- Concrete-filled steel pipe piles

These piles are usually driven or placed in the ground and covered by slabs. Complex for-mulas determine the size of the pile, its depth in the ground, and the number of piles required. The type of pile you use depends on lateral pressures in different types and conditions of soils, as well as on the loads to be carried. This information is listed in UBC Table 18-I-A, *Allowable Foundation and Lateral Pressure* and Table 18-I-B, *Classification of Expansive Soil.* (See Figures 9-4 and 9-5.)

Footing and Foundation Summary

Most small contractors never have to deal with the more sophisticated foundations. If you do, have a structural engineer design them. This prevents problems and can really help when you approach the building inspector for approval of your plans.

In calculating your concrete foundation wall, be sure to make the wall high enough to be at least 6 inches above grade. Here's what I mean. If the footing must go 24 inches below grade, the distance between the top of the wall and the bottom of the footing must be at least 30 inches. That 6 inches above grade helps keep wood framing away from surface moisture.

You can use a stepped footing if the ground slopes too much for a level footing. Section 1806.4 states that the foundation must be level if your ground slopes more than 1 foot in 10. But it may be stepped so that both the top and bottom of the foundation are level. This means that if your lot slopes too much, you can step-down your foundation and use framing material to finish the walls up to the plate line of the first floor.

Remember to protect adjoining property while preparing the foundation on your lot. If leveling your lot creates a finish grade higher than that of adjoining property, protect that property from your fill. Either slope the bank or build a retaining wall. If, on the other hand, you excavate on your lot, you have to protect adjoining property with the same type of cut bank or retaining wall. If the hillside is steep, the procedure shown in Figure 9-3 may be necessary.

Retaining Walls

There isn't too much in the code about retaining walls. Section 1611.6 covers them very briefly:

1611.6 Retaining Walls. Retaining walls shall be designed to resist loads due to the lateral pressure of retained material in accordance with accepted engineering practice. Walls retaining drained soil, where the surface of the retained soil is level, shall be designed for a load, H, equivalent to that exerted by a fluid weighing not less than 30 psf per foot of depth (4.71 kN/ m²/m) and having a depth equal to that of the retained soil. Any surcharge shall be in addition to the equivalent fluid pressure.

Retaining walls shall be designed to resist sliding by at least 1.5 times the lateral force and overturning by at least 1.5 times the overturning moment, using allowable stress design loads.

Most inspectors require the footing of a retaining wall to go at least to the frost line, the same as any footing. They're not really as concerned about the danger of frost heaving as they are about the wall tipping if the load behind it becomes too great.

My rule of thumb is that a retaining wall up to 6 feet high should be at least 8 inches thick. Walls higher than 6 feet should be engineered to determine the thickness and reinforcing steel needed. This applies only to the part of the wall subject to lateral pressure from the soil behind it. Any part of the wall above the dirt line may be reduced in thickness to suit your purposes. If the wall is engineered, include enough reinforcing steel to make up for any lack of thickness.

What's the next step, after the foundation and retaining walls? In the next chapter we'll move on to masonry walls.

A Shot in the Dark

We have high winds in my part of the country, eastern Washington. That's why I'm a stickler on roof installation. But the roofer isn't always to blame when a roof gets blown away. A contractor I know owns an apartment building that had the roof blown off twice before it was a year old. It's a flat roof with a five-layer mopped-on covering. There's a parapet wall three to four feet high all the way around the roof perimeter. I know the roofing subcontractor who did the job both times. He's about as professional and conscientious as they come. So why so much damage in one year?

I went out to check the building after the second storm. Roofing material was scattered a hundred yards up and down both sides of the street. Only about a third of the roof was still on top of the building. And there was something funny about what was left. Almost all roofing still there was around the roof edges. The center of the roof was almost bare. So I knew the wind hadn't found a weak spot at an edge and worked its way in.

The contractor, the roofer and I walked the entire roof and talked about it. My guess was that wind spilling over the top of the parapet wall caused a vacuum at the roof center. You know how dust swirls in the vacuum behind a big truck going down a dirt road? I guessed the same type of vacuum was lifting the roof cover. Most parapet walls have penetrations for drains. This one didn't. Roof drains went down through the exterior wall to ground level. I asked the contractor why.

"I did that to cut down on water stains on exterior walls."

"That's quality construction," I agreed, "but I think it's also turning this roof into an airplane wing in high wind. Why don't you cut a few scupper holes through each parapet wall. That might relieve the vacuum."

We decided to cut three holes along each parapet wall. It was only a shot in the dark. But it must have worked. The roof came through the next winter in perfect shape.

10

Masonry Walls

When the foundation is poured, the next step is to put up the walls. But what kind of walls? Most building walls are either masonry or wood frame. In the next chapter we'll cover the requirements for frame walls. Here we'll focus on masonry.

Masonry walls are covered in Chapter 21 of the UBC. As usual, most of the definitions and formulas are of interest only to designers. But there are a few definitions you'll need to know:

Bedded Area *is the area of the surface of a masonry unit which is in contact with mortar in the plane of the joint.*

Bond Beam *is a horizontal grouted element within masonry in which reinforcement is embedded.*

Bonded Wall *is a masonry wall in which two or more wythes are bonded to act as a structural unit.*

Bonds: *(a) Adhesion bond is the adhesion between masonry units and mortar or grout. (b) Reinforcing bond is the adhesion between steel reinforcement and mortar or grout.*

Cavity Wall *is a wall containing continuous air space with a minimum width of 2 inches (51 mm) and a maximum width of 4½ inches (114 mm) between wythes which are tied with metal ties.*

Cell *is a void space having a gross cross-sectional area greater than 1½ square inches (967 mm²).*

Collar joint *is the mortared or grouted space between wythes of masonry.*

Grout Lift *is an increment of grout height within the total pour.*

Joints: *(a) Bed joint is the mortar joint that is horizontal at the time the masonry units*

Figure 10-1 *Rebar in masonry wall construction*

are placed. *(b) Head joint is the mortar joint having a vertical transverse plane.*

Web *is an interior solid portion of a hollow-masonry unit as placed in masonry.*

Wythe *is the portion of the wall which is one masonry unit in thickness. A collar joint is not considered a wythe.*

Masonry Usually Means Block

Concrete blocks and cinder blocks are the most popular unit masonry today. Very few buildings have walls made entirely of brick. The brick you see in homes is nearly always veneer that covers either concrete block or wood frame walls.

With concrete block walls, there's no 2 x 6 plate on top of the foundation as I explained in Chapter 7. You can even omit the concrete foundation, building with masonry from the footing right up to the roof line.

If you use masonry block for the foundation, you'll probably have to put iron reinforcing dowels in the footing when it's poured.

Space these dowels every 4 feet, as shown in Figure 10-1. When the blocks are in place, fill every cell that has a dowel with concrete grout.

These reinforcing dowels don't have to run the full height of the wall. There's a practical reason for that. Masons don't like dropping blocks over reinforcing dowels 10 to 15 feet long. It takes too long and results in a lot of broken blocks. The code doesn't state that the rebar must be continuous, only that its strength be continuous. This can be done by splicing or welding shorter pieces together.

But inspectors aren't watching as every block is laid. So some masons don't bother to weld their steel. Many don't even wire it. They just jam rebar into the grout in each cell and hope that nobody notices. Don't let the masons get away with that on your jobs. Insist that spliced rebar meet code requirements.

Splicing and Placing Rebar

Splices in a bar should be as strong as an unspliced bar. You do that by lapping bars at least 30 diameters wherever bars join. For example, if you're using $\frac{1}{2}$ inch bar, the lap must be 15 inches. If you are using $\frac{5}{8}$ inch bar, lap $18\frac{3}{8}$ inches. For $\frac{3}{4}$ inch bar, go to $22\frac{1}{2}$ inches. Figure 10-2 shows a good rebar splice.

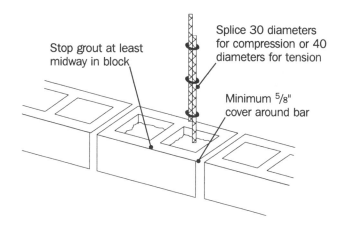

Section 2107 covers most of the requirements for reinforced hollow unit masonry

Figure 10-2 *Properly spliced rebar in hollow unit masonry*

What about the location of the bar in the cell? Do you just stick it anyplace? Not according to the code, although some masons do it that way. Joint reinforcement must have at least ⅝ inch mortar coverage from any face that's exposed to air or the surrounding environment. All other reinforcement must have a minimum mortar coverage of the diameter of the bar, or ¾ inch, whichever is more. If the bars are in the face exposed to the weather or soil, the minimum coverage is 1½ inches in weather-exposed masonry and 2 inches in soil.

Running Pipes or Conduit Through Masonry

Let's say you're building a block basement and you want to put electrical outlets in the exterior wall. There's no problem with that as long as you don't reduce the structural stability of the wall itself. If the outlet has been detailed in the plans, there shouldn't be any structural problems. You can run pipe or conduit through masonry, using a sleeve large enough to pass any hub or coupling on the pipeline. If you use multiple sleeves, they must be at least 3 inches apart. That's for areas where the block must be core-filled or where rebar may be installed. Pipe or conduit placed in the unfilled cores of hollow unit masonry isn't considered embedded.

General Masonry Requirements

The first bed joint (on top of the foundation wall) must be at least ¼ inch thick and not more than 1 inch thick. All subsequent bed joints have the same ¼ inch minimum thickness, but the maximum is ⅝ inch. Most masonry is put up in lifts usually limited to 4 feet high. The code doesn't say this directly — it's just a rule of thumb. But if your wall is much higher than 4 feet, the weight of higher courses may squeeze wet mortar out of joints on lower courses.

Each 4-foot lift should be laid, grouted and allowed to set before the next lift is started.

Always build the wall in lifts when you're grouting, especially around rebar. Remember, though, that the grout should not be level with the top of the block except on the last course. It should stop at least 1½ inches below the top of the block. The wall would have a weak point if the grout joint and the bed joint fell at the same level. With bond beams, however, the grout should stop ½ inch below the bond beam.

Any chases or recesses you're building into the wall should be small enough so they don't reduce the strength or fire resistance of the wall.

Occasionally you'll run across masonry walls built with a stack bond. This is where the blocks are placed directly over each other without the lapped joint used on most masonry work. Walls built with a stack bond must include horizontal reinforcing. This reinforcing must be at least two continuous wires, with a minimum cross-sectional area of 0.017 square inch. Install these wires horizontally between courses and no more than 16 inches apart. There are stricter requirements in Seismic Zone 1.

Corbeling

If you work with masonry, you certainly know about corbeling. Webster's dictionary says that a corbel is an architectural member that projects from within a wall and supports a weight. They're usually stepped upward and outward from a vertical surface. Figure 10-3 illustrates corbeling in masonry construction.

You can only build a corbel in a solid masonry wall that's at least 12 inches thick. The projection of each course can't exceed 1 inch. It can't project more than one-third the total thickness of the wall when used to support a chimney built into the wall. The top course of all corbels must be a header course.

Be careful when building corbels in earthquake zones. The inspector may have some strict regulations. Many areas are requiring owners to remove corbels and cornices that might fall on people below in an earthquake.

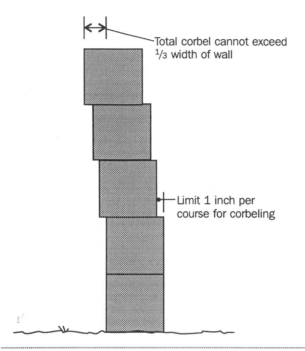

Total corbel cannot exceed ⅓ width of wall

Limit 1 inch per course for corbeling

Figure 10-3 *Corbeling in masonry construction*

Laying Block in Cold Weather

Can you lay concrete masonry units in any kind of weather? Not according to the code, unless you take specific steps to protect the strength of the wall. Check Section 2104.3 of the UBC on Cold Weather Construction:

*1. **General.** All materials shall be delivered in a usable condition and stored to prevent wetting by capillary action, rain and snow.*

The tops of all walls not enclosed or sheltered shall be covered with a strong weather-resistive material at the end of each day or shutdown.

Partially completed walls shall be covered at all times when work is not in progress. Covers shall be draped over the wall and extend a minimum of 2 feet (600 mm) down both sides and shall be securely held in place, except when additional protection is required in Section 2104.3.4

*3. **Construction.** Masonry units shall be dry at time of placement. Wet or frozen masonry units shall not be laid.*

Air temperature 40 degrees F to 32 degrees F. (4.5 degrees C. to 0 degrees C.): Sand or mixing water shall be heated to produce mortar temperature between 40 degrees F and 120 degrees F (4.5 degrees C. and 49 degrees C.).

The code then describes what must be done at air temperatures below 32 degrees. As it gets colder, the code requires more precautions. Furthermore, all work must be protected and heated for 24 hours.

If you work in a cold climate, you've probably seen buildings under construction surrounded by giant plastic cocoons. These cocoons are heated and inflated like a balloon during construction. This heat must be kept on for 24 hours after Type III portland cement is used and for 48 hours after Type I portland cement is used.

Even if the wall will be heated, don't lay brick or block that's got ice or snow clinging to it.

Thickness-to-Height Ratio

Prior to the 1985 edition, the code carried a table of thickness-to-height ratios for both reinforced and unreinforced masonry. These were rules of thumb, not code requirements, and were sometimes misinterpreted. In 1985, they replaced the table with text to explain the table. In my opinion, the explanation didn't help much. The 1991 edition replaced that explanation with text that's even more complex. This is primarily for design purposes. Its use in the field would be limited.

The authors of the code are trying to provide guidance for dealing with earthquake loads. I'm not certain that code recommendations for thickness-to-height ratios will apply in all parts of the country. Only an engineer designing a particular building for particular risk is qualified to decide what's adequate and what isn't. Still, anything the authors can do to promote earthquake safety is commendable. As I've pointed out — earthquakes can occur anyplace.

Most people without an engineering degree won't be able to understand this section on thickness-to-height ratios. Of course, we need better design for earthquake loads. But few building departments have inspectors or plans examiners on staff that can interpret these sections of the code. There's no advantage in requiring what can't be enforced, in my opinion.

In a nutshell, here's what you need to know about Chapter 21: All masonry must be reinforced, with no exceptions except as permitted by a licensed engineer. Of course that's oversimplified, but it's a good beginning point for your planning.

Masonry Standards

The code references to quality of materials changed, starting with the 1994 code. Earlier codes usually referred you to the UBC Standards for information on material specifications. Beginning with the 1991 code, references are to both ASTM Standards and the UBC Standards.

Several points on material standards for masonry are worth emphasizing:

First, used materials must conform to the same standards as new material. This is pretty hard for inspectors to enforce. Other than surface appearance, you can't tell much about used masonry. It's a safe bet that new masonry meets current code requirements. But were the standards the same when used material was made?

Second, metal ties and anchors must have a minimum tensile strength of 30,000 psi. If they are not fully embedded in mortar or grout then they must be corrosion resistant.

Third, water used in mortar or grout should be the same quality as water used in cement. Basically, if you wouldn't drink it, don't use it in mortar or grout.

Use of Mass

Anytime you make a wall higher, it has to be stronger. To make it stronger, you make it thicker. Adding mass adds strength. Architects have known about this for centuries. It's called a *principle of empirical design* because we know

it works even before we start trying to prove that it should work.

Codes before the 1991 edition accepted this principle. But the current edition recognizes the strength inherent in massive walls only in Seismic Zone 0 or 1 and only when wind loads don't exceed 80 miles per hour. Otherwise the engineer will have to demonstrate that the wall is stronger so it can be built higher.

New York City once had a building code that stated the rule very simply. The code required brick walls for buildings to be 12 inches thick for single story buildings and an additional 4 inches thick for each additional floor. So a two-story building had to have a first floor 16 inches thick. The practical limit on the height of masonry walls was 10 stories because at that point the wall on the ground floor had to be 4 feet thick. The rules are a lot more complex today, but at least 10-story buildings don't require 48-inch walls any more.

Types of Masonry

The current code omits the lists of various masonry types that appeared in earlier versions. For your convenience, I've listed the various masonry types in order from strongest to weakest. This list is based on my interpretation of the code and refers primarily to compressive strength, which is usually the most important consideration. You can usually substitute a stronger material for a weaker material, but not vice versa. Of course, all stronger materials aren't necessarily good substitutes for all weaker materials.

1) Brick made with sand-lime

2) Brick made of clay or shale

3) Concrete building blocks

4) Structural clay floor tile

5) Solid load-bearing concrete masonry units

6) Unburned clay

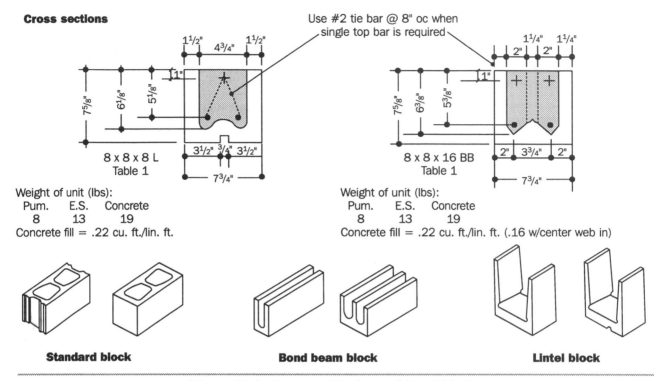

Figure 10-4 *Concrete blocks and lintel blocks*

Masonry Grades

The grade of masonry units is very important. Building bricks made of clay or shale are graded SW, MW and NW. Those made of sand-lime come in only two grades: SW and MW. For bricks made of clay or shale, here's what these grades mean:

SW Bricks have a high resistance to frost. Use them in areas where the brick is exposed and may freeze when wet. These are a good choice in foundation courses and retaining walls in climates where frost is common.

MW Bricks are intended for use where temperatures go below freezing but where brick won't be exposed to water. They have only moderate and non-uniform resistance to frost. Use them in the face of a wall above ground when not exposed to constant moisture.

NW These may be used as backup or interior masonry. You can also use them exposed in areas with no frost, or colder areas where the annual precipitation is less than 20 inches.

Bond Beams

A bond beam is a block cast with three sides and no ends, so it forms an open U. It's laid into a course with the open side up and filled with concrete. Lintel blocks, used to build lintels over doors, windows, and other openings, are a variation of the bond beam. I think lintel blocks are easier to use and look nicer than a cast-in-place concrete lintel.

In both bond beam and lintel blocks, the reinforcing used in the cavity depends on the strength required. Figure 10-4 shows several types of concrete block and lintel block reinforcing.

Face Brick and Veneer Anchorage

The most common use of brick is as face brick veneer. Brick veneer can be used over wood frame, concrete block, or even stone walls. These are clay building bricks, not concrete blocks. The difference is important, even though some people erroneously interchange the terms.

Most masons anchor face brick to a concrete block wall with mortar having a high concrete ratio. This produces a tight, secure bond. But clips are also required. These clips are little strips of corrugated sheet metal used to attach brick veneer to the block wall. On a frame building, they're nailed to the exterior sheathing and bent outward to lay between the courses.

Although most brick veneer is anchored with clips in residential construction, the clips aren't always installed properly. The most common mistake is not using enough clips, or placing clips at random. If someone isn't keeping an eye on the job, you can be sure that clips won't be installed correctly. A good mason will use clips correctly and place them according to code. Make sure it happens that way on your jobs.

Mortar

Mortar has to be applied correctly if a wall is going to have the strength intended. First, all bricks must be laid with a full head and bed joint. Second, all interior joints designed to be mortared should be filled. The average thickness of head and bed joints can't be more than ½ inch.

The mortar mix itself is also critical. There are four types of mortar used in masonry construction: Types M, S, N, and O. Mix proportions are described in UBC Table 21-A (Figure 10-5). UBC Table 21-M (Figure 10-6) gives allowable working stresses for unreinforced unit masonry. These tables will help you choose the right mortar and the proper mix for most masonry work.

Most mortar is mixed at the job, so it's easy to control the quality of the mix. The code now controls how mortar is to be mixed. I suppose that's needed — but there's one major drawback. Section 2104.2 Item 7 applies to every job, whether big or small. You decide if the following is practical on small jobs:

Mortar or grout mixed at the jobsite shall be mixed for a period of time not less than 3 minutes nor more than 10 minutes in a mechanical mixer with the amount of water required to provide the desired workability. Hand mixing of small amounts of mortar is

TABLE 21-A—MORTAR PROPORTIONS FOR UNIT MASONRY

MORTAR	TYPE	Portland Cement or Blended Cement	Masonry Cement¹			Mortar Cement²			Hydrated Lime or Lime Putty	AGGREGATE MEASURED IN A DAMP, LOOSE CONDITION
			M	S	N	M	S	N		
Cement-lime	M	1	—	—	—	—	—	—	¼	
	S	1	—	—	—	—	—	—	over ¼ to ½	
	N	1	—	—	—	—	—	—	over ½ to 1¼	
	O	1	—	—	—	—	—	—	over 1¼ to 2½	
Mortar cement	M	1	—	—	—	—	—	1	—	Not less than 2¼ and not more than 3 times the sum of the separate volumes of cementitious materials.
	M	—	—	—	—	1	—	—	—	
	S	½	—	—	—	—	—	1	—	
	S	—	—	—	—	—	1	—	—	
	N	—	—	—	—	—	—	1	—	
Masonry cement	M	1	—	—	1	—	—	—	—	
	M	—	1	—	—	—	—	—	—	
	S	½	—	—	1	—	—	—	—	
	S	—	—	1	—	—	—	—	—	
	N	—	—	—	1	—	—	—	—	
	O	—	—	—	1	—	—	—	—	

¹Masonry cement conforming to the requirements of UBC Standard 21-11.
²Mortar cement conforming to the requirements of UBC Standard 21-14.

Figure 10-5 *Mortar proportions for unit masonry*

TABLE 21-M—ALLOWABLE COMPRESSIVE STRESSES FOR EMPIRICAL DESIGN OF MASONRY

CONSTRUCTION: COMPRESSIVE STRENGTH OF UNIT, GROSS AREA	ALLOWABLE COMPRESSIVE STRESSES[1] GROSS CROSS-SECTIONAL AREA (psi)	
× 6.89 for kPa	× 6.89 for kPa	
	Type M or S Mortar	Type N Mortar
Solid masonry of brick and other solid units of clay or shale; sand-lime or concrete brick:		
8,000 plus, psi	350	300
4,500 psi	225	200
2,500 psi	160	140
1,500 psi	115	100
Grouted masonry, of clay or shale; sand-lime or concrete:		
4,500 plus, psi	275	200
2,500 psi	215	140
1,500 psi	175	100
Solid masonry of solid concrete masonry units:		
3,000 plus, psi	225	200
2,000 psi	160	140
1,200 psi	115	100
Masonry of hollow load-bearing units:		
2,000 plus, psi	140	120
1,500 psi	115	100
1,000 psi	75	70
700 psi	60	55
Hollow walls (cavity or masonry bonded)[2] solid units:		
2,500 plus, psi	160	140
1,500 psi	115	100
Hollow units	75	70
Stone ashlar masonry:		
Granite	720	640
Limestone or marble	450	400
Sandstone or cast stone	360	320
Rubble stone masonry Coarse, rough or random	120	100
Unburned clay masonry	30	—

[1]Linear interpolation may be used for determining allowable stresses for masonry units having compressive strengths which are intermediate between those given in the table.

[2]Where floor and roof loads are carried upon one wythe, the gross cross-sectional area is that of the wythe under load. If both wythes are loaded, the gross cross-sectional area is that of the wall minus the area of the cavity between the wythes.

From the Uniform Building Code, ©1997, ICBO

Figure 10-6 *Allowable compressive stresses for empirical design of masonry*

permitted. *Mortar may be retempered. Mortar or grout which has hardened or stiffened due to hydration of the cement shall not be used, but under no case shall mortar be used two and one-half hours, nor grout used one and one-half hours, after the initial mixing water has been added to the dry ingredients at the jobsite.*

Exception: *Dry mixes for mortar and grout which are blended in the factory and mixed at the jobsite shall be mixed in mechanical mixers until workable, but not to exceed 10 minutes.*

There's one more serious problem with this regulation. An inspector would have to stand there all the time masons are laying block to be sure mortar is being mixed correctly. That isn't practical.

An inspector can, of course, call for tests on the mortar. According to the UBC, if special inspections are needed, they're done at the expense of the contractor.

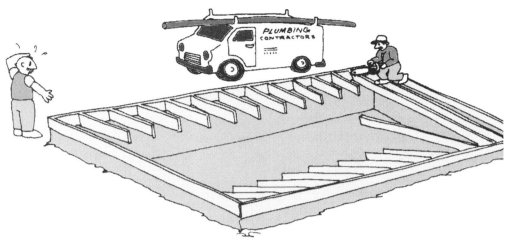

Who's Going to Header That Hole?

Every subcontractor makes mistakes. Maybe that's an understatement. I should say, everybody makes mistakes. But when it comes to mistakes by subs, framers seem to be the worst. I can say that. I was one once. Anything a framer leaves out is probably very important. I'll give an example.

Framers make their living with high production: get the foundation sill down. Install the joists. Get it plated. Tilt up the walls, and so on. The sooner framing is done, the bigger the profit, the sooner we get paid.

And framers have their excuses. But usually the real problem is lack of planning. In this case, the lumber truck dumped the load at the south side of the lot. So Mr. Framer starts setting floor joists right there, on the south side, working north at 16 inch centers. That's the quick way to do it. In a few minutes he's nailing on rim joists and almost ready for decking. This is going slick as a whistle.

Mr. Framer's finished in a few days. And no wonder. He didn't waste a minute, especially in checking the plans. But maybe he should have noticed a few things. Like where plumbing lines have to run through his precious framing. Certainly Mr. Plumber will.

Now, speaking of Mr. Plumber, here he comes. He discovers there's a joist in the way of the closet bend for his toilet. And another one goes smack through where the middle of the bathtub drain trap will come down. By this time there isn't a carpenter anywhere in sight. So he has to fall back on "Plan B." He drags out his trusty chain saw and whacks off several feet of perfectly good joist, leaving it dangling like a limb on a tree.

The writers of the Uniform Building Code, in their wisdom, decided that the ends of joists have to be supported by something solid. So here's what happens when I come along to inspect the job.

"This hole will have to be headed," I say. "What hole is that?" the foreman asks, with his most innocent expression covering his face. So I point it out. "But I didn't cut that hole. It must have been the plumber." True enough. But the code is the code, so it's got to be done.

The whole problem could have been avoided if Mr. Framer were as quick at reading plans as he is at driving nails. For this job floor joists should have been laid out from the north side of the foundation, where the plumbing fixtures are. That's probably what the architect had in mind in the first place. But I won't blame the architect. The framer should know his business. And part of that is planning for work by other trades.

11

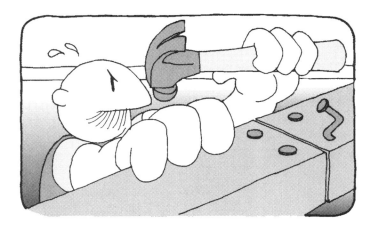

Frame Walls

The code has the same goal for frame walls as it does for masonry walls: a sturdy building that's warm and dry. Chapter 23 of the UBC covers wood framing. Let's start with the first section of Chapter 23:

Sec. 2301.1 Scope. The quality and design of wood members and their fastenings shall conform to the provisions of this chapter.

This covers just about everything involving wood and wood products. Section 2304 governs workmanship and fabrication:

Section 2304.4.1 General. Preparation, fabrication and installation of wood members and their fastenings shall conform to accepted engineering practices and to the requirements of this code. All members shall be framed, anchored, tied and braced so as to develop the strength and rigidity necessary for the purposes for which they are used.

Lumber Grading

Because we have to rely on lumber grades as our guide to the strength of lumber, the grade marks must be clearly visible on all framing members. Notice in Figure 11-1 that lumber grade marks are clearly visible. Unfortunately, a grade stamp doesn't always indicate the strength of that particular piece. Lumber mill grades are based on the judgment of the person grading the lumber. Nearly all framing lumber is graded by eye and the human eye can't see every defect. That makes it your responsibility to reject any material that isn't up to par.

Do you accept all the lumber that's delivered to your job? Just because a piece of wood has a grade mark doesn't mean that it will do the job you want it to do. If it's poor quality lumber, reject it.

If the dealer won't take it back, buy from a dealer who will. Unless you bought the lumber from a stack of bargain material, you should be

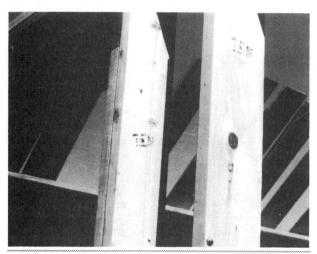

Figure 11-1 *Grade marks clearly visible on framing members*

able to return it. Defective lumber that you can't or don't want to return can be used for blocking or backing where strength and appearance aren't as critical. But be careful. According to Section 2304.8, the building official can reject flawed lumber if he finds it on your job. He can make you replace it even if it's already installed. Here's what the code says:

> **Section 2304.8 Rejection.** *The building official may deny permission for the use of a wood member where permissible grade characteristics or defects are present in such a combination that they affect the serviceability of the member.*

Suppose you have a joist with a knot that's the maximum size allowable for this particular joist. Then your plumber comes along and notches the joist near enough to this knot to weaken the entire member. This is bound to catch the inspector's eye. The inspector has four options: First, he can make you replace it. Second, he can order it cut back and headered in. Third, he can ask you to brace it, either with a post or by scabbing another piece to it. If you don't want to do any of these, the inspector can require you to hire a testing agency. At your considerable expense, they'll sandbag the floor, test it for deflections, and then certify to the inspector that the assembly has the strength required by the code.

Well, that's what the inspector can do. But it shouldn't happen. Anticipate the problem and solve it by bracing before the inspector ever sees it.

Notching Beams and Joists

Because of the changes in Chapter 23, you'll now find that the subject of notching and boring of framing timbers in light wood construction is covered in Sections 2820.8.3, 2820.11.9 and 2320.11.10. Here's what it says about notching and boring joists:

> *Notches on the ends of joists shall not exceed one fourth the joist depth. Holes bored in joists shall not be within 2 inches (51 mm) of the top or bottom of the joist, and the diameter of any such hole shall not exceed one third the depth of the joist. Notches in the top or bottom of joists shall not exceed one sixth the depth and shall not be located in the middle third of the span.*

Figure 11-2 shows joist cuts and notches that meet code requirements.

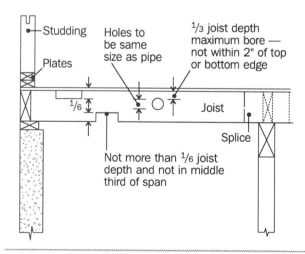

Figure 11-2 *Proper cutting and notching of joists and beams*

Section 313.2 of the 1994 Uniform Plumbing Code states:

313.2 All piping in connection with a plumbing system shall be so installed that piping or connections will not be subject to undue strains and stresses, and provisions shall be made for expansion, contraction, and structural settlement. No piping shall be directly embedded in concrete or masonry. No structural member shall be seriously weakened or impaired by cutting, notching or otherwise.

Plumbers tend to cut away any framing that's in their way, especially around bathrooms. If a plumber discovers that a water closet bend has to run where a joist is installed, he'll get out his saw and make a few alterations. The next thing the general contractor knows, the inspector is knocking on his door demanding that this little problem be taken care of by headering. By this time the pipes are already in place and the plumber is off on another job. Adding a header at this point isn't an easy job.

Of course, a good framer would have spotted the problem and solved it long before the plumber arrived. Simply starting the joist layout from the other side of the foundation might have solved the problem. In too many cases, however, the main problem is lack of supervision. If your framer isn't experienced, go over the layout in detail before cutting any lumber. Show him exactly where pipe chases and cutouts should be and how to header them.

In the final analysis, the owner is responsible. The owner has to select a competent general contractor who selects competent subcontractors who hire competent tradesmen able to do the work correctly. Make sure you meet your responsibilities in that chain of command.

What Should You Do About Holes?

We've talked about cutting holes in joists for pipe, conduit, or wires — but that's not the end of it. The code clearly states that holes should be the size of the pipe or conduit going

through them. But the holes are often made much larger than needed for the convenience of the wire-puller or the person installing the pipe. The UBC covers this in Section 708.2.1 Item 4. It requires you to provide fire blocks:

In openings around vents, pipes, ducts, chimneys, fireplaces, and similar openings which afford a passage for fire at ceiling and floor levels, with noncombustible materials.

This paragraph reflects one of the code's main concerns: fire prevention. Another concern is the strength of the member. Let's take a look at Section 2320.11.7:

Pipes in walls. Stud partitions containing plumbing, heating, or other pipes shall be so framed and the joists underneath so spaced as to give proper clearance for the piping. Where a partition containing such piping runs parallel to the floor joists, the joists underneath such partitions shall be doubled and spaced to permit the passage of such pipes and shall be bridged. Where plumbing, heating or other pipes are placed in or partly in a partition, necessitating the cutting of the soles or plates, a metal tie not less than 0.058 inches (1.47 mm) (16 galvanized gage) and 1½ inches (38 mm) wide shall be fastened to each plate across and to each side of the opening with not less than six 16d nails.

There's still more on pipes in the walls. Section 2320.11.10 approaches it this way:

Bored holes. A hole not greater in diameter than 40 percent of the stud width may be bored in any wood stud. Bored holes not greater than 60 percent of the width of the stud are permitted in nonbearing partitions or in any wall where each bored stud is doubled, provided not more than two such successive doubled studs are so bored.

Figure 11-3 shows pipes running through stud blocking. Note the approximate ⅝-inch space from the edge of the block to the edge of the hole, and the galvanized plates on the edge

Figure 11-3 *Pipes through stud blocking*

of the blocking. The edge of the bored hole can't be less than ⅝ inch from the edge of the stud. And you can't bore holes in a section of stud that already had a cut or a notch.

What the code requires is preventative construction. The ⅛-inch plate and the ⅝-inch setback from the edge serve a single purpose — to keep sheetrock nails and screws from puncturing water lines. This is important. If a nail or screw tip punctures a water line, it might not show up immediately. But normal vibration and shrinkage after a couple of months may eventually enlarge the hole. Then you have a leak that's expensive to repair — and may do a lot of damage before it's repaired.

Determining Wood Strength

The code relies on standard formulas to determine the strength of wood, wood joints, and other wood assemblies. Since most of these formulas apply only to large structures, let's leave them for the engineers and designers. The average contractor will find nearly all the design information needed in span tables in Chapter 23 of the UBC.

Structural design of timber is a complex subject. But you don't have to know anything about timber engineering to frame most houses. Just follow the tables in the code. Occasionally you'll need to know more than most joist and rafter tables show. That's when some understanding of timber engineering will come in handy.

Modulus of Elasticity

This is what I call the "first line of defense." If you know the modulus of elasticity (E factor), you can find most of the other information you'll need to determine wood strength. In most cases, the modulus of elasticity should be about 1,500,000 psi.

The appendix at the back of this manual includes complete wood span tables and other tables that cover wood framing. Here's how to use Table 23-IV-V-1, beginning on page 280. Start with the type of lumber you want to use. In my area most framing material is Douglas fir (North). So I'll assume 2 x 8 Douglas fir joists placed 16 inches on center. We'll check construction grade first since it's the most common.

But can we use it? Go to the second column, *Size Classification.* This column shows that construction grade is only used in timbers 2 to 4 inches thick, 4 inches wide. Our 2 x 8 joists won't fit here. So what grade of lumber can we use? Read down the column until you come to this dimension: 2" to 4" thick, 5" and wider. Here we find that "No. 3 and Stud" has the same modulus of elasticity as construction grade. (Modulus of elasticity is given in the second column from the right.)

Before we make a firm decision, however, let's go to the column called *Extreme Fiber in Bending (Fb).* What do we find? Although the E factor is the same, the Fb factor is not. Is this the one we should use? First, we'll have to do a little more research.

Beams are often used as single members, but joists seldom are. They're usually ganged in groups of four or more. That's what the code

TABLE 23-IV-J-1—FLOOR JOISTS WITH *L*/360 DEFLECTION LIMITS
The allowable bending stress (*F_b*) and modulus of elasticity *(E)* used in this table shall be from Tables 23-IV-V-1 and 23-IV-V-2 only.

DESIGN CRITERIA:
Deflection — For 40 psf (1.92 kN/m^2) live load.
Limited to span in inches (mm) divided by 360.
Strength — Live load of 40 psf (1.92 kN/m^2) plus dead load of 10 psf (0.48 kN/m^2) determines the required bending design value.

Joist Size (In)	Spacing (In)	Modulus of Elasticity, *E*, in 1,000,000 psi $\times$ 0.00689 for N/mm^2																
$\times$ 25.4 for mm		0.8	0.9	1.0	1.1	1.2	1.3	1.4	1.5	1.6	1.7	1.8	1.9	2.0	2.1	2.2	2.3	2.4
2 × 6	12.0	8-6	8-10	9-2	9-6	9-9	10-0	10-3	10-6	10-9	10-11	11-2	11-4	11-7	11-9	11-11	12-1	12-3
	16.0	7-9	8-0	8-4	8-7	8-10	9-1	9-4	9-6	9-9	9-11	10-2	10-4	10-6	10-8	10-10	11-0	11-2
	19.2	7-3	7-7	7-10	8-1	8-4	8-7	8-9	9-0	9-2	9-4	9-6	9-8	9-10	10-0	10-2	10-4	10-6
	24.0	6-9	7-0	7-3	7-6	7-9	7-11	8-2	8-4	8-6	8-8	8-10	9-0	9-2	9-4	9-6	9-7	9-9
2 × 8	12.0	11-3	11-8	12-1	12-6	12-10	13-2	13-6	13-10	14-2	14-5	14-8	15-0	15-3	15-6	15-9	15-11	16-2
	16.0	10-2	10-7	11-0	11-4	11-8	12-0	12-3	12-7	12-10	13-1	13-4	13-7	13-10	14-1	14-3	14-6	14-8
	19.2	9-7	10-0	10-4	10-8	11-0	11-3	11-7	11-10	12-1	12-4	12-7	12-10	13-0	13-3	13-5	13-8	13-10
	24.0	8-11	9-3	9-7	9-11	10-2	10-6	10-9	11-0	11-3	11-5	11-8	11-11	12-1	12-3	12-6	12-8	12-10
2 × 10	12.0	14-4	14-11	15-5	15-11	16-5	16-10	17-3	17-8	18-0	18-5	18-9	19-1	19-5	19-9	20-1	20-4	20-8
	16.0	13-0	13-6	14-0	14-6	14-11	15-3	15-8	16-0	16-5	16-9	17-0	17-4	17-8	17-11	18-3	18-6	18-9
	19.2	12-3	12-9	13-2	13-7	14-0	14-5	14-9	15-1	15-5	15-9	16-0	16-4	16-7	16-11	17-2	17-5	17-8
	24.0	11-4	11-10	12-3	12-8	13-0	13-4	13-8	14-0	14-4	14-7	14-11	15-2	15-5	15-8	15-11	16-2	16-5
2 × 12	12.0	17-5	18-1	18-9	19-4	19-11	20-6	21-0	21-6	21-11	22-5	22-10	23-3	23-7	24-0	24-5	24-9	25-1
	16.0	15-10	16-5	17-0	17-7	18-1	18-7	19-1	19-6	19-11	20-4	20-9	21-1	21-6	21-10	22-2	22-6	22-10
	19.2	14-11	15-6	16-0	16-7	17-0	17-6	17-11	18-4	18-9	19-2	19-6	19-10	20-2	20-6	20-10	21-2	21-6
	24.0	13-10	14-4	14-11	15-4	15-10	16-3	16-8	17-0	17-5	17-9	18-1	18-5	18-9	19-1	19-4	19-8	19-11
F_b	12.0	718	777	833	888	941	993	1,043	1,092	1,140	1,187	1,233	1,278	1,323	1,367	1,410	1,452	1,494
	16.0	790	855	917	977	1,036	1,093	1,148	1,202	1,255	1,306	1,357	1,407	1,456	1,504	1,551	1,598	1,644
	19.2	840	909	975	1,039	1,101	1,161	1,220	1,277	1,333	1,388	1,442	1,495	1,547	1,598	1,649	1,698	1,747
	24.0	905	979	1,050	1,119	1,186	1,251	1,314	1,376	1,436	1,496	1,554	1,611	1,667	1,722	1,776	1,829	1,882

NOTE: The required bending design value, *F_b*, in pounds per square inch ($\times$ 0.00689 for N/mm^2) is shown at the bottom of this table and is applicable to all lumber sizes shown. Spans are shown in feet-inches (1 foot = 304.8 mm, 1 inch = 25.4 mm) and are limited to 26 feet (7925 mm) and less.

From the Uniform Building Code, ©1997, ICBO

Figure 11-4 *Floor joists with deflection limits*

calls *Repetitive-member Uses*, the second column under the *Extreme Fiber in Bending* column. In this column the Fb factor for "No. 3 and Stud" is 850, compared to 1200 for construction grade. Are we still in trouble?

Allowable Spans for Joists and Rafters

Let's go to UBC Table 23-IV-J-1, (Figure 11-4) to find the joists we should use. It's called *Floor Joists with L/360 Deflection Limits*. This table might look tricky, but it's really quite simple.

Look at the first column, *Joist Size*. It lists the common joist dimensions for light frame buildings. Column 2 lists the common spacings (12, 16, and 24 inches). The columns to the right give the E factors, beginning at 800,000 psi and ranging up to 2.4 million psi. Look at the first line of the column headed 0.8. That's 2 x 6 joists, 12 inches on center, with an E factor of 0.8 psi. You'll find a set of numbers that looks like this: 8-6. Translated, that means that a 2 x 6 joist, 12 inches o.c. with an Fb factor of 720 will span 8'6".

The hyphenated number is the span in feet and inches for a 2 x 6 joist when it's placed 12 inches o.c. If we were to space that same timber 16 inches o.c., the span would be reduced to 7'9".

It might depend on how strict the inspector is. I think it would do the job, but it might give you some pretty springy floors. You may be able to push the lighter material past the inspector. But remember that he'll be looking at the same charts we've just been reviewing. And your reputation is on the line. Is a springy floor worth the few dollars you'll save? I recommend going to a larger timber, a 2 x 10, 16 inches o.c.

If you're using a plan prepared by an engineer, the drawings will probably indicate the size of the joists, the spacing, and the direction of run. They should also identify the lumber species and grade.

Diaphragms and Framing

The code recognizes that nailing plywood sheathing to wood framing makes the framing much stronger. The code calls this a *wood diaphragm* and defines it as any assembly of lumber and plywood designed to resist horizontal and vertical pressures and loads. Certain deflections are allowed, as long as the diaphragm can still support the assumed loads without danger to the structure or its occupants.

A roof, floor, or wall can be a diaphragm. UBC Table 23-II-H (Figure 11-5) is called *Allowable Shear in Pounds per Foot for Horizontal Wood Structural Panel Diaphragms*. It shows some typical diaphragms.

Particleboard is accepted more and more in place of plywood. At first its primary function was only as underlayment for floors. But now there's even one type that's occasionally used in finish work. Table 23-II-I-2 covers particleboard diaphragms.

Joists and Joist Problems

Now we know how to determine joist sizes and loading. But there's more involved than just laying them out on top of the foundation plate. Joists must be supported laterally by solid blocking at the ends and at support points unless the joist ends are nailed to a header, band, rim joist, or an adjoining stud. Solid blocking must be at least 2 inches thick and the full depth of the joist. That information comes from Chapter 23 of the UBC.

No cross-bridging or blocking is required between the ends of the joists except as noted in Section 2320 below. Notice that I said between the ends of joists; the ends themselves must still be solid blocked. Here's what Section 2320.8.3 says about blocking:

2320.8.3 Framing details. Joists shall be supported laterally at the ends and at each support by solid blocking except where the ends of the joists are nailed to a header, band or rim joist or to an adjoining stud or by other approved means. Solid blocking shall not be less than 2 inches (51 mm) in thickness and the full depth of joist.

Joist framing from opposite sides of a beam, girder or partition shall be lapped at least 3 inches or the opposing joists shall be tied together in an approved manner.

Joists framing into the side of a wood girder shall be supported by framing anchors or on ledger strips not less that 2 inches by 2 inches (51 mm by 51 mm).

You must double joists running parallel under bearing partitions.

When the span of the header exceeds 4 feet, double the header joists or use lumber that's the same cross section as a doubled header. The ends of header joists more than 6 feet long must be supported by framing anchors or joist hangers unless they're bearing on a beam. This means that if your opening is less than 4 feet, a single header will do. In any case it must be as wide as the joist it supports.

PANEL GRADE	COMMON NAIL SIZE	MINIMUM NAIL PENETRATION IN FRAMING (inches)	MINIMUM NOMINAL PANEL THICKNESS (inches)	MINIMUM NOMINAL WIDTH OF FRAMING MEMBER (inches)	BLOCKED DIAPHRAGMS — Nail spacing (in.) at diaphragm boundaries (all cases), at continuous panel edges parallel to load (Cases 3 and 4) and at all panel edges (Cases 5 and 6)				UNBLOCKED DIAPHRAGMS — Nails spaced 6" (152 mm) max. at supported edges	
					6	4	2½[2]	2[2]	Case 1 (No unblocked edges or continuous joints parallel to load)	All other configurations (Cases 2, 3, 4, 5 and 6)
					Nail spacing (in.) at other panel edges					
					6	6	4	3		
		×25.4 for mm			× 0.0146 for N/mm					
Structural 1	6d	1¼	5/16	2	185	250	375	420	165	125
				3	210	280	420	475	185	140
	8d	1½	3/8	2	270	360	530	600	240	180
				3	300	400	600	675	265	200
	10d[3]	1⅝	15/32	2	320	425	640	730	285	215
				3	360	480	720	820	320	240
C-D, C-C, Sheathing, and other grades covered in UBC Standard 23-2 or 23-3	6d	1¼	5/16	2	170	225	335	380	150	110
				3	190	250	380	430	170	125
			3/8	2	185	250	375	420	165	125
				3	210	280	420	475	185	140
	8d	1½	3/8	2	240	320	480	545	215	160
				3	270	360	540	610	240	180
			7/16	2	255	340	505	575	230	170
				3	285	380	570	645	255	190
			15/32	2	270	360	530	600	240	180
				3	300	400	600	675	265	200
	10d[3]	1⅝	15/32	2	290	385	575	655	255	190
				3	325	430	650	735	290	215
			19/32	2	320	425	640	730	285	215
				3	360	480	720	820	320	240

[1]These values are for short-time loads due to wind or earthquake and must be reduced 25 percent for normal loading. Space nails 12 inches (305 mm) on center along intermediate framing members.

Allowable shear values for nails in framing members of other species set forth in Division III, Part III, shall be calculated for all other grades by multiplying the shear capacities for nails in Structural I by the following factors: 0.82 for species with specific gravity greater than or equal to 0.42 but less than 0.49, and 0.65 for species with a specific gravity less than 0.42.

[2]Framing at adjoining panel edges shall be 3-inch (76 mm) nominal or wider and nails shall be staggered where nails are spaced 2 inches (51 mm) or 2½ inches (64 mm) on center.

[3]Framing at adjoining panel edges shall be 3-inch (76 mm) nominal or wider and nails shall be staggered where 10d nails having penetration into framing of more than 1⅝ inches (41 mm) are spaced 3 inches (76 mm) or less on center.

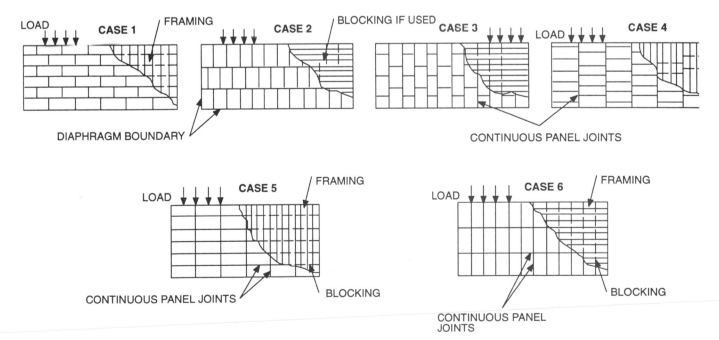

NOTE: Framing may be oriented in either direction for diaphragms, provided sheathing is properly designed for vertical loading.

From the Uniform Building Code, ©1997, ICBO

Figure 11-5 *Allowable shear for horizontal plywood diaphragms*

Framing Floors

Let's first look at subflooring. This is where the trouble usually begins. Squeaky, noisy floors begin with a bad subfloor.

I once owned a house with a squeaking floor in the hall and bathroom. Tiles kept popping up. Finally I tore up the floor to see what the trouble was. The subfloor was nothing but scrap lumber laid (not nailed) on the joists. It wasn't even laid tight. I had to replace the entire floor from the joists up.

Laying Subfloor

Joints in subflooring should all be made over joists unless you're using endmatched lumber. When properly installed, endmatched lumber acts as one continuous piece. Each piece must rest on at least two joists. If you're using plywood for subflooring, as nearly everyone does now, you'll have to meet the requirements shown in Tables 23-II-E-1 or 23-II-E-2 (Figure 11-6).

Figure 11-7 (Table 23-II-D-1) gives allowable spans for lumber floor and roof sheathing. The UBC Standard numbers tell you where these grades are defined in the Standards. But all you usually have to do is check the grade markings on the timber.

UBC Table 23-II-F-1 (Figure 11-8) is a companion table to UBC Table 23-II-D-1. Table 23-II-F-1 is a sneaky little number and might surprise you. Do you see the column called *Species Group*? You have to refer to Table 23-2-A from the UBC Standards (Figure 11-9) to find out what the groups are.

Post and Beam — Plank and Beam

The two names are often used interchangeably although they're not actually the same. Figure 11-10 shows a post and beam floor system. A plank and beam system has planks covering the beams, although today we usually use 5 quarter plywood instead of planks.

Post and beam floors must meet the same general requirements as other types of floors.

But where you were using 2-inch-thick joists on edge and ⅝ inch or ¾ inch subflooring, now you'd use 2-inch-thick planks or decking, then heavier beams and greater spans. Requirements for endmatched lumber are also the same. You don't have to rest the joints on the joists as you would if you used plain unmatched planks.

If you use the usual "5-quarter" or "4-for-1" plywood, check UBC Table 23-II-E-1. If you lay these panels with the long edges across the joists, unsupported spans of 48 inches may be permitted. But I've found that this creates a spongy floor if it has to support loads like a water bed or piano. Most builders now use 32-inch spacing in their floor beams. The extra cost is very small.

Framing Walls

When the subfloor is down, the next step is to get the studding up. When I was an apprentice, all studs were called scantlings. I haven't heard the term for many years — it probably disappeared along with the old-timers who taught me the trade.

Studs (usually 2 x 4s or 2 x 6s) form the building walls. Siding and wallboard hang from the studs and the second floor and roof are supported by wall studs. Whether you call them studding or scantling, they're an important part of every wood-frame building.

Stud Spacing

If studs are supporting floors above, space them not more than 16 inches o.c. But 2 x 4 studs that support only a ceiling and a roof may be spaced up to 24 inches o.c. You can also use 24-inch spacing for nonbearing interior walls. With 24-inch spacing, center the roof trusses directly over the studding. This transfers the vertical roof load directly through the studding to the foundation. Studding sizes and heights are given in Table 23-IV-B (Figure 11-11). Make sure your carpenters place the studs with the wide dimension of the timber at right angles to the wall.

TABLE 23-II-E-1—ALLOWABLE SPANS AND LOADS FOR WOOD STRUCTURAL PANEL SHEATHING AND SINGLE-FLOOR GRADES CONTINUOUS OVER TWO OR MORE SPANS WITH STRENGTH AXIS PERPENDICULAR TO SUPPORTS[1,2]

SHEATHING GRADES		ROOF[3]				FLOOR[4]
		Maximum Span (inches)		Load[5] (pounds per square foot)		
		× 25.4 for mm		× 0.0479 for kN/m²		Maximum Span (inches)
Panel Span Rating	Panel Thickness (inches)	With Edge Support[6]	Without Edge Support	Total Load	Live Load	
Roof/Floor Span	× 25.4 for mm					× 25.4 for mm
12/0	$5/16$	12	12	40	30	0
16/0	$5/16, 3/8$	16	16	40	30	0
20/0	$5/16, 3/8$	20	20	40	30	0
24/0	$3/8, 7/16, 1/2$	24	20[7]	40	30	0
24/16	$7/16, 1/2$	24	24	50	40	16
32/16	$15/32, 1/2, 5/8$	32	28	40	30	16[8]
40/20	$19/32, 5/8, 3/4, 7/8$	40	32	40	30	20[8,9]
48/24	$23/32, 3/4, 7/8$	48	36	45	35	24
54/32	$7/8, 1$	54	40	45	35	32
60/48	$7/8, 1, 1 1/8$	60	48	45	35	48
SINGLE-FLOOR GRADES		ROOF[3]				FLOOR[4]
		Maximum Span (inches)		Load[5] (pounds per square foot)		
		× 25.4 for mm		× 0.0479 for kN/m²		Maximum Span (inches)
Panel Span Rating (inches)	Panel Thickness (inches)	With Edge Support[6]	Without Edge Support	Total Load	Live Load	
× 25.4 for mm						× 25.4 for mm
16 oc	$1/2, 19/32, 5/8$	24	24	50	40	16[8]
20 oc	$19/32, 5/8, 3/4$	32	32	40	30	20[8,9]
24 oc	$23/32, 3/4$	48	36	35	25	24
32 oc	$7/8, 1$	48	40	50	40	32
48 oc	$1 3/32, 1 1/8$	60	48	50	50	48

[1]Applies to panels 24 inches (610 mm) or wider.
[2]Floor and roof sheathing conforming with this table shall be deemed to meet the design criteria of Section 2312.
[3]Uniform load deflection limitations $1/180$ of span under live load plus dead load, $1/240$ under live load only.
[4]Panel edges shall have approved tongue-and-groove joints or shall be supported with blocking unless $1/4$-inch (6.4 mm) minimum thickness underlayment or $1 1/2$ inches (38 mm) of approved cellular or lightweight concrete is placed over the subfloor, or finish floor is $3/4$-inch (19 mm) wood strip. Allowable uniform load based on deflection of $1/360$ of span is 100 pounds per square foot (psf) (4.79 kN/m²) except the span rating of 48 inches on center is based on a total load of 65 psf (3.11 kN/m).
[5]Allowable load at maximum span.
[6]Tongue-and-groove edges, panel edge clips [one midway between each support, except two equally spaced between supports 48 inches (1219 mm) on center], lumber blocking, or other. Only lumber blocking shall satisfy blocked diaphgrams requirements.
[7]For $1/2$-inch (12.7 mm) panel, maximum span shall be 24 inches (610 mm).
[8]May be 24 inches (610 mm) on center where $3/4$-inch (19 mm) wood strip flooring is installed at right angles to joist.
[9]May be 24 inches (610 mm) on center for floors where $1 1/2$ inches (38 mm) of cellular or lightweight concrete is applied over the panels.

TABLE 23-II-E-2—ALLOWABLE LOAD (PSF) FOR WOOD STRUCTURAL PANEL ROOF SHEATHING CONTINUOUS OVER TWO OR MORE SPANS AND STRENGTH AXIS PARALLEL TO SUPPORTS (Plywood structural panels are five-ply, five-layer unless otherwise noted.)[1,2]

PANEL GRADE	THICKNESS (inch)	MAXIMUM SPAN (inches)	LOAD AT MAXIMUM SPAN (psf)	
			× 0.0479 for kN/m²	
	× 25.4 for mm		Live	Total
Structural I	$7/16$	24	20	30
	$15/32$	24	35[3]	45[3]
	$1/2$	24	40[3]	50[3]
	$19/32, 5/8$	24	70	80
	$23/32, 3/4$	24	90	100
Other grades covered in UBC Standard 23-2 or 23-3	$7/16$	16	40	50
	$15/32$	24	20	25
	$1/2$	24	25	30
	$19/32$	24	40[3]	50[3]
	$5/8$	24	45[3]	55[3]
	$23/32, 3/4$	24	60[3]	65[3]

[1]Roof sheathing conforming with this table shall be deemed to meet the design criteria of Section 2312.
[2]Uniform load deflection limitations: $1/180$ of span under live load plus dead load, $1/240$ under live load only. Edges shall be blocked with lumber or other approved type of edge supports.
[3]For composite and four-ply plywood structural panel, load shall be reduced by 15 pounds per square foot (0.72 kN/m²).

From the Uniform Building Code, ©1997, ICBO

Figure 11-6 *Allowable spans and loads for sheathing and single-floor grades*

TABLE 23-II-D-1—ALLOWABLE SPANS FOR LUMBER FLOOR AND ROOF SHEATHING[1, 2]

SPAN (Inches) × 25.4 for mm	MINIMUM NET THICKNESS (Inches) OF LUMBER PLACED			
	Perpendicular to Supports		Diagonally to Supports	
	× 25.4 for mm			
	Surfaced Dry[3]	Surfaced Unseasoned	Surfaced Dry[3]	Surfaced Unseasoned
	Floors			
1. 24	$3/4$	$25/32$	$3/4$	$25/32$
2. 16	$5/8$	$11/16$	$5/8$	$11/16$
	Roofs			
3. 24	$5/8$	$11/16$	$3/4$	$25/32$

[1]Installation details shall conform to Sections 2320.9.1 and 2320.12.8 for floor and roof sheathing, respectively.
[2]Floor or roof sheathing conforming with this table shall be deemed to meet the design criteria of Section 2312.
[3]Maximum 19 percent moisture content.

From the Uniform Building Code, ©1997, ICBO

Figure 11-7 *Allowable spans for lumber floor and roof sheathing*

TABLE 23-II-F-1—ALLOWABLE SPAN FOR WOOD STRUCTURAL PANEL COMBINATION SUBFLOOR-UNDERLAYMENT (SINGLE FLOOR)[1,2] Panels Continuous over Two or More Spans and Strength Axis Perpendicular to Supports

IDENTIFICATION	MAXIMUM SPACING OF JOISTS (Inches)				
	× 25.4 for mm				
	16	20	24	32	48
	Thickness (Inches)				
Species Group[3]	× 25.4 for mm				
1	$1/2$	$5/8$	$3/4$	—	—
2, 3	$5/8$	$3/4$	$7/8$	—	—
4	$3/4$	$7/8$	1	—	—
Span rating[4]	16 o.c.	20 o.c.	24 o.c.	32 o.c.	48 o.c.

[1]Spans limited to value shown because of possible effects of concentrated loads. Allowable uniform loads based on deflection of $1/360$ of span is 100 pounds per square foot (psf) (4.79 kN/m^2), except allowable total uniform load for $1^1/8$-inch (29 mm) wood structural panels over joists spaced 48 inches (1219 mm) on center is 65 psf (3.11 kN/m^2). Panel edges shall have approved tongue-and-groove joints or shall be supported with blocking, unless $1/4$-inch (6.4 mm) minimum thickness underlayment or $1^1/2$ inches (38 mm) of approved cellular or lightweight concrete is placed over the subfloor, or finish floor is $3/4$-inch (19 mm) wood strip.
[2]Floor panels conforming with this table shall be deemed to meet the design criteria of Section 2312.
[3]Applicable to all grades of sanded exterior-type plywood. See UBC Standard 23-2 for plywood species groups.
[4]Applicable to underlayment grade and C-C (plugged) plywood, and single floor grade wood structural panels.

From the Uniform Building Code, ©1997, ICBO

Figure 11-8 *Allowable span for plywood subfloor underlayment*

The code doesn't require double wall plates on nonbearing interior partitions. But since studs are sold in bundles precut to length, many contractors prefer to use double plates even on interior partitions. That saves ordering two different sizes of studs for the job.

Offset joints in double top plates at least 48 inches. Joining partitions must be overlapped on the top plate. Make sure studs bear on a plate or sill not less than 2 inches thick. The bottom plate must be at least as wide as the wall stud.

I once inspected a job where exterior stud spacing varied from 10 to 16 inches on center. The interior walls were even worse — the spac-

ing varied up to 24 inches o.c. I'd never seen anything like it. But checking my code book, I found that I had to pass it. After all, the spacing didn't exceed the code maximums, 16 inches on exterior and 24 inches on interior walls. The code doesn't require even stud spacing. Of course, a magician was needed to hang drywall on that job. Finding studs to nail to under the drywall was sure to be a nightmare.

Boring and Notching Studs

Sections 2320.11.9 and 2320.11.10 set limits for notching and boring studding.

2320.11.9 Cutting and notching. *In exterior walls and bearing partitions, any*

From the Uniform Building Code, ©1991, ICBO

TABLE NO. 25-9-A—CLASSIFICATION OF SPECIES

Group 1	Group 2		Group 3	Group 4

Apitong[a][b]
Beech, American
Birch
  Sweet
  Yellow
Douglas Fir[c]
Kapur[a]
Keruing[a][b]
Larch, Western
Maple, Sugar
Pine
  Caribbean
  Ocote
Pine, Southern
  Loblolly
  Longleaf
  Shortleaf
  Slash
Tanoak
	Cedar, Port Orford
	Cypress
	Douglas Fir 2[c]
	Fir
	  California Red
	  Grand
	  Noble
	  Pacific Silver
	  White
	Hemlock, Western
	Lauan
	  Almon
	  Bagtikan
	  Mayapis
	  Red Lauan
	  Tangile
	  White Lauan
		Maple, Black
		Mengkulang[a]
		Meranti, Red[a][d]
		Mersawa[a]
		Pine
		  Pond
		  Red
		  Virginia
		  Western White
		Spruce
		  Red
		  Sitka
		Sweetgum
		Tamarack
		Yellow-poplar
			Alder, Red
			Birch, Paper
			Cedar, Alaska
			Fir, Subalpine
			Hemlock, Eastern
			Maple, Bigleaf
			Pine
			  Jack
			  Lodgepole
			  Ponderosa
			  Spruce
			Redwood
			Spruce
			  Black
			  Englemann
			  White
				Aspen
				  Bigtooth
				  Quaking
				Cativo
				Cedar
				  Incense
				  Western Red
				Cottonwood
				  Eastern
				  Black (Western Poplar)
				Pine
				  Eastern White
				  Sugar

(a) Each of these names represents a trade group of woods consisting of a number of closely related species.

(b) Species from the genus Dipterocarpus are marketed collectively: Apitong if originating in the Philippines; Keruing if originating in Malaysia or Indonesia.

(c) Douglas fir from trees grown in the states of Washington, Oregon, California, Idaho, Montana, Wyoming, and the Canadian Provinces of Alberta and British Columbia shall be classed as Douglas fir No. 1. Douglas fir from trees grown in the states of Nevada, Utah, Colorado, Arizona and New Mexico shall be classed as Douglas fir No. 2.

(d) Red Meranti shall be limited to species having a specific gravity of 0.41 or more based on green volume and oven dry weight.

Figure 11-9 *Classification of species*

wood stud may be cut or notched to a depth not exceeding 25 percent of its width. Cutting and notching of studs to a depth not greater than 40 percent of the width of the stud is permitted in nonbearing partitions supporting no loads other than the weight of the partition.

2320.11.10 Bored holes. *A hole not greater in diameter than 40 percent of the stud width may be bored in any wood stud. Bored holes not greater than 60 percent of the width of the stud are permitted in nonbearing partitions or in any wall where each bored stud is doubled, provided not more than two such successive doubled studs are so bored.*

In no case shall the edge of the bored hole be nearer than ⅝ inch (16 mm) to the edge of the stud. Bored holes shall not be located at the same section of stud as a cut or notch.

Corner Bracing

All exterior walls must be braced. The most common method is placing plywood panels at each corner. Another method uses a 1 x 4 brace

Figure 11-10 *Post and beam floor system*

TABLE 23-IV-B—SIZE, HEIGHT AND SPACING OF WOOD STUDS

STUD SIZE (inches)	BEARING WALLS				NONBEARING WALLS	
	Laterally Unsupported Stud Height[1] (feet)	Supporting Roof and Ceiling Only	Supporting One Floor, Roof and Ceiling	Supporting Two Floors, Roof and Ceiling	Laterally Unsupported Stud Height[1] (feet)	Spacing (inches)
		Spacing (inches)				
× 25.4 for mm	× 304.8 for mm	× 25.4 for mm			× 304.8 for mm	× 25.4 for mm
1. 2 × 3[2]	—	—	—	—	10	16
2. 2 × 4	10	24	16	—	14	24
3. 3 × 4	10	24	24	16	14	24
4. 2 × 5	10	24	24	—	16	24
5. 2 × 6	10	24	24	16	20	24

[1]Listed heights are distances between points of lateral support placed perpendicular to the plane of the wall. Increases in unsupported height are permitted where justified by an analysis.
[2]Shall not be used in exterior walls.

From the Uniform Building Code, ©1997, ICBO

Figure 11-11 *Wood stud sizes*

Figure 11-12 *Plywood siding installed over aluminized sheathing*

inset at an angle into the studs. This angle brace runs from the floor to the upper plate at an angle not over 60 degrees.

You can use manufactured wallboard of structural quality instead of angle bracing or plywood. But before you buy, check with the inspector. Verify that your brand has been approved and find out how it must be installed. Yes, the code even specifies the number of nails. Figure 11-12 shows plywood siding being attached over aluminized sheathing. This particular brand has qualified as structural grade.

Header All Openings

In Section 2320.11.6 of the UBC, there's an interesting note about the framing of headers. Headers and lintels over openings 4 feet (1219 mm) wide or less can be made of double 2 x 4s on edge. Here's the rule of thumb: For each 2 feet of opening over 4 feet, increase the lumber size 2 inches. In other words, you would use 2 x 4s on edge over a 4-foot opening, 2 x 6s over a 6-foot opening, 2 x 8s over 8 feet, and so on. And you don't have to use doubled 2-inch stock. Solid or 4-inch-thick material will do as well. There's no reason why you can't substitute a 4 x 6 for two 2 x 6s.

All headers and lintels must have at least 2-inch solid bearing at each end to the floor or bottom plate, unless you use other approved framing methods or joint brackets. There are a number of these brackets on the market now. Some are made of plastic but most are galvanized steel.

Some contractors prefer to use solid headers over window and door openings. If you use a narrower size, you need a certain amount of blocking between them and the top plate. Some even extend this header to each side of the window opening instead of using curtain blocking. But it's not required.

Cripples and Cripple Walls

When framing window openings, it's customary to put extra short studs (called cripples) under the lower side of the opening. Cripples double up the stud where the lower framing cross member touches the studs at the sides of the opening. This gives additional support to that member. Although it's not always required by the code, I recommend using cripples to increase the strength of the wall.

Section 2320.11.5 of the code gives requirements for a cripple wall. It states that foundation walls must be framed of studs at least the size of the studding above with a minimum length of 14 inches (356 mm). If the cripple wall exceeds 4 feet (1219 mm) in height, the studs must be the size required for an additional story.

Miscellaneous Requirements

Earlier in this book I mentioned crawl spaces and crawl holes. You may remember that crawl holes have to be at least 18 inches by 24 inches. Even if you have a partial basement, you still must have a crawl hole or access to the unexcavated portion. Incidentally, pipes or heat ducts cannot diminish the size of the crawl space.

Plans often call for beams set in pockets constructed in the foundation wall. Just remember to leave at least ½ inch of clearance at the tops, sides and ends of the beams unless you're using either an approved wood that resists decay, or treated wood. The only woods that I know of with a natural resistance to decay are redwood and cypress.

We've discussed foundation ventilation, so you know the framing material must be 6 inches from any earth unless separated by at least 3 inches of concrete. But what about the planter boxes installed adjacent to wood framing? These are usually masonry boxes built on the ground, often adjacent to the entry. The planter box must have at least 2 inches of space between it and the adjacent wall. And the adjacent wall must have flashing if it's within 6 inches of the planter.

Fire Blocks

Fire blocks are installed between studs to form a barrier to air movement in the framing and between floors. Most framing provides enough fire stops without adding any extra blocks. There are a few areas, however, that may require additional fire blocks. According to Section 708.2.1, use fire blocks in these places (this isn't the complete list):

Item 1. In concealed spaces of stud walls and partitions, including furred spaces, at the ceiling and floor levels and at 10-foot (3048 mm) intervals both vertical and horizontal. See also Section 803, Item 1.

Exception: Fire blocks may be omitted at floor and ceiling levels when approved smoke-actuated fire dampers are installed at these levels.

Item 2. At all interconnections between concealed vertical and horizontal spaces such as occur at soffits, drop ceilings and cove ceilings.

Item 3. In concealed spaces between stair stringers at the top and bottom of the run and between studs along and in line with the run of the stairs if the walls under the stairs are unfinished.

Item 4. In openings around vents, pipes, ducts, chimneys, fireplaces and similar openings which afford a passage for fire at ceiling and floor levels, with noncombustible materials.

Item 5. At openings between attic spaces and chimney chases for factory-built chimneys.

TABLE 23-II-K—WOOD SHINGLE AND SHAKE SIDE WALL EXPOSURES

SHINGLE OR SHAKE	MAXIMUM WEATHER EXPOSURES (inches)			
	× 25.4 for mm			
	Single-Coursing		Double-Coursing	
Length and Type	No. 1	No. 2	No. 1	No. 2
16-inch (405 mm) shingles	7¹/₂	7¹/₂	12	10
18-inch (455 mm) shingles	8¹/₂	8¹/₂	14	11
24-inch (610 mm) shingles	11¹/₂	11¹/₂	16	14
18-inch (455 mm) resaw shakes	8¹/₂	—	14	—
18-inch (455 mm) straight-split shakes	8¹/₂	—	16	—
24-inch (610 mm) resaw shakes	11¹/₂	—	20	—

From the Uniform Building Code, ©1997, ICBO

Figure 11-13 *Wood shingle and shake side wall exposures*

Notice that it refers you to Section 803, Item 1. That gives the requirement in fire-resistive or noncombustible construction that any furring on walls and ceilings required to be fire-resistive must be filled in with inorganic or Class I material or fire-blocked not to exceed 8 feet (2438 mm) in any direction.

Fire blocks must be nominal 2-inch-thick wood, gypsum board, cement asbestos board, mineral fiber, glass fiber or other approved noncombustible materials securely fastened in place. Lap joints must be broken and protected.

Siding

Rustic, drop siding or shiplap siding should be at least ³/₈ inch thick unless you're putting it over sheathing permitted by the code. This thickness is based on a maximum stud spacing of 16 inches on center. There's a movement afoot to get the maximum spacing increased to 24 inches for studding in the exterior walls. In that case you would have to use thicker plywood or use sheathing underneath the siding.

Bevel siding must be at least ⁷/₁₆ inch thick on the butt and ³/₁₆ inch thick on the tip. You may be able to use thinner siding. But first check with your local inspector.

All weatherboarding or siding must be nailed securely to each stud. Use at least one nail every 6 inches on the edges and every 12 inches on the field. For conventional siding, there should be at least one nail per stud.

Conventional siding installed over 1-inch nominal sheathing or ½-inch plywood sheathing must be fastened with nails spaced not more than 24 inches on center in each piece of weatherboarding or siding.

Unless you've applied the siding over sheathing, joints must be over the framing members and covered with a continuous wood batt, lapped horizontally, or otherwise made waterproof to the satisfaction of the inspector. This may be done with caulking or flashing.

Shingles or shakes, whether of wood, asbestos cement or other approved materials, have different rules. They may be applied over furring strips, wood sheathing or approved fiberboard shingle backer. But they must be placed over building paper unless they're applied over solid sheathing. If fiberboard backing is used, they must be attached with corrosion-resistant annular grooved nails.

The weather exposure of wood shingles or shake siding can't exceed the maximums in UBC Table 23-II-K (Figure 11-13).

Nails

UBC Table 23-II-B-1 (Figure 11-14) gives nailing requirements for most carpentry joints used in residential construction.

The code also spells out the spacing for nailing. For wood-to-wood joints, use a center-to-center spacing that's not less than the

TABLE 23-II-B-1—NAILING SCHEDULE

CONNECTION	NAILING[1]
1. Joist to sill or girder, toenail	3-8d
2. Bridging to joist, toenail each end	2-8d
3. 1" × 6" (25 mm × 152 mm) subfloor or less to each joist, face nail	2-8d
4. Wider than 1" × 6" (25 mm × 152 mm) subfloor to each joist, face nail	3-8d
5. 2" (51 mm) subfloor to joist or girder, blind and face nail	2-16d
6. Sole plate to joist or blocking, typical face nail Sole plate to joist or blocking, at braced wall panels	16d at 16" (406 mm) o.c. 3-16d per 16" (406 mm)
7. Top plate to stud, end nail	2-16d
8. Stud to sole plate	4-8d, toenail or 2-16d, end nail
9. Double studs, face nail	16d at 24" (610 mm) o.c.
10. Doubled top plates, typical face nail Double top plates, lap splice	16d at 16" (406 mm) o.c. 8-16d
11. Blocking between joists or rafters to top plate, toenail	3-8d
12. Rim joist to top plate, toenail	8d at 6" (152 mm) o.c.
13. Top plates, laps and intersections, face nail	2-16d
14. Continuous header, two pieces	16d at 16" (406 mm) o.c. along each edge
15. Ceiling joists to plate, toenail	3-8d
16. Continuous header to stud, toenail	4-8d
17. Ceiling joists, laps over partitions, face nail	3-16d
18. Ceiling joists to parallel rafters, face nail	3-16d
19. Rafter to plate, toenail	3-8d
20. 1" (25 mm) brace to each stud and plate, face nail	2-8d
21. 1" × 8" (25 mm × 203 mm) sheathing or less to each bearing, face nail	2-8d
22. Wider than 1" × 8" (25 mm × 203 mm) sheathing to each bearing, face nail	3-8d
23. Built-up corner studs	16d at 24" (610 mm) o.c.
24. Built-up girder and beams	20d at 32" (813 mm) o.c. at top and bottom and staggered 2-20d at ends and at each splice
25. 2" (51 mm) planks	2-16d at each bearing

26. Wood structural panels and particleboard:[2]
   Subfloor and wall sheathing (to framing):
     $1/2$" (12.7 mm) and less
     $19/32$"-$3/4$" (15 mm-19 mm)
     $7/8$"-1" (22 mm-25 mm)
     $1^1/8$"-$1^1/4$" (29 mm-32 mm)
 	
   Combination subfloor-underlayment (to framing):
     $3/4$" (19 mm) and less
     $7/8$"-1" (22 mm-25 mm)
     $1^1/8$"-$1^1/4$" (29 mm-32 mm)
	
	6d[3]
	8d[4] or 6d[5]
	8d[3]
	10d[4] or 8d[5]
	
	6d[5]
	8d[5]
	10d[4] or 8d[5]

27. Panel siding (to framing)[2]:
   $1/2$" (12.7 mm) or less
   $5/8$" (16 mm)
	
	6d[6]
	8d[6]

28. Fiberboard sheathing:[7]
   $1/2$" (12.7 mm)
 	
   $25/32$" (20 mm)
	
	No. 11 ga.[8]
	6d[4]
	No. 16 ga.[9]
	No. 11 ga.[8]
	8d[4]
	No. 16 ga.[9]

29. Interior paneling
   $1/4$" (6.4 mm)
   $3/8$" (9.5 mm)
	
	4d[10]
	6d[11]

[1]Common or box nails may be used except where otherwise stated.

[2]Nails spaced at 6 inches (152 mm) on center at edges, 12 inches (305 mm) at intermediate supports except 6 inches (152 mm) at all supports where spans are 48 inches (1219 mm) or more. For nailing of wood structural panel and particleboard diaphragms and shear walls, refer to Sections 2315.3.3 and 2315.4. Nails for wall sheathing may be common, box or casing.

[3]Common or deformed shank.

[4]Common.

[5]Deformed shank.

[6]Corrosion-resistant siding or casing nails conforming to the requirements of Section 2304.3.

[7]Fasteners spaced 3 inches (76 mm) on center at exterior edges and 6 inches (152 mm) on center at intermediate supports.

[8]Corrosion-resistant roofing nails with $7/16$-inch-diameter (11 mm) head and $1^1/2$-inch (38 mm) length for $1/2$-inch (12.7 mm) sheathing and $1^3/4$-inch (44 mm) length for $25/32$-inch (20 mm) sheathing conforming to the requirements of Section 2304.3.

[9]Corrosion-resistant staples with nominal $7/16$-inch (11 mm) crown and $1^1/8$-inch (29 mm) length for $1/2$-inch (12.7 mm) sheathing and $1^1/2$-inch (38 mm) length for $25/32$-inch (20 mm) sheathing conforming to the requirements of Section 2304.3.

[10]Panel supports at 16 inches (406 mm) [20 inches (508 mm) if strength axis in the long direction of the panel, unless otherwise marked]. Casing or finish nails spaced 6 inches (152 mm) on panel edges, 12 inches (305 mm) at intermediate supports.

[11]Panel supports at 24 inches (610 mm). Casing or finish nails spaced 6 inches (152 mm) on panel edges, 12 inches (305 mm) at intermediate supports.

From the Uniform Building Code, ©1997, ICBO

Figure 11-14 *Nailing schedule*

Figure 11-15 *Typical truss installation*

required penetration. Edge distances may not be less than one-half the required penetration. If you have to bore holes for nails to prevent splitting, make the hole smaller in diameter than the nail you'll use.

Staples

Staples are popular with many tradesmen because they make the work easier and save time. Staples and staplers can be very effective. When there's a problem, it's usually the fault of the operator. No matter how well a tool is designed and built, there's always someone who can foul it up.

Staples are an acceptable replacement for nails in most cases, if the end result is as strong as nailing. But it won't be unless you use the right staple for the particular job at hand. You wouldn't staple down a roof with an ordinary office stapler. Well, using the wrong staple, even in the right gun, can have the same effect. And once the job is finished and the paint is on, it's hard to tell the difference. But the owner will know the difference after the first storm.

Trusses

Manufactured roof trusses are assembled at the factory with metal connectors or gussets instead of nails. They're made of galvanized metal, engineered for a particular application with specific loadings. The strength of the truss depends on both the size and grade of the timber and the size of the connector and the number of spikes it has. Figure 11-15 shows a typical truss installation. Notice the piping for automatic sprinklers.

One problem with these trusses is that some manufacturers don't follow the engineered design. They may cheat on the material grades or on the size of the metal connectors. It's a good idea to get your hands on the engineer's specs and make sure the manufacturer is following them. If he isn't, return the trusses.

True, this may delay your job. But if you use faulty materials and the inspector finds out, it can cost you a lot more than just a short delay. I suggest you use the inspector's Product Evaluation Reports to check the various types and manufacturers.

The 1997 edition contains a number of additional requirements for Seismic Zone 2, 3 and 4, as well as areas of high wind impact. If you're planning to build light frame structures in those seismic zones or if the basic wind speed in your area exceeds 80 miles per hour, the plans may have to be approved by an engineer. Check with your building official.

Hidden away at the very end of Chapter 23 in the UBC is a requirement that's easy to overlook. Turn to Section 2320.13 if you're framing exterior stairs or a balcony in a seismic zone:

Exit Facilities. *In Seismic Zones 3 and 4, exterior exit balconies, stairs and similar exit facilities shall be positively anchored to the primary structure at not over 8 feet (2438 mm) on center or shall be designed for lateral forces. Such attachment shall not be accomplished by use of toenails or nails subject to withdrawal.*

The Traveling Solid Core Door

I suppose there are more ways to fool building inspectors than there are building inspectors to fool. I've learned to never underestimate the ingenuity of an entrepreneur who's determined to save a buck, even if it costs two dollars to do it. Here's a case in point.

Once I issued permits to a local contractor for three single-family residences on three adjoining lots. His practice was to begin one home, get it well along, then start with the next. Most of the time during construction he had three houses at different stages of completion. As he finished each part of the job, he called for the usual inspections.

On the final inspection for the first house, I entered the residence through the door that separated the garage from the entry to the kitchen. The code says any door separating a garage from living space has to be solid core, and for good reason. A solid core door is designed to take heavy use and abuse. It's much more likely to keep garage

fumes out of the living area for the life of the home. Spending an extra $20 on a solid core door is worth the money.

As I came in, I gave the door a couple of raps with my knuckles. The dull thud told me it was solid core, just like the code required. Later I made the same final inspection on each of the other houses. Eventually all three houses passed inspection and were sold.

Several years later the FHA foreclosed on the second of those three houses. They called me in to certify code compliance so the house could be sold under an FHA program. That probably wasn't necessary. After all, I had inspected those houses myself only a few years earlier. Anyhow, I checked the plumbing, made sure kitchen and bath fans exhausted to the outside, counted the foundation vents — all the usual stuff. Everything checked out.

I started back into the house to write up my report for the FHA. As I went through the opening between the garage and the kitchen, I gave the door a rap with my knuckles. It sounded hollow, not solid. Funny, why would anyone remove a solid core door and replace it with a hollow core door? While I was mulling this over, I got another thought.

I went over to the first of the three houses, introduced myself, and asked to check the kitchen door. Sure enough, it was hollow core too. So I went down to the third house in the line and checked the same door. This door was a solid core door. Then it dawned on me — I had inspected the same door when I'd made the final inspection on all three houses.

12

Exits and Clearances

This chapter is about something we all take for granted — getting in and out of buildings. Obviously, having the right kind of door where and when you need it can be very important. In a fire, exiting can be a life or death matter. That's why the code is so particular about doorways and clearances.

I once plan-checked a building that had a room with no door at all. Perfect! Nobody could get in the room so nobody could get trapped inside. I can guess how an oversight like that happened. The owner decided that the original door wasn't in the right place. The draftsman rubbed the door off the plan and was interrupted before drawing the new door. He never got back to it, and the reviewer never caught the mistake. But I did.

What Are Exits?

Every room in every building needs a way in and out, so let's take a closer look at exiting. The 1997 UBC now uses the term "means of egress" to define exiting. Chapter 10 in the UBC covers exiting — including the definition of *means of egress.*

Means of egress is an exit system that provides a continuous, unobstructed and undiminished path of exit travel from any occupied point in a building or structure to a public way.

Aisles, doors, hallways, ramps, stairways, corridors, stair towers, exit passageways, horizontal exits, yards, exit courts and gates are components that can be considered portions of the exit system. Elevators or escalators can't be used as a required exit.

Exit Court is a yard or court providing access to a public way for one or more required exits.

Horizontal Exit is a wall that completely divides a floor of a building into two or more separate exit-access areas to afford safety from fire and smoke in the exit-access area of incident origin.

Exit passageways are similar to hallways and corridors, but they're built to a higher level of fire resistance. They shouldn't be used for any purpose other than as a means of egress.

In other words, a means of egress is all the ways out of a building. But there's more to it than that. The inspector and the fire marshal need to know how many people can get out quickly from any given point. And there's more to this access business than meets the eye. For example, you could have a hangar with a door 40 feet wide, but if one person can't easily get out of the building in an emergency, then you don't have adequate exits.

If a new motion picture theater has been built in your community in the last ten years, it's probably a multitheater complex with several auditoriums showing several movies at the same time. The 1997 code sets special requirements for what it defines as multitheaters. It's defined this way in Section 1002:

> ***Multitheater Complex*** *is a building or portion thereof containing two or more motion picture auditoriums that are served by a common lobby.*

Exit Standards Promote Safety

The definitions of means of egress imply that eventually, all exits lead outdoors and to safety. To be more precise, when you leave a building through an exit system, it will eventually lead to a *public way*. What's a public way? The code defines it this way:

> ***Public Way*** *is any street, alley or similar parcel of land essentially unobstructed from the ground to the sky which is deeded, dedicated or otherwise permanently appropriated to the public for public use and having a clear width of not less than 10 feet (3048 mm).*

To determine the size and number of exits for a building, you must know how many people will normally occupy a given space. In Chapter 3 we learned how to determine the occupant load. For this you must use UBC Table 10-A, *Minimum Egress Requirements* (Figure 3-1 in Chapter 3).

The issue of occupant load is at the root of many arguments over the building code. The owner of a store may try to bargain with the inspector, saying, "You know I probably won't have that many customers in my store on even the busiest day. Why can't we figure it on what I think I'll have?"

There's only one good answer to that question: "Because it says so in The Book!" After all, codes are written to establish safe building standards. Of course, there'll always be those who question these standards. Usually they'll complain that the standards are too strict. But often the regulations are too generous. Most were designed to set minimum standards, leaving the inspector some room for interpretation. That's certainly true of occupant loads.

To find the occupant load permitted in any building or part of a building, divide the floor area by the square feet per occupant required in UBC Table 10-A. If the table doesn't cover a particular occupancy, the building official will decide, based on the occupancy it most nearly resembles. And that can lead to legitimate arguments.

You can increase the occupant load by providing extra exits. But most inspectors are skeptics. You'll need an approved aisle or seating diagram to prove your point.

Determining Occupant Load for Exits

In determining the occupant load, the code assumes that all areas of a building will be occupied at the same time. That means that if you have a building of mixed occupancy with most of the occupants using the same exits, the building must be calculated as though each occupancy was used to the maximum all the time. But that doesn't mean that the most restrictive provisions apply to the entire building. Each separate occupancy is rated on its

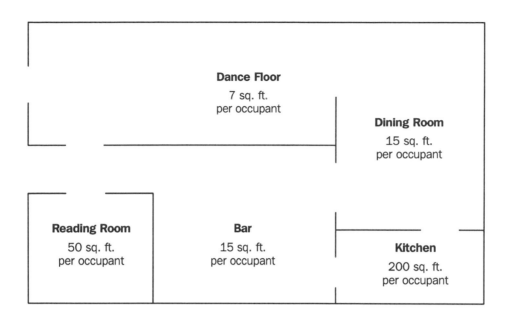

Figure 12-1 *Sketch of lodge*

own usage. But it's assumed that all areas are used simultaneously. Let's look at an example.

Remember the lodge building we discussed back in Chapter 3? It had a dance floor, dining room, reading room, bar and kitchen. We used the figure of 7 square feet per occupant for the dance floor and 15 square feet per occupant for the dining room and the bar. The reading room needed 50 square feet per occupant and the kitchen a whopping 200 square feet per occupant. Let's look at that lodge building again. You'll find it in Figure 12-1.

We decided, back in Chapter 3, that the lodge building could be 9,000 square feet and accommodate 664 people. But the lodge only meets once a week. The dining room is open only from 3 p.m. to midnight and the reading room from 10 a.m. until 5 p.m. They hold a dance once a week.

Do they need an exit designed to handle the whole crowd of 664? Or could they get by with exits to handle the crowd they actually expect to be in the building at any one time? You guessed it. Under the code, exits have to be designed to handle all 664 people.

Overloading an Occupancy

There's one more situation to consider. We originally designed the bar to hold 100 people. But during an intermission at the dance, there might be more than 100 people in there. If the owner hadn't thought of it, the builder should suggest a way to deal with this overflow.

Section 1007.2.6 warns that any room used for an assembly purpose that doesn't have fixed seats must have the capacity of the room posted in a conspicuous place. It must be an approved sign that indicates the number of occupants permitted for each room use, posted near the main exit or exit-access door from the room. The building owner or manager must enforce the maximum capacity. If he doesn't, the fire marshal has the authority to shut them down until the crowd thins out.

If you think this might present an enforcement problem, talk to the fire marshal. Try to work out a better ratio between the bar and the dance floor. This usually isn't a big problem because most dance floors are located in or next to the bar.

Establishing Exit Size

The first point to make here is that every building or usable portion of a building must have at least one exit. There's a column in UBC Table 10-A headed *Minimum of Two Means of Egress Are Required Where Number of Occupants Is At Least . . . .* Suppose your dance floor is 900 square feet. Table 10-A requires 7 square feet per occupant. Divide 900 by 7 to find an occupant load of 128. The table also shows that we need at least two exits. But we still haven't established how big they'll be.

Exit width is discussed in Section 1003.2.3.2 of the UBC:

Minimum width. The width, in inches (mm), of any component in the means of egress system shall not be less than the product determined by multiplying the total occupant load served by such component by the applicable factor set forth in Table 10-B. In no case shall the width of an individual means of egress component be less than the minimum required for such component as specified elsewhere in this chapter.

Where more than one exit or exit-access doorway serves a building or portion thereof, such calculated width may be divided approximately equally among the means of egress components serving as exits or exit-access doorways for that area.

Looks easy, doesn't it? Seems like you'll need only 3 feet of exit width. But the book says you must have two exits. What happens now? Do you put in two 18-inch doors? Of course not. Section 1003.3.1.3 states that every required exit doorway must allow the installation of a door at least 3 feet wide. In other words, what you thought was going to be 3 feet of exit has now become 6 feet.

Not only is there a minimum size for a door, there's also a maximum size. No leaf of an exit door may be more than 4 feet wide. In other words, if you have a double door, the width of the opening would have to be at least 6 feet and not more than 8 feet. Here's another way to

look at it. If you need 5 feet of exit width, you'll have to install two 3-foot doors, because no door may be 5 feet wide.

All exit doors must be clearly marked. We don't want strangers in the building winding up in a broom closet in an emergency. And the hardware for these doors must be designed so that it doesn't require any unusual skill or strength to open the door.

Establishing Exit Position

So you'll need two 3-foot doors where you originally thought that 3 feet of total doorway area would be enough. Why not just put in a double door? Because if you do, you'll have the inspector breathing down your neck. The code says that if two or more doors are required, they must be positioned apart from each other. Here's a quote from Section 1004.2.4:

Separation of exits or exit-access doorways. Where two or more exits or exit-access doorways are required from any level or portion of the building, at least two of the exits or exit-access doorways shall be placed a distance apart equal to not less than one half of the length of the maximum overall diagonal dimension of the area served measured in a straight line between the center of such exits or exit-access doorways. Additional exits or exit-access doorways shall be arranged a reasonable distance apart so that if one becomes blocked, the others will be available.

Exception: The separation distance determined in accordance with this section may be measured along a direct path of exit travel within a corridor serving exit enclosures. The walls of any such exit enclosure shall not be less than 30 feet (9144 mm), measured in a straight line, from the walls of another exit enclosure.

Let's look at a sketch of a dance floor (Figure 12-2). It's 30 feet wide by 30 feet long, or 900 square feet. The longest diagonal measurement of this square dance floor will be

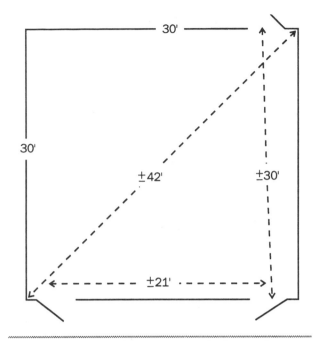

Figure 12-2 *Placing exits on dance floor*

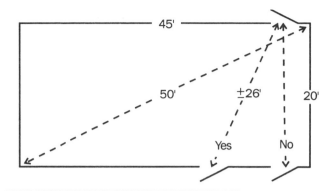

Figure 12-3 *Exits on long narrow buildings*

about 42 feet. To find this, find the square of the length of the two sides, add them, then find the square root of the total.

The doors must be separated by half the diagonal, or 21 feet. That means you could put both exits on one wall, as shown in Figure 12-2. But wouldn't it be better to have a door at the front and one at the rear? Yes — if both would have access to a public way. In fact, I highly recommend it.

Check the code first, though. Is it allowed? The code only specifies the distance. So one door at the front and one at the rear would conform to the code because they would be at least 30 feet apart. Our minimum separation was 21 feet.

What If the Building Isn't Square?

Suppose your building is 20 feet wide by 45 feet long, as shown in Figure 12-3. It's still 900 square feet. Could you put two doors directly opposite each other on the long sides? Probably not. Because the building has different dimensions, we have to recalculate the diagonal.

Take the new length and width and do some squaring. Twenty squared is 400; 45 squared is 2025. Together they add up to 2425. The square root of 2425 is almost 50 feet. Remember, we have to use at least one-half of that distance as a minimum distance between two exits. So our two exits would have to be at least 25 feet apart. Figure 12-3 shows one possible arrangement of exits. Or you could put them at each end of the building.

What About Three Exits?

If you were to put three exits in that building, you could have two exits directly opposite or even on the same wall at opposite corners. If three or more exits are required, at least two have to conform to the diagonal formula. The third may be a reasonable distance away, so that if one is blocked, the others will be available. If the building doesn't have sprinklers, no part of it may be more than 200 feet from an exterior exit door, a horizontal exit, an exit passageway, or an enclosed stairway. This distance can be measured along a direct line to the exit. Even if you have to go around objects such as desks, files, bookcases, or any movable or temporary fixtures, the 150 feet can be a direct measurement.

On the other hand, if your building has sprinklers (and I hope it has), this distance may be increased to 250 feet.

Exits may lead into adjoining or intervening rooms or areas if they're easily accessible and

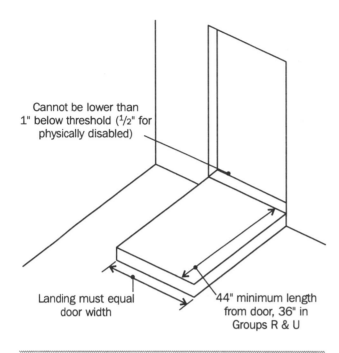

Cannot be lower than
1" below threshold (¹/₂" for
physically disabled)

Landing must equal
door width

44" minimum length
from door, 36" in
Groups R & U

Figure 12-4 *Approved landing*

provide a direct route to an outside exit. Exits cannot pass through kitchens, storerooms, rest rooms, closets, or spaces used for similar purposes.

Landings Required

Most exit requirements are based on an occupancy of ten or more. But notice the difference between occupancy and occupant load. Landings are required, regardless of occupant load.

Floor level at doors. *Regardless of the occupant load served, there shall be a floor or landing on each side of a door. Where access for persons with disabilities is required by Chapter 11, the floor or landing shall not be more than ¹/₂ inch (12.7 mm) lower than the threshold of the doorway. Where such access is not required, the threshold shall not exceed 1 inch (25 mm). Landings shall be level except that exterior landings may have a slope not to*

exceed ¹/₄ unit vertical in 12 units horizontal (2% slope).

Section 1003.3.1.7 says that landings must be at least as wide as the stairway or door, and that the door can't reduce that dimension by more than 7 inches when it's fully opened. If you have an occupant load of 50 or more, then doors in any position can't reduce the width of the landing more than 50 percent. The landing length in the direction of travel must be at least 44 inches. But before you panic, there is an exception:

Exception: *In Group R, Division 3, and Group U Occupancies and within individual units of Group R, Division 1 Occupancies, such length need not exceed 36 inches (914 mm).*

Figure 12-4 shows an approved landing. The code lists four exceptions that cover private residences. A stair opening is excepted if the door doesn't swing over the top step or open over a landing that is more than 8 inches lower than the floor level. Other landings in homes need not be wider than the door. Screen or storm doors don't require a landing.

Requirements for Exterior Exit Doors

The code has some rigid requirements for exit doors. It says you normally can't use revolving, sliding and overhead doors as a required exit, even though you see them all over town. You've probably seen pneumatically-operated doors, overhead doors and various forms of sliding doors. But take a good look at those sliding and pneumatically-operated doors. You'll find a little note, probably in one of the upper corners, that says something like: "In case of emergency, push on door panel."

That means that in case of a power outage or equipment failure, the door panel will either push out or swivel out so that people inside can get out. Occasionally you'll run across an older model that doesn't operate this way.

Doors like that met the regulations in force at the time, and were grandfathered in when the code changed. If they're ever replaced, it must be with the newer style doors with warnings and armor plate glass.

Rolling Overhead Doors

You've probably been to a modern shopping mall where the shops are secured at night by overhead rolling doors or sliding doors. They're legal because they're not used during the day when the business is open. They're only closed at night for security reasons. Figure 12-5 shows a rolling overhead door typical of what you find at shopping malls.

But what about power-operated doors? Here's what Section 1003.3.1.2 says:

Special doors. *Revolving, sliding and overhead doors serving an occupant load of 10 or more shall not be used as required exit doors.*

Exceptions: 1. Approved revolving doors having leaves that will collapse under opposing pressures may be used, provided:

1.1 Such doors have a minimum width of 6 feet 6 inches (1981 mm).

1.2 At least one conforming exit door is located adjacent to each revolving door.

1.3 The revolving door shall not be considered to provide any required width when computing means of egress width in accordance with Section 1003.2.3.

2. Horizontal sliding doors complying with UBC Standard 7-8 may be used:

2.1 In elevator lobby separations.

2.2 In other than Groups A and H Occupancies, where smoke barriers are required.

2.3 In other than group H Occupancies, where serving an occupant load of less than 50.

Figure 12-5 *Rolling overhead door*

Power-operated doors complying with UBC Standard 10-1 may be used for egress purposes. Such doors, where swinging, shall have two guide rails installed on the swing side projecting out from the face of the door jambs for a distance not less than the widest door leaf. Guide rails shall be not less than 30 inches (762 mm) in height with solid or mesh panels to prevent penetration into door swing and shall be capable of resisting a horizontal load at top of rail of not less than 50 pounds per lineal foot (730 N/m).

The guide rails are designed to keep people from walking into swinging doors.

Exit Enclosures

When does an exit have to be enclosed? Section 1005.3.3.1 says you don't have to enclose interior stairways, ramps, or escalators that serve only one adjacent floor and aren't connected with corridors or stairways serving other floors except in Group H and I occupancies.

An exit enclosure, which is a fire-safe exit way, usually means an emergency exit. Though they may never be needed for an emergency, they must be ready. That's the reason for the strict requirements. Consequently, you can't have any openings into exit enclosures, except for exit doorways and at landings and parts of floors connecting stairway flights. Also there must be a continuation of the enclosure on the ground floor leading outside from the stairway. All exit doors must be either one-hour or 90-minute fire protection assemblies with self-closing or automatic closing devices.

Pressurized Enclosures

If a floor is more than 75 feet above the highest grade, all of the required exits must be pressurized enclosures. They must have a vestibule at least 44 inches by 72 inches. Both the vestibule and the adjacent stairway must be enclosed by walls that are fire-resistive for at least two hours. The ceiling of the vestibule serves as a smoke and heat trap.

The pressurized enclosure must have mechanical ventilation to create required pressure differences. Emergency lights are also required.

know when these lamps are going to burn out. It's unlikely both will burn out at the same time.

There used to be a lot of arguing about whether exit signs should be red or green. Some said that red would be easy to spot. Others pointed out that in a dark, smoked-filled room, fire fighters had occasionally wasted time and water on a red glow that turned out to be an exit sign. Both sides must have compromised because the code doesn't specify which color to use. It can be any color if it's in high contrast with its background.

The code does say, however, that all graphics, whether arrows, letters, or other symbols, must be high contrast and letters must be at least 6 inches high with a stroke not less than ¾ inch wide.

Certain high-density occupancies are required to have two separate power sources for the exit lights and signs. These are sources, not circuits. The second source is usually a battery system. If the emergency and sign lighting are on a separate circuit, they can be attached to a generator.

Exit Lights and Signs

For occupancies other than Group R-3, you've got to provide exit lights and signs. Any time the building is occupied, the exits must be illuminated by at least one foot-candle of light at floor level. For some areas of a building, the light must have separate power sources so the exits will be lit in an emergency.

Any room or area requiring two or more exits shall be provided with exit signs. They must also have exit signs at each doorway and anywhere the direction of the exit may be in question. The lettering has to be at least 6 inches high.

When exit signs are provided, they must always be illuminated. Illuminated signs must have at least two 15-watt lamps. Why two lamps? It's a safety precaution. You never

Hallways and Corridors

A hallway or corridor in a public building, according to Sections 1004.3.3.2 and 1004.3.4.2, must be at least 44 inches wide and must be unobstructed. In private residences, or for occupant loads of 49 or less, 36 inches is the minimum width. There are a few special conditions relating to trim, handrails, and some forms of hardware. Nonstructural trim and similar decorative features can't reduce the width more than 1½ inches on each side.

Doors opening into corridors may not reduce the required width of the corridor by more than 7 inches when fully opened. Doors in any position may not obstruct more than half of the corridor. That means that if you have a 3-foot-wide door and a 44-inch-wide hallway, you'll either have to reverse the swing

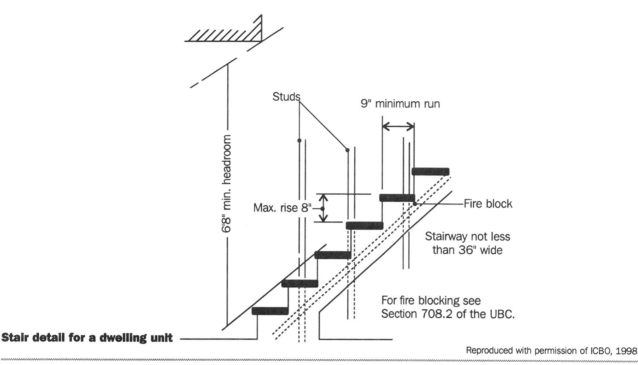

Studs

9" minimum run

6'8" min. headroom

Max. rise 8"

Fire block

Stairway not less
than 36" wide

For fire blocking see
Section 708.2 of the UBC.

Stair detail for a dwelling unit

Reproduced with permission of ICBO, 1998

Figure 12-6 *ICBO's stair detail for a private residence*

of your door, or the doorway itself will have to be inset into the room.

If you decide to reverse the swing of your door, check your occupant load. Remember? Occupant loads over 50 require that the door swing in the direction of exit travel.

Partitions, rails, counters and similar space dividers that aren't over 5'9" don't form corridors. And here's one final word about hallways and corridors: A dead-end corridor may not be more than 20 feet long.

Stairways and Ramps

The rise of each step must not be less than 4 inches or more than 7 inches. The tread can't be less than 11 inches deep. There are, of course, exceptions. Stairs or ladders used only for equipment are exempt. Stairs in private residences have a whole new set of rules — the maximum rise is 8 inches and the minimum tread only 9 inches.

Stairs, generally, may not rise more than 12 feet without a landing at least as wide as the stairs. But the run of the landing doesn't have to be more than 44 inches, unless the stairway is not a straight run. You need a minimum of 6'8" of headroom between a line drawn over the nose of the treads and any ceiling or projection in the ceiling above. This is shown in Figure 12-6.

Stairways serving an occupant load of up to 50 must be at least 36 inches wide. If the occupant load is greater than 50, you must go to a 44-inch stairway.

Section 1003.3.3.13 requires that all stairways in buildings four or more stories in height have stairway identification signs at each floor stating the floor number, whether there is roof access, and the upper and lower terminus of the stairway. The sign must be readily visible and approximately 5 feet above the landing.

Figure 12-7 *Ramp providing access for the disabled*

Spiral and Circular Stairs

There are two differences between a spiral and a circular stairway: the radius, and where you can use them. You can use a circular stairway as a public stairway if the minimum width of the run is at least 10 inches and the smallest radius is not less than twice the width of the stair. For example, if you had a 5-foot-wide circular stairway in a commercial building, it couldn't curve any faster than it would take to circle a 10-foot column or circular space.

The spiral stairway, on the other hand, may only be used in Group R, Division 1 and 3 occupancies. The run must be least 7½ inches at a point 12 inches from the side of the stairs where the tread is narrowest. The rise can't exceed 9½ inches, and you need at least 6'6" headroom.

Spiral stairs are used in many homes and for access to mechanical rooms (rooms where heating and air conditioning equipment is located). But you can't use them for a public exit.

That's the code's stair requirements in a nutshell. There's just one more thing. On public stairs the floor number, the terminus of the top and bottom levels, and the identification of the stairs must appear at each floor in buildings over four stories high.

Understair Space

If the stairs in your building go down to the basement or any area below grade level, you need an approved barrier at grade level. That's to prevent anyone from accidentally winding up in the basement during an emergency. Also, any usable space under the stairways in an exit enclosure must be open and unused. That's to prevent the storage of anything under the stairs that could cause a fire and block the exit.

But what about closets under the stairs in private homes? Are they legal? Yes, provided the enclosed space is of fire-rated construction.

Get to know Chapter 10 of the UBC. Many of the items I've discussed are exempt in Group R and U occupancies. So go ahead and store your Christmas ornaments under the stairs at home. But don't do it in your office!

Ramps

You have to build a ramp for any change in elevation in an exit path if the change is less than 12 inches vertically. The width and clearance requirements for corridors also apply to ramps. These requirements are discussed in Section 1003.3.4 of the code and Chapter 19 in this book.

Figure 12-7 shows a typical ramp. The slope of the ramp must not exceed 1 vertical inch to 12 horizontal inches. Ramps that aren't specifically for the disabled can have a slightly steeper slope, 1 inch vertically to 8 inches horizontally.

If your ramp exceeds 1 vertical to 20 horizontal, you must install a handrail. Also, the surface must be roughened or covered with a non-slip material.

Aisles and Aisleways

Aisles between furniture, equipment, merchandise, or other obstructions must be at least 3 feet wide if they serve one side of the aisle, or 3⅔ feet wide if they serve both sides. Regardless of the width of the aisle, the distance to the nearest exit can't be more than 200 feet. If the building has fire sprinklers, you can increase the travel distance to 250 feet.

Aisles and aisleways are fairly well covered in Section 1004.3.2 of the 1997 Edition. Except for some rearranging of requirements, they are pretty well condensed into the following items:

1) The clear width of aisles must be based on the number of occupants within the seated areas.

2) Clear width of aisles in inches shall be the occupant load served by the aisles times 0.3 for aisles with steps or stairways.

3) Clear width in inches where slopes are less than 1 vertical to 8 horizontal is occupant load times 0.2.

4) If you have fixed seats, the aisle width is 42 inches for leveled or ramped aisles (48 inches for steps or stairways) serving both sides and 36 inches serving seating on one side only.

5) Aisles must terminate at a cross aisle, foyer, doorway or vomitory.

6) The slope of ramped aisles can't be more than 1 vertical to 8 horizontal and must have a slip-resistant surface.

What the above means is *be careful*. Suppose you had an auditorium that seated 250 people. That could require an aisle of 75 inches. If you only had one aisle then, it would have to be 75 inches wide, not 42 inches as shown in Item 4 above. If you had two aisles, then they must each be 42 inches or a total of 84 inches and not the 75 inches indicated above. Sometimes requirements can be tricky.

The formula previously used to determine the width of cross aisles has been removed from the code. To find that number now requires a great deal of searching in the following sections: Sect. 1004.3.2, Sect. 1008.5.4, Sect. 1008.5.5 and Tables 10-C and 10-E.

Let's assume that you have an auditorium seating 500 people. Sect. 1004.3.2.3 says we'll need a total of 100 inches of exit aisle width which must be divided as follows: aisles serving only one side must be at least 36 inches wide and aisles serving both sides are a minimum of 42 inches.

Table 10-C states that you multiply 500 by 0.220 to get an exit dimension of 110 inches, minimum. If you had side aisles, you would deduct 72 inches (2 x 36) from your required minimum of 110 inches. That would leave you 38 inches for a center aisle — and that isn't enough. Your center aisle needs to be 42 inches. But wait a minute. Can you do it with only one center aisle? That depends on your seating arrangement. You see, Table 10-E says you can only have 14 seats between aisles. You may have to put in another aisle.

Fixed Seating

For rooms with fixed seating, such as auditoriums and theaters, it's pretty easy to determine occupancy loads. Just count the seats. For benches or pews, you're allowed one person for each 18 inches of bench or pew. For booths in dining arcas, you can figure one person for each 24 inches of the length of the booth.

Here's what the code says about seating in Section 1004.3.2.3.2:

Seat spacing. Where seating rows have 14 or less seats, the minimum clear width of aisle accessways shall not be less than 12 inches (305 mm) measured as the clear horizontal distance from the back of the row or guardrail ahead and the nearest projection of the row behind. Where seats are automatic or self-rising, measurement may be made with the seats in the raised position. Where seats are not automatic or self-rising, the minimum clear width shall be measured with the seat in the down position.

That's pretty clear. If the seats rise automatically, like theater seats, measure with the seats up. If they're not automatic, measure with the seat down.

This whole section on fixed seating applies only to seats inside a building. Outdoor grandstands and bleachers are a whole new ball game.

Grandstands and Bleachers

Let's begin with the code definitions of bleachers and grandstands. The definitions are found in Section 1008.2:

Bleachers *are tiered or stepped seating facilities without backrests.*

Grandstands *are tiered or stepped seating facilities.*

Figure 12-8 shows typical outdoor seating. The code considers bleachers temporary if they won't be used in one location for more than 90 days. But most rules for outdoor seating are the same whether the grandstands or bleachers are temporary or permanent.

Exit requirements are based on the number of occupants, which is based on the number of seats. For chairs, just count the chair backs,

For benches, assume each person will occupy 18 inches of bench.

Stairs and ramps must conform to Sections 1008.5.6 and 1008.5.7. Many of the regulations on aisles are the same as for interior auditoriums. You need guardrails on all portions of elevated seating more than 30 inches above grade. The guardrails must be at least 42 inches high. You also need a 4-inch-high barrier below the guardrail on the edge of all walking platforms. Cross aisles and vomitories must be at least 54 inches wide and terminate at an exit or exterior perimeter ramp.

Row Spacing

The spacing for rows of outdoor seating differs from that of indoor seating. Section 1008.5.1 covers the subject. You need clear space of 12 inches or more between the front of the seat and the back or backrest of the seat in front of it. And measuring from back to back, the minimum distances are:

- 22 inches for seats without backrests
- 30 inches for seats with backrests
- 33 inches for chair seating

Figure 12-8 *Grandstands and bleachers*

Who'll Cast the First Stone?

In 1972 I bought a house that had been built in 1955. The last few years hadn't been kind to it. Part of my deal with the VA was that I would "earn" part of my down payment. I agreed to paint the house inside and out and reroof it. My real estate agent furnished the shingles and I went to work on it. My wife and the youngest of my eight kids did most of the painting. I led the roofing crew (my oldest kids).

Believe it or not, I'd never laid T-lock asphalt shingles before. When one of my kids asked a question I couldn't answer, I went looking for the product information slip that has to be included in every package of roofing. Boy, was I in for a surprise.

The code makes it clear: all roofing must come with the name of the manufacturer, the type of roofing, fire rating, and weight per square, among other things. The slips I found had none of this information. Nothing was printed on the cartons either. So there I was, roof half done with non-code materials. And I was the building inspector! You know what I'd have to do if I caught a roofer doing that.

I traced the roofing supplier through the real estate agent. He couldn't remember who his dealer was but insisted the manufacturer was a reputable firm. It's just that he couldn't remember the name. I found more of the material in his yard and advised him to get rid of it. But not in my town, because if I found any on a job, I'd make him pick it up.

I shouldn't have, but I finished my roof with the materials we had. As it turned out, the T-locks must have been OK. I still own the house and we haven't seen a leak yet. I'll say this, though. The experience makes me feel a little more humble when I see non-code materials on a job. It can happen to anyone, even the building inspector!

13

Keeping Your Building Warm and Dry

So far we've covered foundations, walls, exits and occupancies — which gives us a box without a lid. Before we go much farther, we need a roof.

Roof Construction

Chapter 15 of the UBC deals with roof construction and covering. The chapter was revised in the 1988 edition to reflect new materials, standards and methods of installation. Related areas are covered in other chapters: skylights (Chapter 24), penthouses (Section 1511 of Chapter 15), use of plastics (Chapter 26) and solar energy collectors (Section 2603.14 and Chapter 13).

Section 1501.1 says:

General. *Roofing assemblies, roof coverings and roof structures shall be as specified in this code and as otherwise required by this chapter.*

Subject to the requirements of this chapter, combustible roofing and roof insulation may be used in any type of construction.

The first part of that sounds pretty simple, but watch out for that second paragraph. It can be misleading. Remember, Chapter 6 of the UBC states that an entire building will be reduced to a lower grade if even one part of the building doesn't meet requirements of a higher grade. So if your building type calls for a one-hour fire resistiveness, your roof assembly must be one-hour rated. If you use a combustible deck or a nonrated roofing, your building could be reduced to a lower type classification. That could be an expensive mistake.

Each package of roofing material must be labeled to show the type of material and the name and address of the manufacturer. This applies to all shakes, shingles, or manufactured roofing. The label should also include the grade, and in the case of manufactured roofing, the weight per roofing square.

Definitions

I won't quote all the definitions here — just the key ones you'll need most often:

Base Ply *is one layer of felt secured to the deck over which a built-up roof is applied.*

Base Sheet *is a product used as the base ply in a built-up roofing membrane.*

Built-up Roofing *is two or more layers of felt cemented together and surfaced with a cap sheet, mineral aggregate, smooth coating or similar surfacing material.*

Built-up Roofing Ply *is a layer of felt in built-up roofing.*

Cap Sheet *is roof covering made of organic or inorganic fibers, saturated and coated on both sides with a bituminous compound, surfaced with mineral granules, mica, talc, ilmenite, inorganic fibers or similar material.*

Wood Shakes and Shingles, Fire-retardant (treated), *are wood shakes and shingles complying with UBC Standard 15-3 or 15-4 impregnated by the full-cell vacuum-pressure process with fire-retardant chemicals, complying with UBC Standard 15-2 for use on Class A, B or C roofs.*

Modified Bitumen Membrane Roof Covering *is one or more layers of polymer modified asphalt sheet membranes complying with UBC Standard 15-6. The sheet materials may be fully adhered or mechanically attached to the substrate, or held in place with an appropriate ballast layer.*

Thermoplastic Membrane Roof Covering *is a sheet membrane composed of polymers and other proprietary ingredients, in compliance with UBC Standard 15-6, whose chemical composition allows the sheet to be welded together by either heat or solvent throughout its service life.*

Thermoset Membrane Roof Covering *is a sheet membrane composed of polymers and other proprietary ingredients, in compliance with UBC Standard 15-6, whose*

chemical composition vulcanizes or cross-links during manufacturing or during its service life.

Vapor Retarder *is a layer of material or a laminate used to appreciably reduce the flow of water vapor into the roofing system.*

Roof Covering Classifications

Roof coverings are broken down into three different classifications to fit different types of construction. There's no longer any "ordinary" roofing. Look at Table 15-A (Figure 13-1).

Then read Section 1504:

1504.1 Fire-retardant Roofing. *Fire-retardant roofs are roofing assemblies complying with UBC Standard 15-2 and listed as Class A, B or C roofs.*

1504.2 Noncombustible Roof Covering. *Noncombustible roof covering shall be one of the following:*

1. *Cement shingles or sheets.*

2. *Exposed concrete slab roof.*

3. *Ferrous or copper shingles or sheets.*

4. *Slate shingles.*

5. *Clay or concrete roofing tile.*

1504.3 Nonrated Roofing. *Nonrated roofing is approved material that is not listed as a Class A, B or C roofing assembly.*

Class B and C roof coverings are just defined as any Class B or C roofing assembly. A nonrated roof covering is a mineral aggregate surface built-up roof with a slope of not more than 3 inches in 12 inches applied according to Table 15-E. It must have at least three layers of felt and 300 pounds per roofing square of gravel or other approved material or 250 pounds per square of crushed slag. Modified bitumen, thermoplastic and thermoset membrane

TABLE 15-A—MINIMUM ROOF CLASSES

OCCUPANCY	TYPES OF CONSTRUCTION								
	I	II			III		IV	V	
	F.R.	F.R.	One-hour	N	One-hour	N	H.T.	One-hour	N
A-1	B	B	—	—	—	—	—	—	—
A) 2-2.1	B	B	B	—	B	—	B	B	—
A-3	B	B	B	B	B[1]	C	B[1]	B[1]	C
A-4	B	B	B	B	B	B	B	B	B[1]
B	B	B	B	B	B[1]	C	B[1]	B[1]	C
E	B	B	B	B	B	B	B	B	B[1]
F	B	B	B	B	B[1]	C	B[1]	B[1]	C
H-1	A	A	A	A	—	—	—	—	—
H) 2-3-4-5-6-7	A	B	B	B	B	B	B	B	B
I) 1.1-1.2-2	A	B	B	—	B	—	B	B	—
I-3	A	B	B[1]	—	B[2]	—	—	B[3]	—
M	B	B	B	B	B[1]	C	B[1]	B[1]	C
R-1	B	B	B	B	B[1,3]	C[3]	B[1,3]	B[1,3]	C[2,3]
R-3	B	B	B	B	NR	NR	NR	NR	NR
S-1, S-3	B	B	B	B	B[1]	C	B[1]	B[1]	C
S-2, S-5	B	B	B	B	B	B	B	B	B[1]
S-4	B	B	B	B	—	—	—	—	—
U	B	B	B	B	NR[4]	NR[4]	NR[4]	NR[4]	NR[4]

A—Class A roofing.
B—Class B roofing.
C—Class C roof covering.
F.R.—Fire resistive.
H.T.—Heavy timber.
N—No requirements for fire resistance.
NR—Nonrated roof coverings.

[1]Buildings that are not more than two stories in height and have not more than 6,000 square feet (557 m^2) of projected roof area and where there is a minimum of 10 feet (3048 mm) from the extremity of the roof to the property line or assumed property line on all sides except for street fronts may have Class C roof coverings that comply with UBC Standard 15-2.

[2]See Section 308.2.2.

[3]Nonrated roof coverings may be used on buildings that are not more than two stories in height and have not more than 3,000 square feet (279 m^2) of projected roof area and where there is a minimum of 10 feet (3048 mm) from the extremity of the roof to the property line on all sides except for street fronts.

[4]Unless otherwise required because of location, Group U, Division 1 roof coverings shall consist of not less than one layer of cap sheet, or built-up roofing consisting of two layers of felt and a surfacing material of 300 pounds per roofing square (14.6 kg/m^2) of gravel or other approved surfacing material, or 250 pounds (12.2 kg/m^2) of crushed slag.

From the Uniform Building Code, ©1997, ICBO

Figure 13-1 *Minimum roof classes*

assemblies that don't meet Class A, B or C requirements are also nonrated, as are wood shingles and wood shakes.

Classes of Roofing

These are fire-retardancy ratings, as set forth in the UBC Standard 15-2:

Class A *roofing assemblies are effective against severe fire test exposures. Under such exposures, roofing assemblies of this class are not readily flammable, afford a fairly high degree of fire protection to the roof deck, do not slip from position, and are not expected to produce flying brands.*

Class B *roofing assemblies are effective against moderate fire test exposures. Under such exposures, roofing assemblies of this class are not readily flammable, afford a moderate degree of fire protection to the roof deck, do not slip from position, and are not expected to produce flying brands.*

Class C roofing assemblies are effective against light fire test exposures. Under such exposures, roofing assemblies of this class are not readily flammable, afford a measurable degree of fire protection to the roof deck, do not slip from position, and are not expected to produce flying brands.

Testing Methods

These are the tests used to determine the classification of the materials:

1) Intermittent-flame test
2) Spread-of-flame test
3) Burning-brand test
4) Flying-brand test
5) Rain test
6) Weathering test

For the burning-brand and intermittent-flame tests, the material is applied to a test deck just as it would be installed on the job. The only difference is that the edges of the deck are mortared with a mixture of asbestos-gypsum and water. This keeps heated gases produced by the test from getting to both sides of the material at once. The test deck is 3⅓ feet wide by 4⅓ feet long. The roofing material used is all store-grade as defined in Standard 15.201.2, UBC Standards. The exact construction of the deck is also outlined so tests can be done the same way.

Air is directed over the sample in a prescribed direction at 12 miles per hour. For shingle roofs the deck is inclined at least 5 inches per horizontal foot; for built-up roofs the maximum slope is 5 inches per horizontal foot. The test applies a luminous gas flame over the width of the deck at the bottom edge. It must heat the sample uniformly, except for the two upper corners.

The flame develops a temperature of 1400 degrees for Class A and B roofing and 1300 degrees for Class C roofing. It's applied to the test sample for a specified time and then shut off for a specified time. This cycle is repeated throughout the test.

The spread-of-flame test is similar. The amount of combustion is measured against flame spread, production of flaming or glowing brands, and the displacement of portions of the test sample.

The last three tests are used only on treated wood shingles and shakes. Of all the tests, the weathering test takes the most time.

Marquees and Mansards

What about architectural appendages such as marquees and pseudo-mansard designs, the ones with shakes and shingles? Well, the code sections I'm describing here apply only to roofs. Even though a mansard might look like a roof, it's actually more of a decoration. Chapter 6 of the UBC allows mansards attached to the side of a building facing a street or adequate adjoining space (like a parking lot) — *if* constructed as for a projection.

How do marquees and mansards affect the fire resistance of a building? Except for the electrical wiring in a marquee, there's little in a marquee or mansard that can cause a fire. A marquee or mansard attached to a noncombustible surface wouldn't damage the rest of the building even if it burned for a considerable time.

Roof Application Methods

UBC Chapter 15 also covers the approved ways to apply the roofing materials. First, let's look at built-up roofing.

Built-up Roofing

Built-up roofing is appropriate only on flat or near-flat roofs — and flat roofs always bother me. Apparently they also bothered the code people because Section 1506.1 requires a slope of not less than ¼ inch per foot. But buildings settle in time, and materials don't always shrink evenly. That means the roof will eventually develop low spots that trap water unless the installation is first class. Let's look at the code requirements, which depend on whether the roof deck is nailable (such as wood) or non-nailable (such as metal)

On *mechanically-fastened roofs*, nail the base sheet with at least one nail for each $1^1/3$ square feet, using nails specified by the roofing material manufacturer. Then cement the following layers to the base sheets, using the specified type and amount of cementing material.

For an *adhesively-fastened roof*, you must mop the base sheet with at least 20 pounds of hot asphalt per roofing square for solid cementing, or at least 20 pounds of coal tar pitch per roofing square.

On mineral-aggregate surfaced roofs, apply at least 50 pounds of hot asphalt or other cementing material per roofing square. Then embed at least 400 pounds of gravel or 300 pounds of crushed slag. Cement cap sheets to the base sheets with the same amount of cementing material used on other layers. See Table 15-F.

Hot asphalt must be between 375 degrees and 425 degrees F. Table 15-G states that cementing material should not be heated above 25 degrees F below flash point.

Applying heat to asphalt can be like putting a match to a dynamite fuse: it's safe if it doesn't go too far. Heating the material beyond its *flash point* — the point at which it will ignite — creates a dangerous fire hazard. The flash point should be clearly printed on the label.

The inspector may require a layer of weather-resistant sheetrock between the roofing material and the sheathing. It's a good idea to check with the inspector before you begin.

What Is a Roofing Square?

Roofing materials are sold by the *square*, the quantity needed to cover 100 square feet of roof surface when laid to the manufacturer's

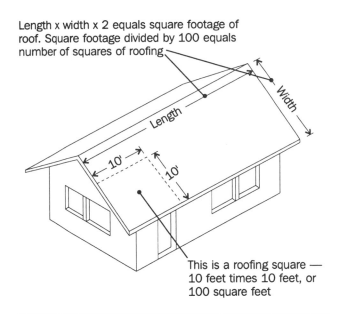

Length x width x 2 equals square footage of roof. Square footage divided by 100 equals number of squares of roofing.

Length

Width

10'

10'

This is a roofing square — 10 feet times 10 feet, or 100 square feet

Figure 13-2 *Calculating roof coverage*

specs. It usually takes three bundles of composition shingles to cover one square.

Figure 13-2 shows how to determine roof coverage. To calculate the quantity of material needed, divide the roof area by 100. This gives the number of squares required to cover the roof. If there are many ridges and valleys, as much as 15 percent more material may be required.

Applying Asphalt Shingles

Apply asphalt shingles only to solidly sheathed roofs with a slope of more than 2 inches in 12 inches in temperate climates. Use only approved self-sealing shingles as indicated in UBC Table 15-B-1 (Figure 13-3).

Fasten asphalt shingles according to the manufacturer's instructions, using at least four nails for each strip shingle 36 to 40 inches wide and two nails for each shingle 9 to 18 inches wide. You must have an underlayment of at least two layers of 15-pound felt for a roof pitch of less than 4 inches in 12 inches. For a steeper roof, you can use just one layer of 15-pound felt.

TABLE 15-B-1—ASPHALT SHINGLE APPLICATION

	ASPHALT SHINGLES	
	Not Permitted below 2 Units Vertical in 12 Units Horizontal (16.7% Slope)	
Roof Slope	**2 Units Vertical in 12 Units Horizontal (16.7% Slope) to Less than 4 Units Vertical in 12 Units Horizontal (33.3% Slope)**	**4 Units Vertical in 12 Units Horizontal (33.3% Slope) and Over**
1. Deck requirement	Asphalt shingles shall be fastened to solidly sheathed roofs. Sheathing shall conform to Sections 2312.2 and 2320.12.9.	
2. Underlayment Temperate climate	Asphalt strip shingles may be installed on slopes as low as 2 units vertical in 12 units horizontal (16.7% slope), provided the shingles are approved self-sealing or are hand sealed and are installed with an underlayment consisting of two layers of nonperforated Type 15 felt applied shingle fashion. Starting with an 18-inch-wide (457 mm) sheet and a 36-inch-wide (914 mm) sheet over it at the eaves, each subsequent sheet shall be lapped 19 inches (483 mm) horizontally.	One layer nonperforated Type 15 felt lapped 2 inches (51 mm) horizontally and 4 inches (102 mm) vertically to shed water.
Severe climate: In areas subject to wind-driven snow or roof ice buildup	Same as for temperate climate, and the two layers shall be solid cemented together with approved cementing material between the plies extending from the eave up the roof to a line 24 inches (610 mm) inside the exterior wall line of the building. As an alternative to the two layers of cemented Type 15 felt, an approved self-adhering, polymer modified, bituminous sheet may be used.	Same as for temperate climate, except that one layer No. 40 coated roofing or coated glass base shall be applied from the eaves to a line 12 inches (305 mm) inside the exterior wall line with all laps cemented together. As an alternative to the layer of No. 40 felt, a self-adhering, polymer modified, bituminous sheet may be used.
3. Attachment Combined systems, type of fasteners	Corrosion-resistant nails, minimum 12-gage $^3/_8$-inch (9.5 mm) head, or approved corrosion-resistant staples, minimum 16-gage $^{15}/_{16}$-inch (23.8 mm) crown width. Fasteners shall comply with the requirements of Chapter 23, Division III, Part III. Fasteners shall be long enough to penetrate into the sheathing $^3/_4$ inch (19 mm) or through the thickness of the sheathing, whichever is less.	
No. of fasteners[1]	4 per 36-inch to 40-inch (914 mm to 1016 mm) strip 2 per 9-inch to 18-inch (229 mm to 457 mm) shingle	
Exposure Field of roof Hips and ridges	Per manufacturer's instructions included with packages of shingles. Hip and ridge weather exposures shall not exceed those permitted for the field of the roof.	
Method	Per manufacturer's instructions included with packages of shingles.	
4. Flashing Valleys Other flashing	Per Section 1508.2 Per Section 1509	

[1]Figures shown are for normal application. For special conditions, such as mansard application and where roofs are in special wind regions, shingles shall be attached per the manufacturer's instructions.

From the Uniform Building Code, ©1997, ICBO

Figure 13-3 *Shingle application*

Applying Wood Shingles or Shakes

You can apply wood shingles on a roof with either solid sheathing or spaced sheathing. For spaced sheathing on wood roofs, the boards must be spaced on centers equal to the weather exposure and nailing pattern. In any case, the sheathing board must be at least 1 x 4 nominal dimensions. Figure 13-4 shows the technique for laying and nailing wood shingle roofs.

Wood shingles vary from 3 inches to 14 inches wide and from 16 inches to 24 inches long. UBC Table 23-II-D-1 (Figure 11-7 in Chapter 11) shows sheathing sizes and spans.

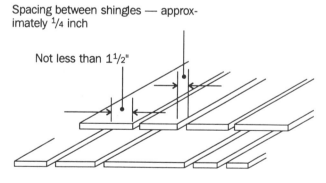

Spacing between shingles — approximately $^1/_4$ inch

Not less than $1^1/_2$"

Two nails per shingle only $^3/_4$" from edge — 1" above exposure line

Figure 13-4 *Shingle laying diagram*

TABLE 15-B-2—WOOD SHINGLE OR SHAKE APPLICATION

ROOF SLOPE	WOOD SHINGLES Not Permitted below 3 Units Vertical in 12 Units Horizontal (25% Slope) See Table 15-C	WOOD SHAKES Not Permitted below 4 Units Vertical in 12 Units Horizontal (33.3% Slope)[1] See Table 15-C
1. Deck requirement	Shingles and shakes shall be applied to roofs with solid or spaced sheathing. When spaced sheathing is used, sheathing boards shall not be less than 1 inch by 4 inches (25 mm by 102 mm) nominal dimensions and shall be spaced on centers equal to the weather exposure to coincide with the placement of fasteners. When 1-inch-by-4-inch (25 mm by 102 mm) spaced sheathing is installed at 10 inches (254 mm) on center, additional 1-inch-by-4-inch (25 mm by 102 mm) boards must be installed between the sheathing boards. Sheathing shall conform to Sections 2312.2 and 2320.12.9.	
2. Interlayment	No requirements.	One 18-inch-wide (457 mm) interlayment of Type 30 felt shingled between each course in such a manner that no felt is exposed to the weather below the shake butts and in the keyways (between the shakes).
3. Underlayment Temperate climate	No requirements.	No requirements.
Severe climate: In areas subject to wind-driven snow or roof ice buildup	Two layers of nonperforated Type 15 felt applied shingle fashion shall be installed and solid cemented together with approved cementing material between the plies extending from the eave up the roof to a line 36 inches (914 mm) inside the exterior wall line of the building.	Sheathing shall be solid and, in addition to the interlayment of felt shingled between each course in such a manner that no felt is exposed to the weather below the shake butts, the shakes shall be applied over a layer of nonperforated Type 15 felt applied shingle fashion. Two layers of nonperforated Type 15 felt applied shingle fashion shall be installed and solid cemented together with approved cementing material between the plies extending from the eave up the roof to a line 36 inches (914 mm) inside the exterior wall line of the building.
4. Attachment Type of fasteners	Corrosion-resistant nails, minimum No. $14^1/2$-gage, $^7/_{32}$-inch (5.6 mm) head, or corrosion-resistant staples, when approved by the building official.	Corrosion-resistant nails, minimum No. 13-gage, $^7/_{32}$-inch (5.6 mm) head, or corrosion-resistant staples, when approved by the building official.
	Fasteners shall comply with the requirements of Chapter 23, Division III, Part III. Fasteners shall be long enough to penetrate into the sheathing $^3/_4$ inch (19 mm) or through the thickness of the sheathing, whichever is less.	
No. of fasteners	2 per shingle	2 per shake
Exposure Field of roof Hips and ridges	Weather exposures shall not exceed those set forth in Table 15-C. Hip and ridge weather exposure shall not exceed those permitted for the field of the roof.	
Method	Shingles shall be laid with a side lap of not less than $1^1/_2$ inches (38 mm) between joints in adjacent courses, and not in direct alignment in alternate courses. Spacing between shingles shall be approximately $^1/_4$ inch (6.4 mm). Each shingle shall be fastened with two nails only, positioned approximately $^3/_4$ inch (19 mm) from each edge and approximately 1 inch (25 mm) above the exposure line. Starter course at the eaves shall be doubled.	Shakes shall be laid with a side lap of not less than $1^1/_2$ inches (38 mm) between joints in adjacent courses. Spacing between shakes shall not be less than $^3/_8$ inch (9.5 mm) or more than $^5/_8$ inch (15.9 mm) except for preservative-treated wood shakes, which shall have a spacing not less than $^1/_4$ inch (6.4 mm) or more than $^3/_8$ inch (9.5 mm). Shakes shall be fastened to the sheathing with two nails only, positioned approximately 1 inch (25 mm) from each edge and approximately 2 inches (51 mm) above the exposure line. The starter course at the eaves shall be doubled. The bottom or first layer may be either shakes or shingles. Fifteen-inch or 18-inch (381 mm or 457 mm) shakes may be used for the starter course at the eaves and final course at the ridge.
5. Flashing Valleys Other flashing	Per Section 1508.5 Per Section 1509	

[1]When approved by the building official, wood shakes may be installed on a slope of not less than 3 units vertical in 12 units horizontal (25% slope) when an underlayment of not less than nonperforated Type 15 felt is installed.

From the Uniform Building Code, ©1997, ICBO

Figure 13-5 *Shingle or shake application*

For laying wood shingles, refer to UBC Table 15-B-2 (Figure 13-5). Table 15-C (Figure 13-6) shows the maximum exposure to the weather for each shingle length and roof slope. And don't forget you have to double the beginning course of shingles.

The requirements for shakes are similar, except that the spacing between shakes can't be less than $^3/_8$ inch. Because most shakes are split instead of sawed, they don't always have straight edges. The code just requires them to be parallel within 1 inch. Nail shakes within 1

TABLE 15-C—MAXIMUM WEATHER EXPOSURE

GRADE LENGTH	3 UNITS VERTICAL TO LESS THAN 4 UNITS VERTICAL IN 12 UNITS HORIZONTAL (25% ≤ 33.3% SLOPE)	4 UNITS VERTICAL IN 12 UNITS HORIZONTAL (33.3% SLOPE)
	× 25.4 for mm	
Wood Shingles		
1. No. 1 16-inch	$3^3/_4$	5
2. No. 2^1 16-inch	$3^1/_2$	4
3. No. 3^1 16-inch	3	$3^1/_2$
4. No. 1 18-inch	$4^1/_4$	$5^1/_2$
5. No. 2^1 18-inch	4	$4^1/_2$
6. No. 3^1 18-inch	$3^1/_2$	4
7. No. 1 24-inch	$5^3/_4$	$7^1/_2$
8. No. 2^1 24-inch	$5^1/_2$	$6^1/_2$
9. No. 3^1 24-inch	5	$5^1/_2$
Wood Shakes[2]		
10. No. 1 18-inch	$7^1/_2$	$7^1/_2$
11. No. 1 24-inch	10	10
12. No. 2 18-inch tapersawn shakes	—	$5^1/_2$
13. No. 2 24-inch tapersawn shakes	—	7^1_2

[1]To be used only when specifically permitted by the building official.
[2]Exposure of 24-inch by $^3/_8$-inch (610 mm by 9.5 mm) resawn handsplit shakes shall not exceed 5 inches (127 mm) regardless of the roof slope.

Figure 13-6 *Maximum weather exposure*

inch of the edge of the shake and approximately 2 inches above the exposure line.

You have to double the beginning course of shakes, also, but the bottom course can be shingles. Shakes must have a layer of Type 30 felt between each course, with no felt exposed below the butts.

Snow is a special problem for shake roofs. In more severe climates, there are additional requirements, including solid sheathing and two layers of felt from the eave to 36 inches inside the exterior wall line. See UBC Table 15-B-2 (Figure 13-5).

In some areas (particularly in southern California) flammable roofs are not permitted because of the fire danger. It's usually prudent to check with your local building official.

Applying Tile Roofing

Tile roofs, either slate, ceramic or concrete, must be applied according to UBC Table 15-D-1 or 15-D-2 (Figure 13-7). The requirements are clear and straightforward.

Valley Flashing

Complex roofs, with many ridges and valleys, mean extra work — including the valley flashing. Flashing requirements for most roofs are about the same. It has to be underlaid with Type 15 felt, and the valley iron must be 28-gauge galvanized sheet metal. Application details are in Tables 15-B-1 and 15-B-2 (Figures 13-3 and 13-5) and Tables 15-D-1 and D-2 (Figure 13-7).

There are, however, some variations:

Wood shingles and shakes: Sections of flashing must overlap at least 4 inches and

TABLE 15-D-1—ROOFING TILE APPLICATION[1] FOR ALL TILES

	ROOF SLOPE 2½ UNITS VERTICAL IN 12 UNITS HORIZONTAL (21% Slope) TO LESS THAN 3 UNITS VERTICAL IN 12 UNITS HORIZONTAL (25% Slope)	ROOF SLOPE 3 UNITS VERTICAL IN 12 UNITS HORIZONTAL (25% Slope) AND OVER
1. Deck requirements	Solid sheathing per Sections 2312.2 and 2320.12.9	
2. Underlayment In climate areas subject to wind-driven snow, roof ice damming or special wind regions as shown in Chapter 16, Figure 16-1.	Built-up roofing membrane, three plies minimum, applied per Section 1507.6. Surfacing not required.	Same as for other climate areas, except that extending from the eaves up the roof to a line 24 inches (610 mm) inside the exterior wall line of the building, two layers of underlayment shall be applied shingle fashion and solidly cemented together with an approved cementing material.
Other climate areas		One layer heavy-duty felt or Type 30 felt side lapped 2 inches (51 mm) and end lapped 6 inches (153 mm).
3. Attachment[2] Type of fasteners	Corrosion-resistant nails not less than No. 11 gage, $^5/_{16}$-inch (7.9 mm) head. Fasteners shall comply with the requirements of Chapter 23, Division III, Part III. Fasteners shall be long enough to penetrate into the sheathing $^3/_4$ inch (19 mm) or through the thickness of the sheathing, whichever is less. Attaching wire for clay or concrete tile shall not be smaller than 0.083 inch (2.11 mm) (No. 14 B.W. gage).	
Number of fasteners[2,3]	One fastener per tile. Flat tile without vertical laps, two fasteners per tile.	Two fasteners per tile. Only one fastener on slopes of 7 units vertical in 12 units horizontal (58.3% slope) and less for tiles with installed weight exceeding 7.5 pounds per square foot (36.6 kg/m^2) having a width no greater than 16 inches (406 mm).[4]
4. Tile headlap	3 inches (76 mm) minimum.	
5. Flashing	Per Sections 1508.4 and 1509.	

[1]In snow areas, a minimum of two fasteners per tile are required.
[2]In areas designated by the building official as being subject to repeated wind velocities in excess of 80 miles per hour (129 km/h) or where the roof height exceeds 40 feet (12 192 mm) above grade, all tiles shall be attached as follows:
  2.1 The heads of all tiles shall be nailed.
  2.2 The noses of all eave course tiles shall be fastened with approved clips.
  2.3 All rake tiles shall be nailed with two nails.
  2.4 The noses of all ridge, hip and rake tiles shall be set in a bead of approved roofer's mastic.
[3]In snow areas, a minimum of two fasteners per tile are required, or battens and one fastener.
[4]On slopes over 24 units vertical in 12 units horizontal (200% slope), the nose end of all tiles shall be securely fastened.

From the Uniform Building Code, ©1997, ICBO

Figure 13-7 *Roofing tile application*

extend 8 inches from the center line each way for shingles and 11 inches for shakes.

Asphalt shingles: Use metal flashing and either laced asphalt shingles or a 90-pound mineral cap sheet if they are cemented together. The bottom layer should be 12 inches wide and laid face down, the top layer 24 inches wide and laid face up.

Metal shingles: Extend metal flashing 8 inches from the center line, with a splash diverter as part of the flashing. The splash diverter must be at least ¾ inch high at the flow line.

Asbestos-cement shingles, slate shingles, clay and concrete tile: Extend metal flashing 11 inches from center line, with a splash diverter

rib at the flow line at least 1 inch high formed as part of the flashing.

Attics

Any house with an attic that has more than 30 inches in vertical clear height (from the top of the joist to the underside of the rafter) must have an attic opening. This opening must be at least 22 inches by 30 inches, with at least 30 inches of clear headroom above the access opening. Section 1505.1 describes the location this way:

Access. An attic access opening shall be provided to attics of buildings with combustible ceiling or roof construction.

TABLE 15-D-2—CLAY OR CONCRETE ROOFING TILE APPLICATION INTERLOCKING TILE WITH PROJECTING ANCHOR LUGS— MINIMUM ROOF SLOPE 4 UNITS VERTICAL IN 12 UNITS HORIZONTAL (33.3% Slope)

ROOF SLOPE	4 UNITS VERTICAL IN 12 UNITS HORIZONTAL (33.3% Slope) AND OVER
1. Deck requirements	Spaced structural sheathing boards or solid roof sheathing.
2. Underlayment In climate areas subject to wind-driven snow, roof ice or special wind regions as shown in Chapter 16, Figure 16-1.	Solid sheathing one layer of Type 30 felt lapped 2 inches (51 mm) horizontally and 6 inches (152 mm) vertically, except that extending from the eaves up the roof to line 24 inches (610 mm) inside the exterior wall line of the building, two layers of the underlayment shall be applied shingle fashion and solid cemented together with approved cementing material.
Other climates	For spaced sheathing, approved reinforced membrane. For solid sheathing, one layer heavy-duty felt or Type 30 felt lapped 2 inches (51 mm) horizontally and 6 inches (152 mm) vertically.
3. Attachment[1] Type of fasteners	Corrosion-resistant nails not less than No. 11 gage, 5/16-inch (7.9 mm) head. Fasteners shall comply with the requirements of Chapter 23, Division III, Part III. Fasteners shall be long enough to penetrate into the battens[2] or sheathing 3/4 inch (19 mm) or through the thickness of the sheathing, whichever is less. Attaching wire for clay or concrete tile shall not be smaller than 0.083 inch (2.11 mm) (No. 14 B.W. gage). Horizontal battens are required on solid sheathing for slopes 7 units vertical in 12 units horizontal (58.3% slope) and over.[2] Horizontal battens are required for slopes over 7 units vertical in 12 units horizontal (58.3% slope).[2]
No. of fasteners with: Spaced/solid sheathing with battens, or spaced sheathing[3]	Below 5 units vertical in 12 units horizontal (41.7% slope), fasteners not required. Five units vertical in 12 units horizontal (41.7% slope) to less than 12 units vertical in 12 units horizontal (100% slope), one fastener per tile every other row. Twelve units vertical in 12 units horizontal (100% slope) to 24 units vertical in 12 units horizontal (200% slope), one fastener every tile.[4] All perimeter tiles require one fastener.[5] Tiles with installed weight less than 9 pounds per square foot (4.4 kg/m²) require a minimum of one fastener per tile regardless of roof slope.
Solid sheathing without battens[3]	One fastener per tile.
4. Tile headlap	3-inch (76 mm) minimum.
5. Flashing	Per Sections 1508.4 and 1509.

[1]In areas designated by the building official as being subject to repeated wind velocities in excess of 80 miles per hour (129 km/h), or where the roof height exceeds 40 feet (12 192 mm) above grade, all tiles shall be attached as set forth below:
  1.1 The heads of all tiles shall be nailed.
  1.2 The noses of all eave course tiles shall be fastened with a special clip.
  1.3 All rake tiles shall be nailed with two nails.
  1.4 The noses of all ridge, hip and rake tiles shall be set in a bead of approved roofer's mastic.
[2]Battens shall not be less than 1-inch-by-2-inch (25 mm by 51 mm) nominal. Provisions shall be made for drainage beneath battens by a minimum of 1/8-inch (3.2 mm) risers at each nail or by 4-foot-long (1219 mm) battens with at least 1/2-inch (12.7 mm) separation between battens. Battens shall be fastened with approved fasteners spaced at not more than 24 inches (610 mm) on center.
[3]In snow areas, a minimum of two fasteners per tile are required, or battens and one fastener.
[4]Slopes over 24 units vertical in 12 units horizontal (200% slope), nose ends of all tiles must be securely fastened.
[5]Perimeter fastening areas include three tile courses but not less than 36 inches (914 mm) from either side of hips or ridges and edges of eaves and gable rakes.

From the Uniform Building Code, ©1997, ICBO

Figure 13-7 *Roofing tile application (Continued)*

Exception: *Attics with a maximum vertical height of less than 30 inches (762 mm).*

The opening shall not be less than 22 inches (559 mm) by 30 inches (762 mm) and shall be located in a corridor, hallway or other readily accessible location. Thirty-inch-minimum (762 mm) unobstructed headroom in the attic space shall be provided at or above the access opening.

How would you define "readily accessible?" Many contractors put these openings in a closet to keep them out of sight. Is this readily accessible? The building inspector and the fire marshal probably wouldn't think so. But your choice may be limited where headroom is the required 30 inches.

Roof Insulation, Draft Stops and Ventilation

Every roof needs insulation, either under or over the sheathing. In most houses, it's installed between the rafters where it doesn't interfere with the roofing. But when you use rigid insulation as a base for roof covering, there's a whole new set of rules. Section 1510 covers it this way:

Roof Insulation. *Roof insulation shall be of a rigid type suitable as a base for application of a roof covering. Foam plastic roof insulation shall conform to the requirements of Section 2602. The use of insulation in fire-restrictive construction shall comply with Section 710.1.*

The roof insulation, deck material and roof covering shall meet the fire retardancy requirements of Section 1504 and Table 15-A.

Insulation for built-up roofs shall be applied in accordance with Table 15-E. Insulation for modified bitumen, thermoplastic and thermoset membrane roofs shall be applied in accordance with the roofing manufacturer's recommendations. For other roofing materials such as shingles or tile, the insulation shall be covered with a suitable nailing base secured to the structure.

Figure 13-8 shows Tables 15-E, F, and G which cover built-up roof application. You'll have to read and follow these sections carefully. Each step is critical. And there's also some room for interpretation. For instance, when do you need a vapor retarder over an insulated deck? When the average January temperature is under 45 degrees or you anticipate excessive moisture conditions inside the building? It's up to you and the building inspector to define "excessive moisture."

Draft Stops

Any enclosed attic with more than 3,000 square feet must be divided by partitions extending from the ceiling to the roof. The partitions must be at least ½-inch-thick gypsum wallboard, 1-inch nominal tight-fitting wood, or ⅜-inch-thick plywood. There are other materials you can use, if you check with the inspector first. If you have to install doors to provide access from one section of the attic to another, they must be self-closing and have the same fire resistance as the partition.

Ventilation

You can provide air through vents in the eaves or cornice, but these areas may be plugged if insulation is blown in. A blocking strip between the rafters prevents this and helps move the air over the insulation.

The formula for venting area is simple: Vent area should be $\frac{1}{150}$ of the horizontal roof area. If your attic area is 1,200 square feet, for example, you need 8 square feet of attic ventilation (1,200 divided by 150 is 8).

There's an exception, as usual. If you locate 50 percent of the ventilators at least 3 feet above the eaves or cornice area, you can reduce the free ventilating area to $\frac{1}{300}$. The other 50 percent of the openings must be the cornice or eave vents. So that 1,200 square foot attic would only need 4 square feet of vent area. Cover all openings with corrosion-resistant metal mesh with ¼-inch openings.

In some occupancies, you also have to provide smoke and heat ventilation. These occupancies are single-story Groups B, F, M, S-1 and S-2 (moderate hazard) with more than 50,000 square feet of undivided area, and Group H occupancies (hazardous) with over 15,000 square feet on a single floor.

You can vent these occupancies with open or openable skylights or windows that open directly to the exterior. Because this ventilation is so important, the code goes into considerable detail about how many vents are required and where they should go. Still, it's a good idea to contact your local inspector and fire marshal for advice before beginning construction.

Roof Drainage

If a roof isn't designed to support accumulated water, it has to be sloped for drainage. Here are a few guidelines:

- Install roof drains at the lowest point on the roof.
- Roof drains must be capable of handling the water flowing to them.

TABLE 15-E—BUILT-UP ROOF-COVERING APPLICATION

	MECHANICALLY FASTENED SYSTEMS	ADHESIVELY FASTENED SYSTEMS
1. Deck conditions	Decks shall be firm, broom-clean, smooth and dry. Insulated decks shall have wood insulation stops at all edges of the deck, unless an alternative suitable curbing is provided. Insulated decks with slopes greater than 2 units vertical in 12 units horizontal (16.7% slope) shall have wood insulation stops at not more than 8 feet (2438 mm) face to face. Wood nailers shall be provided where nailing is required for roofing plies.	
	Solid wood sheathing shall conform to Sections 2312.2 and 2320.12.9.	Provide wood nailers where nailing is required for roofing plies (see below).
2. Underlayment	One layer of sheathing paper, Type 15 felt or other approved underlayment nailed sufficiently to hold in place, is required over board decks where openings between boards would allow bitumen to drip through. No underlayment requirements for plywood decks. Underlayment on other decks shall be in accordance with deck manufacturer's recommendations.	Not required.
3. Base ply requirements Over noninsulated decks	Over approved decks, the base ply shall be nailed using not less than one fastener for each $1^1/_3$ square feet (0.124 m²).	Decks shall be primed in accordance with the roofing manufacturer's instructions. The base ply shall be solidly cemented or spot mopped as required by the type of deck material using adhesive application rates shown in Table 15-F.
4. Mechanical fasteners	Fasteners shall be long enough to penetrate $^3/_4$ inch (19 mm) into the sheathing or through the thickness of the sheathing, whichever is less. Built-up roofing nails for wood board decks shall be minimum No. 12 gage, $^7/_{16}$-inch (11.1 mm) head driven through tin caps or approved nails with integral caps. For plywood, No. 11 gage ring-shank nails driven through tin caps or approved nails with integral caps shall be used. For gypsum, insulating concrete, cementitious wood fiber and other decks, fasteners recommended by the manufacturer shall be used.	When mechanical fasteners are required for attachment of roofing plies to wood nailers or insulation stops (see below), they shall be as required for wood board decks.
5. Vapor retarder Over insulated decks	A vapor retarder shall be installed where the average January temperature is below 45°F (7°C), or where excessive moisture conditions are anticipated within the building. It shall be applied as for a base ply.	
6. Insulation	When no vapor retarder is required, roof insulation shall be fastened in an approved manner. When a vapor retarder is required, roof insulation is to be solidly mopped to the vapor retarder using the adhesive application rate specified in Table 15-F. See manufacturer's instructions for the attachment of insulation over steel decks.	When no vapor retarder is required, roof insulation shall be solid mopped to the deck using the adhesive application rate specified in Table 15-F. When a vapor retarder is required, roof insulation is to be solidly mopped to the vapor retarder, using the adhesive application rate specified in Table 15-F. See manufacturer's installation instructions for attachment of insulation over steel decks.
7. Roofing plies	Successive layers shall be solidly cemented together and to the base ply or the insulation using the adhesive rates shown in Table 15-F. On slopes greater than 1 unit vertical in 12 units horizontal (8.3% slope) for aggregate-surfaced, or 2 units vertical in 12 units horizontal (16.7% slope) for smooth-surfaced or cap sheet surfaced roofs, mechanical fasteners are required. Roofing plies shall be blind-nailed to the deck, wood nailers or wood insulation stops in accordance with the roofing manufacturer's recommendations. On slopes exceeding 3 units vertical in 12 units horizontal (25% slope), plies shall be laid parallel to the slope of the deck (strapping method).	
8. Cementing materials	See Table 15-G.	
9. Curbs and walls	Suitable cant strips shall be used at all vertical intersections. Adequate attachment shall be provided for both base flashing and counterflashing on all vertical surfaces. Reglets shall be provided in wall or parapets receiving metal counterflashing.	
10. Surfacing	Mineral aggregate surfaced roofs shall comply with the requirements of UBC Standard 15-1 and Table 15-F. Cap sheets shall be cemented to the roofing plies as set forth in Table 15-F.	

TABLE 15-F—BUILT-UP ROOFING CEMENTING ADHESIVE AND SURFACING APPLICATION RATES

	MINIMUM APPLICATION RATE, MATERIAL/100 FT.² (9.3 m²) ROOF AREA		
	Hot Asphalt (pounds)	Hot Coal-tar (pounds)	Cold-process Cement (gallons)
MATERIAL TO BE ADHERED	× 0.45 for kg	× 0.45 for kg	× 3.785 for liters
Base ply or vapor retarder 1. Spot mopping 2. Solid cementing	 15 20	 15 20	 1 $1^1/_2$
Insulation 1. Solid cementing	 20	 20	 $1^1/_2$
Roofing plies (and between layers of vapor retarder) 1. Felts 2. Coated felts	 20 20	 20 20	 Not permitted $1^1/_2$
Cap sheets 1. Solid cementing	 20	 Not permitted	 $1^1/_2$

Mineral aggregate[1,2]
1. Fire-retardant roof coverings
  1.1 Gravel, 400 lb./sq. (20.1 kg/m²)
  1.2 Slag, 300 lb./sq. (15.1 kg/m²)
  1.3 Granules, 60 lb./sq. (3 kg/m²)
2. Nonrated roof coverings
  2.1 Gravel, 300 lb./sq. (15.1 kg/m²)
  2.2 Slag, 250 lb./sq. (12.6 kg/m²)
  2.3 Granules, 60 lb./sq. (3 kg/m²)
	
	50
	50
	—
	
	40
	40
	—
		
		60
		60
		—
		
		50
		50
		—
			
			4
			4
			3
			
			4
			4
			3

[1]Mineral aggregate shall not be used for built-up roofing membranes at roof slopes greater than 3 units vertical in 12 units horizontal (25% slope).
[2]A minimum of 50 percent of the required aggregate shall be embedded in the pour coat.

Figure 13-8 *Built-up roofing*

TABLE 15-G—APPLICATION OF CEMENTING MATERIALS

APPLICATION	MAXIMUM SLOPE, VERTICAL UNITS PER 12 UNITS HORIZONTAL				
	Asphalt Type				Coal-tar Pitch
	Type I	Type II	Type III	Type IV	
1. Insulation to deck	—	—	All	All	—
2. Felt or vapor retarder to deck	—	¹/₂ (4% slope) or less	3 (25% slope) or less	All	¹/₂ (4% slope) or less
3. Felt to felt	—	¹/₂ (4% slope) or less	¹/₂ -3 (4%-25% slope)	All	¹/₂ (4% slope) or less
4. Cap sheet to felt	—	—	3 (25% slope) or less	All	—
5. Gravel to felts	¹/₂ (4% slope) or less	¹/₂ (4% slope) or less	¹/₂ -3 (4%-25% slope)	N.P.	¹/₂ (4% slope) or less
6. Heating of cementing material,[1] °F Temperature at kettle[2] (maximum)	475 (246°C)	525 (274°C)	525 (274°C)	525 (274°C)	425 (218°C)
Application temperature,[3] °F	375-425 (190-218°C)	375-425 (190-218°C)	375-425 (190-218°C)	400-450 (204-232°C)	350-400 (177-204°C)

N.P.—Not permitted.

[1]Bulk tanker temperatures shall be reduced to 320°F to 350°F (160°C to 177°C) at night or during periods when no roofing will occur.
[2]Cementing material shall not be heated above a temperature that is 25°F (14°C) below its flash point.
[3]Bitumen identified with the equiviscous temperature (EVT) shall be applied at the EVT ± 25°F (14°C).

From the Uniform Building Code, ©1997, ICBO

Figure 13-8 *Built-up roofing (Continued)*

- In most areas, a roof drain may not drain into the sanitary sewer.

- In many areas, roof drainage water can't flow over public property or into adjacent property.

- Concealed roof drainage must conform to the plumbing code.

Figure 13-9 shows a roof drain on a built-up roof. The grated cover is a leaf strainer. Place the drains so that they drain the water from the roof as quickly as possible.

Figure 13-9 *Roof drain on built-up roof*

Chimneys and Fireplaces

Not every house needs a chimney, of course. But if there is a chimney, it has to meet code requirements. Chapter 31 of the UBC lists four classes of chimneys:

Residential Appliance-type, *is a factory-built or masonry chimney suitable for removing products of combustion from residential-type appliances producing combustion gases not in excess of 1,000°F (538°C) measured at the appliance flue outlet.*

Low-heat Industrial Appliance-type, *is a factory-built, masonry or metal chimney suitable for removing the products of combustion from fuel-burning low-heat appliances producing combustion gases not in excess of 1,000°F (538°C) under normal operating conditions but capable of producing combustion gases of 1,400°F (760°C) during intermittent forced firing for periods up to one hour. All temperatures are measured at the appliance flue outlet.*

TABLE 31-A—MINIMUM PASSAGEWAY AREAS FOR MASONRY CHIMNEYS[1]

Type of Masonry Chimney	MINIMUM CROSS-SECTIONAL AREA		
	× 645 for mm²		
	Tile Lined		Lined with Firebrick or Unlined
	Round	Square or Rectangle	
1. Residential	50 square inches	50 square inches	85 square inches
2. Fireplace	See Figure 31-1	See Figure 31-1	1/8 of opening minimum 100 square inches
3. Low heat	50 square inches	57 square inches	135 square inches

4. Incinerator Apartment type
  1 opening
  2 to 6 openings
  7 to 14 openings
  15 or more openings
	196 square inches
	324 square inches
	484 square inches
	484 square inches plus 10 square inches for each additional opening
			Not applicable

NOTE: For altitudes over 2,000 feet (610 m) above sea level, the building official shall be consulted in determining the area of the passageway.
[1] Areas for medium- and high-heat chimneys shall be determined using accepted engineering methods and as approved by the building official.

From the Uniform Building Code, ©1997, ICBO

Figure 13-10 *Passageway areas for masonry chimneys*

Medium-heat Industrial Appliance-type, *is a factory-built, masonry or metal chimney suitable for removing the products of combustion from fuel-burning medium-heat appliances producing combustion gases not in excess of 2,000°F (1093°C) measured at the appliance flue outlet.*

High-heat Industrial Appliance-type, *is a factory-built masonry or metal chimney suitable for removing the products of combustion from fuel-burning high-heat appliances producing combustion gases in excess of 2,000°F (1093°C) measured at the appliance flue outlet.*

Residential and low-heat chimneys are about the same. The only important difference is that residential chimneys may have walls 4 inches thick and a flue liner, while low-heat chimneys require 8-inch-thick walls and a flue liner. The liner in both cases should extend from a point 8 inches below the lowest inlet to a point above the enclosing walls. UBC Tables 31-A and 31-B (Figures 13-10 and 13-11) give dimensions and construction details for most chimneys.

Every chimney must rise from its own foundation, which must be on solid ground, to a point at least 2 feet higher than any point of a building within 10 feet horizontally. Bracket flues are not permitted. A chimney can't support any portion of the building unless it was specifically designed as a supporting member.

Construction Standards

The area of the chimney passageway must be at least as large as the vent connection. Figure 13-10 shows the minimum passageway areas. Note that these are cross-section dimensions made after the flue liner is installed.

You can omit the liner on residential chimneys that have at least 8-inch solid masonry walls. Does that mean you can use any old concrete block? No, you can't. You still have to follow UBC Table 31-B (Figure 13-11), which shows the wall thickness you need for each type of masonry unit.

Smoke doesn't go straight up a chimney, it spirals up. This is why a round chimney is the ideal shape. A square flue is also good, since only the corners are dead space. A long, narrow, rectangular flue needs more area to get

TABLE 31-B—CONSTRUCTION, CLEARANCE AND TERMINATION REQUIREMENTS FOR MASONRY AND CONCRETE CHIMNEYS

CHIMNEYS SERVING	THICKNESS (min. inches) × 25.4 for mm		HEIGHT ABOVE ROOF OPENING (feet) × 304.8 for mm	HEIGHT ABOVE ANY PART OF BUILDING WITHIN (feet) × 304.8 for mm			CLEARANCE TO COMBUSTIBLE CONSTRUCTION (inches) × 25.4 for mm	
	Walls	Lining		10	25	50	Int. Inst.	Ext. Inst.
1. **RESIDENTIAL-TYPE APPLIANCES**[1,2] (Low Btu input) Clay, shale or concrete brick Reinforced concrete Hollow masonry units Stone	4[3] 4[3] 4[4] 12	⅝ fire-clay tile or 2 firebrick	2	2			2	1 or ½ gypsum[5]
Unburned clay units	8	4½ firebrick						
2. **BUILDING HEATING AND INDUSTRIAL-TYPE LOW-HEAT APPLIANCES**[1,2] [1,000°F (538°C) operating temp.—1,400°F (760°C) maximum] Clay, shale or concrete brick Hollow masonry units Reinforced concrete Stone	8 8[4] 8 12	⅝ fire-clay tile or 2 firebrick	3	2			2	2
3. **MEDIUM-HEAT INDUSTRIAL-TYPE APPLIANCES**[1,6] [2,000°F (1093°C) maximum] Clay, shale or concrete brick Hollow masonry units (Grouted solid) Reinforced concrete Stone	8 8 8 12	4½ medium-duty firebrick	10		10		4	4
4. **HIGH-HEAT INDUSTRIAL-TYPE APPLIANCES**[1,6] [Over 2,000°F (1093°C)] Clay, shale or concrete brick Hollow masonry units (Grouted solid) Reinforced concrete	16[7] 16[7] 16[7]	4½ high-duty firebrick	20			20	8	8
5. **RESIDENTIAL-TYPE INCINERATORS**	Same as for residential-type appliances as shown above.							
6. **CHUTE-FED AND FLUE-FED INCINERATORS WITH COMBINED HEARTH AND GRATE AREA 7 SQ. FT. (0.65 m²) OR LESS** Clay, shale or concrete brick or hollow units Portion extending to 10 ft. (3048 mm) above combustion chamber roof Portion more than 10 ft. (3048 mm) above combustion chamber roof	4 8	4½ medium-duty firebrick ⅝ fire-clay tile liner	3	2			2	2
7. **CHUTE-FED AND FLUE-FED INCINERATORS—COMBINED HEARTH AND GRATE AREAS LARGER THAN 7 SQ. FT. (0.65 m²)** Clay, shale or concrete brick or hollow units grouted solid or reinforced concrete Portion extending to 40 ft. (12 192 mm) above combustion chamber roof Portion more than 40 ft. (12 192 mm) above combustion chamber roof Reinforced concrete	4 8 8	4½ medium-duty firebrick ⅝ fire-clay tile liner 4½ medium-duty firebrick laid in medium-duty refract mortar		10			2	2
8. **COMMERCIAL OR INDUSTRIAL-TYPE INCINERATORS**[2] Clay or shale solid brick Reinforced concrete	8 8	4½ medium-duty firebrick laid in medium-duty refract mortar		10			4	4

[1]See Table 9-A of the Mechanical Code for types of appliances allowed with each type of chimney.
[2]Lining shall extend from bottom to top of chimney.
[3]Chimneys having walls 8 inches (203 mm) or more in thickness may be unlined.
[4]Equivalent thickness including grouted cells when grouted solid. The equivalent thickness may also include the grout thickness between the liner and masonry unit.
[5]Chimneys for residential-type appliances installed entirely on the exterior of the building. For fireplace and barbecue chimneys, see Section 3102.7.8.
[6]Lining to extend from 24 inches (610 mm) below connector to 25 feet (7620 mm) above.
[7]Two 8-inch (203 mm) walls with 2-inch (51 mm) airspace between walls. Outer and inner walls may be of solid masonry units or reinforced concrete or any combination thereof.
[8]Clearance shall be approved by the building official and shall be such that the temperature of combustible materials will not exceed 160°F (710°C).

From the Uniform Building Code, ©1997, ICBO

Figure 13-11 *Requirements for masonry and concrete chimneys*

Figure 13-12 *Zero clearance fireplace*

the same results. It's a good idea to consider Section 3102.3.2 when designing a chimney:

> **Construction.** *Each chimney shall be so constructed as to safely convey flue gases not exceeding the maximum temperatures for the type of construction as set forth in Table 31-B and shall be capable of producing a draft at the appliance not less than that required for safe operation.*

That's what it all boils down to. If it doesn't work, you've wasted a lot of time.

Fireplaces

Many "zero clearance" factory-built metal fireplace inserts are now available. These are prefabricated fireplaces and can be set directly in wood framing. See Figure 13-12. They must be installed exactly as the manufacturer specifies. Often the fireplace is listed by ICBO Evaluation Services or another organization for use under specified conditions. It's too early to say if they'll prove to be as durable as masonry fireplaces, but they should last a long time. And they have the advantage of being much cheaper to install than a standard masonry fireplace.

If you're installing a masonry fireplace, there are a number of things to consider. First, the depth of the firebox may not be less than 20 inches. The width of the opening isn't too important, but don't make the height of the opening more than the size of the fire contemplated. A small fire in a large, high firebox is usually a smoky fire.

The shape of the back and sides of the firebox determines how well it will reflect heat into a room. The shapes of the smoke chamber, throat and smoke shelf are also important. The damper, when fully opened, can't restrict the flue beyond the dimensions shown in UBC Table 31-A (Figure 13-10). The damper blade, when fully opened, can't extend past the line of the inside of the flue.

Earthquakes and chimneys — During an earthquake, a chimney can become the most dangerous part of the house. In many cases the only serious damage to a home is the chimney, usually an exterior one. That's why Section 3102.4.3 says:

> **Section 3102.4.3 Reinforcing and Seismic Anchorage.** *Unless a specific design is provided, every masonry or concrete chimney in Seismic Zones 2, 3, and 4 shall be reinforced with not less than four No. 4 reinforcing bars conforming to the provisions of Chapter 19 or 21 of this code. The bars shall extend the full height of the chimney and shall be spliced in accordance with the applicable requirements of Chapters 19 and 21. In masonry chimneys the vertical bars shall have a minimum cover of ½-inch (12.7 mm) of grout or mortar tempered to a pouring consistency. The bars shall be tied horizontally at 18-inch (457 mm) intervals with not less than ¼-inch (6.4 mm) steel ties. The slope of the inclined portion of the offset in vertical bars shall not exceed 2 units vertical in 1 unit horizontal (200% slope). Two ties shall also be placed at each bend in vertical bars. When the width of the chimney exceeds 40 inches (1016 mm), two additional No. 4 ver-*

tical bars shall be provided for each additional flue incorporated in the chimney or for each additional 40 inches (1016 mm) in width or fraction thereof.

The code goes on to require that the chimney be anchored at each floor or ceiling line more than 6 feet above grade. Further, masonry chimneys may be offset at a slope of not more than 4 inches in 24 inches, but not more than one third of the dimension of the chimney, in the direction of the offset.

Hearths — The hearth of a masonry fireplace must be at least 4 inches thick of brick, concrete, stone or other approved noncombustible slab. It has to be supported by noncombustible materials or reinforced to carry its own weight and whatever loads it will carry. Make sure the hearth extends at least 16 inches beyond the front of the opening and at least 8 inches beyond the sides of the opening. If your hearth opening exceeds 6 square feet, the hearth has to be bigger. Then the hearth needs to extend 20 inches in the front and 12 inches on the sides.

Hearth extensions for factory-built fireplaces or fireplace stoves are a little different. These must conform to the manufacturer's installation instructions.

Metal damper hoods — Most masonry fireplaces have metal damper hoods. These hoods usually come complete with smoke shelf, damper, and a properly-sized flue outlet. According to the code, they must be made of 19-gauge corrosion-resistant metal (copper, galvanized steel or other equivalent ferrous metal). All seams must be smokeproof and unsoldered. Hoods must be sloped 45 degrees or less and extend horizontally at least 6 inches beyond the front of the firebox. Don't install the hood closer than 18 inches to any combustible material unless its design is approved for that.

Line the top side of the hood with several inches of fiberglass to keep from losing heat into the chimney cavity. And always mortar the hood in place. This wasn't always done in the past. It was common practice to just stuff the space with fiberglass. But fiberglass, although noncombustible, can melt, leaving room for flame to enter the chimney cavity. Since that's a fire danger, all hoods must now be mortared in.

You can't place combustible material within 2 inches of a firebox, smoke chamber or chimney wall, or within 12 inches of the fireplace opening.

I'll talk more about fireplaces in Chapter 15, Combustion Air.

Rolling Out the Rock

I don't think any building inspector likes to shut a job down. I know I don't. It's heavy handed (sort of a last resort after everything else has failed). Negotiation is always better than confrontation. And stopping all work is the worst type of confrontation. But I've had to order work stopped a few times. Once I did it as a favor to the contractor. There wasn't even a code violation. Here's the story.

A few years ago I had an out-of-town developer apply for a permit on a 22-home tract. I hadn't heard of this developer before, so I mentioned his name at a regional conference of building inspectors. No one had anything good to say about him. Some predicted trouble right from the start. I decided to keep an eye on him, visiting the tract daily.

Most of the time I couldn't find anything wrong. When I noticed something that needed attention, I'd note it on a piece of paper and give it to the foreman. He would either fix the problem right away or explain that the work was scheduled and suggest when it would be finished. I was having no trouble at all with this builder. He seemed very professional in every way.

Then a funny thing happened. I was making a routine inspection on one of the homes. The sheetrock hangers had been working since morning. As I walked through, I had a feeling that something was wrong. But I couldn't put my finger on it. I went through the place item by item and found nothing unusual. Still, my intuition said to keep looking. I counted the nails in each sheet of drywall, checked the blocking on joints, and everything else I could think of. Still nothing.

I started to leave through the kitchen into an attached garage. As I went through the opening, I ran my hand along the wall where the trim would go. "Here's where the light switch will probably be," I told myself. But, surprise, there was no opening in the wallboard for the switch. I couldn't believe it! There were no electrical openings anywhere in the wallboard. I checked some rooms that hadn't been rocked yet. The house hadn't been wired! There was no electrical wiring in the walls and the sheetrock hangers were covering up the framing! My intuition hadn't let me down.

How did that happen? Was the foreman making a horrible mistake? Or was the developer hoping to find a buyer who wanted electrical wiring run on the wall surface? That's ridiculous. No one wants a home that's wired like a barn. It had to be a mistake.

But what should I do? I had no right to stop work. There was no code violation. Neither the UBC nor the NEC require that wiring be run inside walls. But everyone does it. I've never seen a new home with exposed wiring. Someone had to tell the sheetrock crew to stop work immediately. Should I do it?

I decided to take the heat. I shut the job down. That brought the foreman to me with fire in his eyes. I had no authority to shut down his job, he screamed. And he was right. He'd been told to "rock" that house, and that's what he was going to do.

I suggested to the foreman that we take a break, consider the situation, and make a few calls. He cooled down after a while, and admitted that I was right. The wiring should go in first. It was nice of him to admit that — but he still had a house to wire.

14

Finish Materials and Installation Procedures

UBC Chapter 25 is called *Gypsum Board and Plaster*. It covers plaster, lath, exposed aggregate plaster (stucco) and pneumatically placed cement plaster (gunite).

Before we begin, let me clarify something. A vertical assembly is anything you assemble out of building materials that rises vertically — commonly called a wall. A horizontal assembly is anything you assemble that's laid and used in a horizontal position — in other words, floors and ceilings. We'll start at the top, with ceilings.

Suspended Ceilings

Ceiling members aren't always attached. Sometimes they're simply laid in place and held there by gravity. A suspended ceiling is a good example. The panels are laid in runners suspended from the structural framing above. The panels may be light diffusers or solid panels.

Some buildings use the space between the suspended ceiling and the structural framing above for an *extended plenum* or *plenum chamber* to circulate either heated or cooled air. That lets you install air diffusers wherever you want them. The air is forced under pressure into the space between the two ceilings and then forced out through the diffusers.

The hangers must be saddle-tied around the main runner to develop their full strength. UBC Table 25-A (Figure 14-1) gives specifications for suspended ceilings weighing less than 10 pounds per square foot.

TABLE 25-A—SUSPENDED AND FURRED CEILINGS[1]
[For support of ceilings weighing not more than 10 pounds per square foot (4.89 kg/m²)]

MINIMUM SIZES FOR WIRE AND RIGID HANGERS			
Size and Type		**Maximum Area Supported (square feet)** × 0.09 for m²	**Size** × 25.4 for mm
Hangers for suspended ceilings		12.5	0.148-inch (3.76 mm) (No. 9 B.W. gage) wire
		16	0.145-inch (4.19 mm) (No. 8 B.W. gage) wire
		18	$^3/_{16}$" diameter, mild steel rod[2]
		20	$^7/_{32}$" diameter, mild steel rod[2]
		22.5	$^1/_4$" diameter, mild steel rod[2]
		22.0	1" × $^3/_{16}$" mild steel flats[3]
Hangers for attaching runners and furring directly to beams and joists	For supporting runners	Single hangers between beams[4]	8	0.109-inch (2.77 mm) (No. 12 B.W. gage) wire
			12	0.134-inch (3.40 mm) (No. 10 B.W. gage) wire
			16	0.165-inch (4.19 mm) (No. 8 B.W. gage) wire
		Double wire loops at beams or joists[3]	8	0.083-inch (2.11 mm) (No. 14 B.W. gage) wire
			12	0.109-inch (2.77 mm) (No. 12 B.W. gage) wire
			16	0.120-inch (3.05 mm) (No. 11 B.W. gage) wire
	For supporting furring without runners[4] (wire loops at supports)	Type of support: Concrete	8	0.083-inch (2.11 mm) (No. 14 B.W. gage) wire
		Steel		0.065-inch (1.65 mm) (No. 16 B.W. gage) wire (2 loops)[5]
		Wood		0.065-inch (1.65 mm) (No. 16 B.W. gage) wire (2 loops)[5]

MINIMUM SIZES AND MAXIMUM SPANS FOR MAIN RUNNERS[6,7]		
Size and Type × 25.4 for mm × 1.49 for kg/m	**Maximum Spacing of Hangers or Supports (Along Runners)** × 304.8 for mm	**Maximum Spacing of Runners (Transverse)** × 304.8 for mm
$^3/_4$" — 0.3 pound per foot, cold- or hot-rolled channel	2'	3'
$1^1/_2$" — 0.475 pound per foot, cold-rolled channel	3'	4'
$1^1/_2$" — 0.475 pound per foot, cold-rolled channel	3.5'	3.5'
$1^1/_2$" — 0.475 pound per foot, cold-rolled channel	4'	3'
$1^1/_2$" — 1.12 pounds per foot, hot-rolled channel	4'	5'
2" — 1.26 pounds per foot, hot-rolled channel	5'	5'
2" — 0.59 pounds per foot, cold-rolled channel	5'	3.5'
$1^1/_2$" × $1^1/_2$" × $^3/_{16}$" angle	5'	3.5'

MINIMUM SIZES AND MAXIMUM SPANS FOR CROSS FURRING[6,7]		
Size and Type of Cross-furring × 25.4 for mm × 1.49 for kg/m	**Maximum Spacing of Runners or Supports** × 304.8 for mm	**Maximum Spacing of Cross-furring Members (Transverse)** × 25.4 for mm
$^1/_4$" diameter pencil rods	2'	12"
$^3/_8$" diameter pencil rods	2'	19"
$^3/_8$" diameter pencil rods	2.5'	12"
$^3/_4$" — 0.3 pound per foot, cold- or hot-rolled channel	3'	24"
	3.5'	16"
	4'	12"
1" — 0.410 pound per foot, hot-rolled channel	4'	24"
	4.5'	19"
	5'	12"

[1]Metal suspension systems for acoustical tile and lay-in panel ceiling systems weighing not more than 4 pounds per square foot (19.5 kg/m²), including light fixtures and all ceiling-supported equipment and conforming to UBC Standard 25-2, are exempt from Table 25-A.

[2]All rod hangers shall be protected with a zinc or cadmium coating or with a rust-inhibitive paint.

[3]All flat hangers shall be protected with a zinc or cadmium coating or with a rust-inhibitive paint.

[4]Inserts, special clips or other devices of equal strength may be substituted for those specified.

[5]Two loops of 0.049-inch (1.24 mm) (No. 18 B.W. gage) wire may be substituted for each loop of 0.065-inch (1.65 mm) (No. 16 B.W. gage) wire for attaching steel furring to steel or wood joists.

[6]Spans are based on webs of channels being erected vertically.

[7]Other sections of hot- or cold-rolled members of equivalent strength may be substituted for those specified.

Figure 14-1 *Suspended and furred ceilings*

TABLE 25-B[1]—TYPES OF LATH—MAXIMUM SPACING OF SUPPORTS

TYPE OF LATH[2]		MINIMUM WEIGHT (per square yard) (× 0.38 for kg/m²) GAGE AND MESH SIZE (× 25.4 for mm)	VERTICAL (Inches) × 25.4 for mm			HORIZONTAL (inches) × 25.4 for mm	
			Wood	Metal Solid Plaster Partitions	Other	Wood or Concrete	Metal
1. Expanded metal lath (diamond mesh)		2.5 3.4	16[3] 16[3]	16[3] 16[3]	12 16	12 16	12 16
2. Flat rib expanded metal lath		2.75 3.4	16 19	16 24	16 19	16 19	16 19
3. Stucco mesh expanded metal lath		1.8 and 3.6	16[4]	—	—	—	—
4. ³/₈" (9.5 mm) rib expanded metal lath		3.4 4.0	24 24	24[5] 24[5]	24 24	24 24	24 24
5. Sheet lath		4.5	24	[5]	24	24	24
6. Wire fabric lath	Welded	1.95 pounds, 0.120 inch (No. 11 B.W. gage), 2" x 2" 1.16 pounds, 0.065 inch (No. 16 B.W. gage), 2" x 2" 1.4 pounds, 0.049 inch (No. 18 B.W. gage), 1" x 1"[6]	24 16 16[4]	24 16 —	24 16 —	24 16 —	24 16 —
	Woven	1.1 pounds, 0.049 inch (No. 18 B.W. gage), 1¹/₂" hexagonal[6] 1.4 pounds, 0.058 inch (No. 17 B.W. gage), 1¹/₂" hexagonal[6] 1.4 pounds, 0.049 inch (No. 18 B.W. gage), 1" hexagonal[6]	24 24 24	16 16 16	16 16 16	24 24 24	16 16 16
7. ³/₈" (9.5 mm) gypsum lath (plain)			16	—	16[7]	16	16
8. ¹/₂" (12.7 mm) gypsum lath (plain)			24	—	24	24	24

[1]For fire-resistive construction, see Tables 7-A, 7-B and 7-C. For shear-resisting elements, see Table 25-I.
[2]Metal lath and wire fabric lath used as reinforcement for cement plaster shall be furred out away from vertical supports at least ¹/₄ inch (6.4 mm). Self-furring lath meets furring requirements.
   EXCEPTION: Furring of expanded metal lath is not required on supports having a bearing surface width of 1⁵/₈ inches (41 mm) or less.
[3]Span may be increased to 24 inches (610 mm) with self-furred metal lath over solid sheathing assemblies approved for this use.
[4]Wire backing required on open vertical frame construction except under expanded metal lath and paperbacked wire fabric lath.
[5]May be used for studless solid partitions.
[6]Woven wire or welded wire fabric lath not to be used as base for gypsum plaster without absorbent paperbacking or slot-perforated separator.
[7]Span may be increased to 24 inches (610 mm) on vertical screw or approved nailable assemblies.

From the Uniform Building Code, ©1997, ICBO

Figure 14-2 *Maximum spacing of supports for lath*

Lath

The UBC no longer recognizes wood lath. Look at the types of lath listed in UBC Table 25-B (Figure 14-2); wood is not among them. This signals the end of an era. That can create problems when remodeling older homes, as the new lath may not be the same thickness as the old wood lath.

We'll look at metal lath first, since it's listed first in the UBC. If you're using metal lath or wire fabric lath, attach it with at least 18-gauge wire ties spaced not more than 6 inches apart or with an approved fastener.

Apply metal lath with the long dimension of the sheets perpendicular to the supports. Lap joints at least one mesh at the sides and ends, but not less than 1 inch. You can lap metal rib lath with edge ribs wider than ¹/₈ inch by nesting the outside ribs. If the edge ribs are less than ¹/₈ inch, lap it ¹/₂ inch at the sides or nest the outside ribs. If the laps don't fall over supports, tie them with 18-gauge wire.

UBC Tables 25-B (Figure 14-2) and 25-C (Figure 14-3) give the type and weight of metal lath, the gauge and spacing of wire in welded or woven lath, the spacing of supports, and how to attach lath to wood supports.

TABLE 25-C—TYPES OF LATH—ATTACHMENT TO WOOD AND METAL[1] SUPPORTS

TYPE OF LATH	NAILS[2,3] Type and Size	NAILS Max Spacing Vertical	NAILS Max Spacing Horizontal	SCREWS[3,4] Max Spacing Vertical	SCREWS Max Spacing Horizontal	STAPLES[3,5] Wire Gage No.	STAPLES Crown	STAPLES Leg	STAPLES Max Spacing Vertical	STAPLES Max Spacing Horizontal
1. Diamond mesh expanded metal lath and flat rib metal lath	4d blued smooth box $1^1/_2$"[7] No. 14 gage $^7/_{32}$" head (clinched)[8] 1" No. 11 gage $^7/_{16}$" head, barbed $1^1/_2$" No. 11 gage $^7/_{16}$" head, barbed	6 6 6	— — 6	6	6	16	$^3/_4$	$^7/_8$	6	6
2. $^3/_8$" (9.5 mm) rib metal lath and sheet lath	$1^1/_2$" No. 11 gage $^7/_{16}$" head, barbed	6	6	6	6	16	$^3/_4$	$1^1/_4$	At ribs	At ribs
3. $^3/_4$" (19.1 mm) rib metal lath	4d common $1^1/_2$" No. $12^1/_2$ gage $^1/_4$" head 2" No. 11 gage $^7/_{16}$" head, barbed	At ribs	— At ribs	At ribs	At ribs	16	$^3/_4$	$1^5/_8$	At ribs	At ribs
4. Wire fabric lath[9]	4d blued smooth box (clinched)[8] 1" No. 11 gage $^7/_{16}$" head, barbed $1^1/_2$" No. 11 gage $^7/_{16}$" head, barbed $1^1/_4$" No. 12 gage $^3/_8$" head, furring 1" No. 12 gage $^3/_8$" head	6 6 6 6 6	— — 6 6	6	6	16 16	$^3/_4$ $^7/_{16}$[9]	$^7/_8$ $^7/_8$	6 6	6 6
5. $^3/_8$" (9.5 mm) gypsum lath	$1^1/_8$" No. 13 gage $^{19}/_{64}$" head, blued	8[10]	8[10]	8[10]	8[10]	16	$^3/_4$	$^7/_8$[11]	8[10]	8[10]
6. $^1/_2$" (12.7 mm) gypsum lath	$1^1/_4$" No. 13 gage $^{19}/_{64}$" head, blued	8	8[10] 6[7]	8[10]	8[10] 6[7]	16	$^3/_4$	$1^1/_8$[11]	8[10]	8[10] 6[7]

[1]Metal lath, wire lath, wire fabric lath and metal accessories shall conform to approved standards.

[2]For nailable nonload-bearing metal supports, use annular threaded nails or approved staples.

[3]For fire-resistive construction, see Tables 7-B and 7-C. For shear-resisting elements, see Table 25-I. Approved wire and sheet metal attachment clips may be used.

[4]Screws shall be an approved type long enough to penetrate into wood framing not less than $^5/_8$ inch (15.9 mm) and through metal supports adaptable for screw attachment not less than $^1/_4$ inch (6.4 mm).

[5]With chisel or divergent points.

[6]Maximum spacing of attachments from longitudinal edges shall not exceed 2 inches (51 mm).

[7]Supports spaced 24 inches (610 mm) on center. Four attachments per 16-inch-wide (406 mm) lath per bearing. Five attachments per 24-inch-wide (610 mm) lath per bearing.

[8]For interiors only.

[9]Attach self-furring wire fabric lath to supports at furring device.

[10]Three attachments per 16-inch-wide (406.4 mm) lath per bearing. Four attachments per 24-inch-wide (610 mm) lath per bearing.

[11]When lath and stripping are stapled simultaneously, increase leg length of staple $^1/_8$ inch (3.2 mm).

From the Uniform Building Code, ©1997, ICBO

Figure 14-3 *Attaching lath to wood and metal supports*

When you're lathing exterior stud walls with metal or gypsum lath, you need a "weep screed" at or below the foundation line. Place the screed at least 4 inches above grade. It allows water to drain to the exterior of the building.

You can't use all types of gypsum lath for exterior lathing. And remember not to install interior lath until there's complete weather protection. Apply gypsum lath with the long dimension perpendicular to the supports. Stagger end joints in successive courses. If adjacent panels have end joints on the same support, apply joint stripping to the full length of the joint. If the lath joints don't touch or if the space between them is greater than $^3/_8$ inch, you have to strip the joint.

Weather-Resistive Barriers

Section 2506.4 requires that you install a weather-resistant barrier in exterior walls. Section 1402.1 explains the requirement. You'll

TABLE 25-D—THICKNESS OF PLASTER[1]

PLASTER BASE	FINISHED THICKNESS OF PLASTER FROM FACE OF LATH, MASONRY, CONCRETE	
	× 25.4 for mm	
	Gypsum Plaster	Portland Cement Plaster
1. Expanded metal lath	5/8" minimum[2]	5/8" minimum[2]
2. Wire fabric lath	5/8" minimum[2]	3/4" minimum (interior)[3] 7/8" minimum (exterior)[3]
3. Gypsum lath	1/2" minimum	
4. Masonry walls[4]	1/2" minimum	1/2" minimum
5. Monolithic concrete walls[4,5]	5/8" maximum[6]	7/8" maximum[6]
6. Monolithic concrete ceilings[4,5]	3/8" maximum[6,7,8]	1/2" maximum[7,8]

[1]For fire-resistive construction, see Tables 7-A, 7-B and 7-C.
[2]When measured from back plane of expanded metal lath, exclusive of ribs, or self-furring lath, plaster thickness shall be 3/4 inch (19 mm) minimum.
[3]When measured from face of support or backing.
[4]Because masonry and concrete surfaces may vary in plane, thickness of plaster need not be uniform.
[5]When applied over a liquid bonding agent, finish coat may be applied directly to concrete surface.
[6]An approved skim-coat plaster 1/16 inch (1.6 mm) thick may be applied directly to concrete.
[7]On concrete ceilings, where the base coat plaster thickness exceeds the maximum thickness shown, metal lath or wire fabric lath shall be attached to the concrete.
[8]Approved acoustical plaster may be applied directly to concrete, or over base coat plaster, beyond the maximum plaster thickness shown.

From the Uniform Building Code, ©1997, ICBO

Figure 14-4 *Thickness of plaster*

need to hang two layers of Grade D paper over wood base sheathing. Here's what 1402.1 says:

Section 1402.1 Weather-resistive Barriers.
All weather-exposed surfaces shall have a weather-resistive barrier to protect the interior wall covering. Such barrier shall be equal to that provided for in UBC Standard 14-1 for kraft waterproof building paper or asphalt-saturated rag felt. Building paper and felt shall be free from holes and breaks other than those created by fasteners and construction system due to attaching of the building paper, and shall be applied over studs or sheathing of all exterior walls. Such felt or paper shall be applied horizontally, with the upper layer lapped over the lower layer not less than 2 inches (51 mm). Where vertical joints occur, felt or paper shall be lapped not less than 6 inches (152 mm).

You can omit the weather-protective barriers when:

- The exterior covering is approved weatherproof panels

- The construction is back-plastered

- There's no human occupancy

- The panel sheathing is water-repellent

- There's approved paperbacked metal or wire fabric lath

- There's lath and portland cement plaster on the underside of roof and eave projections

Plaster

There are generally two types of plaster used in construction today. You can use portland cement plaster for both outdoor and indoor work. Use gypsum plaster only on interior work. Both require three coats when applied over metal lath or wire fabric lath. You must apply at least two coats over any other material allowed by the code. Remember this, though: You can never apply plaster directly to fiber insulation board.

Three tables set the requirements for plaster. UBC Table 25-D (Figure 14-4) gives the minimum thickness of both kinds of plaster over plaster bases. (Plaster thickness is measured

TABLE 25-E—GYPSUM PLASTER PROPORTIONS[1]

| NUMBER | COAT | PLASTER BASE OR LATH | MAXIMUM VOLUME AGGREGATE PER 100 POUNDS (45.4 kg) NEAT PLASTER[2,3] (cubic feet) | |
| | | | × 0.028 for m³ | |
			Damp Loose Sand[4]	Perlite or Vermiculite[4]
1. Two-coat work	Base coat	Gypsum lath	$2\frac{1}{2}$	2
	Base coat	Masonry	3	3
2. Three-coat work	First coat	Lath	2[5]	2
	Second coat	Lath	3[5]	2[6]
	First and second coats	Masonry	3	3

[1]Wood-fibered gypsum plaster may be mixed in the proportions of 100 pounds (45.4 kg) of gypsum to not more than 1 cubic foot (0.028 m³) of sand where applied on masonry or concrete.

[2]For fire-resistive construction, see Tables 7-A, 7-B and 7-C.

[3]When determining the amount of aggregate in set plaster, a tolerance of 10 percent shall be allowed.

[4]Combinations of sand and lightweight aggregate may be used, provided the volume and weight relationship of the combined aggregate to gypsum plaster is maintained.

[5]If used for both first and second coats, the volume of aggregate may be $2\frac{1}{2}$ cubic feet (0.07 m³).

[6]Where plaster is 1 inch (25 mm) or more in total thickness, the proportions for the second coat may be increased to 3 cubic feet (0.08 m³).

From the Uniform Building Code, ©1997, ICBO

Figure 14-5 *Gypsum plaster proportions*

from the face of the base it's applied over.) Table 25-E (Figure 14-5) shows the proportions of aggregate to cementitious materials in gypsum plaster. Table 25-F (Figure 14-6) does the same thing for portland cement plaster and portland cement-lime plaster. Curing times for portland cement or cement-lime plaster are shown in UBC Table 25-F.

To ensure proper bonding, concrete or masonry surfaces must be clean and free from efflorescence, sufficiently damp, and rough. If the surface isn't rough, apply bonding agents or a portland cement dash bond coat. Mix the dash bond coat in the proportions of 1½ cubic feet of sand to 1 cubic foot of portland cement.

You can't apply portland cement plaster to frozen surfaces or use any frozen ingredients. Protect all work from freezing for 24 hours. If you have to work in cold weather, I recommend that you follow the procedures in Chapter 10 for laying concrete block during cold weather.

Exposed Aggregate Plaster

You probably know this material as stucco. It's used almost the same way as standard interior plaster except that more sand aggre-gate is added to a bedding coat. For exterior work, this bedding coat consists of one part portland cement, one part Type S lime and a maximum three parts of graded white or natural sand by volume. It must have a minimum compressive strength of 1,000 pounds per square inch. The composition of the interior bedding coat is 100 pounds of neat gypsum plaster and a maximum 200 pounds of graded white sand.

Section 2509 covers exposed aggregate plaster:

2509.1 General. *Exposed natural or integrally colored aggregate may be partially embedded in a natural or colored bedding coat of cement or gypsum plaster, subject to the provisions of this section.*

2509.2 Aggregate. *The aggregate may be applied manually or mechanically and shall consist of marble chips, pebbles, or similar durable, nonreactive materials, moderately hard (three or more on the Mohs scale).*

TABLE 25-F—CEMENT PLASTERS[1]

PORTLAND CEMENT PLASTER							
Coat	Volume Cement	Maximum Weight (or Volume) Lime per Volume Cement	Maximum Volume Sand per Combined Volumes Cement and Lime[2]	Approximate Minimum Thickness[3]	× 25.4 for mm	Minimum Period Moist Curing	Minimum Interval between Coats
First	1	20 lbs. (9.07 kg)	4		$3/8$"[4]	48 hours[5]	48 hours[6]
Second	1	20 lbs. (9.07 kg)	5		1st and 2nd coats total $3/4$"	48 hours	7 days[7]
Finish	1	1[8]	3		1st, 2nd and finish coats $7/8$"	—	7

PORTLAND CEMENT-LIME PLASTER[9]							
Coat	Volume Cement	Maximum Volume Lime per Volume Cement	Maximum Volume Sand per Combined Volumes Cement and Lime[3]	Approximate Minimum Thickness[3]	× 25.4 for mm	Minimum Period Moist Curing	Minimum Interval between Coats
First	1	1	4		$3/8$"[4]	48 hours[5]	48 hours[6]
Second	1	1	$4^1/_2$		1st and 2nd coats total $3/4$"	48 hours	7 days[7]
Finish	1	1[8]	3		1st, 2nd and finish coats $7/8$"	—	7

PLASTIC CEMENT PLASTER[9]							
Coat	Volume Cement	Maximum Weight (or Volume) Lime per Volume Cement	Maximum Volume Sand per Volume Cement[2]	Approximate Minimum Thickness[3]	× 25.4 for mm	Minimum Period Moist Curing	Minimum Interval between Coats
First	1	—	4		$3/8$"[4]	48 hours[5]	48 hours[6]
Second	1	—	5		1st and 2nd coats total $3/4$"	48 hours	7 days[7]
Finish	1	—	3		1st, 2nd and finish coats $7/8$"	—	7

[1]Exposed aggregate plaster shall be applied in accordance with Section 2509. Minimum overall thickness shall be $3/4$ inch (19 mm).
[2]When determining the amount of sand in set plaster, a tolerance of 10 percent may be allowed.
[3]See Table 25-D.
[4]Measured from face of support or backing to crest of scored plaster.
[5]See Section 2507.3.3.
[6]Twenty-four-hour minimum interval between coats of interior cement plaster. For alternate method of application, see Section 2508.6.
[7]Finish coat plaster may be applied to interior portland cement base coats after a 48-hour period.
[8]For finish coat plaster, up to an equal part of dry hydrated lime by weight (or an equivalent volume of lime putty) may be added to Types I, II and III standard portland cement.
[9]No additions of plasticizing agents shall be made.

From the Uniform Building Code, ©1997, ICBO

Figure 14-6 *Portland cement plaster*

Pneumatically Placed Plaster

Section 2510 describes pneumatically placed plaster, usually known as gunite.

Pneumatically placed portland cement plaster shall be a mixture of portland cement and sand, mixed dry, conveyed by air through a pipe or flexible tube, hydrated at the nozzle at the end of the conveyor and deposited by air pressure in its final position.

"Hydrated at the nozzle" means that the water is added to the dry gunite mixture as it leaves the tube.

You almost always have to apply two coats of gunite. Together, the two coats must be at least $7/8$ inch thick. Curing time between coats is specified in UBC Table 25-F (Figure 14-6).

There's one refinement that doesn't apply to other types of plaster. You can screen and reuse the rebound material as long as it doesn't exceed 25 percent of the total sand used in any batch.

Gypsum Wallboard

I've seen sheetrock put up almost every way possible. Some installers would probably sew it on if they could. I think the main reason for sloppy installation is that most installers are paid by the unit rather than by the hour. If they can take shortcuts or omit a few nails here and there, they can put up more material and make more money.

That may be why the code regulates wallboard. It must be inspected, as outlined in Section 108.5.5:

> **Lath or gypsum board inspection:** *To be made after all lathing and gypsum board, interior and exterior, is in place, but before any plastering is applied or before gypsum board joints and fasteners are taped and finished.*

There are several points to note about installation of gypsum board and laths. Take a look at Section 2505.1.

> **General.** *Gypsum lath shall not be installed until weather protection for the installation is provided. . . .*

The code says gypsum lath, but the same rule also applies to wallboard. Now we'll see what Section 2512 says:

> *When gypsum is used as a base for tile or wall panels for tub, shower or water closet compartment walls (see Sections 807.1.2 and 807.1.3), water-resistant gypsum backing board shall be used. Regular gypsum wallboard is permitted under tile or wall panels in other wall and ceiling areas when installed in accordance with Table 25-G. Water-resistant gypsum board shall not be used in the following locations:*
>
> *1. Over a vapor retarder.*
>
> *2. In areas subject to continuous high humidity, such as saunas, steam rooms or gang shower rooms.*
>
> *3. On ceilings where frame spacing exceeds 12 inches (305 mm) on center.*

Fastening Gypsum Wallboard

There are three common ways to hang wallboard. The most common is nailing, second is attaching with screws, and third is using adhesives. About the only difference between using nails and screws is that you can space screws 12 inches apart. Nails can't exceed 7- or 8-inch spacing. Screws are commonly used in commercial areas for Type I construction with steel studding. In commercial applications the wallboard will be thicker to get the required fire rating.

There are two ways to install sheetrock where a fire rating is required: single-ply and two-ply application. Specifications are given in UBC Table 25-G (Figure 14-7) for single-ply and Table 25-H (Figure 14-8) for two-ply application.

The Gypsum Association, which wrote most of the section on wallboard application, lists twelve steps for proper application. Although this applies to wallboard that's nailed, many of the same rules apply to screw-fastened wallboard.

Nailing — The footnotes on UBC Table 25-G mention two methods of nailing. The first is outlined in the table itself where it indicates that spacing of single nails will be generally 7 inches both along edges and in the field (middle) of the panel. Footnote 3 covers double-nailing:

> *Two nails spaced 2 inches to 2½ inches (51 mm to 64 mm) apart may be used where the pairs are spaced 12 inches (305 mm) on center except around the perimeter of the sheets.*

You can find the Gypsum Association's nailing recommendations in their handbook. Although the code doesn't quote them directly, most of them have made their way into the code. If you follow the Gypsum Association recommendations, you won't have any trouble with the inspector.

TABLE 25-G—SINGLE-PLY GYPSUM WALLBOARD APPLIED PARALLEL (‖) OR PERPENDICULAR (⊥) TO FRAMING MEMBERS

THICKNESS OF GYPSUM WALLBOARD (Inch) × 25.4 for mm	PLANE OF FRAMING SURFACE	MAXIMUM SPACING OF FRAMING MEMBER[1] (Center to Center) (inches) × 25.4 for mm	LONG DIMENSION OF GYPSUM WALLBOARD SHEETS IN RELATION TO DIRECTION OF FRAMING MEMBERS ‖	⊥	MAXIMUM SPACING OF FASTENERS[1] (Center to Center) (inches) × 25.4 for mm Nails[3]	Screws[4]	NAILS[2]—TO WOOD × 25.4 for mm
1/2	Horizontal	16	P	P	7	12	No. 13 gage, 1 3/8" long, 19/64" head; 0.098" diameter, 1 1/4" long, annular ringed; 5d, cooler (0.086" dia., 1 5/8" long, 15/64" head) or wallboard (0.086" dia., 1 5/8" long, 9/32" head) nail.
		24	NP	P	7	12	
	Vertical	16	P	P	8	16	
		24	P	P	8	12	
5/8	Horizontal	16	P	P	7	12	No. 13 gage, 1 5/8" long, 19/64" head; 0.098" diameter, 1 3/8" long, annular ringed; 6d, cooler (0.092" dia., 1 7/8" long, 1/4" head) or wallboard (0.0915" dia., 1 7/8" long, 19/64" head) nail.
		24	NP	P	7	12	
	Vertical	16	P	P	8	16	
		24	P	P	8	12	

Nail or Screw Fastenings with Adhesives (Maximum Center to Center in Inches)

× 25.4 for mm

(Column headings as above)					End	Edges	Field	
1/2 or 5/8	Horizontal	16	P	P	16	16	24	As required for 1/2" and 5/8" gypsum wallboard, see above.
		24	NP	P	16	24	24	
	Vertical	24	P	P	16	24	NR	

NOTES: Horizontal refers to applications such as ceilings. Vertical refers to applications such as walls.

‖ denotes parallel.

⊥ denotes perpendicular.   P—Permitted.   NP—Not permitted.   NR—Not required.

[1] A combination of fasteners consisting of nails along the perimeter and screws in the field of the gypsum board may be used with the spacing of the fasteners shown in the table.

    For fire-resistive construction, see Tables 7-B and 7-C. For shear-resisting elements, see Table 25-I.

[2] Where the metal framing has a clinching design formed to receive the nails by two edges of metal, the nails shall not be less than 5/8 inch (15.9 mm) longer than the wallboard thickness, and shall have ringed shanks. Where the metal framing has a nailing groove formed to receive the nails, the nails shall have barbed shanks or be 5d, No. 13 1/2 gage, 1 5/8 inches (41 mm) long, 15/64-inch (6.0 mm) head for 1/2-inch (12.7 mm) gypsum wallboard; 6d, No. 13 gage, 1 7/8 (48 mm) inches long, 15/64-inch (6.0 mm) head for 5/8-inch (15.9 mm) gypsum wallboard.

[3] Two nails spaced 2 inches to 2 1/2 inches (51 mm to 64 mm) apart may be used where the pairs are spaced 12 inches (305 mm) on center except around the perimeter of the sheets.

[4] Screws shall be long enough to penetrate into wood framing not less than 5/8 inch (15.9 mm) and through metal framing not less than 1/4 inch (6.4 mm).

From the Uniform Building Code, ©1997, ICBO

Figure 14-7 *Application of single-ply gypsum wallboard*

The Institute says this about nailing:

1) Drive nails at least 3/8 inch from ends and edges of the wallboard.

2) Position nails on adjacent ends or edges opposite each other.

3) Begin nailing from the center of the wallboard and proceed toward edges or outer ends.

4) When nailing, apply pressure on wallboard adjacent to the nail you're driving to ensure that the wallboard is secured tightly on the framing member.

5) Drive nails with the shank perpendicular to the face of the board.

6) Use a crown-head hammer.

7) With the last blow of the hammer, seat the nail so the head is in a slight uniform dimple formed by the last blow of the hammer.

8) Don't break the paper at the nail head or around the circumference of the dimple by over-driving it. And don't use a nail set. The dimple shouldn't be over 1/32 inch deep.

9) If you tear the face paper, set an additional nail or fastener not more than 2 inches from the tear.

TABLE 25-H—APPLICATION OF TWO-PLY GYPSUM WALLBOARD[1]

Thickness of Gypsum Wallboard (Each Ply) (inch) × 25.4 for mm	Plane of Framing Surface	Long Dimension of Gypsum Wallboard Sheets	Maximum Spacing of Framing Members (Center to Center) (inches) × 25.4 for mm	Maximum Spacing of Fasteners (Center to Center) (inches) × 25.4 for mm				
				Base Ply			Face Ply	
				Nails[2]	Screws[3]	Staples[4]	Nails[2]	Screws[3]
FASTENERS ONLY								
3/8	Horizontal	Perpendicular only	16	16	24	16	7	12
	Vertical	Either direction	16				8	
1/2	Horizontal	Perpendicular only	24				7	
	Vertical	Either direction	24				8	
5/8	Horizontal	Perpendicular only	24				7	
	Vertical	Either direction	24				8	
FASTENERS AND ADHESIVES								
3/8	Horizontal	Perpendicular only	16	7	12	5	Temporary nailing or shoring to comply with Section 2511.4	
Base ply	Vertical	Either direction	24	8		7		
1/2	Horizontal	Perpendicular only	24	7		5		
Base ply	Vertical	Either direction	24	8		7		
5/8	Horizontal	Perpendicular only	24	7		5		
Base ply	Vertical	Either direction	24	8		7		

[1]For fire-resistive construction, see Tables 7-B and 7-C. For shear-resisting elements, see Table 25-I.

[2]Nails for wood framing shall be long enough to penetrate into wood members not less than 3/4 inch (19.1 mm), and the sizes shall comply with the provisions of Table 25-G. For nails not included in Table 25-G, use the appropriate size cooler or wallboard nails. Nails for metal framing shall comply with the provisions of Table 25-G.

[3]Screws shall comply with the provisions of Table 25-G.

[4]Staples shall not be less than No. 16 gage by 3/4-inch (19.1 mm) crown width with leg length of 7/8 inch (22.2 mm), 1 1/8 inches (28.6 mm) and 1 3/8 inches (34.9 mm) for gypsum wallboard thicknesses of 3/8 inch (9.5 mm), 1/2 inch (12.7 mm) and 5/8 inch (15.9 mm), respectively.

From the Uniform Building Code, ©1997, ICBO

Figure 14-8 *Application of two-ply gypsum wallboard*

10) Follow the nailing schedule even when you're using adhesives.

11) You can use screws if they're approved sizes. Spacing may be altered if screws are used. Check with your building inspector.

12) Gypsum wallboard may be applied parallel or perpendicular to the studs.

Screws — Both UBC Tables 25-G and 25-H show maximum spacing required for fastening gypsum wallboard with screws. Footnote 4 in Table 25-G says that screws "shall be long enough to penetrate into wood framing not less than 5/8 inch (15.9 mm) and through metal framing not less than 1/4 inch (6.4 mm)." There aren't too many surprises in UBC Standards about screws. Here are some of the main requirements:

■ The head of the screw must be at least 0.315 inch in diameter.

■ The driving recess must be a No. 2 Phillips design with a minimum depth of 0.105 inch.

■ Screws must be self drilling and drive into the stud in less than five seconds.

■ Screw threads must be capable of pulling the head of the screw below the surface of the wallboard through four layers of 0.010-inch-thick kraft paper over 5/8 inch Type X gypsum wallboard.

Adhesives — As a building inspector I made a few people unhappy by not allowing them to use adhesives on wallboard unless a full-time inspector was there to check each step of the job. To do a good job, you must apply the adhesive according to the manufacturer's recommendations. The code says you must put down a bead of adhesive that will spread to at least 1 inch wide and $\frac{1}{16}$ inch thick. This calls for a continuous bead at least ¼ inch to ⅜ inch for all framing members, except top and bottom plates.

I found that some installers were only putting down spots or thin beads of adhesive, especially when the tube was about to run out (after all, adhesives cost money, and if you don't have another tube on hand, getting one wastes time). Once the wallboard's in place, there's no easy way of telling how wide, thick or continuous the adhesive is. That's why I wanted constant supervision.

It really wasn't a very big deal. The installers found they didn't save a lot of time, anyway. For practical reasons, they had to apply the adhesive on the reverse side of the panel. That meant marking the panel for the stud locations. Then the panel had to be held in place while the adhesive dried. Back then the code didn't require nailing. But as you can see in UBC Table 25-G, the code now requires a certain amount of nailing on single-ply applications.

Two-ply installation — Two-ply is usually used where extra thickness is required for fire-resistiveness. Sheetrock is heavy. It's much easier to lay up two pieces of ⅜-inch wallboard than one piece that's ¾ inch thick. If you need 1 or 1½ inches of wallboard thickness, two-ply installation is the only way to go.

Another advantage of two-ply installation is that you get a smoother wall. You lay up the first layer just like a single layer, then put up the second coat with adhesives. You don't need to nail the second layer. You'll have to hold this layer in place until the adhesive sets up, but that usually doesn't take long. The amount of taping is reduced, and the overall finish is neater. To get the required fire-resistiveness, the second layer must be applied perpendicular to the base layer.

How Is Sheetrock Fire Resistive?

At first it's difficult to understand how a white powder encased in two layers of paper could be fire resistive. But it's just a simple chemical reaction. As fire burns through the paper and reaches the gypsum, the heat causes a thin layer of water vapor to form over the surface. This repels the fire and cools the surface. But the effect doesn't last long. That's why you need additional thickness to get longer fire-resistiveness. The water vapor evaporates, slowing the spread of fire.

A Woman's Place

A young woman contractor came into my office a few years ago to apply for a permit. She said she'd drawn the plans herself. And she'd done a pretty good job. I found one or two little details she'd missed. Then she got her permit.

We didn't talk again until after I'd made the last inspection. I was curious about how she got into the construction business. "My dad was a carpenter in Arkansas," she told me, "and I worked a lot with him. When my kids were old enough for school, I looked around for something to do. I had three choices: Stay home and wash dishes, get an office job at a computer terminal, or build houses. I like building houses."

At the next home builder's association meeting I took a little good natured kidding. What was I doing issuing a permit to a woman? Some of the newer contractors there didn't understand that many of my applicants were women — but usually contractor's wives helping out with the paperwork. There aren't many female contractors. This is mostly a man's business. And I suppose that's the way some of my contractor friends like it. Maybe they can't take the competition.

Anyhow, the woman I'm talking about eventually moved away from the area. But while she was here she designed and built some fine houses. And I never had any code enforcement problems with her. She was as professional and capable as any contractor I know.

When you think about it, there's nothing in construction contracting that keeps a woman from being every bit as good as a man. You don't have to be 6'2" and weigh 225 to make it in this business.

Of course, there are far more male contractors than female. And I don't expect that will change in my lifetime. But if you're a woman (and I hope at least a few of readers are), let me encourage you with this note:

I've checked the building code very carefully, from cover to cover, I haven't found a single section, not a single word, not a shred of a trace of anything that gives any kind of a preference to men.

This industry can always use one more dedicated professional, whether male or female.

15

Combustion Air

As a building inspector I was constantly running into problems over "combustion air." How much was enough? Here's what Section 701.1 of the Uniform Mechanical Code (UMC) has to say about it:

701.1 Air Supply. *Fuel-burning equipment shall be assured a sufficient supply of combustion air. The methods of providing combustion air in this chapter do not apply to direct vent appliances, appliances listed as having separated combustion systems, enclosed furnaces, listed cooking appliances, refrigerators and domestic clothes dryers.*

In buildings of unusually tight construction, combustion air shall be obtained from outside. In buildings of ordinary tightness insofar as infiltration is concerned, all or a portion of the combustion air for fuel-burning appliances may be obtained from infiltration when the requirement for 50 cubic feet (1.42 m³) per 1000 Btu/h (293.1 W) input is met.

701.4 Existing Buildings. *When fuel-burning appliances are installed in an existing building containing other fuel-burning appliances, the room or space shall be provided with combustion air as required by this chapter for all fuel-burning appliances contained therein.*

This whole chapter in the UMC is vague. I can foresee more than a few disputes with building inspectors who haven't thought it out.

Most new or recently-remodeled buildings have combustion air inlets for fuel-burning appliances. But older buildings may not have combustion air inlets, or the inlets may be blocked. For instance, louvered vents that provide air can be blocked by dampers or by items stored in front of them. Combustion air inlets may be obstructed when rooms are remodeled.

Did you notice the term "ordinary tightness" in Section 701.1? How would you define it? Let's look at some definitions from Chapter 2 of the UMC to help us:

Confined Space *is a room or space having a volume less than 50 cubic feet (1.42 m³) per 1000 Btu/h (293.1 W) of the aggregate input rating of all fuel-burning appliances installed in that space.*

Unconfined Space *is a room or space having a volume equal to at least 50 cubic feet (1.416 m³) per 1000 Btu/h (0.293 kW) of the aggregate input rating of all fuel-burning appliances installed in that space. Rooms communicating directly with the space in which the appliances are installed, through openings not furnished with doors, are considered a part of the unconfined space.*

Unusually Tight Construction *is construction where:*

1. *Walls and ceilings exposed to the outside atmosphere have a continuous water vapor retarder with a rating of one perm or less with any openings gasketed or sealed;*

2. *Weatherstripping is on openable windows and doors; and*

3. *Caulking or sealants are applied to areas such as joints around window and door frames, between sole plates and floors, between wall-ceiling joints, between wall panels and at penetrations for plumbing, electrical and gas lines and at other openings.*

A building is of "ordinary tightness" if it doesn't meet the definition of "unusually tight construction."

Computing Combustion Air Requirements

Take time to read this next section very carefully. There are very specific steps in the way you compute combustion air requirements.

This is what Section 703 of the UMC offers:

703.4 Interior Spaces. *In buildings of ordinary tightness, combustion air provided by infiltration may be obtained from freely communicating interior spaces, provided the combined volume in cubic feet complies with the following conditions:*

703.4.1 Adequate Volume — Gas and Liquid. *If the volume of the room or space in which fuel-burning appliances are installed is equal to or greater than 50 cubic feet (1.416 m³) per 1000 Btu/h (0.293 kW) of aggregate input rating of appliances, infiltration may be regarded as adequate to provide combustion air. Exclude from the calculation the input ratings of listed direct vent appliances, enclosed furnaces, cooking appliances, refrigerators and domestic clothes dryers.*

703.4.2 Insufficient Volume — Gas and Liquid. *Rooms or spaces containing gas- or liquid-fuel-burning appliances which do not have the volume as specified above shall be provided with minimum unobstructed combustion air openings as specified in Section 707.0 and arranged as specified in Section 702.0.*

You'll hear a lot about British thermal units (Btu) whenever you get involved with heat-producing appliances such as furnaces, water heaters, ovens or hot plates. A Btu is the amount of heat required to raise the temperature of 1 pound of water 1 degree Fahrenheit at or near its point of maximum density. Btu/h is the Btu per hour of input.

Consider the Size of the Enclosure

Let's look at a common example. Your home measures 24 feet by 36 feet and you have the usual 8-foot ceilings. You've got about 7,000 cubic feet of space. Let's say your furnace is in an unfinished basement with the same dimensions as the house, so it's also in a space of about 7,000 cubic feet.

TABLE 7-A—SIZE OF COMBUSTION-AIR OPENINGS OR DUCTS[1]

COLUMN I		COLUMN II	
Buildings of Ordinary Tightness		Buildings of Unusually Tight Construction[2]	
Condition	Size of Openings or Ducts × 0.293 for W × 645.2 for mm²	Condition	Size of Openings or Ducts × 0.293 for W × 645.2 for mm²
Appliance in unconfined[2] space:	May rely on infiltration alone.	Appliance in unconfined[2] space: Obtain combustion air from outdoors or from space freely communicating with outdoors.	Provide two openings, each having 1 sq. in. per 5,000 Btu/h input. Ducts admitting outdoor air may be connected to the cold-air return.
Appliance in confined[3] space: 1. All air from inside building.	Provide two openings into enclosure each having 1 sq. in. per 1,000 Btu/h input freely communicating with other unconfined interior spaces. Minimum 100 sq. in. each opening.[4]	Appliance in confined[3] space: Obtain combustion air from outdoors or from space freely communicating with outdoors.	1. Provide two vertical ducts or plenums; 1 sq. in. per 4,000 Btu/h input each duct or plenum. 2. Provide two horizontal ducts or plenums; 1 sq. in. per 2,000 Btu/h input each duct or plenum.
2. Part of air from inside building.	Provide two openings into enclosure[4] from other freely communicating unconfined[2] interior spaces each having an area of 100 sq. in. plus one duct or plenum opening to outdoors having an area of 1 sq. in. per 5,000 Btu/h input rating. The outdoor duct or plenum opening may be connected to the cold-air return.		3. Provide two openings in an exterior wall of the enclosure; each opening 1 sq. in. per 4,000 Btu/h input. 4. Provide one ceiling opening to ventilated attic and one vertical duct to attic; each opening 1 sq. in. per 4,000 Btu/h input. 5. Provide one opening or one vertical duct or one horizontal duct in the enclosure; 1 sq. in. per 3,000 Btu/h input but no smaller than vent flow area.
3. All air from outdoors. Obtain from outdoors or from space freely communicating with outdoors.	Use any of the methods listed for confined space in unusually tight construction as indicated in Column II.		6. Provide one opening in enclosure ceiling to ventilated attic and one opening in enclosure floor to ventilated crawl space; each opening 1 sq. in. per 4,000 Btu/h input.

[1]For location of openings, see Section 702.

[2]As defined in Section 223.

[3]As defined in Section 205.

[4]When the total input rating of appliances in enclosure exceeds 100,000 Btu/h (29.3 kW), the area of each opening into the enclosure must be increased 1 square inch (645 mm²) for each 1,000 Btu/h (293 W) over 100,000 (29.3 kW).

From the Uniform Mechanical Code, ©1997, ICBO

Figure 15-1 *Size of combustion-air openings or ducts*

Let's further assume that your fuel needs are 140,000 Btu per hour. Using the figures from Section 703.4, you need 50 cubic feet for each 1,000 Btu. Multiply 140 by 50. That's 7,000 cubic feet of combustion air — just what you have. This is with no partitions in your basement.

You may have a problem, though. An unfinished basement simply screams for the family handyman to finish it. When he does, the furnace usually ends up in a furnace room or a corner of the utility room. But that furnace, squeezed into a smaller area, still needs to have an adequate supply of air. So how much is "adequate"?

Air Required

Here again we've got to start with the size of the area where your fuel-burning appliance is located. UMC Table 7-A (Figure 15-1) addresses this subject.

First, the table breaks it down into the two types of construction; Column I, Buildings of Ordinary Tightness and the second category, Buildings of Unusually Tight Construction. It's up to you to select the condition that most nearly typifies your installation. That will give you the requirements you must follow.

Remember, that's for unconfined spaces. For appliances in confined spaces with all combustion air coming from inside the building, you need at least 1 square inch for each 1,000 Btu input rating. That's five times as much. Each of the combustion air openings has to be at least 100 square inches — only 10 inches by 10 inches, probably the smallest size made.

When we have to bring in all the air from outdoors, the vertical ducts must have a free area of 1 square inch for each 4,000 Btu/h of input (Figure 15-1). Horizontal ducts, on the other hand, require 1 square inch of free area for each 2,000 Btu/h of input, or twice as much. Ducts combining outdoor air and indoor air need only 1 square inch of free area for each 5,000 Btu per hour. Where ducts are admitting outdoor air, they may be connected to the cold-air return of the heating system.

Supplying the Air

According to Section 702.1 of the UMC, half of the required air must come from an opening located within the upper 12 inches of the enclosure. The other half comes from an opening located within the lower 12 inches of the enclosure.

There's an exception to Section 702.1 that allows for only one combustion air opening within the upper 12 inches of the enclosure if the appliance has a minimum clearance of 1 inch on the sides and back and 6 inches on the front. Figure 15-2 shows some different methods of supplying combustion air. It should also be noted that the International Mechanical Code allows for some different ways of supplying combustion air that aren't mentioned in the UMC.

Sources of Air

Section 707.2 is an interesting one as the following tale will tell you. But first, let's see what this section will tell the inspector:

707.2 Designed Installations. *Compliance with Table 7-1 is not required for an installation which has been professionally designed to ensure an adequate supply of combustion air.*

The source and condition of the air are important. While I was a building official, a hospital in my town converted its furnaces and boilers from oil to natural gas. Because of other remodeling, they closed the combustion air duct and opened another hole in the wall of the furnace room directly to the outside. This was properly fitted with a louvered vent electrically interlocked with the gas burner. When the thermostat called for heat, the louvers were electrically opened at the same time ignition took place. This is mentioned in Section 702.2.

It had been designed by a heating engineer who did a beautiful job. When the boiler fired, I was on hand to check the system and the louvers responded perfectly. The job was approved.

About the middle of January, I received calls from both the contractor and the hospital. Everything in the boiler room was frozen. Why? Several steam lines and a main water line passed in front of the combustion air vent. With below-freezing weather outside and the boiler calling for heat, the icy wind blowing through the vent had frozen all the pipes in front of it. The problem was solved by placing heaters in the passageway where the cold wind entered. But it took a freeze-up to point out the problem. I couldn't find anything about it in the code except a warning that exposed pipes should be protected. But who would anticipate that pipes would need to be protected from freezing inside a room with two boilers? Experts have been known to overlook vital points, too.

The code requires you to insulate ducts. It describes what must be done in hanging ducts, but in no place that I could find does it require duct heaters in ducts supplying below-freezing air for combustion purposes. That's one of the things you have to learn by experience. Usually your local gas company will be of assistance.

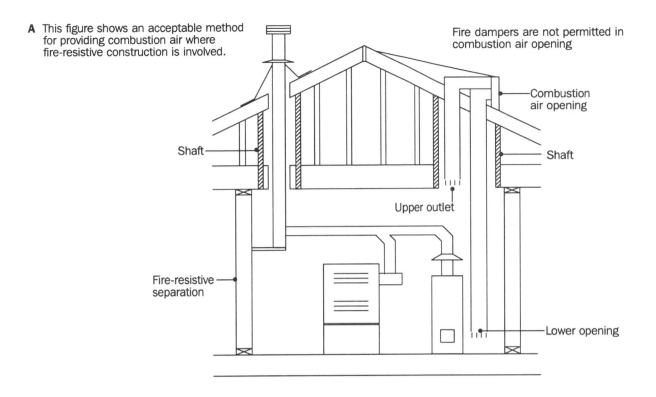

A This figure shows an acceptable method for providing combustion air where fire-resistive construction is involved.

Fire dampers are not permitted in combustion air opening

Combustion air opening

Shaft

Shaft

Upper outlet

Fire-resistive separation

Lower opening

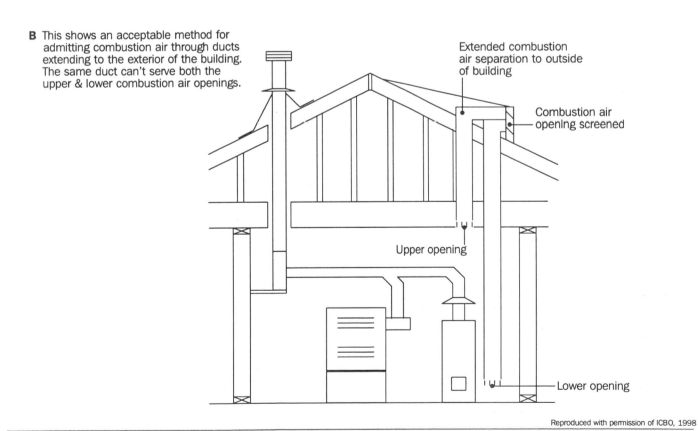

B This shows an acceptable method for admitting combustion air through ducts extending to the exterior of the building. The same duct can't serve both the upper & lower combustion air openings.

Extended combustion air separation to outside of building

Combustion air opening screened

Upper opening

Lower opening

Figure 15-2 *Sources of combustion air*

C This figure shows an acceptable method for admitting combustion air through ducts extending to the exterior of the building. Combustion air openings shall be covered with ¼" screen. See Sec. 702.3.

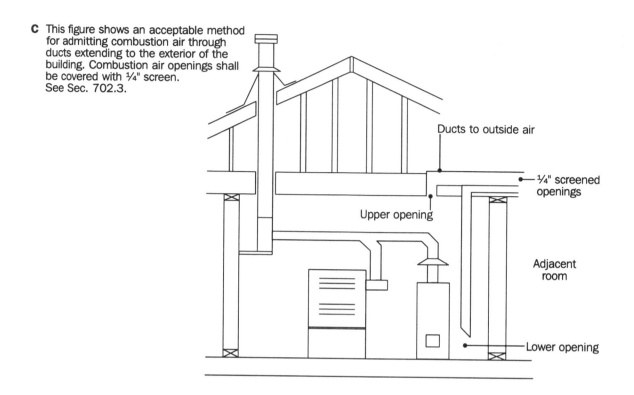

Ducts to outside air

¼" screened openings

Upper opening

Adjacent room

Lower opening

D Inside closet installation

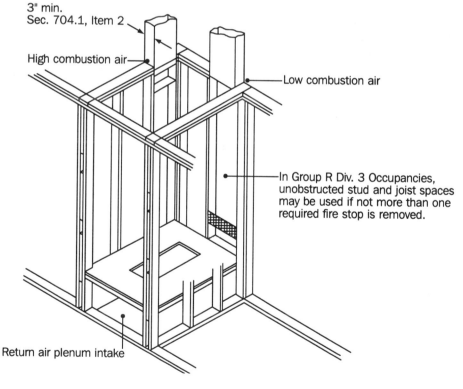

3" min. Sec. 704.1, Item 2

High combustion air

Low combustion air

In Group R Div. 3 Occupancies, unobstructed stud and joist spaces may be used if not more than one required fire stop is removed.

Return air plenum intake

Figure 15-2 *Sources of combustion air (Continued)*

E This shows acceptable methods for admitting combustion air through permanent openings to the outside of the building.

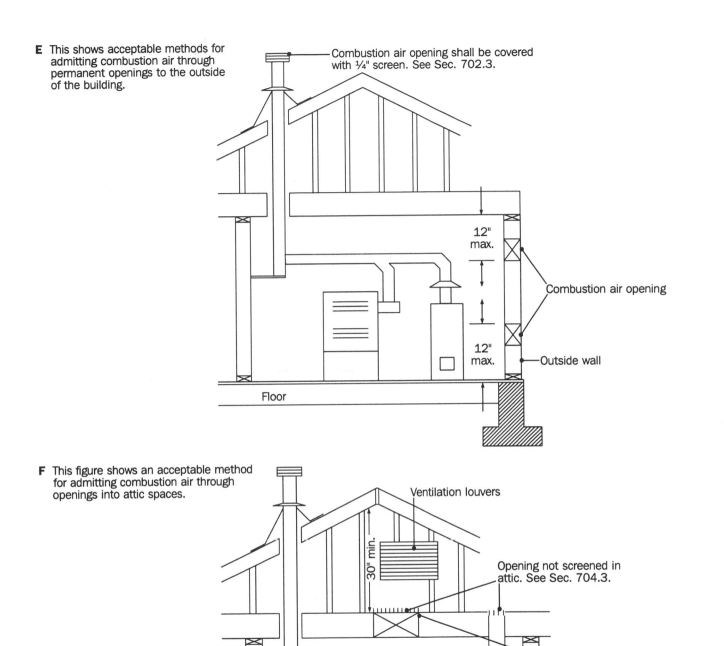

Combustion air opening shall be covered with ¼" screen. See Sec. 702.3.

12" max.

12" max.

Combustion air opening

Outside wall

Floor

F This figure shows an acceptable method for admitting combustion air through openings into attic spaces.

Ventilation louvers

30" min.

Opening not screened in attic. See Sec. 704.3.

Upper outlet

No. 26 gauge galvanized steel 6" above joists and insulation.

12" max.

Reproduced with permission of ICBO, 1998

Figure 15-2 *Sources of combustion air (Continued)*

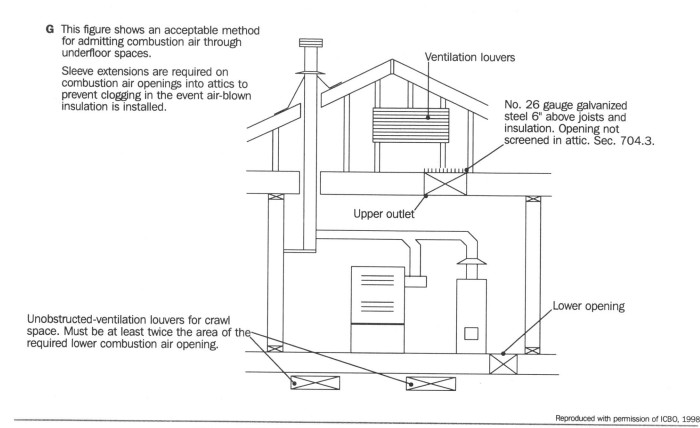

G This figure shows an acceptable method for admitting combustion air through underfloor spaces.

Sleeve extensions are required on combustion air openings into attics to prevent clogging in the event air-blown insulation is installed.

Ventilation louvers

No. 26 gauge galvanized steel 6" above joists and insulation. Opening not screened in attic. Sec. 704.3.

Upper outlet

Lower opening

Unobstructed-ventilation louvers for crawl space. Must be at least twice the area of the required lower combustion air opening.

Figure 15-2 *Sources of combustion air (Continued)*

Section 703.3 of the UMC specifies where you can't get your combustion air:

> ***Prohibited Sources.*** *Openings and ducts shall not connect appliance enclosures with space in which the operation of a fan may adversely affect the flow of combustion air. Combustion air shall not be obtained from a hazardous location or from any area in which objectionable quantities of flammable vapor, lint or dust are released. Combustion air shall not be taken from a refrigeration machinery room.*

According to the UMC, you can't use combustion air openings or ducts where fire dampers are required. And you can't install volume dampers in combustion air openings or ducts. But the International Mechanical Code allows the use of fire dampers in combustion air openings.

That leaves you with three primary sources of combustion air:

1) Outside of the building

2) The underfloor area, provided there's sufficient ventilation

3) Inside the building or conditioned space

Outside — Size your duct to the volume of air needed because you can't install dampers. To use outside air, you must screen your entry duct with a corrosion-resistant screen of not more than ¼-inch mesh. For both outside and underfloor vents, make sure the screens are kept clean. All screened openings must be kept free of dust, leaves, and other debris that will restrict the opening.

For some reason attic space is included under "outside air" instead of in a category of its own. But you can only use attic air if there are sufficient openings to the outside. You must have a minimum vertical clear space of 30 inches at the maximum height of the attic.

Underfloor — You can use underfloor space if there's sufficient free flow of air. That's provided by foundation vents or other special vents with unobstructed openings to the outside.

Inside — You can take combustion air from an interior space if all of the following conditions are met:

1) The space or freely communicating spaces have to be of ordinary tightness. Combustion air can't be obtained from inside of a building of unusually tight construction.

2) The interior freely communicating spaces must have a volume of at least 50 cubic feet per 1,000 Btu/h combined input rating of all the appliances in the space, according to Section 703.4.1. An easy way to find the maximum Btu/h is to multiply the volume by 20. Let's look at an example. Assume a building of ordinary tightness measures 25 feet by 25 feet, and has an 8-foot ceiling. It's all freely communicating space. The building contains 5,000 cubic feet (25 x 25 x 8). Can we install a 100,000 Btu/h furnace? This installation would comply with the code (5,000 x 20 = 100,000).

Now that we have you spooked, there's a ray of sunshine. The code gives you an out. You don't have to comply with the combustion air requirements if the installation has been designed by a qualified engineer.

Consider Other Air Users

There are many other air users in your house — common household items such as fireplaces, kitchen fans and bathroom vents. Each removes air from a confined space. I doubt seriously if many people are aware of how great this air loss is. Recirculating kitchen fans draw air across a charcoal filter to remove cooking odors and grease, then put the air back into the room. They're not a problem. But if your fan discharges to the exterior of the building, then it's reducing the amount of available combustion air.

While we're at it, here's a little advice. Check the attic to make sure the kitchen fan isn't dumping kitchen grease into the attic. The same caution applies to bath vents. Make sure these vents discharge outside.

Section 706.0 of the UMC states:

Operation of exhaust fans, kitchen ventilation systems, clothes dryers or fireplaces shall be considered in determining combustion air requirements to avoid unsatisfactory operation of installed gas appliances.

Fireplaces

As an inspector I was often called out to investigate smoking fireplaces, especially in new homes. There are many reasons for a smoky fireplace, but fireplace construction is seldom the culprit. Houses today are more airtight than they used to be. Single-wall construction with plywood sheathing or siding doesn't admit as much exterior air as diagonal sheathing or shiplap siding. Storm windows, weatherstripping and plastic vapor barriers further reduce air leakage.

In a tight home, furnaces, kitchen and bath fans and fireplaces compete for whatever air is trapped inside the house. During the day, when windows are open and doors are being opened and closed, this isn't a problem. There's a lot of air coming into the house. But it can be a problem at night when all windows and doors are shut. I usually found that a fireplace was smoking because it was starved for oxygen. The flames were licking out for any available air.

Many fireplaces are now designed with vents and tubes to provide combustion air from the outside.

Commercial Air Users

Commercial establishments such as restaurants also have combustion air problems. The vent hoods (and many are required) take a lot of air out of most kitchens. And there are gas-flame grills, water heaters and other appliances gobbling up air.

In winter, the problem usually gets worse. Windows are kept shut and air conditioning units are plugged. But venting of kitchen vapor and steam continues. The kitchen becomes an airless box until someone opens a door and momentarily relieves the condition.

The same thing can happen in your home. If, on some windless night, you open a door or window and a gust of air blows in, you've got a problem. You're living in a vacuum created by your fireplace, furnace and other air-consuming devices. A properly-designed house (and one that doesn't draw cold air) is one with a slightly positive pressure.

Combustion air is probably the least considered of all of a house's ills. But, with the many devices competing for air, it's something that can't be ignored.

In the next chapter, we'll take a look at the Uniform Mechanical Code requirements for heating and cooling homes and small commercial buildings.

The Day I Got Spooked

In most cities and counties an inspection is required when new gas, water or electric lines are installed or reopened. One day I got a call from a young lady who had just moved into an older home. A new gas line had been installed and she needed an inspection before the gas company would begin service. Would I please come out and do whatever was required?

After I'd checked the gas line, she asked me to take a look in the basement. She didn't use it, she told me, but there must be something wrong down there. She heard strange noises coming from under the house at night. She seemed completely serious. My guess was that neighborhood kids were playing down there. "No problem," I told her.

She pointed to a place in the hall where the freezer stood. The basement door was behind it and was both locked and nailed shut. I borrowed a hammer and pried the door open. I tried the light switch just inside the door, but it didn't work.

Dim light coming from the basement showed the outline of furnace duct and an old furnace. The basement must have been a coal bin and furnace room when the home was first built. Judging by the damp, moldy smell, the furnace hadn't been used in many years. Most likely, no one had gone down those stairs into the basement in years.

I stood just inside the basement door for a minute while my eyes became accustomed to the dim light. The door I came through opened onto a small landing at the top of a flight of stairs. Squatting down, I could see two windows at the far end of the basement. They must have been obscured by bushes on the outside, as very little light was coming through. From where I stood, I couldn't see any way in or out except the stairway I was standing on and the two small windows.

I put my weight on the first step down the flight of stairs. It felt solid. I tested the next. The stairs seemed safe enough. But the further I got from the door at the top of the stairs, the more uncomfortable I felt. The hair on the back of my neck was standing straight up. I remember wondering, "Do I get paid for exploring haunted houses?" No doubt about it, I was scared.

I turned to look back up the stairs. The lady was still there, watching from the basement door. If she hadn't been there, I would have been up the stairs and gone, quick as a wink. Instead, I gave her a weak smile, then turned to take another cautious step down. A dozen more steps and I was on the basement floor. I went straight to one window, checked the latch, then did the same on the second window. Both window latches were stuck in the locked position. The cobwebs around the window frames showed the windows hadn't been opened in years. I turned briskly and went back up the stairs, climbing just slowly enough so I didn't look like I was running.

"Nothing to worry about," I said reassuringly. "Looks fine to me. I'll tell the gas company it's OK to start service."

Then I walked, not ran, to my car and drove away.

Several weeks later I was telling the story to some friends who live just down the street from that house. They both laughed. "Didn't you know?" they asked. "That house is haunted. You should hear some of the ghost stories the tenants tell. One couple even moved out. They couldn't sleep at night. But the lady there now says she had someone from the city come out to check the basement. She says it's fine now."

16

Heating, Ventilating & Air Conditioning

Every building code is complex. They have to be. Construction is a complex subject. And codes try to cover it all. To do that, many sections refer to other sections which refer to still more sections. To answer a specific question, you may have to understand what each of the referenced sections requires. That's no problem if you've spent a lifetime working with the code — as many inspectors have. They take pride in having mastered the complexity and subtleties in the code. Builders who haven't had a lifetime to do that, and don't want to, are at a big disadvantage. That's the reason why I wrote this book — to level the playing field a little so you can anticipate problems before they become expensive mistakes.

Heating, ventilating and air conditioning (HVAC) proves my point. The Uniform Building Code doesn't even cover HVAC work. You have to refer to the Uniform Mechanical Code. That's a separate book published by the International Conference of Building Officials. Since nearly every building has heating, cooling or ventilating equipment, you can have UMC problems on nearly any job. After reading this chapter, you should be able to avoid the most common types of code problems on residential and light commercial HVAC work.

We learned in the last chapter how to be sure a furnace has enough combustion air. The next step is installing HVAC equipment so it will pass inspection under the Uniform Mechanical Code.

The UMC, like the UBC, is a complex code. It would take another book this size to explain it completely. You don't need that. So I'll focus on what you do need: installing fuel-using appliances (excluding electrical appliances).

Let's start with a very important section of the UMC. Chapter 3, General Requirements, says that all mechanical equipment that provides space heating, ventilating, air conditioning or refrigeration has to comply with the requirements of the code.

Section 305.1 is a little more specific:

Equipment shall not be installed or altered in violation of the provisions of this code nor shall the fuel input rate be increased beyond or decreased below the approved rating for the altitude at which the equipment is installed.

In simpler terms — don't mess up good equipment with a bad installation job.

Heating equipment gets hot. That's unavoidable. It can also be deadly. An installer who tries to get a little more than the designed heat output, or a little better than the designed air circulation, may be creating work for your local firemen. Don't do it. There are good reasons for following the code and the manufacturer's design limits.

Every appliance you install or service has a data plate showing the intended function and capacity. Take the manufacturer's word on what they know best: their appliance. The data plate on gas, oil and electric heaters and heat pumps has to show serial and model numbers as well as rated capacities. If the tag is missing, return the equipment. Don't install it.

305.1. General. *Fuel-burning equipment shall be designed for use with the type of fuel to which it will be connected and the altitude at which it is installed.*

There's more to that section, but that's the meat of it. If you have natural gas, don't try to hook up a butane or propane appliance. It won't work. If it lights at all, it'll just sputter along at a fraction of the design capacity. You might not burn the house down, but you won't heat it either. Using butane or propane on an appliance intended for natural gas can be deadly. The gas orifice is too big. A natural gas appliance running on butane is a blowtorch.

In any event, you're required to install two approved shutoff valves: one within 3 feet of the appliance and another at the service meter. In each case, provide a union connection, an approved appliance connector, or an approved, listed, quick-disconnect device between the appliance and the valve. That makes it easier to exchange appliances. Connectors for residential ranges and clothes dryers can't be over 6 feet long.

The shutoff valve near the appliance must be in the same room or enclosure and within sight of the furnace. It can't interfere with the maintenance or removal of the furnace. An exception states that the shutoff valve can be inside or under the appliance as long as it's accessible and you can remove the appliance without removing the shutoff valve.

Here's a note about safety: In California and wherever earthquakes are common, authorities recommend keeping a tool near the service entrance for closing the gas shutoff valve. If there's any sign of a leak after a severe earthquake, gas should be shut off until the gas system has been checked.

You can't conceal or extend appliance connectors through a wall, partition, floor or ceiling, or through the equipment housing or casing. The connectors must be large enough to provide the total demand of the connected appliance, according to Tables 3-D-1 and 3-D-2 (Figure 16-1). Only appliance connectors listed for outdoor installation can be installed outdoors. They can't be in contact with soil. Aluminum alloy connectors are limited to interior locations. They can't contact masonry, plaster or insulation, and can't be subject to repeated corrosive wettings.

Installing HVAC Equipment

I'll say this again because it's so important: When installing any appliance, always do what the manufacturer recommends. Every appli-

TABLE 3-D-1—CAPACITIES OF LISTED METAL APPLIANCE CONNECTORS[1]
For use with gas pressures 8-inch (2 kPa) or more water column.

SEMIRIGID CONNECTOR O.D.[2] (inch)	FLEXIBLE CONNECTOR NOMINAL I.D.[3] (inch)	MAXIMUM CAPACITIES IN THOUSANDS Btu/h [Based on pressure drop of 0.4-inch water column (1 kPa)] NAT. GAS[4] OF 1,100 Btu/cu. ft. (41 MJ/m³)							
		1′	1¹/₂′	2′	2¹/₂′	3′	4′	5′	6′
		× 304.8 for mm							
		All Gas Appliances					Ranges and Clothes Dryers		
× 25.4 for mm		× 293.07 for W							
³/₈	¹/₄	40	33	29	27	25			
¹/₂	³/₈	93	76	66	62	58			
⁵/₈	¹/₂	189	155	134	125	116	101	90	80
—	³/₄	404	330	287	266	244			
—	1	803	661	573	534	500			

[1]Gas connectors are certified by the testing agency as complete assemblies including the fittings and valves. Capacities shown are based on the use of fittings and valves supplied with the connector.
[2]Semirigid connector listings are based on outside diameter.
[3]Flexible connector listings are based on nominal diameter.
[4]For liquefied petroleum gas, use 1.6 times the natural gas capacities shown.

TABLE 3-D-2—CAPACITIES OF LISTED METAL APPLIANCE CONNECTORS[1]
For use with gas pressures less than 8-inch (2 kPa) water column.

SEMIRIGID CONNECTOR O.D.[2] (inch)	FLEXIBLE CONNECTOR NOMINAL I.D.[3] (inch)	CAPACITIES FOR VARIOUS LENGTHS IN THOUSANDS Btu/h [Based on pressure drop of 0.2-inch water column (500 Pa)] NAT. GAS[4] OF 1,100 Btu/cu. ft. (41 MJ/m³)							
		1′	1¹/₂′	2′	2¹/₂′	3′	4′	5′	6′
		× 304.8 for mm							
		All Gas Appliances					Ranges and Clothes Dryers		
× 25.4 for mm		× 293.07 for W							
³/₈	¹/₄	28	23	20	19	17			
¹/₂	³/₈	66	54	47	44	41			
⁵/₈	¹/₂	134	110	95	88	82	72	63	57
—	³/₄	285	233	202	188	174			
—	1	561	467	405	378	353			

[1]Gas connectors are certified by the testing agency as complete assemblies including the fittings and valves. Capacities shown are based on the use of fittings and valves supplied with the connector.
[2]Semirigid connector listings are based on outside diameter.
[3]Flexible connector listings are based on nominal diameter.
[4]For liquefied petroleum gas, use 1.6 times the natural gas capacities shown.

From the Uniform Mechanical Code, ©1997, ICBO

Figure 16-1 *Capacities of metal appliance connectors*

ance is tested the way it's intended to be used. Using it any other way may be dangerous. If your appliance was installed by a dealer, chances are it was done correctly. Just check it over and make sure the installer left a copy of the installation and operating instructions attached to the appliance.

But if you're doing the job yourself, where are you going to install this equipment? That information is in Sections 303.1 and 304.6: Unless the equipment was designed for a closet or alcove, it must be installed in a room with a volume at least 12 times the total volume of the furnace. If you're installing a central heating boiler, the room must be at least 16 times the volume of the boiler. And there's another thing: Even if the room or space is higher than 8 feet, you still have to calculate the volume as if it had an 8-foot ceiling.

If there's a conflict between the code and the manufacturer's installation instructions, follow the more restrictive provisions, after checking with your local building department.

Unlisted appliances are only allowed with prior approval from the building department.

The guidelines are in UMC Section 303.2. You'll find the required clearances from unlisted appliances to combustibles in Section 304.6, which refers you to Tables 3-A and 3-B (Figures 16-2 and 16-3).

Equipment Supports and Restraints

Make sure all equipment is supported by substantial bases or hangers capable of supporting the loads they'll be subjected to. If the appliance is designed to be permanently mounted, it must be fixed in position by substantial means that will prevent accidental movement. The restraint has to accommodate both vertical and lateral loads, including wind, snow and seismic loads.

Last but not least, appliances must be accessible for inspection, service, repair and replacement. If you have an under-floor installation, remember that the access hole must be large enough to remove the appliance under the floor. If the access hole is within the building, it can't be covered with carpeting or hidden in a closet. "Readily accessible" means just that.

If you're installing equipment that burns liquid petroleum gas (LPG) or liquid fuel, the inspector won't let you put it under the floor anyway. Such equipment can't be placed in pits, in an under-floor space or below grade where heavier-than-air gases might be trapped. But there's an *if*. If you install an approved method for the safe collection, removal and containment or disposal of the vapors or fuel, you may get approval.

In areas subject to flooding, equipment which would be damaged or create hazardous conditions if inundated can't be installed at or below grade unless it's protected by an approved means.

Automatic Control Devices

All heating appliances have to be equipped with safety controls to shut off the fuel supply to the main burner in case of unsafe conditions. These may occur from out of limits operation or failure of the pilot or ignition. Nearly all heaters come with a device that meets code requirements. It's best to check, though, to be sure.

Heating appliances connected to ducts have to have two separate temperature limiting controls:

■ An automatically-resetting control to prevent the discharge temperature from exceeding 200 degrees F (93 degrees C)

■ A manually-resetting control to prevent the discharge temperature from exceeding 250 degrees F (121 degrees C)

Fuel-burning equipment must be equipped with an approved automatic means that will shut off the fuel supply to the equipment in case of ignition or flame failure. But there are exceptions to this rule.

Exceptions: The listed shutoff devices shall not be required on range or cooking tops, log lighters, lights or other open-burner manually operated appliances or listed appliances not requiring such devices and specific industrial appliances as approved by the Building Official.

Condensate

Now we come to a sticky wicket. Section 309.3 says this:

Chilled Water and Evaporator Coils. Condensate, defrost and overflow discharges from cooling coils shall be collected and discharged to an approved plumbing fixture or disposal area. Approved corrosion-resistant discharge piping shall not be smaller than the drain pan connection of the approved equipment and shall maintain a minimum horizontal slope of not less than 1/8 vertical unit in 12 units horizontal (1%). When serving shop or field-fabricated drain pans or more than one piece of equipment, such drains shall be sized as required by Chapter 11 of this code.

TABLE 3-A—STANDARD INSTALLATION CLEARANCES, IN INCHES, FOR UNLISTED HEAT-PRODUCING APPLIANCES
See Section 304.

RESIDENTIAL-TYPE APPLIANCES	Fuel	Above Top of Casing or Appliance	From Top and Sides of Warm-air Bonnet or Plenum	From Front[1]	From Back	From Sides
				$\times$ 25.4 for mm		
Boilers and water heaters Steam boilers—15 psi (103.4 Pa) Water boilers—250°F. (121°C) Water heaters—200°F. (93°C) All water walled or jacketed	Automatic oil or comb. gas-oil	6		24	6	6
	Automatic gas	6		18	6	6
	Solid	6		48	6	6
Furnaces—central; or heaters—electric central Warm-air furnaces Gravity, upflow, downflow, horizontal and duct Warm-air—250°F (121°C) max.	Automatic oil or comb. gas-oil	6	6	24	6	6
	Automatic gas	6	6	18	6	6
Furnaces—floor For mounting in combustible floors	Solid	18[2]	18[2]	48	18	18
	Electric	6	6	18	6	6
	Automatic oil or comb. gas-oil	36		12	12	12
	Automatic gas	36		12	12	12
Heat exchanger Steam—15 psi max. (103.4 Pa max.) Hot water—250°F (121°C) max.		1	1	1	1	1
Room heaters[3] Circulating type	Oil or solid	36		24	12	12
	Gas	36		24	12	12
Radiant or other type	Oil or solid	36		36	36	36
	Gas	36		36	18	18
	Gas with double metal or ceramic back	36		36	12	18
Fireplace stove	Solid	48[4]		54	48[4]	48[4]
Radiators Steam or hot water[5]		36		6	6	6

Ranges—cooking stoves					Firing Side	Opp. Side
	Oil	30[6]			9	24	18
	Gas	30[6]			6	6	6
	Solid clay-lined firepot	30[6]			24	24	18
	Solid unlined firepot	30[6]			36	36	18
	Electric	30[6]			6	6

| Incinerators
Domestic types | | 36[7] | | 48 | 36 | 36 |

(Continued)

From the Uniform Mechanical Code, ©1997, ICBO

Figure 16-2 *Standard installation clearances*

TABLE 3-A—STANDARD INSTALLATION CLEARANCES, IN INCHES, FOR UNLISTED HEAT-PRODUCING APPLIANCES—(Continued)
See Section 304.

COMMERCIAL INDUSTRIAL-TYPE LOW-HEAT APPLIANCES ANY AND ALL PHYSICAL SIZES EXCEPT AS NOTED	Fuel	APPLIANCE				
		Above Top of Casing or Appliance[8]	From Top and Sides of Warm-air Bonnet or Plenum	From Front[1]	From Back[8]	From Sides[8]
		× 25.4 for mm				
Boilers and water heaters 100 cu. ft. (2.83 m³) or less Any psi steam	All fuels	18		48	18	18
50 psi (342 Pa) or less Any size	All fuels	18		48	18	18
Unit heaters Floor mounted or suspended—any size	Steam or hot water	1		1	1	
Suspended—100 cu. ft. (2.83 m³) or less	Oil or comb. gas-oil	6		24	18	18
Suspended—100 cu. ft. (2.83 m³) or less	Gas	6		18	18	18
Suspended—Over 100 cu. ft. (2.83 m³)	All fuels	18		48	18	18
Floor mounted—any size	All fuels	18		48	18	18
Ranges—restaurant-type Floor mounted	All fuels	48		48	18	18
Other low-heat industrial appliances Floor mounted or suspended	All fuels	18	18	48	18	18

COMMERCIAL INDUSTRIAL-TYPE MEDIUM-HEAT APPLIANCES	Fuel	APPLIANCE				
		Above Top of Casing or Appliance[9]	From Top and Sides of Warm-air Bonnet or Plenum	From Front[1]	From Back[9]	From Sides[9]
		× 25.4 for mm				
Boilers and water heaters Over 50 psi (345 Pa) Over 100 cu. ft. (2.83 m³)	All fuels	48		96	36	36
Other medium-heat industrial appliances All sizes	All fuels	48	36	96	36	36
Incinerators All sizes		48		96	36	36
INDUSTRIAL-TYPE HIGH-HEAT APPLIANCES						
High-heat industrial appliances All sizes	All fuels	180		360	120	120

[1]The minimum dimension shall be that necessary for servicing the appliance, including access for cleaning and normal care, tube removal, etc.

[2]The dimension may be 6 inches (152 mm) for an automatically stoker-fired forced-warm-air furnace equipped with 250°F (121°C) limit control and with barometric draft control operated by draft intensity and permanently set to limit draft to a maximum intensity of 0.13-inch water gage (32 Pa).

[3]Approved appliances shall be installed on noncombustible floors and may be installed on protected combustible floors. Heating appliances approved for installation on protected combustible flooring shall be so constructed that flame and hot gases do not come in contact with the appliance base. Protection for combustible floors shall consist of 4-inch (102 mm) hollow masonry covered with sheet metal at least 0.021 inch (0.5 mm) thick (No. 24 manufacturer's standard gage). Masonry shall be permanently fastened in place in an approved manner with the ends unsealed and joints matched so as to provide free circulation of air through the masonry. Floor protection shall extend 12 inches (305 mm) at the sides and rear of the appliance, except that at least 18 inches (457 mm) shall be required on the appliance-opening side or sides measured horizontally from the edges of the opening.

[4]The 48-inch (1219 mm) clearance may be reduced to 36 inches (914 mm) when protection equivalent to that provided by Items 1 through 8 of Table 3-A is applied to the combustible construction.

[5]Steampipes and hot-water-heating pipes shall be installed with a clearance of at least 1 inch (25 mm) to all combustible construction or material, except that at the points where pipes carrying steam at not over 15 pounds gage pressure (103 kPa) or hot water emerge from a floor, wall or ceiling, the clearance at the opening through the finish floorboards or wall-ceiling boards may be reduced to not less than $1/2$ inch (13 mm). Each such opening shall be covered with a plate of noncombustible material.

Such pipes passing through stack shelving shall be covered with not less than 1 inch (25 mm) of approved insulation.

Wood boxes or casings enclosing uninsulated steam or hot-water-heating pipes or wooden covers to recesses in walls in which uninsulated pipes are placed shall be lined with metal or insulating millboard.

Where the temperature of the boiler piping does not exceed 160°F (71°C), the provisions of this table do not apply.

Coverings or insulation used on steam or hot-water pipes shall be of material suitable for the operating temperature of the system. The insulation or jackets shall be of noncombustible materials, or the insulation or jackets and lap-seal adhesives shall be tested as a composite product. Such composite product shall have a flame-spread rating of not more than 25 and a smoke-developed rating not to exceed 50 when tested in accordance with UBC Standard 8-1.

[6]To combustible material or metal cabinets. If the underside of such combustible material or metal cabinet is protected with insulating millboard at least $1/4$ inch (6 mm) thick covered with sheet metal of not less than 0.013 inch (0.3 mm) (No. 28 gage), the distance may be reduced to 24 inches (610 mm).

[7]Clearance above charging door must be at least 48 inches (1219 mm).

[8]If the appliance is encased in brick, the 18-inch (457 mm) clearance above and at sides and rear may be reduced to 12 inches (305 mm).

[9]If the appliance is encased in brick, the clearance above may be reduced to 36 inches (914 mm) and at sides and rear may be reduced to 18 inches (457 mm).

From the Uniform Mechanical Code, ©1997, ICBO

Figure 16-2 *Standard installation clearances (Continued)*

TABLE 3-B—CLEARANCES, IN INCHES, WITH SPECIFIED FORMS OF PROTECTION[1,2]

TYPE OF PROTECTION Applied to the Combustible Material Unless Otherwise Specified and Covering All Surfaces within the Distance Specified as the Required Clearance with No Protection (Thicknesses are Minimum) × 25.4 for mm	WHERE THE STANDARD CLEARANCE IN TABLE 5-A WITH NO PROTECTION IS:											
	36 Inches			18 Inches			12 Inches			6 Inches		
	× 25.4 for mm											
	Above	Sides and Rear	Chimney or Vent Connector	Above	Sides and Rear	Chimney or Vent Connector	Above	Sides and Rear	Chimney or Vent Connector	Above	Sides and Rear	Chimney or Vent Connector
1. $1/4''$ in insulating millboard spaced out $1''$[3]	30	18	30	15	9	12	9	6	6	3	2	3
2. 0.013″ (No. 28 manufacturer's standard gage) steel sheet on $1/4''$ insulating millboard	24	18	24	12	9	12	9	6	4	3	2	2
3. 0.013″ (No. 28 manufacturer's standard gage) steel sheet spaced out $1''$[3]	18	12	18	9	6	9	6	4	4	2	2	2
4. 0.013″ (No. 28 manufacturer's standard gage) steel sheet on $1/8''$ insulating millboard spaced out $1''$[3]	18	12	18	9	6	9	6	4	4	2	2	2
5. $1^{1}/_{2}''$ insulating cement covering on heating appliance	18	12	36	9	6	18	6	4	9	2	1	6
6. $1/4''$ insulating millboard on $1''$ mineral fiber batts reinforced with wire mesh or equivalent	18	12	18	6	6	6	4	4	4	2	2	2
7. 0.027″ (No. 22 manufacturer's standard gage) steel sheet on $1''$ mineral fiber batts reinforced with wire or equivalent	18	12	12	4	3	3	2	2	2	2	2	2
8. $1/4''$ insulating millboard	36	36	36	18	18	18	12	12	9	4	4	4

[1]For appliances complying with Sections 304.2 and 304.3.

[2]Except for the protection described in Item 5, all clearances shall be measured from the outer surface of the appliance to the combustible material, disregarding any intervening protection applied to the combustible material.

[3]Spacers shall be of noncombustible material.

NOTE: Insulating millboard is a factory-made product formed of noncombustible materials, normally fibers, and having a thermal conductivity of 1 Btu-inch per square foot per degree Fahrenheit [1.73W/(m·K)] or less.

From the Uniform Mechanical Code, ©1997, ICBO

Figure 16-3 *Clearances with specified forms of protection*

Section 1105.13 gives the sizing criteria for condensate lines. See Table 11-E (Figure 16-4), Condensate waste size.

This can get you in a lot of trouble. In humid climates air-conditioning units give off a lot of condensate. You've got to get rid of it — legally. If your unit is above grade, the disposal problem is easier than if it's in a basement. To handle condensate in a basement with no floor drain, you can locate the under-floor sewer and connect it to that, or you can install a sump and a pump.

My city and many others require a floor drain or floor sink whenever plumbing fixtures are installed below grade. A lot of plumbers resisted this at first, but it didn't take them long to see the advantage. Think about it; every clothes washer, water heater, and toilet is going to fail some day. And when that happens, the first thing you'll have to do is get rid of the water. It's no picnic replacing an appliance if you have to begin by bailing water out the window.

Two final words of warning: Place your air-conditioning unit where the condensate dripping out of the unit won't run down into the furnace heat exchanger. Wet heat exchangers rust out very quickly. And if your heater is in a garage at floor level, protect it from car bumpers and fenders with a curb to stop the front wheels, or steel posts in the floor.

Warm-Air Heating Systems

Most single-family homes are heated with forced or gravity air systems. Chapter 3 of the UMC covers these systems, providing requirements that are in addition to what we've already covered. Before getting into Chapter 3, let me mention Chapters 8 and 6 of the UMC. Chapter 8 covers vents for fuel-burning

TABLE 11-E—CONDENSATE WASTE SIZE

EQUIPMENT CAPACITY	MINIMUM CONDENSATE PIPE DIAMETER
Up to 20 tons (70.3 kW) of refrigeration	$^3/_4$ inch (19 mm)
Over 20 (70.3 kW) to 40 tons (141 kW) of refrigeration	1 inch (25 mm)
Over 40 (141 kW) to 90 tons (317 kW) of refrigeration	$1^1/_4$ inches (32 mm)
Over 90 (317 kW) to 125 tons (440 kW) of refrigeration	$1^1/_2$ inches (38 mm)
Over 125 (440 kW) to 250 tons (879 kW) of refrigeration	2 inches (51 mm)

From the Uniform Mechanical Code, ©1997, ICBO

Figure 16-4 *Condensate waste size*

warm-air furnaces. Chapter 6 specifies the air ducts and plenums you have to use. We'll look at Chapters 8 and 6 later in this chapter. But first, let's consider the access requirements in Chapter 3.

Access and Service Space

307.1 General. Equipment requiring routine inspection or maintenance shall be provided with sufficient access to allow inspection, maintenance and replacement without removing permanent construction or other equipment or disabling the function of required fire-resistant construction.

307.2 Equipment in Rooms. Rooms containing equipment requiring access shall be provided with a door and an unobstructed passageway measuring not less than 36 inches (914 mm) wide and 80 inches (2032 mm) high.

Exception: Residential-type appliances installed in a compartment, alcove, basement or similar space may be accessed by an opening or door and an unobstructed passageway measuring not less than 24 inches (610 mm) wide and large enough to permit removal of the largest appliance in the space, provided that a service space of not less than 30 inches (762 mm) deep and the height of the appliance, but not less than 30 inches (762 mm) is present at the front or service side of the appliance with the door open.

Here are the code sections that govern access to warm-air furnaces:

■ Installed in under-floor spaces, Section 307.4

■ Installed in an attic or furred space, Section 307.3

■ Installed on a roof or an outside wall structure, Section 307.5

Figures 16-5 through 16-8 show what these sections require. All of these sections address the same problem: Anything you install will probably have to be replaced some

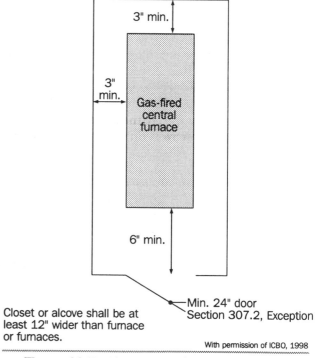

Closet or alcove shall be at least 12" wider than furnace or furnaces.

With permission of ICBO, 1998

Figure 16-5 *Clearances for maintenance and replacement — furnace in a compartment*

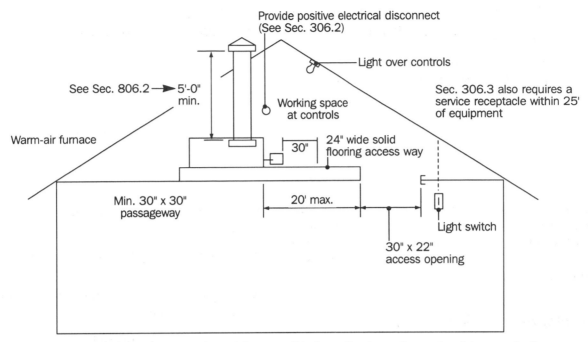

Central warm-air furnaces installed in an attic must be accessible for routine inspection and maintenance by the owner/occupant and for service and repair as needed. Changing filters, lubricating motor and fan bearings, checking belt tension, and relighting the pilot following a service interruption are normal owner functions. Adequate light, an electrical outlet, safe access way and sufficient working space on the control side all encourage and facilitate maintenance and also enable rapid egress in an emergency.

With permission of ICBO, 1998

Figure 16-6 *Furnace in attic*

day, so you might as well plan for that during installation. Another thing to take into consideration during installation: Unless a furnace is designed for outdoor use, it must be protected from the elements. That means that an underfloor furnace must rest on a concrete pad, not on the ground.

A central warm-air furnace installed in an attic also has to be accessible for inspection, maintenance and repair. You have to provide adequate light, an electrical outlet, safe access and enough space to work on the control side. Figure 16-6 shows an installation that meets all the code requirements.

Installation

Installing a furnace seems like such a simple thing. You take it out of the box, set it upright and connect the fuel lines and the duct work. Well, almost. Sections 303 and 304 cover

the installation and location of furnaces. Section 303 begins with this general statement:

Equipment shall be installed as required by the terms of its approval. The conditions of listing and the manufacturer's installation instructions shall be the minimum requirements for installation.

■ It can't be placed on the discharge side of the refrigerant evaporator unless it's specifically designed to go there.

■ As mentioned above, it can't rest on the ground. It has to be on a concrete pad not less than 3 inches above the adjoining ground level.

■ You can't convert an existing furnace for use with cooling coils unless it's authorized by the manufacturer for that particular model and approved by the building official.

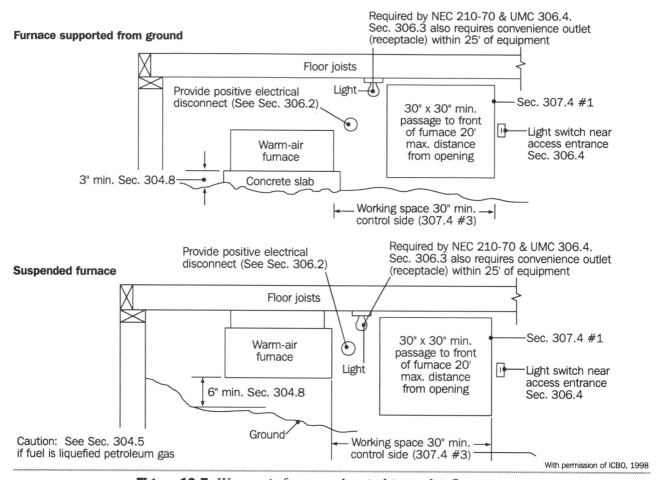

Furnace supported from ground

Required by NEC 210-70 & UMC 306.4. Sec. 306.3 also requires convenience outlet (receptacle) within 25' of equipment

Floor joists

Light

Provide positive electrical disconnect (See Sec. 306.2)

Sec. 307.4 #1

30" x 30" min. passage to front of furnace 20' max. distance from opening

Light switch near access entrance Sec. 306.4

Warm-air furnace

3" min. Sec. 304.8

Concrete slab

Working space 30" min. control side (307.4 #3)

Suspended furnace

Provide positive electrical disconnect (See Sec. 306.2)

Required by NEC 210-70 & UMC 306.4. Sec. 306.3 also requires convenience outlet (receptacle) within 25' of equipment

Floor joists

Warm-air furnace

Light

30" x 30" min. passage to front of furnace 20' max. distance from opening

Sec. 307.4 #1

Light switch near access entrance Sec. 306.4

6" min. Sec. 304.8

Ground

Caution: See Sec. 304.5 if fuel is liquefied petroleum gas

Working space 30" min. control side (307.4 #3)

With permission of ICBO, 1998

Figure 16-7 *Warm-air furnaces located in under-floor spaces*

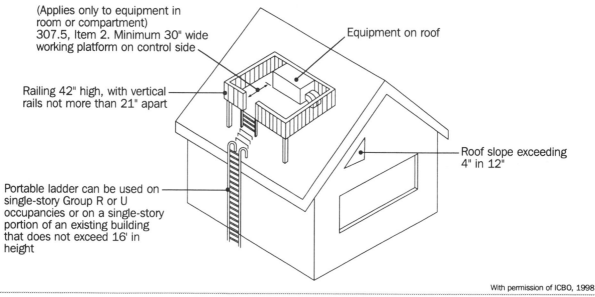

(Applies only to equipment in room or compartment) 307.5, Item 2. Minimum 30" wide working platform on control side

Equipment on roof

Railing 42" high, with vertical rails not more than 21" apart

Portable ladder can be used on single-story Group R or U occupancies or on a single-story portion of an existing building that does not exceed 16' in height

Roof slope exceeding 4" in 12"

With permission of ICBO, 1998

Figure 16-8 *Equipment on roofs*

Section 906.1 further states that you must provide the furnace with return air, outside air, or both. Later in this chapter we'll discuss the source of outside air as well as duct construction and insulation.

Section 907.1 restricts the duct size. A duct for a forced air furnace must have an unobstructed area on the supply side of not less than 2 square inches per 1000 Btu/h of furnace output. For a gravity-type furnace, you've got to have 7 square inches of duct area per 1000 Btu/h output. Dampers, grilles and registers aren't considered obstructions for the purposes of this section. If you're using a heat pump, provide 6 square inches per 1000 Btu/h of nominal output rating.

Miscellaneous Heating Devices

Miscellaneous heating devices include vented decorative appliances, floor furnaces, vented wall furnaces, unit heaters and room heaters. Most are approved for use in any house or small commercial building. You can't use them in surgical operating rooms, hazardous locations, Group H, Division 1, 2, or 3 (hazardous) occupancies, or any room where an open flame is prohibited. Overhead heaters installed in aircraft hangars must be at least 10 feet above the upper surface of wings or engine enclosures of the tallest aircraft using the hanger.

Always follow the manufacturer's installation instructions, unless the building inspector has more stringent regulations.

Venting Appliances

Venting is important for all gas-fired appliances. Although natural gas, by itself, isn't toxic, it can replace all the oxygen in a room. That can lead to asphyxiation. Following the manufacturer's recommendations will nearly eliminate that risk. Section 801.1 of the UMC describes the venting systems you can use:

Venting systems shall consist of approved chimneys, Type B vents, Type BW vents, Type L vents, plastic pipe recommended by the manufacturer of listed condensing appliances for use with specified models, or a venting assembly which is an integral part of a listed appliance.

All vents have to be generally vertical, but you can use offsets that aren't over 45 degrees from the vertical. Support all offset vents. An angle that exceeds 45 degrees is considered a horizontal run. The total length of a horizontal run, including the vent connector, can't exceed 75 percent of the vertical height of the vent. You can't put manually-operated dampers in chimneys, although automatically-operated ones are acceptable. And make sure all unused openings in a vent are sealed.

Section 806 of the UMC covers vent terminations. Basically, the type of vent you're using determines how far above the roof surface it must extend.

- *Gravity-type vents:* Except for Type BW gas-venting systems, and built-in venting systems for listed appliances, the vent has to extend at least 5 feet above the highest vent collar it serves.

- *Wall furnaces:* A Type BW vent serving a vented wall furnace has to terminate at least 12 vertical feet above the bottom of the furnace, except as provided for in Section 807.0. We'll look at that section a bit later.

- *Type B or BW gas vents:* If they have listed caps that are 12 inches or smaller, you can terminate Type B or BW gas vents according to Table 8-A, provided they are located at least 8 feet from a vertical wall or other obstruction. Any Type B vent that doesn't meet that requirement must terminate at least 2 feet above the highest point where it passes through the roof and at least 2 feet higher than any portion of a building within 10 feet. See Figure 16-9.

- *Type L gas vents:* They must terminate at least 2 feet above any portion of the building that's within 10 feet of the vent.

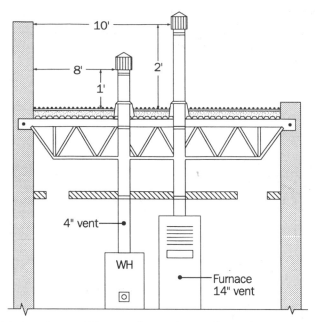

Type B or BW gas vents with listed vent caps 12" or smaller can be terminated in accordance with Table 8-A, provided they are located at least 8' from a vertical wall or similiar obstruction. All other Type B gas vents shall terminate not less than 2' (610 mm) above the highest point where they pass through the roof and at least 2' higher than any portion of a building within 10' feet.

Figure 16-9 *Vent termination*

■ *Vent terminals:* The required distance for a vent terminal is at least 1 foot above, 4 feet below, or 4 feet horizontally away from any door, window, or gravity air inlet into the building (Figure 6-10).

Wall Furnaces

Vents for wall furnaces are usually placed within the wall cavity. Figures 16-11 and 16-12 show typical installations. UMC Section 807 lists nine requirements that must be met:

1) Attach Type BW gas vents to a solid header plate designed for the furnace you're installing. Use the base plate furnished with the equipment.

2) The stud space where you're installing the Type BW vent must be free of obstructions, except required fire-stop spacers in multistory buildings. All ceiling and floor plates must be cut flush.

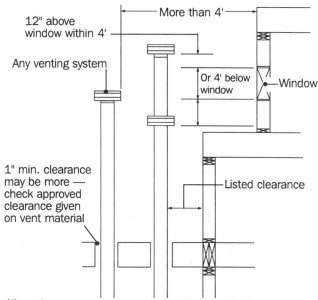

All venting systems are regulated with regard to the location of vent terminations relative to openings into buildings through which products of combustion might enter.

Figure 16-10 *Vent terminals*

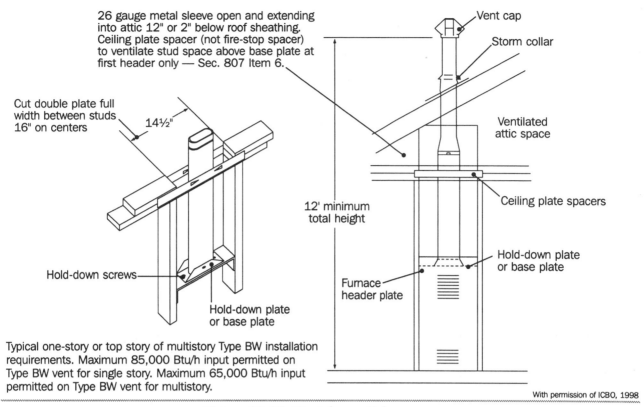

26 gauge metal sleeve open and extending into attic 12" or 2" below roof sheathing. Ceiling plate spacer (not fire-stop spacer) to ventilate stud space above base plate at first header only — Sec. 807 Item 6.

Cut double plate full width between studs 16" on centers

14½"

Vent cap

Storm collar

Ventilated attic space

12' minimum total height

Ceiling plate spacers

Hold-down plate or base plate

Hold-down screws

Hold-down plate or base plate

Furnace header plate

Typical one-story or top story of multistory Type BW installation requirements. Maximum 85,000 Btu/h input permitted on Type BW vent for single story. Maximum 65,000 Btu/h input permitted on Type BW vent for multistory.

With permission of ICBO, 1998

Figure 16-11 *Vent for wall furnaces*

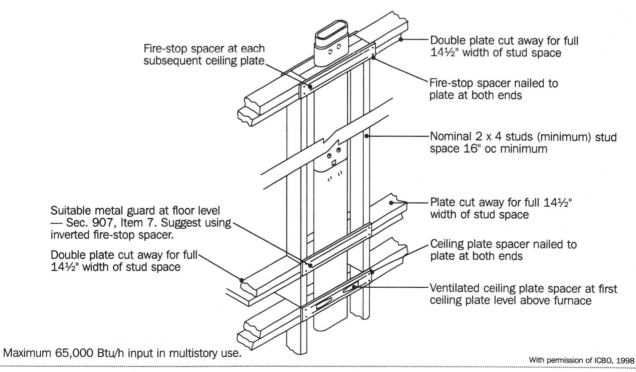

Fire-stop spacer at each subsequent ceiling plate

Double plate cut away for full 14½" width of stud space

Fire-stop spacer nailed to plate at both ends

Nominal 2 x 4 studs (minimum) stud space 16" oc minimum

Plate cut away for full 14½" width of stud space

Ceiling plate spacer nailed to plate at both ends

Ventilated ceiling plate spacer at first ceiling plate level above furnace

Suitable metal guard at floor level — Sec. 907, Item 7. Suggest using inverted fire-stop spacer.

Double plate cut away for full 14½" width of stud space

Maximum 65,000 Btu/h input in multistory use.

With permission of ICBO, 1998

Figure 16-12 *Type BW vent installation, multistory use*

3) The vent clearance provided by the base plate, ceiling space spacer straps and fire-stop spacers must be maintained after all wall coverings are in place. If the wall covering is perforated lath, metal lath or building paper, install a sheet metal barrier between the vent and the wall covering.

4) If the vent is listed only for single-story use, you can't use it in a multistory building except on the top floor. But a multistory vent can go in either single- or multistory structures.

5) The stud space in a single-story building or the top floor of a multistory building has to be open to an attic space or to a ventilated roof flashing equipped with a storm collar. There's one exception: Instead of a ventilated roof flashing, you can vent the stud space with an opening into the room heated by the wall heater. The opening must be within 12 inches of the top of the space.

6) If you're installing a vented recessed wall furnace in a stud space, ventilate it at the first ceiling plate above the furnace with the ceiling plate spacer furnished with the vent. Use the fire-stop space at each floor or ceiling.

7) Install a suitable metal guard at the floor line of each floor to assure required clearance from combustible material.

8) When a Type BW gas vent is installed in an existing building, remove the wall covering on one side of the vent so it's open for installation and inspection.

9) Type BW gas vents must extend from the header plate of the vented wall furnace to the highest ceiling plate through which the vent passes, including any offsets or crossovers. From that point, you can complete the vent with a Type B gas vent.

Follow the manufacturer's instructions for all fuel-burning appliances, controls, vents and accessories. As a builder, I know it's tempting to make some economies. But as a building inspector, I know that building inspectors look hard at appliance installations. A non-approved economy here can cost you a bundle.

Selecting the Chimney

Check UMC Table 8-B to find the right chimney for your appliance installation. Table 8-C covers the vent types you'll need. Both tables are in Figure 16-13.

Ductwork

Chapter 6 of the Uniform Mechanical Code covers ductwork:

601.5. Factory-made Air Ducts. Factory-made air ducts shall be approved for the use intended or shall conform to the requirements of UL 181. Each portion of a factory-made air duct system shall be identified by the manufacturer with a label or other suitable identification indicating compliance with UL 181 and its class designation. These ducts shall be listed and shall be installed in accordance with the terms of their listing, and the requirements of UL 181. Flexible air connectors are not permitted.

Section 601.1.2 goes on to say that you can use the concealed building space or independent construction within a building for ductwork. Figures 16-14 and 16-15 show Tables 6-A through 6-C from the UMC containing construction details for metal ducts. When gypsum wallboard is exposed in ducts or plenums, the air temperature can only range between 50 degrees F and 125 degrees F. Both the temperature and moisture content must be controlled to keep the gypsum dry. That's one reason why you can't use it to enclose evaporative cooler ductwork.

The flame-spread index of material exposed within ductwork is limited to 25, and the smoke-developed rating can't exceed 50. Venting systems must not extend into or pass through ducts or plenums.

TABLE 8-B—CHIMNEY SELECTION CHART

CHIMNEYS FOR RESIDENTIAL APPLIANCES	CHIMNEYS FOR LOW-HEAT APPLIANCES		CHIMNEYS FOR MEDIUM-HEAT APPLIANCES	CHIMNEYS FOR HIGH-HEAT APPLIANCES
	Building-Heating Appliances	Industrial-Type Low-Heat Appliances		
1. Factory-built (residential) 2. Masonry (residential) 3. Metal (residential)	1. Factory-built (low-heat type) 2. Masonry (low-heat type) 3. Metal (smokestack)	1. Factory-built (industrial low-heat type) 2. Masonry (low-heat type) 3. Metal (smokestack)	1. Factory-built (medium-heat type) 2. Masonry (medium-heat type) 3. Metal (smokestack)	1. Masonry (high-heat type) 2. Metal (smokestack)
TYPES OF APPLIANCES TO BE USED WITH EACH TYPE CHIMNEY				
Column I	**Column II**	**Column III**	**Column IV**	**Column V**
A. Residential-type appliances, such as: 1. Ranges 2. Warm-air furnaces 3. Water heaters 4. Hot-water-heating boilers 5. Low-pressure steam-heating boilers [not over 15 psig (103.4 kPa)] 6. Domestic incinerators 7. Floor furnaces 8. Wall furnaces 9. Room heaters 10. Fireplace stoves 11. Closed-combustion-type solid-fuel-burning stoves or room heaters.[1] B. Fireplaces	A. All appliances shown in Column I B. Nonresidential-type building-heating appliances for heating a total volume of space exceeding 25,000 cubic feet (707.75 m^3) C. Steam boilers operating at not over 1,000°F (538°C) flue gas temperature; pressing machine boilers	All appliances shown in Columns I and II, and appliances such as: 1. Annealing baths for hard glass (fats, paraffin, salts or metals) 2. Bake ovens (in bakeries) 3. Boiling vats, for wood fibre, straw, lignin, etc. 4. Candy furnaces 5. Coffee roasting ovens 6. Core ovens 7. Cruller furnaces 8. Feed drying ovens 9. Fertilizer drying ovens 10. Fireplaces, other than residential type 11. Forge furnaces (solid fuel) 12. Gypsum kilns 13. Hardening furnaces (below dark red) 14. Hot-air engine furnaces 15. Ladle-drying furnaces 16. Lead-melting furnaces 17. Nickel plate (drying) furnaces 18. Paraffin furnaces 19. Recuperative furnaces (spent materials) 20. Rendering furnaces 21. Restaurant-type cooking appliances using solid or liquid fuel 22. Rosin-melting furnaces 23. Stereotype furnaces 24. Sulphur furnaces 25. Tripoli kilns (clay, coke and gypsum) 26. Type foundry furnaces 27. Wood-drying furnaces 28. Wood-impregnating furnaces 29. Zinc-amalgamating furnaces	All appliances shown in Columns I, II and III, and appliances such as: 1. Alabaster gypsum kilns 2. Annealing furnaces (glass or metal) 3. Charcoal furnaces 4. Cold stirring furnaces 5. Feed driers (direct-fire-heated) 6. Fertilizer driers (direct-fire-heated) 7. Galvanizing furnaces 8. Gas producers 9. Hardening furnaces (cherry to pale red) 10. Incinerators, commercial and industrial-type 11. Lehrs and glory holes 12. Lime kilns 13. Linseed-oil-boiling furnaces 14. Porcelain biscuit kilns 15. Pulp driers (direct-fire-heated) 16. Steam boilers operating at over 1,000°F (538°C) flue gas temperature 17. Water-glass kiln 18. Wood-distilling furnaces 19. Wood-gas retorts	All appliances shown in Columns I, II, III and IV, and appliances such as: 1. Bessemer retorts 2. Billet and bloom furnaces 3. Blast furnaces 4. Bone calcining furnaces 5. Brass furnaces 6. Carbon point furnaces 7. Cement brick and tile kilns 8. Ceramic kilns 9. Coal and water gas retorts 10. Cupolas 11. Earthenware kilns 12. Glass blow furnaces 13. Glass furnaces (smelting) 14. Glass kilns 15. Open hearth furnaces 16. Ore-roasting furnaces 17. Porcelain-baking and glazing kilns 18. Pot-arches 19. Puddling furnaces 20. Regenerative furnaces 21. Reverberatory furnaces 22. Stacks, carburetor or superheating furnaces (in water-gas works) 23. Vitreous enameling oven (ferrous metals) 24. Wood-carbonizing furnaces

[1]When this appliance is vented with a factory-built chimney, the chimney must be a listed Type HT chimney.

TABLE 8-C—VENT SELECTION CHART

COLUMN I TYPE B, GAS Round or Oval	COLUMN II TYPE BW GAS	COLUMN III TYPE L	COLUMN IV PLASTIC PIPE
All listed gas appliances with draft hoods such as: 1. Central furnaces 2. Floor furnaces 3. Heating boilers 4. Ranges and ovens 5. Recessed wall furnaces (above wall section) 6. Room and unit heaters 7. Water heaters	1. Gas-burning wall heaters listed for use with Type BW vents	1. Oil-burning appliances listed for use with Type L vents 2. Gas appliances as shown in first column	1. Condensing appliances listed for use with a specific plastic pipe recommended and identified in the manufacturer's installation instructions

From the Uniform Mechanical Code, ©1997, ICBO

Figure 16-13 *Chimney and vent selection charts*

**TABLE 6-A—CONSTRUCTION DETAILS FOR RECTANGULAR SHEET METAL DUCTS
FOR STATIC AIR PRESSURES UP TO 2 INCHES WC**

For pressures in excess of 2-inch water column (498 Pa), duct wall thickness shall be
two gages (for sheet gage equivalents see Appendix D) heavier than set forth in this table.

Duct specifications shown here are applicable when ducts larger than 18 inches (457 mm) are cross broken. Where cross breaking is not used,
duct wall thickness shall be two gages (for sheet gage equivalents see Appendix D) heavier on ducts 19 inches through 60 inches (483 mm
through 1524 mm) wide unless longitudinal standing seams are used.

MINIMUM METAL GAGES				
Steel—U.S. Standard, inches (gage)	Aluminum B.&S., inches (gage)	Copper Cold Rolled	Duct Dimension (inches)	Permissible Girth Joints and Longitudinal Seams
× 25.4 for mm	× 0.0026 for kg/m²	× 25.4 for mm	× 25.4 for mm
0.019 (26)	0.020 (24)	16 oz.	Up through 12	Drive slip, plain "S" slip, or 1″ pocket lock
0.024 (24)	0.025 (22)	24 oz.	13 through 18	Drive slip, plain "S" slip, or 1″ pocket lock
			19 through 30	Hemmed "S" slip, 1″ bar slip, or 1″ pocket lock on 5′ centers Hemmed "S" slip, 1″ bar slip, or 1″ pocket lock on 10′ centers with 1″ × 1″ × 1/8″ angles on center line between Hemmed "S" slip, 1″ bar slip, or 1″ pocket lock on 10′ centers with cross break 1″ standing seam on 5′ centers
0.030 (22)	0.032 (20)	32 oz.	31 through 42	1″ bar slip, reinforced bar slip, or pocket lock, on 5′ centers 1″ bar slip, reinforced bar slip, or pocket lock on 10′ centers with 1″ × 1″ × 1/8″ angles on center line between 1″ standing seam on 5′ centers Inside longitudinal standing seams with 1″ × 1″ × 1/8″ angles on 5′ center on exterior
			43 through 54	1 1/2″ bar slip, reinforced bar slip, or pocket lock on 4′ centers 1 1/2″ bar slip, reinforced bar slip, or pocket lock on 8′ centers with 1 1/2″ × 1 1/2″ × 1/8″ angles on center line between 1 1/2″ bar slip, reinforced bar slip, or pocket lock on 4′ centers with cross break
0.036 (20)	0.040 (18)	36 oz.	55 through 60	1 1/2″ standing steam on 3′ centers Inside longitudinal standing seam with 1 1/2″ × 1 1/2″ × 1/8″ angles on 4′ centers on exterior
			61 through 84	Reinforced bar slip, angle slip, alternate bar slip, or angle reinforced pocket lock on 4′ centers using 1 1/2″ × 1 1/2″ × 1/8″ reinforcing angles and with 1 1/2″ × 1 1/2″ × 1/8″ angles on center line between Reinforced bar slip, angle slip, alternate bar slip, or angle reinforced pocket lock on 8′ centers using 1 1/2″ × 1 1/2″ × 1/8″ reinforcing angles and with 1 1/2″ × 1 1/2″ × 1/8″ angles 2′ on centers in between 1 1/2″ angle reinforced standing seam on 2′ centers using 1 1/2″ × 1 1/2″ × 1/8″ reinforcing angles Inside longitudinal standing seams with 1 1/2″ × 1 1/2″ × 1/8″ angles on 2′ centers on exterior
0.047 (18)	0.050 (16)	48 oz.	85 through 96	Companion angles, angle slip, or angle reinforced pocket lock using 1 1/2″ × 1 1/2″ × 3/16″ companion or reinforcing angles on 4′ centers with 1 1/2″ × 1 1/2″ × 3/16″ angles on center line between Companion angles, angle slip, or angle reinforced pocket lock using 1 1/2″ × 1 1/2″ × 3/16″ companion or reinforcing angles on 8′ centers with 1 1/2″ × 1 1/2″ × 3/16″ angles on 2′ centers in between 1 1/2″ angle reinforced standing seam on 2′ centers using 1 1/2″ × 1 1/2″ × 3/16″ reinforcing angles Inside longitudinal standing seams with 1 1/2″ × 1 1/2″ × 3/16″ angles on 2′ centers on exterior
			Over 96	Companion angles, angle slip, or angle reinforced pocket using 2″ × 2″ × 1/4″ companion or reinforcing angles on 4′ centers with 2″ × 2″ × 1/4″ angles on center line between Companion angles, angle slip, or angle reinforced pocket lock using 2″ × 2″ × 1/4″ companion or reinforcing angles on 8′ centers with 2″ × 2″ × 1/4″ angles 2′ on center line between 1 1/2″ angle reinforced standing seam on 2′ centers using 2″ × 2″ × 1/4″ reinforcing angles Inside longitudinal standing seams with 2″ × 2″ × 1/4″ angles on 2′ centers on exterior

Figure 16-14 *Construction details for rectangular sheet metal ducts*

TABLE 6-B—CONSTRUCTION DETAILS FOR ROUND AND FLAT-OVAL DUCTS

DUCT DIAMETER MAXIMUM WIDTH (Inches)	ALUMINUM B.&S. GAGE	STEEL—THICKNESS IN INCHES (STEEL—GALVANIZED SHEET GAGE)					GIRTH JOINTS[1]	
	Pressure ≤ 2″ WC	Pressure ≤ 2″ WC[2] (498 Pa)		Pressure > 2″ ≤ 10″ WC (498 Pa ≤ 2.5 kPa)				Minimum Girth Reinforcing, Maximum Spacing and Angle Size
	Round	Round	Flat-Oval	Spiral Seam	Longitudinal Seam	Welded Fittings	Pressure > 2″ ≤ 10″ WC	
		×25.4 for mm						
Up to 9	24	0.019 (26)	0.024 (24)	0.019 (26)	0.024 (24)	0.030 (22)	2″ slip	None
Over 9 Up to 14	24	0.019 (26)	0.024 (24)	0.024 (24)	0.030 (22)	0.036 (20)	4″ slip	None
Over 14 Up to 23	22	0.024 (24)	0.030 (22)	0.024 (24)	0.030 (22)	0.036 (20)	4″ slip	None
Over 23 Up to 37	20	0.030 (22)	0.036 (20)	0.030 (22)	0.036 (20)	0.036 (20)	4″ slip	None
Over 37 Up to 51	18	0.036 (20)	0.047 (18)	0.036 (20)	0.036 (20)	0.047 (18)	$1^1/_4″ × 1^1/_4″ × ^1/_8″$ flange	$1^1/_4″ × 1^1/_4″ × ^1/_8″$ on 72″
Over 51 Up to 61	16	0.047 (18)	0.058 (16)	X	0.047 (18)	0.047 (18)	$1^1/_4″ × 1^1/_4″ × ^1/_8″$ flange	$1^1/_4″ × 1^1/_4″ × ^1/_8″$ on 72″
Over 61 Up to 84	14	0.058 (16)	0.070 (14)	X	0.058 (16)	0.058 (16)	$1^1/_2″ × 1^1/_2″ × ^1/_8″$ flange	$1^1/_2″ × 1^1/_2″ × ^1/_8″$ on 48″

[1]For pressure ≤ 2 inches WC (498 Pa) any of the following joints are acceptable: butt slip, pipe slip, pipe lock, roll slip, snap slip, plenum lock and companion flange.

[2]Acceptable longitudinal seams for pressure ≤ 2 inches WC (498 Pa): Acme (grooved), snap lock, standing and spiral.

TABLE 6-C—THICKNESS OF METAL DUCTS AND PLENUMS USED FOR HEATING OR COOLING FOR A SINGLE DWELLING UNIT

SIZE AND SHAPE OF DUCT	GALVANIZED STEEL		APPROXIMATE ALUMINUM B.&S. GAGE
	Minimum Thickness (Inches) ×25.4 for mm	Equivalent Galvanized Sheet Gage No.	
Round ducts and enclosed rectangular ducts 14″ (356 mm) or less Over 14″ (356 mm)	0.013 0.016	30 28	26 24
Exposed rectangular ducts 14″ (356 mm) or less Over 14″ (356 mm)	0.016 0.019	28 26	24 22

From the Uniform Mechanical Code, ©1997, ICBO

Figure 16-15 *Construction details for metal ducts*

Insulating the Ducts

604.1 Amount of Insulation. *Supply- and return-air ducts and plenums of a heating or cooling system shall be insulated with not less than the amount of insulation set forth in Table 6-D, except for ducts and plenums used exclusively for evaporative cooling systems.*

Table 6-D appears here as Figure 16-16. You can use only approved materials with a mold-, humidity-, and erosion-resistant face. If your duct is handling velocities in excess of 2000 feet per minute, all liners must be securely fastened with both adhesive and mechanical fasteners. When you install insulation on the exterior of the duct, the material is limited to a flame spread of 25 and a smoke-density of 50.

Under-Floor Space

According to Section 607 of the UMC, you can use under-floor areas as a supply plenum in residences of one or two stories if the area is free of combustible materials and tightly sealed. Section 607 then goes on to list further requirements.

TABLE 6-D—INSULATION OF DUCTS

DUCT LOCATION	INSULATION TYPES MECHANICALLY COOLED	HEATING ZONE[1]	INSULATION TYPES HEATING ONLY
On roof on exterior of building	C, V[2] and W	I	A and W
		II	B and W
		III	C and W
Attics, garages and crawl spaces	A and V[2]	I	A
		II	A
		III	B
In walls,[3] within floor-ceiling spaces[3]	A and V[2]	I	A
		II	A
		III	B
Within the conditioned space or in basements; return ducts in air plenums	None required		None required
Cement slab or within ground	None required		None required

NOTE: Where ducts are used for both heating and cooling, the minimum insulation shall be as required for the most restrictive condition.

[1]Heating Degree Days:

Zone I	below 4,500 D.D.
Zone II	4,501 to 8,000 D.D.
Zone III	over 8,001 D.D.

[2]Vapor retarders shall be installed on supply ducts in spaces vented to the outside in geographic areas where the summer dew point temperature based on the $2\frac{1}{2}$ percent column of dry-bulb and mean coincident wet-bulb temperature exceeds 60°F (15.4°C).

[3]Insulation may be omitted on that portion of a duct which is located within a wall- or a floor-ceiling space where:

    3.1 Both sides of the space are exposed to conditioned air.
    3.2 The space is not ventilated.
    3.3 The space is not used as a return plenum.
    3.4 The space is not exposed to unconditioned air.
Ceilings which form plenums need not be insulated.

INSULATION TYPES[4]:

    A—A material with an installed conductance of 0.48 (2.72 W/(m·K)] or the equivalent thermal resistance of 2.1 [0.367 (m·K)/W].
        Examples of materials capable of meeting the above requirements:
          1-inch (25 mm), 0.60 lb./cu. ft. (9.6 kg/m³) mineral fiber, rock, slag or glass blankets.
          $\frac{1}{2}$-inch (13 mm), 1.5 to 3 lb./cu. ft. (24 to 48 kg/m³) mineral fiber blanket duct liner.
          $\frac{1}{2}$-inch (13 mm), 3 to 10 lb./cu. ft. (48 to 160 kg/m³) mineral fiber board.
    B—A material with an installed conductance of 0.24 [1.36W/(m·K)] or the equivalent thermal resistance of 4.2 (0.735 m·K/w).
        Examples of materials meeting the above requirements:
          2-inch (51 mm), 0.60 lb./cu. ft. (9.6 kg/m³) mineral fiber blankets.
          1-inch (25 mm), 1.5 to 3 lb./cu. ft. (24 to 48 kg/m³) mineral fiber blanket duct liner.
          1-inch (25 mm), 3 to 10 lb./cu. ft. (48 to 160 kg/m³) mineral fiber board.
    C—A material with an installed conductance of 0.16 [0.9 W/(m·K)] or the equivalent thermal resistance of 6.3 [1.1 (m·K)/W].
        Examples of materials meeting the above requirements:
          3-inch (76 mm), 0.60 lb./cu. ft. (9.6 kg/m³) mineral fiber blankets.
          $1\frac{1}{2}$-inch (38 mm), 1.5 to 3 lb./cu. ft. (24 to 48 kg/m³) mineral fiber blanket duct liner.
          $1\frac{1}{2}$-inch (38 mm), 3 to 10 lb./cu. ft. (48 to 160 kg/m³) mineral fiber board.
    V—Vapor Retarders: Material with a perm rating not exceeding 0.5 perm [29 ng/(Pa·s·m²)]. All joints to be sealed.
    W—Approved weatherproof barrier.
[4]The example of materials listed under each type is not meant to limit other available thickness and density combinations with the equivalent installed conductance or resistance based on the insulation only.

From the Uniform Mechanical Code, ©1997, ICBO

Figure 16-16 *Insulation of ducts*

A furnace located in under-floor space must have an automatic control that starts an air-circulating fan whenever the bonnet temperature reaches 150 degrees F. The furnace must also have a temperature limit control that keeps the outlet air temperature below 200 degrees F. Fuel-gas lines and plumbing waste cleanouts can't be located in the same area. Cover the entire ground surface area with a vapor barrier.

As usual, you have to provide access to the equipment. Cut an opening in the floor that's at least 24 by 24 inches. Hang noncombustible receptacles that measure 3 inches beyond each side of the opening not more than 18 inches below each floor opening. Most installers use sheet metal pans to catch refuse that falls through the opening. The registers for each opening must be easily removable for cleaning the receptacles.

Cooling

New homes in many parts of the U.S. come with cooling systems (air conditioning) already installed. There are two common cooling methods. If you live in the arid southwest, you might be quite comfortable with an evaporative cooler. In a humid climate, an evaporative cooler is nearly worthless; you need a refrigeration cooler.

Refrigerated Coolers

Refrigeration cooling is usually done with cooling coils located on the upstream side of the furnace. These cooling coils may contain the refrigerant itself, but that's not the most common method. Normally, the cooling agent is cooled by the refrigeration unit and then piped into the furnace. The air is then blown over the coils, cooled, and transported to where it's needed. In humid climates, this can create a moisture problem. As the warm humid air passes over the coils, moisture condenses on the coils and must be collected.

Table 11-E shows the size of condensate drains required for various sizes of air-cooling systems. Look back to Figure 16-4 for this table.

Access

Leave plenty of space for servicing and inspecting the unit. The code calls for a space no less than 36 inches wide by 6 feet, 8 inches high. There's one exception: If the unit is in an attic, you can reduce servicing and inspecting space to 30 inches in length and width if the unit can be replaced through this opening.

All filters, fuel valves and air handlers must have an unobstructed access space. If access is immediately adjacent to the equipment, the space must measure at least 22 inches by 30 inches.

If your unit is located under the floor or in an attic or furred space, you must provide a light and an electrical outlet at or near the equipment. But you can omit the light if the building lighting is adequate.

Return Air and Outside Air

Sections 403.2 and 404.1 list the prohibited sources of outside or return air, or both. You can't take air from the following areas:

1) Where it will pick up objectionable odors, fumes or flammable vapors.

2) Any hazardous or unsanitary location or a refrigeration machinery room.

3) A closet, bathroom, toilet room or kitchen.

4) A corridor, exit passageway or exit enclosure that's required to be of fire-resistive construction.

5) Any dwelling unit, guest room or patient room other than the room where the air originates.

6) A room or space that contains fuel-burning equipment, except for the listed exceptions. Exceptions include fireplaces, and residential cooking appliances and clothes dryers, among others.

7) Any area with a volume less than 25 percent of the entire volume served by the supply air system unless there are permanent openings to areas that have the required 25 percent volume.

You can't discharge return air from one dwelling unit into another dwelling unit through the cooling system. You also need to make sure the air velocity doesn't exceed the filter manufacturer's recommendation. Cover all required outside-air inlets with screen that has ¼-inch openings.

That's the end of our brief look at the Uniform Mechanical Code. In the next chapter we'll cover what you need to know about the Uniform Plumbing Code.

The Plugged Sewer

Once in a while something happens on a construction site that really couldn't happen. You've probably got a favorite story of your own. Here's mine.

A developer was building an enclosed shopping mall in Kennewick (one of the first in eastern Washington). As usual, the city ran the utilities to the property line. From there, piping to each unit was the developer's responsibility. The shopping center required hundreds of feet of mainline sewer, feeder lines, and lines to individual shops.

Sewer lines, manholes and cleanouts have to be inspected before they're covered with backfill and compacted. The best way to inspect a sewer is to shine a flashlight straight down the line. If the inspector at one end can see the beam at the other end, the line must be straight, on grade and clear of obstructions.

The work on the lines continued for several months. As each section of line was completed, I checked it carefully. This was a major project and I wanted it to be as good and trouble-free as we could make it. Finally I was able to certify that the line was constructed properly and would flow in the right direction.

Eighteen months later, with the mall nearly ready to open, the main sewer line stopped flowing, not just once but regularly. Running a Roto-Rooter through the line would get it flowing again (but only for a few days). That shouldn't happen. In fact, it couldn't happen. The line was perfect. I checked every foot of it myself.

After about a month of removing blockages, the superintendent invited me to help him recheck the grade at each manhole. We checked carefully and couldn't find anything wrong with the line pitch. It should have worked perfectly. Still, sewage would not flow through that line!

Completely by accident a workman noticed a length of 2 x 4 floating in a manhole one afternoon. It was too long to pull out, so he called the foreman, who notified the superintendent, who called me to the job. We had to cut the 2 x 4 into short lengths to get it out of the line. When the pieces were placed end to end on the sidewalk, we had assembled a 2 x 4 eighteen feet long. Solids would gather on the end of the timber and gradually build a dam. Removing the timber solved the blockage problem, but how did that 2 x 4 get into the line?

I'd certified the line as clear. There was no way the timber could have been placed in the line after my inspections. I'm afraid we'll never know the answer to that mystery. But I always double-checked for stray lumber when I inspected sewer lines after that.

When the mall was completed, the developer held an opening ceremony for everyone involved in construction. To commemorate the city's participation, the superintendent presented me with the offending 2 x 4. I thanked him and his crew, but had to decline the souvenir. Our office has a strict policy on accepting gifts from contractors.

17

Plumbing for Small Buildings

The Uniform Plumbing Code, published by the International Association of Plumbing and Mechanical Officials (IAPMO), isn't organized in a start-to-finish order. The information you need for any particular job is spread throughout the book. That makes it harder to use the code as a guide when planning your plumbing jobs.

I'll try to organize the material in this chapter a little better — starting with the underground utilities and ending with installing the fixtures. That's probably the order you'd follow when constructing a residential or small commercial building. Let's begin with the building sewers.

Building Sewers

Let me take a minute to define building sewer. It starts 2 feet from the building and extends to either a public or private disposal system. The building drainage system is that part within a building and extending 2 feet beyond the building, where it hooks to the building sewer.

UPC Section 713 begins the subject this way:

713.0 Sewer Required

713.1 *Every building in which plumbing fixtures are installed and every premises having drainage piping thereon, shall have a connection to a public or private sewer, except as provided in Section 101.4.1.3, 713.2 and 713.4.*

Section 713.2 merely states that if there's no public sewer system available, you have to install a private disposal system. Section 713.4 tells us that a public system is considered available if it's within 200 feet of any proposed building. Section 101.4.1.3 is a grandfather clause. It exempts existing buildings if their system was legal at the time it was constructed unless the old plumbing is unsafe, unsanitary, or a nuisance.

Building Sewer Materials

All materials must be approved by the building department. Unless you're experimenting with something exotic, this approval should be pretty routine. Most common sewer items are accepted if they're marked with the manufacturer's name, the weight and quality of the product, and any other markings required by the code.

Section 701.1 has what appears to be some contradiction until you look at it closely. The exceptions give it away.

Drainage piping shall be cast iron, galvanized steel, galvanized wrought iron, lead, copper, brass, Schedule 40 ABS DWV, Schedule 40 PVC DWV, extra strength vitrified clay pipe, or other approved materials having a smooth and uniform bore, except that: . . .

It then goes on to say that you can't use galvanized wrought iron or galvanized steel underground. They must be installed at least 6 inches above ground. The second exception states that ABS and PVC DWV can be used only in buildings up to three stories in height. There's a very good reason for this. The expansion and contraction of these plastic materials is so great that to go above three stories could put your system in jeopardy. The expansion and contraction under extreme conditions might pull a lot of fixtures loose.

You can't use vitrified clay pipe above ground or in a pressurized system. For underground use install it at least 12 inches below the surface.

If you use copper tube either above ground or underground for drainage or vent piping, its weight must not be less than the weight of DWV type copper drainage tube.

The Uniform Plumbing Code has complete material standards in the back of the book, not in a separate volume like the UBC.

Estimating Sewer Size

The size of your building sewer is based on the number of units on your system. Notice I said *units*, not fixtures. The units are based on an estimated amount of water that each fixture will use. You'll have to count the units assigned to the fixtures. UPC Table 7-3 (Figure 17-1) lists the common fixtures, the size of the trap and trap arm, and the number of units assigned to it. If you have a fixture that's not listed here, the inspector would probably work from UPC Table 7-4 (Figure 17-2).

The plans examiner checking your plans will count the fixture units and check your proposed trap arm sizes. Then he'd use UPC Table 7-5 (Figure 17-3) to see if your proposed building sewer line is big enough to carry the load. Of course, the designer has to figure all of this out before the inspector ever sees the plans. The inspector's job is just to check the numbers to make sure it's done right.

Grade, Support and Protection of Building Sewers

Section 718.1 states that building sewers must run in practical alignment toward the point of disposal and at a uniform slope of no less than ¼ inch per foot. The code doesn't give a maximum slope, and for very good reason. What if the building sewer dropped straight down? No problem. But there are slopes that are too steep to work well. The liquids have a tendency to run away from the solids. The solids that are left behind can build up dams, causing stoppages.

I recommend using the ¼ inch slope across the property up to the property line. Then, if the sewer is deep under the street, the line should drop at about a 45-degree angle to the sewer connection. That saves money because you don't have to dig a deep trench across the property.

What if your street sewer is quite shallow, too shallow for a ¼ inch per foot slope? The code allows a shallower slope if you increase the pipe size. If the street sewer is still too shallow, the only solution is to install a sewage pump.

One more requirement: Your sewer line must run at least 2 feet below any building or structure, and no less than one foot below the

TABLE 7-3
Drainage Fixture Unit Values (DFU)

Individual Fixtures	Min.Size Trap and Trap Arm[7]	Private — Individual Dwelling	Private — 3 or more Dwellings	Public — General Use	Public — Heavy-Use Assembly
Bar Sink	1-1/2"	1.0	1.0		
Bar Sink	1-1/2"[2]			2.0	
Bathtub or Combination Bath/Shower	1-1/2"	3.0	3.0		
Bidet, 1-1/4" trap	1-1/4"	1.0	1.0		
Clinical Sink, 3" trap	3"			6.0	
Clothes Washer, domestic, 2" standpipe[5]	2"	3.0	3.0	3.0	
Dental Unit, cuspidor	1-1/4"			1.0	
Dishwasher, domestic, with independent drain	1-1/2"	2.0	2.0	2.0	
Drinking Fountain or Watercooler	1-1/4"			0.5	
Food-waste-grinder, commercial	2"			3.0	
Floor Drain, emergency				0.0	
Kitchen Sink, domestic, with one 1-1/2" trap	1-1/2"[2]	2.0	2.0	2.0	
Kitchen Sink, domestic, with food-waste-grinder	1-1/2"[2]	2.0	2.0	2.0	
Kitchen Sink, domestic, with dishwasher	1-1/2"[2]	3.0	3.0	3.0	
Kitchen Sink, domestic, w/grinder and dishwasher	1-1/2"[2]	3.0	3.0	3.0	
Laundry Sink, one or two compartments	1-1/2"	2.0	2.0	2.0	
Laundry Sink, with discharge from clothes washer	1-1/2"	2.0	2.0	2.0	
Lavatory, single	1-1/4"	1.0	1.0	1.0	1.0
Lavatory in sets of two or three	1-1/2"	2.0	2.0	2.0	2.0
Mobile Home, trap	3"	12.0	12.0		
Mop Basin 3" trap	3"			3.0	
Receptor, indirect waste, 1-1/2" trap[1,3]	1-1/2"			(1)	
Receptor, indirect waste, 2" trap[1,4]	2"			(1)	
Receptor, indirect waste, 3" trap[1]	3"			(1)	
Service Sink, 2" trap	2"			3.0	
Service Sink, 3" trap	3"			3.0	
Shower Stall, 2" trap	2"	2.0	2.0	2.0	
Showers, group, per head (continuous use)	2"			5.0	
Sink, commercial, 1-1/2" trap, with food waste	1-1/2"[2]			3.0	
Sink, service, flushing rim	3"			6.0	
Sink, general, 1-1/2" trap	1-1/2"	2.0	2.0	2.0	
Sink, general, 2" trap	2"	3.0	3.0	3.0	
Sink, general, 3" trap	3"			5.0	
Urinal, 1.0 GPF				4.0	5.0
Urinal, greater than 1.0 GPF				5.0	6.0
Urinal, 1-1/2" trap	1-1/2"[2]			4.0	5.0
Washfountain, 1-1/2" trap	1-1/2"			2.0	
Washfountain, 2" trap	2"			3.0	
Wash Sink, each set of faucets				2.0	
Water Closet, 1.6 GPF Gravity Tank[6]	3"	3.0	3.0	4.0	6.0
Water Closet, 1.6 GPF Flushometer Tank[6]	3"	3.5	3.5	5.0	8.0
Water Closet, 1.6 GPF Flushometer Valve[6]	3"	3.0	3.0	4.0	6.0
Water Closet, 3.5 GPF Gravity Tank[6]	3"	4.0	4.0	6.0	8.0
Water Closet, 3.5 GPF Flushometer Valve[6]	3"	4.0	4.0	6.0	8.0
Whirlpool Bath or Combination Bath/Shower	2"	3.0	3.0		

[1]Indirect waste receptors shall be sized based on the total drainage capacity of the fixtures that drain therein to, in accordance with Table 7-4.

[2]Provide a 2" (51 mm) minimum branch drain beyond the trap arm.

[3]For refrigerators, coffee urns, water stations, and similar low demands.

[4]For commercial sinks, dishwashers, and similar moderate or heavy demands.

[5]Buildings having a clothes washing area with clothes washers in a battery of three (3) or more, clothes washers shall be rated at six (6) fixture units each for purposes of sizing common horizontal and vertical drainage piping.

[6]Water closets shall be computed as six (6) fixture units when determining septic tank sizes based on Appendix K of this Code.

[7]Trap sizes shall not be increased to the point where the fixture discharge may be inadequate to maintain their self-scouring properties.

Figure 17-1 *Drainage fixture unit values (DFU)*

TABLE 7-4
Discharge Capacity In Gallons per Minute
(Liters per Second)
For Intermittent Flow Only

GPM	(l/sec.)		
Up to 7-1/2	(Up to 0.47)	Equals	1 Unit
8 to 15	(0.50 to 0.95)	Equals	2 Units
16 to 30	(1.00 to 1.89)	Equals	4 Units
31 to 50	(1.95 to 3.15)	Equals	6 Units

Discharge capacity for over 50 gallons per minute (3.15 L/sec.) shall be determined by the Administrative Authority.

For a continuous flow into a drainage system, such as from a pump, sump ejector, air conditioning equipment, or similar device, two (2) fixture units shall be allowed for each gallon per minute (0.06 L/sec.) of flow.

Reprinted from the UPC® with permission of the IAPMO, ©1996

Figure 17-2 *Discharge capacities*

ground surface. As defined by the code a "structure" includes: porches and steps (both covered and uncovered), breezeways, roofed patios, carports, and any other covered walk or driveway. But I don't recommend putting a sewer under any building but your own. Repairing a sewer line under a foundation can be a very expensive project.

Dual Use Trenching

When I was a building inspector, one of my most common questions was, "Can I use the same trench for both the water service and the sewer?" A qualified "yes" goes with this question. If you're using a clay pipe or a pipe not authorized for use inside the building, you can put them both in the same trench providing:

720.0 (1) The bottom of the water pipe, at all points, shall be at least twelve (12) inches (0.3 m) above the top of the sewer or drain line.

(2) The water pipe shall be placed on a solid shelf excavated at one side of the

common trench with a minimum clear horizontal distance of at least twelve (12) inches (0.3 m) from the sewer or drain line.

This also applies to a water service line that crosses a sewer. It must be laid 12 inches above the sewer at the point where it crosses the sewer.

Cleanouts and Manholes

719.0 Cleanouts

719.1 Cleanouts shall be placed inside the building near the connection between the building drain and the building sewer or installed outside the building at the lower end of the building drain and extended to grade.

If your building is a long way from the public sewer, you may have to use several cleanouts — or even install a manhole. The code limits the distance between cleanouts to 100 feet. The maximum distance between manholes, however, is 300 feet. But remember that sewers must run in a straight line. If your sewer doesn't, the code requires an additional cleanout for each aggregate horizontal change in direction over 135 degrees. Section 719.6 gives you an alternative. If it's approved in advance, you can install a manhole instead of cleanouts. This section of the code goes on to explain that the inlet and outlet connections must be made with flexible compression joints located more than 12 inches but less than 3 feet away from the manhole. Don't embed these joints in the manhole base.

Each cleanout must extend upward to grade level. I never liked to see cleanouts installed in a basement unless they were at the base of a vertical stack. Cleanouts in a basement floor can be a serious problem. The code says they have to be accessible. When they're installed, there's no basement floor yet. So the inspector notes that a cleanout is installed and goes on his way. Several weeks or months later, when the basement floor is installed, the cleanout is stuck under a stairway, covered with carpet — or even covered with concrete.

TABLE 7-5
Maximum Unit Loading and Maximum Length of Drainage and Vent Piping

Size of Pipe, inches (mm)	1-1/4 (32)	1-1/2 (38)	2 (51)	2-1/2 (64)	3 (76)	4 (102)	5 (127)	6 (152)	8 (203)	10 (254)	12 (305)
Maximum Units Drainage Piping[1]											
Vertical	1	2[2]	16[3]	32[3]	48[4]	256	600	1380	3600	5600	8400
Horizontal	1	1	8[3]	14[3]	35[4]	216[5]	428[5]	720[5]	2640[5]	4680[5]	8200[5]
Maximum Length Drainage Piping											
Vertical, feet (m)	45 (14)	65 (20)	85 (26)	148 (45)	212 (65)	300 (91)	390 (119)	510 (155)	750 (228)		
Horizontal (Unlimited)											
Vent Piping (see note) Horizontal and Vertical											
Maximum Units	1	8[3]	24	48	84	256	600	1380	3600		
Maximum Lengths, feet (m)	45 (14)	60 (18)	120 (37)	180 (55)	212 (65)	300 (91)	390 (119)	510 (155)	750 (228)		

1 Excluding trap arm.
2 Except sinks, urinals, and dishwashers.
3 Except six-unit traps or water closets.
4 Only four (4) water closets or six-unit traps allowed on any vertical pipe or stack; and not to exceed three (3) water closets or six-unit traps on any horizontal branch or drain.
5 Based on one-fourth (1/4) inch per foot (20.9 mm/m) slope. For one-eighth (1/8) inch per foot (10.4 mm/m) slope, multiply horizontal fixture units by a factor of 0.8.

Note: The diameter of an individual vent shall not be less than one and one-fourth (1-1/4) inches (31.8 mm) nor less than one-half (1/2) the diameter of the drain to which it is connected. Fixture unit load values for drainage and vent piping shall be computed from Tables 7-3 and 7-4. Not to exceed one-third (1/3) of the total permitted length of any vent may be installed in a horizontal position. When vents are increased one (1) pipe size for their entire length, the maximum length limitations specified in this table do not apply.

Figure 17-3 *Unit loading and length of drainage and vent piping*

Backwater Valves

There's a chance for some misunderstandings here. The code requires a backflow preventer to keep pollutants from being siphoned back into the water system if water pressure fails. But we're not talking about backflow preventers here. Backwater valves are something different. This is the way the code defines them:

Backflow Preventer — *A backflow preventer is a device or means to prevent backflow into the potable water system.*

Backwater Valve — *A backwater valve is a device installed in a drainage system to prevent reverse flow.*

For any house with plumbing in the basement, I heartily recommend a backwater valve. It keeps the basement from filling with sewage if the sewer line gets stopped up. Many jurisdictions do require them, however. Check with your inspector about backwater valves if the job includes a basement.

Backwater valves must be near the place where your sewer leaves the building, and they must be readily accessible. Sewage flows downstream past a flapper valve as long as the main is flowing normally. If there's a stoppage downstream, the flapper valve swings shut, keeping sewage out of the basement. At least, that's the theory, and it usually works fine.

It works, that is, until the first time the pipes stop up and the homeowner calls Roto-Rooter. A powerful drain snake will usually go right through the backwater valve, ripping it to shreds. And you'll never know it until the city sewer stops up and the basement fills with sewage. Insurance may not cover the loss if a backwater valve has been destroyed. Make sure the homeowner understands the importance of having the valve checked after drains have been cleaned out.

Inspections

Each section of your plumbing must be inspected before it's concealed. Sewers are normally tested with air or water under pressure to be sure the joints don't leak. To test with water, plug all the outlets (special plugs are available at plumbing supply stores) and add a section of vent stack. This stack must be at least 10 feet higher than any portion of the system to be tested. Then fill the vent stack with water and watch for leaks. The inspector is usually satisfied if it doesn't leak after about 15 minutes.

For an air test, plug all outlets and pump the system up to 5 pounds per square inch. This pressure must be maintained for at least 15 minutes. Whichever test you use, the inspector will want to see it done.

Vents and Venting

901.0 Vents Required Each plumbing fixture trap, except as otherwise provided in this Code, shall be protected against siphonage and back-pressure, and air circulation shall be assured throughout all parts of the drainage system by means of vent pipes installed in accordance with the requirements of this chapter and as otherwise required by this Code.

Venting gives your drainage system a chance to breathe so waste flows freely. Yes, your system may drain if it isn't vented — eventually. But the whole system works much better if it is vented. That's why the code requires

venting. You can use vent pipe and fittings made of any material approved for the rest of the system. The sizes are listed back in Figure 17-3.

Vent Pipe Grades and Connections

Vents help keep the waste system at normal air pressure so liquids drain smoothly. There are a few do's and don'ts when it comes to vent construction.

1) They have to be level or drain by gravity back into the drainage pipe. Drops and sags aren't allowed.

2) The invert of the vent should be above the centerline of a horizontal drain.

3) The vent must rise vertically to a point at least 6 inches above the flood level of the fixture being served.

4) Vents must extend full size above the roof.

5) Vents opening from a soil or waste pipe, except for water closets and similar fixtures, can't be below the weir of the trap.

6) Vents have to extend through roof flashing and terminate vertically at least 6 inches above the roof and no less than 1 foot from any vertical surface.

7) They can't terminate within 10 feet of or less than 3 feet above any openable window, door, air intake, vent shaft or other opening. Along lot lines terminations must have 3 feet of clearance in every direction. The only exceptions are alleys and streets.

8) On outdoor installations, vent pipes must extend 10 feet above the surrounding ground and be adequately supported.

9) In high snow load areas, vents must be at least 2 inches in diameter and extend no less than 10 inches above the roof.

Indirect Wastes

According to Section 211.0 an indirect waste pipe doesn't connect directly with the drainage system. Instead it discharges liquid waste into a plumbing fixture, interceptor or receptacle which is connected directly to the drainage system.

The condensate drain from your air conditioning system is an example of an indirect waste. Water from the air conditioner may go directly into a floor drain in a basement. The bar in your local saloon probably has a sink drain that runs into a floor sink. The advantage is that you don't have to install vent lines for these indirect connections.

For indirect wastes you don't need a vent, but you do need an airgap between the drain and the flood line of the receptor. This airgap keeps drain water from being siphoned into the plumbing fixture. Section 202.0 defines it this way:

Airgap, Drainage — An airgap, drainage is the unobstructed vertical distance through the free atmosphere between the lowest opening from any pipe, plumbing fixture, appliance or appurtenance conveying waste to the flood level rim of the receptor.

Many appliances have an airgap device or anti-siphonage system built in. The domestic dishwasher is one example.

You've probably noticed that the faucets in your kitchen sink, tub, and lavatory are high enough above the sink so they can't siphon water back into the tap even if the sink is full. That's an airgap.

Traps and Interceptors

1001.0 Traps Required

1001.1 Each plumbing fixture, excepting those having integral traps, shall be separately trapped by an approved type waterseal trap. Not more than one (1) trap shall be permitted on a trap arm.

That's the general requirement. Section 1001.2 then goes on to say that you can't connect more than three sinks, laundry tubs or lavatories to a single trap. Even then, the trap arm can't be longer than 30 inches.

TABLE 10-1
Horizontal Distance of Trap Arms
(Except for water closets and similar fixtures)*

Trap Arm Inches	Distance Trap to Vent Feet	Inches	Trap Arm mm	Distance Trap to Vent mm
1-1/4	2	6	32	762
1-1/2	3	6	38	1067
2	5	0	51	1524
3	6	0	76	1829
4 & larger	10	0	102 & larger	3048

Slope one-fourth (1/4) inch per foot (20.9 mm/m)

*The developed length between the trap of a water closet or similar fixture (measured from the top of the closet ring [closet flange] to the inner edge of the vent) and its vent shall not exceed six (6) feet (1829 mm).

Figure 17-4 *Horizontal distance of trap arms*

The vertical distance between the fixture outlet and the trap weir must be as short as possible. The tailpiece must never be longer than 24 inches.

Every trap must have a vent pipe to protect against siphonage and back pressure. This vent assures free air circulation throughout the system. UPC Table 10-1 (Figure 17-4) shows the maximum length of the trap arm from the trap weir to the inner edge of the vent.

A trap arm can change direction as long as the change doesn't exceed 90 degrees. Last but not least, the vent pipe opening from a waste pipe must not be below the weir of the trap.

Water Distribution

601.0 Running Water Required

601.1 Except where not deemed necessary for safety or sanitation by the Administrative Authority, each plumbing fixture shall be provided with an adequate

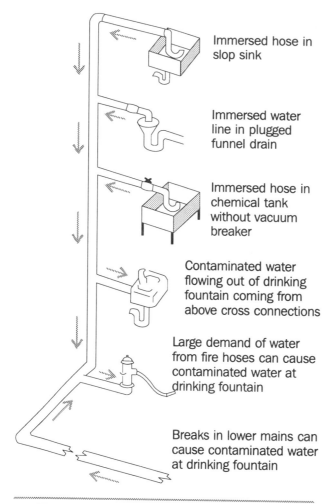

Immersed hose in slop sink

Immersed water line in plugged funnel drain

Immersed hose in chemical tank without vacuum breaker

Contaminated water flowing out of drinking fountain coming from above cross connections

Large demand of water from fire hoses can cause contaminated water at drinking fountain

Breaks in lower mains can cause contaminated water at drinking fountain

Figure 17-5 *How cross connections can create health hazards*

supply of potable running water piped thereto in an approved manner, so arranged as to flush and keep it in a clean and sanitary condition without danger of backflow or cross-connection. Water closets and urinals shall be flushed by means of an approved flush tank or flushometer valve. . .

601.3 Faucets and diverters shall be connected to the water distribution system so that hot water corresponds to the left side of the fittings.

Here's a little gem you have to watch out for: cross-connection. Suppose you have more

than one type of piped water. For example, some areas have both irrigation water systems and drinking water systems. Irrigation water may be provided only during the growing season. But what if someone needs to irrigate earlier or later than the normal growing season? Can you connect your domestic water supply to your yard sprinklers?

In most communities the answer is an unqualified "no." Section 602 says that you can't install or connect potable water supply piping or any plumbing fixture in any way that makes it possible for used, unclean, polluted or contaminated water to enter any portion of the potable water system.

Maybe I should define potable water. It's water that's intended for drinking, cooking or cleaning and meets the requirements of the local health authority.

But how could watering a lawn with potable water contaminate the drinking water system? Your hose doesn't carry germs, does it? Who hasn't taken a drink from a garden hose?

But suppose someone runs down a fire hydrant somewhere and the valve on a water main has to be closed until repairs are made. The water's off. No pressure anywhere. In fact maybe there's a negative pressure. Open the valve anywhere and air is sucked back into the pipe. The hose you were using to spray insecticide in the garden is now sucking insecticide back into the hose and maybe all the way back to the water main. When the hydrant is fixed, that insecticide is going to be delivered through piping systems all over the neighborhood. I know that sounds far-fetched, but it's happened. An approved vacuum breaker installed on the discharge side of the last valve will prevent this.

Figure 17-5 illustrates some ways cross connections can create a health hazard.

Size of Potable Water Piping

Unless you're installing an unusual number of fixtures in the house, you shouldn't have too much trouble with this one. UPC Table 6-4 (Figure 17-6) lists water fixture units assigned to most of the fixtures you'll see in a residence

TABLE 6-4
Water Supply Fixture Units (WSFU) and Minimum Fixture Branch Pipe Sizes

Individual Fixtures[2]	Minimum Fixture Outlet Pipe Size[1]	Private		Public	
		Individual Dwelling	3 or More Dwellings	General Use	Heavy-Use Assembly
Bar Sink...	1/2"	1.0	1.0	2.0	
Bathtub or Combination Bath/Shower........................	1/2"	4.0	3.5		
Bidet	1/2"	1.0	0.5		
Clinic Sink..	1/2"			8.0	
Clotheswasher, domestic.......................................	1/2"	4.0	2.5	4.0	
Dental Unit, cuspidor...	1/2"			1.0	
Dishwasher, domestic	1/2"	1.5	1.0	1.5	
Drinking Fountain or Watercooler............................	1/2"			0.5	0.75
Hose Bibb..	1/2"	2.5	2.5	2.5	
Hose Bibb, each additional....................................	1/2"	1.0	1.0	1.0	
Kitchen Sink, domestic...	1/2"	1.5	1.0	1.5	
Laundry Sink	1/2"	2.0	1.0	2.0	
Lavatory...	1/2"	1.0	0.5	1.0	1.0
Lawn Sprinkler, each head.....................................		1.0	1.0	1.0	
Mobile Home, each		12.0	12.0		
Service Sink or Mop Basin.....................................	1/2"			3.0	
Shower	1/2"	2.0	2.0	2.0	
Shower, continuous use	1/2"			5.0	
Urinal, 1.0 GPF				4.0	5.0
Urinal, greater than 1.0 GPF				5.0	6.0
Urinal, flush tank	1/2"			3.0	4.0
Washfountain, circular spray	3/4"			4.0	
Washup Sink, each set of faucets............................	1/2"			2.0	
Water Closet, 1.6 GPF Gravity Tank	1/2"	2.5	2.5	2.5	4.0
Water Closet, 1.6 GPF Flushometer Tank....................	1/2"	2.5	2.5	2.5	3.5
Water Closet, 1.6 GPF Flushometer Valve...................	1"	5.0	5.0	5.0	8.0
Water Closet, 3.5 GPF Gravity Tank	1/2"	3.0	3.0	5.5	7.0
Water Closet, 3.5 GPF Flushometer Valve...................	1"	7.0	7.0	8.0	10.0
Whirlpool Bath or Combination Bath/Shower................	1/2"	4.0	4.0		

Notes:

1 Size of the cold branch outlet pipe, or both the hot and cold branch outlet pipes.

2 For unlisted fixtures, refer to a listed fixture with a similar flow rate and frequency of use.

3 The listed fixture unit values represent their total load on the cold water service. The separate cold water and hot water fixture unit value for fixtures having both cold and hot water connections shall each be taken as three-quarters (3.4) of the listed total value of the fixture.

4 The listed minimum supply branch pipe sizes for individual fixtures are the nominal (I.D.) pipe size.

5 "General use" applies to business, commercial, industrial, and assembly occupancies other than those defined under "Heavy-use." Included are the public and common areas in hotels, motels, and multi-dwelling buildings.

6 "Heavy-use assembly" applies to toilet facilities in occupancies which place a heavy, but intermittent, time-based demand on the water supply system, such as schools, auditoriums, stadiums, race courses, transportation terminals, theaters, and similar occupancies where queuing is likely to occur during periods of peak use.

7 For fixtures or supply connections likely to impose continuous demands, determine the required flow in gallons per minute (GPM) and add it separately to the demand (in GPM) for the distribution system or portions thereof.

Reprinted from the UPC® with permission of the IAPMO, ©1996

Figure 17-6 *Fixture water demand units*

Table 6-5
Fixture Unit Table for Water Pipe and Meter Sizes

Inch	mm
1/2	12.7
3/4	19.1
1	25.4
1-1/4	31.8
1-1/2	38.1
2	50.8
2-1/2	63.5

Pressure Range — 30 to 45 psi (207 to 310 kPa)**

Meter and Street Service, Inches	Building Supply and Branches, Inches	40 (12)	60 (18)	80 (24)	100 (30)	150 (46)	200 (61)	250 (76)	300 (91)	400 (122)	500 (152)	600 (183)	700 (213)	800 (244)	900 (274)	1000 (305)
3/4	1/2***	6	5	4	3	2	1	1	1	0	0	0	0	0	0	0
3/4	3/4	16	16	14	12	9	6	5	5	4	4	3	2	2	2	1
3/4	1	29	25	23	21	17	15	13	12	10	8	6	6	6	6	6
1	1	36	31	27	25	20	17	15	13	12	10	8	6	6	6	6
3/4	1-1/4	36	33	31	28	24	23	21	19	17	16	13	12	12	11	11
1	1-1/4	54	47	42	38	32	28	25	23	19	17	14	12	12	11	11
1-1/2	1-1/4	78	68	57	48	38	32	28	25	21	18	15	12	12	11	11
1	1-1/2	85	84	79	65	56	48	43	38	32	28	26	22	21	20	20
1-1/2	1-1/2	150	124	105	91	70	57	49	45	36	31	26	23	21	20	20
2	1-1/2	151	129	129	110	80	64	53	46	38	32	27	23	21	20	20
1	2	85	85	85	85	85	85	82	80	66	61	57	52	49	46	43
1-1/2	2	220	205	190	176	155	138	127	120	104	85	70	61	57	54	51
2	2	370	327	292	265	217	185	164	147	124	96	70	61	57	54	51
2	2-1/2	445	418	390	370	330	300	280	265	240	220	198	175	158	143	133

Pressure Range — 46 to 60 psi (317 to 414 kPa)**

Meter and Street Service, Inches	Building Supply and Branches, Inches	40 (12)	60 (18)	80 (24)	100 (30)	150 (46)	200 (61)	250 (76)	300 (91)	400 (122)	500 (152)	600 (183)	700 (213)	800 (244)	900 (274)	1000 (305)
3/4	1/2***	7	7	6	5	4	3	2	2	1	1	1	0	0	0	0
3/4	3/4	20	20	19	17	14	11	9	8	6	5	4	4	3	3	3
3/4	1	39	39	36	33	28	23	21	19	17	14	12	10	9	8	8
1	1	39	39	39	36	30	25	23	20	18	15	12	10	9	8	8
3/4	1-1/4	39	39	39	39	39	39	34	32	27	25	22	19	19	17	16
1	1-1/4	78	78	76	67	52	44	39	36	30	27	24	20	19	17	16
1-1/2	1-1/4	78	78	78	78	66	52	44	39	33	29	24	20	19	17	16
1	1-1/2	85	85	85	85	85	85	80	67	55	49	41	37	34	32	30
1-1/2	1-1/2	151	151	151	151	128	105	90	78	62	52	42	38	35	32	30
2	1-1/2	151	151	151	151	150	117	98	84	67	55	42	38	35	32	30
1	2	85	85	85	85	85	85	85	85	85	85	85	85	85	83	80
1-1/2	2	370	370	340	318	272	240	220	198	170	150	135	123	110	102	94
2	2	370	370	370	370	368	318	280	250	205	165	142	123	110	102	94
2	2-1/2	654	640	610	580	535	500	470	440	400	365	335	315	285	267	250

Pressure Range — Over 60 psi (414 kPa)**

Meter and Street Service, Inches	Building Supply and Branches, Inches	40 (12)	60 (18)	80 (24)	100 (30)	150 (46)	200 (61)	250 (76)	300 (91)	400 (122)	500 (152)	600 (183)	700 (213)	800 (244)	900 (274)	1000 (305)
3/4	1/2***	7	7	7	6	5	4	3	3	2	1	1	1	1	1	0
3/4	3/4	20	20	20	20	17	13	11	10	8	7	6	6	5	4	4
3/4	1	39	39	39	39	35	30	27	24	21	17	14	13	12	12	11
1	1	39	39	39	39	38	32	29	26	22	18	14	13	12	12	11
3/4	1-1/4	39	39	39	39	39	39	39	39	34	28	26	25	23	22	21
1	1-1/4	78	78	78	78	74	62	53	47	39	31	26	25	23	22	21
1-1/2	1-1/4	78	78	78	78	78	74	65	54	43	34	26	25	23	22	21
1	1-1/2	85	85	85	85	85	85	85	85	81	64	51	48	46	43	40
1-1/2	1-1/2	151	151	151	151	151	151	130	113	88	73	51	51	46	43	40
2	1-1/2	151	151	151	151	151	151	142	122	98	82	64	51	46	43	40
1	2	85	85	85	85	85	85	85	85	85	85	85	85	85	85	85
1-1/2	2	370	370	370	370	360	335	305	282	244	212	187	172	153	141	129
2	2	370	370	370	370	370	370	370	340	288	245	204	172	153	141	129
2	2-1/2	654	654	654	654	654	650	610	570	510	460	430	404	380	356	329

** Available static pressure after head loss.
*** Building supply, three-quarter (3/4) inch (19.1 mm) nominal size minimum.

Figure 17-7 *Fixture unit table for determining pipe and meter sizes*

Figure 17-8 *Typical piping rough-in*

or small commercial building. If you install something that isn't listed here, get the unit count from the building inspector.

Find the unit value for each fixture in your building. Total these numbers. Then use UPC Table 6-5 (Figure 17-7) to size the piping.

Water piping outlets, as well as drains and traps, must be secured in place. Figure 17-8 shows a typical washing machine rough-in. Note the gas line in place for the dryer.

Fixtures

There isn't much I can say about fixtures except that they must be installed properly.

Even if the building sewer rough-in is done correctly, careless installation of fixtures can make a mess of the job.

Here's the point to remember: Nearly every fixture you install will have to be repaired some day. Repair and replacement will be much easier if the original installation is done right. Make sure fixture shutoffs are readily accessible. Retaining rings and brackets should be mounted square and snug. Supply and waste lines should connect smoothly without straining either side of the joint. Threaded couplings should be turned snug without over-tightening or cross-threading.

Before we get out of here I think we should look at Section 401:

401.0 Materials — General Requirements

401.1 Quality of Fixtures. *Plumbing fixtures shall be constructed of dense, durable, non-absorbent materials and shall have smooth, impervious surfaces, free from unnecessary concealed fouling surfaces. Except as permitted elsewhere in this Code, all fixtures shall conform in quality and design to nationally recognized applicable standards or to other approved standards acceptable to the Administrative Authority...*

Attention to details like these will make repairs much easier. And it's details like these that identify true professional craftsmanship.

Treehouses Are Buildings, Too

Most building codes require a permit for nearly any type of structure. The Uniform Building Code defines structure as any two or more parts designed to act as a whole. That means nearly anything you can throw a hammer at needs a permit.

I live in a part of Washington where nearly every kid needs (and probably has) at least one treehouse. Construction of treehouses in Kennewick is a pretty serious business. And it isn't just the kids that get involved. Moms and Dads usually help with design and purchase of materials, and sometimes with construction.

Some of these tree houses are works of art, something to be proud of. But some considered them eyesores and wanted them removed. I'll admit that in the winter, when many trees are bare, they were very noticeable. But in the summer they were usually hidden within the leaves of the host tree.

Well, eventually the city got enough complaints about tree houses that the city fathers had to take official notice. They asked me to research the code and come up with a proposal. I took the police chief and the fire chief into my confidence. We began to tour the town treehouses, talking to kids and parents and their neighbors.

We found not one tree house that was built with a permit. Some had electrical power from extension cords run up from the house below. Several even had small heaters in them.

After making our survey, the three of us drafted an exception to the code. Treehouses would be legal as long as they didn't exceed 36 square feet of floor, had no artificial lights except flashlights, and were built in trees behind the setback line of the house. That kept them out of the front yards.

The city council took our suggested ordinance, held the necessary pubic hearings (at which no one showed up) and duly enacted our draft into law. It didn't cause much of a stir in the town but it did make the national press. I heard from places all around the country about my "treehouse ordinance."

And to think it all started in Kennewick.

18

Glass, Skylights and Miscellaneous Components

Every building has at least a few small construction items that make it unique. Some buildings have major custom-designed items that add substantially to the cost. This chapter is a catch-all. We'll look at glass and glazing and some of these miscellaneous components, including skylights.

Glass and Glazing

You and I might call it glass and glazing, but architects and engineers call it fenestration. The word is derived from the Latin *fenestra*, which means window. So, of course, to fenestrate is to install windows. When I was a builder, I can't remember ever fenestrating. I put in a lot of windows though.

Chapter 24 of the UBC regulates the use of glass by area and type. Look at UBC Graph 24-1 (Figure 18-1), which defines the allowable area of glass in relation to the thickness of the glass and the wind load. Use UBC Tables 16-F, G, H and K (Figures 7-4 through 7-7, Chapter 7) and UBC Section 1620 to determine wind load. Pay particular attention to the height above grade in determining this load.

UBC Table 24-A (Figure 18-2) gives you the adjustment factors for the wind load. Be sure to read the footnotes. They explain how to apply this factor to your particular situation.

The code simply states that glass must be firmly supported on all four edges. If it's not, you'll have to submit the design to the building official for approval. Glass supports are considered firm when support deflections at design

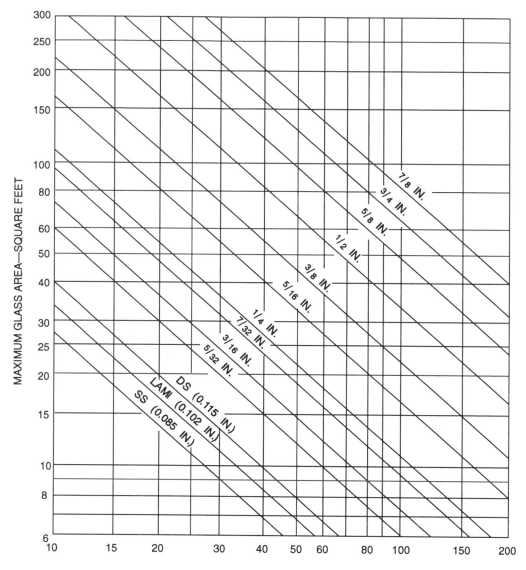

DESIGN WIND PRESSURE FROM CHAPTER 16, DIVISION III—POUNDS PER SQUARE FOOT

For **SI:** 1 inch = 25.4 mm, 1 square foot = 0.0929 m², 1 pound per square foot = 0.479 kN/m².

[1]Applicable for ratios of width to length of 1:1 to 5:1. Design safety factor = 2.5.

GRAPH 24-1—MAXIMUM ALLOWABLE AREA OF GLASS[1]

Figure 18-1 *Maximum allowable area of glass*

TABLE 24-A—ADJUSTMENT FACTORS—RELATIVE RESISTANCE TO WIND LOADS

GLASS TYPE	ADJUSTMENT FACTOR[1]
Laminated[2]	0.75
Fully tempered	4.00
Heat strengthened	2.00
Wired	0.50
Insulating glass[3]—2 panes —3 panes	1.70 2.55
Patterned[4]	1.00
Regular (annealed)	1.00
Sandblasted	0.40[5]

[1]Loads determined from Chapter 16, Division III, shall be divided by this adjustment factor for use with Graph 24-1.
[2]Applies when two plies are identical in thickness and type; use total glass thickness, not thickness of one ply.
[3]Applies when each glass panel is the same thickness and type; use thickness of one panel.
[4]Use minimum glass thickness, i.e., measured at the thinnest part of the pattern; if necessary, interpolation of curves in Graph 24-1 may be required.
[5]Factor varies depending on depth and severity of sandblasting; value shown is minimum.

From the Uniform Building Code, ©1997, ICBO

Figure 18-2 *Relative resistance to wind load*

load don't exceed $1/175$ of the span. Determining deflection in the field may be difficult. Here's the rule of thumb I use. Lean on the support. If you feel any give, it won't pass inspection.

Glazing Subject to Human Impact

Section 2406 is one of the most important sections in Chapter 24. It covers the type of glazing you can use in windows and doors subject to human impact. This means the glazing next to glass doors, the glass doors themselves, the glazing near any walking surfaces, sliding glass doors, shower doors, tub enclosures and storm doors.

Instead of listing areas where protection from human impact is essential, Section 2406.4 excludes areas where there's little danger of human impact. The exceptions include leaded or decorative glass used for decorative purposes, curved panels in revolving doors, and openings in doors that are too small for a 3-inch sphere to pass through. Read Section 2406 carefully before installing anything but safety glass.

Glass for bathtub and shower enclosures must be laminated safety glass or approved plastic. How do you know if a piece of glass has been tempered? The manufacturer's brand name must be on the corner of each piece. On other than single- or double-strength glass, look for that brand name if you're thinking about cutting any glass. It might save you the embarrassment and cost of shattering a perfectly good piece of tempered glass. You don't cut tempered glass. You buy it in stock sizes.

Other Glass Applications

Skylights

Skylights are covered in two different chapters of the UBC. Chapter 24 covers glass skylights; Chapter 26 looks at plastic skylights.

Glass Skylights

The code says all glass in skylights must be wired, laminated or tempered glass. If you use heat-strengthened or fully-tempered glass in a single-layer glazing system, you have to include protective screens below the glazing and within 4 inches of it. The screens must be able to support the weight of the glass, be of noncombustible material no thinner than 0.08 inches,

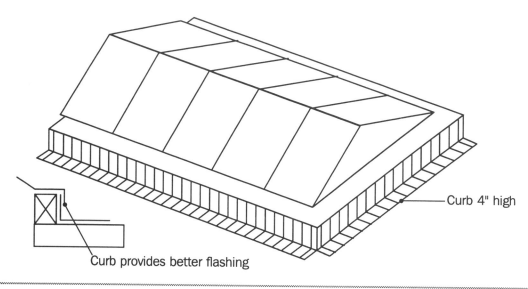

Curb 4" high

Curb provides better flashing

Curb provides better flashing

Figure 18-3 *Construction of glass skylight*

with a mesh not larger than 1 inch by 1 inch. There are several exceptions, so by all means read them if you're tempted to install these skylights with no screens.

In all buildings except Types III, IV and V, you have to build all skylight frames of non-combustible materials. A skylight must be able to carry any roof load that's channeled to it. Skylights set at an angle of less than 45 degrees must be mounted at least 4 inches above the plane of the roof on a suitable curb. Figure 18-3 shows a 4-inch curb. Even where it's not required, curbing is a good idea on any skylight. It's neater and more leak-resistant. But if your roof slope is 45 degrees or greater, skylights may be installed in the plane of the roof.

Plastic Skylights

Preformed skylights are almost entirely Plexiglas or similar plastic. But how would you classify the corrugated plastic panels used in most modern metal buildings? Would you consider these translucent panels a form of skylight? The code does. It covers them in Section 2603.6 where it allows them providing:

1. *Individual roof panels or units shall be separated from each other by distances of not less than 4 feet (1219 mm) measured in a horizontal plane.*

2. *Roof panels or units shall not be installed within that portion of a roof located within a distance to property line or public way where openings in exterior walls are prohibited or required to be protected, whichever is most restrictive.*

It then goes on to describe the type of plastic you can use and the maximum area. It also states that swimming pool shelters under 5,000 square feet are exempt.

There's one more item to consider: You can't install plastic roof material in any area of the roof where openings in exterior walls are prohibited. Look at Table 5-A in the UBC.

Greenhouses

Chapter 24 also governs the construction of greenhouses. But the code says surprisingly little about greenhouses, probably because the normal occupant load is so low. A height of 20 feet above the grade at the ridge is the dividing line for several regulations. Up to 20 feet, you can use ordinary glass and a wood framework. For higher greenhouses, you need metal frames and sash bars, and screening below the glass. Approved plastics may also be used in lieu of glass.

Notice that I said the greenhouse can be 20 feet above grade. That's not the first time we've run into the word grade in the code. It has a specific definition:

> **Grade (Adjacent Ground Elevation)** is the lowest point of elevation of the finished surface of the ground, paving or sidewalk within the area between the building and the property line or, when the property line is more than 5 feet (1524 mm) from the building, between the building and a line 5 feet (1524 mm) from the building.

Sidewalk Light Ports

Once it was common to place glass panels in sidewalks to let light into the basements below. I haven't seen any glass sidewalk light ports lately, but the ones I remember were tinted green and usually chipped. At night the light from underneath would make the glass sparkle like emeralds. The code still permits them if they're in a metal frame and at least ½ inch thick. If the area of the glass is over 16 square inches, it must be wire reinforced.

Floor lights or sidewalk lights must be able to carry the floor or sidewalk load unless protected by a railing at least 42 inches high. With the required railing, the design load need be no more than the roof design load.

On private property, you can build basements under sidewalks. But you might want to build a basement under a public sidewalk so a freight elevator can take deliveries directly to the basement. That usually requires an easement and a relaxation of the zoning ordinance.

Other Plastic Applications

The word *plastic* is a broad term that covers many materials. Chapter 26 of the UBC at one time covered only plastic glazing material. Now it uses the term *light-transmitting plastics*. That's to differentiate it from the other definition of "plastic" that just means capable of being molded. Even concrete in its liquid state is referred to as being plastic.

Rapid changes in plastics in the last several decades have kept the code-writing people on their toes. Chapter 26 of the UBC includes foam plastic insulation, light-transmitting exterior wall and roof panels, skylights, light-diffusing systems for electrical fixtures, partitions, awnings, patio covers, canopies, and solar collectors.

Installation requirements for plastics aren't clearly defined in the code. The main requirement is that it have enough strength and durability to withstand the mandatory design loads. The code isn't too specific on fastenings, either. They must be able to withstand design load and include space for expansion and contraction of the materials. Your job is to satisfy the inspector with the quality of your material. If you're using one of the popular brands on the market, this shouldn't be a problem. The inspector is probably already familiar with them.

Plastic Glazing Material

In a Type V-N building, doors, sash and framed openings that don't have to be fire protected may be glazed with any approved plastic material. But the use of plastics is more regulated in other building types. For instance, the plastic glazing can't cover more than 25 percent of any wall surface on any story. No single pane of glazing material above the first story can be higher than 4 feet or have an area larger than 16 square feet. You can increase this area by 50 percent in a sprinklered building.

You can't go above 65 feet from grade with any plastic glazing. And there's one unusual requirement for plastic glazing: You have to install an approved flame barrier extending 30 inches beyond the exterior wall in the plane of the floor or vertical panel located in adjacent stories. This is to deflect heat from any fire below so the plastic won't melt.

Patio Covers

Section 3116 defines patio covers:

Patio covers are one-story structures not exceeding 12 feet (3657 mm) in height. Enclosure walls may have any configuration, provided the open area of the longer wall and one additional wall is equal to at least 65 percent of the area below a minimum of 6 feet 8 inches (2032 mm) of each wall, measured from the floor. Openings may be enclosed with insect screening or plastic that is readily removable translucent or transparent plastic not more than 0.125 inch (3.2 mm) in thickness.

In the next paragraph it states what they can and can't be used for:

. . . Patio covers shall be used only for recreational, outdoor living purposes and not as carports, garages, storage rooms or habitable rooms.

This is very important. Many manufacturers claim you can use their patio covers for carports, but the code doesn't allow it. To find out if the unit is a patio cover or a carport (especially when you're facing a fast-talking salesman), get the make and model number, the manufacturer's name, and any product specs. Then call the inspector. It will only take him a minute or two to check his Evaluation Reports and find out if the cover is approved for your application. If it's a common national brand, he'll have the information on hand. You'll need his blessing anyway when you apply for a permit, so you might as well start off on the right foot.

Patio covers don't need to be installed on a footing. But the concrete slab under the patio cover must be a minimum of 3½ inches thick. Forming the slab with a 2 x 4 will give it this thickness. Of course, all this assumes that the

cover doesn't support live or dead loads exceeding 750 pounds per column.

Patio covers and carports are exposed to many stresses and strains that aren't common with other structures. They must be designed to withstand the stress limits of the code, all dead loads, and a minimum vertical live load of 10 pounds per square inch — plus one other very critical load: the uplift load. Because of their construction, patio covers and carports are more susceptible to this load than most structures. They must be designed to support a minimum wind uplift load equal to the horizontal wind load pushing upward against the roof surface. But if your patio is less than 10 feet above grade, the uplift load may be only three-fourths the horizontal wind load.

Theaters and Stages

Chapter 4 of the UBC covers theaters and stages. It requires one-hour fire protection in most areas. In fact, nearly all accessory rooms must now have that protection.

Section 405.3.2 requires that dressing room sections, workshops, and storerooms be separated from each other, and from the stage, by a one-hour fire-resistive separation.

We covered fly galleries and proscenium walls in Chapter 2, so we won't repeat it here. But there is one more important subject: ventilation.

Proper ventilation is one of the first and most important considerations in designing a stage. Lights and human activity on the stage generate a great deal of heat. And most stages have a lot of flammable material. The two together create a very volatile situation. For that reason most permanent items on a stage must be as fire resistive as possible.

The ventilators in a theater serve two purposes. The first is obvious — drawing off excess hot air. Modern air conditioning has greatly reduced the need for ventilation alone. The second purpose is fire venting. The code requires special vents to release heat and smoke in case of a fire. Skylights serve this purpose. They must be readily opened, either by spring action or force of gravity sufficient to overcome the effects of neglect, rust, dirt, frost, snow, or expansion and warping of the framework. They must be controlled by a fusible link so they open automatically in case of fire.

Projection Rooms

Originally, theaters were for stage productions. When movies became popular, they started building theaters primarily for movies, but they still included facilities for stage productions. Gradually, the stages disappeared from new movie houses.

UBC Section 406 covers projection rooms. Projection rooms have separate rules even if they're in a theater with a stage. The section on projection rooms also applies to school projection rooms and drive-in theaters. Every projection room must have this sign with 1-inch block letters: Safety Film Only Permitted In This Room.

Motion picture projection rooms must have at least 80 square feet of floor area for one projection machine and 40 square feet for each additional machine. The minimum ceiling height is 7'6". The ceiling must be of the same construction required for the rest of the building. Exits must conform to Chapter 10 of the UBC, but don't have to be surfaced with fire-rated materials.

Openings in the wall between the projection room and the auditorium can't exceed 25 percent of the wall area. The openings must be framed with fire-rated materials.

In a drive-in theater, many inspectors will waive this 25 percent maximum. And ventilation isn't as important because most projection rooms are now air conditioned. But the code requires each projection room to have a lavatory and a water closet. Check the exit and fire requirements for the snack bar and its connection with the projection room. Between shows these places get quite crowded. However, drive-in theaters are a dying breed so even this consideration may be a moot point.

Temporary Use of Public Property

Any permanent use of public property is usually prohibited by either the building code or zoning ordinances. With few exceptions, any structure that's going to stay where it's built can't be built on public property. But fences, barricades and shelters used during construction or demolition are considered temporary structures and may be built on public property. Your jurisdiction may require special permits to use public property, but the UBC doesn't. Structures built for fairs, exhibitions and carnivals are also considered temporary.

Most temporary structures used during the construction or demolition of a building are for the protection of the public. You can use part of the sidewalk area in front of a job site if you leave pedestrians a walkway 4 feet wide. If you need to use the entire walkway, it's O.K. to detour pedestrians into the street if you provide a 4-foot walkway with a railing on the traffic side and a fence on the construction side. Lights are required during dark hours. UBC Table 33-A (Figure 18-4) shows the protection needed for pedestrians.

Install signs and railings to direct pedestrians. Railings must be at least 42 inches high, built of new 2 x 4s or larger lumber. Railings adjacent to excavations must have a mid-rail.

The fence between the walkway and the site must be solid, substantial and at least 8 feet high. It has to extend the full length of the site. Plywood fences must be made of exterior grade plywood. Support plywood ¼ to ⁵⁄₁₆ inch thick with studs at least 2 feet on center unless you add a horizontal stiffener at mid-height. Plywood thicker than ⁵⁄₈ inch can span 8 feet.

Sidewalk canopies (to protect pedestrians from overhead work) must have a clear height of 8 feet, a tightly-sheathed roof of 2-inch nominal wood plankings, and must be lighted during hours of darkness. Incidentally, you have to protect any opening in a temporary fence or shield it with a door that will latch or lock.

TABLE 33-A—TYPE OF PROTECTION REQUIRED FOR PEDESTRIANS

HEIGHT OF CONSTRUCTION	DISTANCE FROM CONSTRUCTION	PROTECTION REQUIRED
	× 304.8 for mm	
8 feet or less	Less than 6 feet	Railing
	6 feet or more	None
More than 8 feet	Less than 6 feet	Fence and canopy
	6 feet or more, but not more than one fourth the height of construction	Fence and canopy
	6 feet or more, but between one fourth to one half the height of construction	Fence
	6 feet or more, but exceeding one half the construction height	None

From the Uniform Building Code, ©1997, ICBO

Figure 18-4 *Protection required for pedestrians*

Be careful when mixing or handling mortar, concrete, or other material on public property. The code says this work can't deface public property or create a nuisance. All utility lines and their frames, standards, and catch basins must be protected against interference.

Permanent Use of Public Property

The permanent use of public property is usually restricted to projections over the property line. Cornices, architectural features, eave overhangs and exterior private balconies that project beyond the floor area are governed by Section 705 of the UBC. Projections in Type I or II buildings must be of noncombustible material. Projections in other buildings can be either noncombustible or combustible. But if you use combustible materials where protected openings are required, they must be one-hour fire-resistive, or heavy timber.

Chapter 32, Section 3204 discusses some of these projections:

Section 3204. *Oriel windows, balconies, sun-control devices, unroofed porches, cornices, belt courses and appendages such as water tables, sills, capitals, bases and architectural projections may project over the public property of the building site a distance as determined by the clearance of*

the lowest point of the projection above the grade immediately below, as follows:

Clearance above grade less than 8 feet (2438 mm)— no projection is permitted.

Clearance above grade over 8 feet (2438 mm)— 1 inch (25 mm) of projection is permitted for each additional inch of clearance, provided that no such projection shall exceed a distance of 4 feet (1219 mm).

Awnings and Marquees

Remember the old-fashioned striped canvas awnings that used to grace Main Street? For many years they were in disrepute. The UBC didn't even recognize them because they were considered a fire hazard. Now they're back in vogue. But they can't encroach on public property further than 7 feet from the face of the building or within 2 feet of the face of the curb. The main awning must be at least 8 feet high. The frames, but not the covers, must be noncombustible. The awning frame must be totally supported from the exterior wall.

Marquees are a little different. They must be constructed of noncombustible material and supported entirely by the building. They can't be more than 3 feet thick when the marquee extends more than two-thirds the distance to the curb. If they're less than two-thirds of that distance, they can go to 9 feet thick.

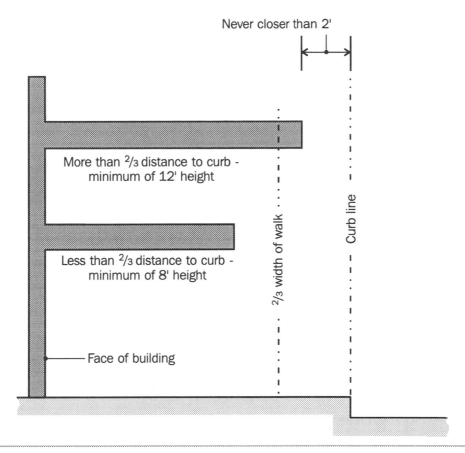

Never closer than 2'

More than ²/₃ distance to curb -
minimum of 12' height

Less than ²/₃ distance to curb -
minimum of 8' height

Face of building

²/₃ width of walk

Curb line

Figure 18-5 *Marquee construction measurements*

Figure 18-5 shows the marquee requirements. Notice that no marquee can project within 2 feet of the curb. That's to prevent damage from tall trucks parking at curbside. The minimum height is 8 feet if it extends less than two-thirds the way to the curb. If it's wider, it can't be less than 12 feet high.

Doors, when fully open, can't project more than 1 foot beyond the property line. In alleys, no projection is allowed.

Agricultural Buildings

Recognizing that the code would eventually be used in most rural and agricultural areas, the UBC covers agricultural buildings in Chapter 3 of the Appendix. Here's what Section 326 says:

The provisions of this appendix shall apply exclusively to agricultural buildings. Such buildings shall be classified as a Group U, Division 3 Occupancy and shall include the following uses:

1. *Storage, livestock and poultry.*

2. *Milking barns.*

3. *Shade structures.*

4. *Horticultural structures (greenhouses and crop protection).*

The allowable height and area of agricultural buildings are greatly increased and exit requirements are generally relaxed compared to other building types. UBC Table A-3-A shows basic allowable areas. Because of their lower occupancy rate, the setbacks, occupancy separations and most other restrictions are vastly different from other types of buildings. But Appendix Chapter 3 doesn't cover any residences, private garages, or commercial or quasi-commercial buildings; the main code sections apply to them.

Prefabricated Buildings

These can include everything from small metal tool sheds to barns and equipment storage facilities. Most of the smaller structures are exempt from permit requirements. Section 106.2 of the UBC exempts detached accessory buildings under 120 square feet.

Prefab buildings larger than that are covered in Section 1704 of the UBC:

Section 1704.1.1 Purpose. The purpose of this chapter is to regulate materials and establish methods of safe construction where any structure or portion thereof is wholly or partially prefabricated.

1704.1.2 Scope. Unless otherwise specifically stated in this section, all prefabricated construction and all materials used therein shall conform to all the requirements of this code. (See Section 104.2.8.)

1704.1.3 Definition. Prefabricated Assembly is a structural unit, the integral parts of which have been built up or assembled prior to incorporation in the building.

Most of the prefabricated steel and aluminum structures sold today meet the code requirements. Other than the interior improvements in these structures (sanitation, insulation, interior finish), there's nothing to inspect except the footings and foundations. If your prefab structure is very big or has a high occupant load, the building official may require tests to determine its durability or weather resistiveness.

That raises the question of whether you could prefab a building in your back yard that you might use later as a house. It might work except for some sneaky little provisions in Section 1704.6.2. It says a certificate of approval must be obtained from an approved agency for each structure.

Sound Transmission Control

Standards for sound transmission control appear in Section 1208 of the Appendix. Group R occupancies now have some protection from noisy neighbors.

After reading through that chapter and the standards that go with it, I'm afraid it's still going to be difficult to enforce compliance, especially in apartment buildings. To do so you'd need a sound engineer with a battery of equipment. To make sure you're meeting the code requirements, check to see if your city has adopted Chapter 35. If it has, ask the building inspector what you have to do.

Swimming Pools, Spas and Hot Tubs

I'll start by explaining that the code doesn't have much to say about swimming pools and spas. This section regulates only the barriers and safety devices around a pool or spa, not the pool itself. In the UBC Appendix, Chapter 4 Division I is called Barriers for Swimming Pools, Spas and Hot Tubs:

419.1 Scope. The provisions of this section apply to the design and construction of barriers for swimming pools located on the premises of Group R, Division 3 Occupancies.

In other words, this covers dwellings and lodging houses only — not apartment buildings or commercial pools. Notice that the code lumps spas, hot tubs, and swimming pools (both indoors and outdoors) under a single heading. Here's the definition of a swimming pool in Section 420:

Swimming pool is any structure intended for swimming or recreational bathing that contains water over 24 inches (610 mm) deep. This includes in-ground, aboveground and on-ground swimming pools, and fixed-in-place wading pools.

Section 421 regulates barriers around these pools. It states that the barrier must be a minimum of 48 inches above grade and the bottom of the barrier must be within 2 inches of grade on the side of the barrier that faces away from the pool. If you have an aboveground pool, either install the barrier at grade level or at pool-top level.

Here are some other considerations:

- Openings in the barrier must be small enough to prevent passage of a 1¾-inch-diameter sphere.

- Solid barriers without openings, like masonry or stone walls, must be smooth except for tooled masonry joints. They can't have indentations or protrusions that would make the wall easy to climb.

- If the barrier has horizontal and vertical members, such as line posts and rails, the requirements vary if the tops of the horizontal members are more or less than 45 inches apart. If it's less than 45 inches, the vertical members can't be more than 1¾ inches apart. Horizontal members must be on the pool side. If horizontal members are more than 45 inches apart, the vertical members can't be more than 4 inches apart. There are additional requirements for decorative cutouts.

- For chain link fences, minimum gauge size is 11.

- Lattice barriers can't have openings greater than 1¾ inches.

- Access gates must open away from the pool, be self-closing and self-locking.

- If the house forms one wall of the barrier, any opening from the house must be protected by an alarm device, a self-closing, self-latching device or separation fence.

That's the gist of it. A 48-inch barrier won't keep all children out, but it will keep out the tots and slow down the rest. That's why any openings in the barrier have to be so small — to keep the little ones from climbing. Maybe the authors of the code figure that any child big enough to climb over a 4-foot fence can climb out of a pool.

That's the end of the miscellaneous components covered by the UBC. In the final chapter, we'll look at a rapidly evolving subject — accessibility by the disabled.

What's Your Category?

I've been inspecting buildings since 1965. I try not to, but I can't avoid putting the contractors I deal with into one of five categories. Normally I don't talk about this. But I want to share it with you. There's a reason. I suspect most building inspectors do something similar. You should know enough to stay out of the wrong categories.

Category A Contractors could get a permit from me on their say-so alone. I've even looked the other way when one of these guys had to start a job in a hurry, before the plans were drawn or permit issued. You get to be a Category A Contractor by knowing as much or more about building and the code as anyone in the community. You do nothing but quality work that meets the highest professional standards, no matter what the situation and no matter who's watching. Category A Contractors usually get the best jobs from owners with the deepest pockets. They're nearly always busy. Though this is a small group, they set a good example for everyone in the industry.

Category B Contractors know as much about construction as Category A Contractors. But they have to buy most jobs with low bids or by hustling a little harder. If nothing bad happens, Category B Contractors turn out good jobs at bargain prices. But when the fat hits the fire, Category B guys will cut corners. They'll compromise on quality to save their margin. They'll let a few things slide by if no one is going to notice. That's why I have to notice. This is a large group.

Category C Contractors don't know as much about construction as either Category A or Category B Contractors. Most would like to be as skilled as their more experienced brethren. But they don't know how. Very few would try to cheat the owner or confuse the inspector. But inexperience and carelessness show in their work. Not all Category C Contractors are new at building. Some have been at it for many years. They just haven't learned very fast. That's why I'm very patient with these builders. I'll explain anything as often as necessary. And I keep my eyes open. Again, this is a large group.

Category D Contractors just don't seem to care. They usually know what they should be doing. But they aren't going to do it until someone makes them. That someone is usually me. I won't use the word lazy for these guys. Maybe the word sluggish is better.

Category F Contractors stand alone. I sometimes wonder what makes these guys tick. You could camp in the middle of the project and Category F contractors would still try to cheat all around you. It's almost like a game: get away with everything you can.

A couple of years ago I gave a talk to our local home builder's association. I explained my five construction categories. That was a mistake. I was too candid. My little talk hurt the pride of some good builders and good friends who don't happen to rate at the top of my list. So I don't say much about categories any more. In fact, I wish I'd never said anything. But you should know that everyone in the construction industry is earning a reputation every day (either for craftsmanship and professionalism or for the lack of it). My advice is simple. Guard your professional reputation like you protect your favorite skill saw. Nothing you're likely to own is more valuable.

19

Accessibility
for the Disabled

The addition of accessible facilities has changed the way you construct buildings these days. You can't just put up a set of steps at a structure and say that they're an entrance or exit. Chapter 11 on Accessibility for the 1994 edition was completely rewritten so there's more for you to be concerned about.

Here's a warning: What you see in the code are minimum standards. You may want to do more. And your local building department may insist on more. I recommend asking your inspector about local regulations that may be more stringent than what's in the UBC.

Definitions

We'll start with the definitions, because they determine to a large extent what we must look for. They're in Section 1102.

Accessible describes a site, building, facility or portion thereof that complies with this chapter and that can be approached, entered, and used by persons with physical disabilities.

Accessible Means of Egress is a path of travel, usable by a mobility-impaired person, that leads to a public way.

Accessible Route is a continuous path connecting accessible elements and spaces in a building or facility that is usable by persons with disabilities

Adaptability is the capability of altering or adding to certain building spaces and elements, such as kitchen counters, sinks and grab bars, to accommodate the needs of persons with and without disabilities, or to accommodate the needs of persons with different types or degrees of disability.

Area of Refuge *is an area with direct access to an exit or an elevator where persons unable to use stairs can remain temporarily in safety to await instructions or assistance during emergency evacuation.*

Dwelling Unit-Type A *is a dwelling unit that is designed and constructed for accessibility in accordance with CABO/ANSI A117.1.*

Dwelling Unit-Type B *is a dwelling unit that is designed and constructed for accessibility in accordance with Section 1106.*

Person With Disability *is an individual who has an impairment, including a mobility, sensory or cognitive impairment, which results in a functional limitation in access to and use of a building or facility.*

All Disabilities?

Note that the code refers to sensory, manual or speaking disabilities. But as a practical matter, there's little in the code to affect a blind or mute person. There is one thing you should remember, however. A deaf or mute person who has to leave a building in an emergency in the daytime should be directed out by visible signs, arrows, or stripes on the floor. That puts them on a par with people who don't have these disabilities.

The federal government has enacted laws to benefit the disabled. Like many regulations, the effort is well-intended but loaded with unintended consequences. All transit systems, for instance, must install wheelchair lifts within a certain time period, even in parts of the country where they can be expected to freeze in place and become unusable.

Arthritis has made me highly experienced in the use of wheelchairs, crutches and canes. So I'm all for making life as easy as possible for people who have to use them. That's what the code authors are trying to do. Expect regulations on access for the disabled to continue evolving as the needs of the disabled are better understood.

Where Is Accessibility Required?

Section 1101.1 pretty well establishes this when it states:

1101.1 General. *Buildings or portions of buildings shall be accessible to persons with disabilities as required by this chapter.*

See also Appendix Chapter 11 for requirements governing the provision of accessible site facilities not regulated by this chapter. See Section 101.3 for applicability of appendix.

Appendix Chapter 11 deals mostly with renovation of existing buildings. You will find that the public is beginning to become quite concerned about accessibility for disabled people and this is quite clearly shown in schools, churches, and entertainment facilities. Although why any businessman would be adverse to making his store or building accessible is a bit hard to understand.

There are, however, certain situations where it is not technically feasible for this to be done and the code allows for that. That is addressed in Section 1111, Definitions, of the appendix:

Technically Infeasible *is an alteration of a building or facility that has little likelihood of being accomplished because existing structural conditions would require removing or altering a load-bearing member which is an essential part of the structural frame, or because existing physical or site constraints prohibit modification or addition of elements, spaces or features which are in full and strict compliance with the minimum requirements for new construction and which are necessary to provide accessibility.*

What isn't said is how this decision will be made. It's assumed the building official will be the one making this decision, and he may require an engineer's certification.

Then it lists all the occupancy classifications and the specific requirements that apply. Most of the regulations are based on the maneuverability of a wheelchair. Generally, anywhere a wheelchair can go, a person on crutches or a cane can go.

All public buildings must be accessible either by ramp or elevator and all facilities inside the building (except for certain areas that aren't usually occupied) must be accessible. These "not usually occupied" areas include elevator pits, piping and equipment catwalks and machinery rooms.

The code permits some deviation from the basic rule of 100 percent accessibility based on the type of usage and occupant load. Here are some specifics:

Group A Occupancy: For seating requirements for dining and drinking establishments, check with your local building official. Stadiums and auditoriums must have at least four wheelchair spaces for the first 300 seats, six for the first 500 seats, and one for each additional 200 seats. Table 11-A shows the number of wheelchair spaces for all assembly areas.

Groups B, E, H, I, M, S and U Occupancy: Except for Group E occupancies, these must be fully accessible.

Group R Occupancy: All private dwellings are exempt, along with structures containing three or fewer living units for less than 10 people. This exemption also applies to Group R-3 for all floors above the primary level if they're not served by elevators. All common or public use areas must be accessible.

The primary entrance of any structure required to be accessible must be accessible as well as any other entrances within 6 inches of grade. An accessible route of travel, properly signed, must also be provided. Groups A, B, E, and M also require assistive listening systems in certain areas. This, of course, is for the hard of hearing. Furthermore, in the Group R occupancies all apartment houses with more than 20 units must have at least one accessible unit.

Evacuation Assistance

This is a topic that's easy to overlook. Elevators, as you know, are generally unusable during a fire. So provisions must be made to protect the disabled in case of fire, earthquake or any condition that might make normal evacuation difficult or impossible. This could be a smokeproof enclosure, an exterior exit balcony, or some other arrangement to allow the disabled to await assistance.

These areas must have communications approved by the fire authorities and a sign stating: "Area For Evacuation Assistance."

Accessibility of Building Facilities

When bathing facilities are provided, at least 2 percent of the facilities, but not less than one bathtub or shower, must be accessible. There must be accessible toilet facilities. There must be at least one accessible water closet. If more than ten water closets are required, two of them must be accessible. Proper grab bars must be installed for all baths, showers and toilets where accessible features are required. At least one accessible lavatory, mirror and towel facility must be provided.

I once visited a state park where the rest room facilities were accessible, according to the signs. Then I noticed a row of concrete wheel bumpers that completely blocked access. I took a picture and sent it to the proper state agency. They never acknowledged the letter, but they corrected the problem. A government that enforces rules also has to follow the rules.

On any floor where there are drinking fountains or telephones, make sure one of each is accessible.

Site Provisions

Appendix Chapter 11 covers site considerations such as disabled parking and access to the building from the parking lot. It also covers

TABLE A-11-A—NUMBER OF ACCESSIBLE PARKING SPACES

TOTAL PARKING SPACES IN LOT OR GARAGE	MINIMUM REQUIRED NUMBER OF ACCESSIBLE SPACES
1-25	1
26-50	2
51-75	3
76-100	4
101-150	5
151-200	6
201-300	7
301-400	8
401-500	9
501-1,000	2% of total spaces
Over 1,000	20 spaces plus 1 space for every 100 spaces, or fraction thereof, over 1,000

From the Uniform Building Code, ©1997, ICBO

Figure 19-1 *Number of accessible parking spaces*

access in remodeled buildings. Section 1107.1 says:

> **1107.1 General.** *Accessible exterior routes shall be provided from public transportation stops, accessible parking and accessible passenger loading zones and public sidewalks to the accessible building entrance they serve.*

When more than one building or facility is located on a site, at least one accessible route shall connect accessible elements, facilities and buildings that are on the same site. The accessible route between accessible parking and accessible building entrances shall be the most practical direct route.

Here's Section 1108.1:

> **Accessible Parking Required.** *When parking lots or garage facilities are provided, accessible parking spaces shall be provided in accordance with Table A-11-A . . .* (See Figure 19-1.)

The code also requires one van-accessible parking space for each eight accessible parking spaces or fraction thereof.

The parking spaces must be located on the shortest route to the nearest accessible entrance to a building or facility. Avoid placing them where the route of travel crosses traffic lanes. If they have to cross traffic, the route of travel must be designated and marked as a crosswalk.

There's a conflict here in most shopping mall parking lots. Other regulations require a fire lane next to the building. Disabled parking can't be in a fire lane. Some traffic engineers feel that marked crosswalks are dangerous because people put too much faith in the stripes on pavement. Kids think they're safe in a crosswalk and may dart out without looking.

Here's something else to consider. Table A-11-A doesn't provide nearly enough accessible parking for some types of buildings. How much disabled parking do you need at an outpatient clinic for the elderly? Lots more than at an elementary school. The code doesn't require it. But you should. The code isn't a replacement for common sense.

Passenger drop-off and loading zones, if provided, must also be signed and located on a direct route to an accessible route of travel.

Accessibility for Existing Buildings

Appendix Chapter 11 also covers providing accessibility when remodeling existing buildings. There are several definitions you should know.

Alterations

Alteration is any change, addition or modification in construction or occupancy.

Any existing elements, spaces, essential features or common areas that are altered or remodeled must meet accessibility standards. That means that you could remodel the first floor, provide accessible features as required there, and not be required to bring the entire building up to code.

The code also permits the alteration or updating of electrical, mechanical or plumbing systems without adhering to Chapter 11. This also applies to any substantial alterations of a building — except that you must provide at least one accessible route of travel, one accessible entrance, and one accessible toilet for each sex in each building or on each floor of a multi-floor structure.

Modifications

Section 1112.2 sets standards for modification of older buildings where it would be structurally impractical to meet access standards. This section also reduces access standards in restored historic buildings. Here's a summary:

■ You don't have to provide full extension of stair handrails if the extension would be hazardous.

■ If elevators are provided, you don't have to modify the stairs.

■ If a safety door edge is provided on elevator doors, you can omit automatic opening devices.

■ You can reduce elevator floor space, but it can't be less than 48 inches by 48 inches.

■ If the existing building prevents strict compliance with the clearance requirement for doors, a ⅝-inch projection is allowed for a door stop.

■ If the existing threshold is ¾ inch high or less, it has to be beveled.

■ A shared toilet facility is acceptable on a floor when it's structurally impractical to meet the requirements of Chapter 11.

■ In assembly areas, seating has to adjoin an accessible route of travel.

Historic Preservation

Appendix Section 1114 sets requirements for historic buildings — and it's loaded with trouble. It's up to the building official to determine if accessibility will or will not destroy the historic significance of a building. If he determines that it will, then conditions in Section 1112.2 apply. If he thinks it won't, you'll have to make it conform. If you're not happy with the building official's decision, of course, you have the right to appeal.

In any event there must be at least one accessible entrance and route of travel at all levels or floors of a building. You can get by with an accessible unisex toilet if it's impractical to install one for each sex.

Appendix

Span Tables

The following pages contain most of the wood span information you're likely to need. Detailed instructions on how to use these tables can be found in Chapter 11.

TABLE 23-II-C—HARDBOARD SIDING

SIDING	MINIMAL NOMINAL THICKNESS (Inch)	FRAMING (2" x 4") MAXIMUM SPACING	NAIL SIZE[1,2]	NAIL SPACING General	NAIL SPACING Bracing Panels[3]
			× 25.4 for mm		
1. LAP SIDING					
Direct to studs	$3/8$	16" o.c.	8d	16" o.c.	Not applicable
Over sheathing	$3/8$	16" o.c.	10d	16" o.c.	Not applicable
2. SQUARE EDGE PANEL SIDING					
Direct to studs	$3/8$	24" o.c.	6d	6" o.c. edges; 12" o.c. at intermed. supports	4" o.c. edges; 8" o.c. intermed. supports
Over sheathing	$3/8$	24" o.c.	8d	6" o.c. edges; 12" o.c. at intermed. supports	4" o.c. edges; 8" o.c. intermed. supports
3. SHIPLAP EDGE PANEL SIDING					
Direct to studs	$3/8$	16" o.c.	6d	6" o.c. edges; 12" o.c. at intermed. supports	4" o.c. edges; 8" o.c. intermed. supports
Over sheathing	$3/8$	16" o.c.	8d	6" o.c. edges; 12" o.c. at intermed. supports	4" o.c. edges; 8" o.c. intermed. supports

[1]Nails shall be corrosion resistant in accordance with Division III, Part III.
[2]Minimum acceptable nail dimensions (inches).

	Panel Siding (inch)	Lap Siding (inch)
	× 25.4 for mm	
Shank diameter	0.092	0.099
Head diameter	0.225	0.240

[3]When used to comply with Division IV, Section 2320.11.3.

TABLE 23-II-D-1—ALLOWABLE SPANS FOR LUMBER FLOOR AND ROOF SHEATHING[1,2]

SPAN (inches)	MINIMUM NET THICKNESS (inches) OF LUMBER PLACED Perpendicular to Supports		Diagonally to Supports	
× 25.4 for mm	× 25.4 for mm			
	Surfaced Dry[3]	Surfaced Unseasoned	Surfaced Dry[3]	Surfaced Unseasoned
Floors				
1. 24	$3/4$	$25/32$	$3/4$	$25/32$
2. 16	$5/8$	$11/16$	$5/8$	$11/16$
Roofs				
3. 24	$5/8$	$11/16$	$3/4$	$25/32$

[1]Installation details shall conform to Sections 2320.9.1 and 2320.12.8 for floor and roof sheathing, respectively.
[2]Floor or roof sheathing conforming with this table shall be deemed to meet the design criteria of Section 2312.
[3]Maximum 19 percent moisture content.

TABLE 23-II-D-2—SHEATHING LUMBER SHALL MEET THE FOLLOWING MINIMUM GRADE REQUIREMENTS: BOARD GRADE

SOLID FLOOR OR ROOF SHEATHING	SPACED ROOF SHEATHING	GRADING RULES
1. Utility	Standard	NLGA, WCLIB, WWPA
2. 4 common or utility	3 common or standard	NLGA, WCLIB, WWPA, NHPMA or NELMA
3. No. 3	No. 2	SPIB
4. Merchantable	Construction common	RIS

From the Uniform Building Code, ©1997, ICBO

TABLE 23-II-E-1—ALLOWABLE SPANS AND LOADS FOR WOOD STRUCTURAL PANEL SHEATHING AND SINGLE-FLOOR GRADES CONTINUOUS OVER TWO OR MORE SPANS WITH STRENGTH AXIS PERPENDICULAR TO SUPPORTS[1,2]

SHEATHING GRADES		ROOF[3]				FLOOR[4]
		Maximum Span (inches)		Load[5] (pounds per square foot)		
		× 25.4 for mm		× 0.0479 for kN/m²		Maximum Span (inches)
Panel Span Rating	Panel Thickness (inches)	With Edge Support[6]	Without Edge Support	Total Load	Live Load	
Roof/Floor Span	× 25.4 for mm					× 25.4 for mm
12/0	$5/16$	12	12	40	30	0
16/0	$5/16, 3/8$	16	16	40	30	0
20/0	$5/16, 3/8$	20	20	40	30	0
24/0	$3/8, 7/16, 1/2$	24	20[7]	40	30	0
24/16	$7/16, 1/2$	24	24	50	40	16
32/16	$15/32, 1/2, 5/8$	32	28	40	30	16[8]
40/20	$19/32, 5/8, 3/4, 7/8$	40	32	40	30	20[8,9]
48/24	$23/32, 3/4, 7/8$	48	36	45	35	24
54/32	$7/8, 1$	54	40	45	35	32
60/48	$7/8, 1, 1 1/8$	60	48	45	35	48
SINGLE-FLOOR GRADES		ROOF[3]				FLOOR[4]
		Maximum Span (inches)		Load[5] (pounds per square foot)		
Panel Span Rating (inches)	Panel Thickness (inches)	× 25.4 for mm		× 0.0479 for kN/m²		Maximum Span (inches)
× 25.4 for mm		With Edge Support[6]	Without Edge Support	Total Load	Live Load	× 25.4 for mm
16 oc	$1/2, 19/32, 5/8$	24	24	50	40	16[8]
20 oc	$19/32, 5/8, 3/4$	32	32	40	30	20[8,9]
24 oc	$23/32, 3/4$	48	36	35	25	24
32 oc	$7/8, 1$	48	40	50	40	32
48 oc	$1 3/32, 1 1/8$	60	48	50	50	48

[1]Applies to panels 24 inches (610 mm) or wider.
[2]Floor and roof sheathing conforming with this table shall be deemed to meet the design criteria of Section 2312.
[3]Uniform load deflection limitations $1/180$ of span under live load plus dead load, $1/240$ under live load only.
[4]Panel edges shall have approved tongue-and-groove joints or shall be supported with blocking unless $1/4$-inch (6.4 mm) minimum thickness underlayment or $1 1/2$ inches (38 mm) of approved cellular or lightweight concrete is placed over the subfloor, or finish floor is $3/4$-inch (19 mm) wood strip. Allowable uniform load based on deflection of $1/360$ of span is 100 pounds per square foot (psf) (4.79 kN/m²) except the span rating of 48 inches on center is based on a total load of 65 psf (3.11 kN/m).
[5]Allowable load at maximum span.
[6]Tongue-and-groove edges, panel edge clips [one midway between each support, except two equally spaced between supports 48 inches (1219 mm) on center], lumber blocking, or other. Only lumber blocking shall satisfy blocked diaphragms requirements.
[7]For $1/2$-inch (12.7 mm) panel, maximum span shall be 24 inches (610 mm).
[8]May be 24 inches (610 mm) on center where $3/4$-inch (19 mm) wood strip flooring is installed at right angles to joist.
[9]May be 24 inches (610 mm) on center for floors where $1 1/2$ inches (38 mm) of cellular or lightweight concrete is applied over the panels.

TABLE 23-II-E-2—ALLOWABLE LOAD (PSF) FOR WOOD STRUCTURAL PANEL ROOF SHEATHING CONTINUOUS OVER TWO OR MORE SPANS AND STRENGTH AXIS PARALLEL TO SUPPORTS
(Plywood structural panels are five-ply, five-layer unless otherwise noted.)[1,2]

PANEL GRADE	THICKNESS (inch)	MAXIMUM SPAN (inches)	LOAD AT MAXIMUM SPAN (psf)	
			× 0.0479 for kN/m²	
	× 25.4 for mm	× 25.4 for mm	Live	Total
Structural I	$7/16$	24	20	30
	$15/32$	24	35[3]	45[3]
	$1/2$	24	40[3]	50[3]
	$19/32, 5/8$	24	70	80
	$23/32, 3/4$	24	90	100
Other grades covered in UBC Standard 23-2 or 23-3	$7/16$	16	40	50
	$15/32$	24	20	25
	$1/2$	24	25	30
	$19/32$	24	40[3]	50[3]
	$5/8$	24	45[3]	55[3]
	$23/32, 3/4$	24	60[3]	65[3]

[1]Roof sheathing conforming with this table shall be deemed to meet the design criteria of Section 2312.
[2]Uniform load deflection limitations: $1/180$ of span under live load plus dead load, $1/240$ under live load only. Edges shall be blocked with lumber or other approved type of edge supports.
[3]For composite and four-ply plywood structural panel, load shall be reduced by 15 pounds per square foot (0.72 kN/m²).

From the Uniform Building Code, ©1997, ICBO

TABLE 23-II-F-1—ALLOWABLE SPAN FOR WOOD STRUCTURAL PANEL COMBINATION SUBFLOOR-UNDERLAYMENT (SINGLE FLOOR)[1,2] Panels Continuous over Two or More Spans and Strength Axis Perpendicular to Supports

IDENTIFICATION	MAXIMUM SPACING OF JOISTS (inches)				
	× 25.4 for mm				
	16	20	24	32	48
Species Group[3]	Thickness (inches)				
	× 25.4 for mm				
1	$^1/_2$	$^5/_8$	$^3/_4$	—	—
2, 3	$^5/_8$	$^3/_4$	$^7/_8$	—	—
4	$^3/_4$	$^7/_8$	1	—	—
Span rating[4]	16 o.c.	20 o.c.	24 o.c.	32 o.c.	48 o.c.

[1]Spans limited to value shown because of possible effects of concentrated loads. Allowable uniform loads based on deflection of $^1/_{360}$ of span is 100 pounds per square foot (psf) (4.79 kN/m^2), except allowable total uniform load for $1^1/_8$-inch (29 mm) wood structural panels over joists spaced 48 inches (1219 mm) on center is 65 psf (3.11 kN/m^2). Panel edges shall have approved tongue-and-groove joints or shall be supported with blocking, unless $^1/_4$-inch (6.4 mm) minimum thickness underlayment or $1^1/_2$ inches (38 mm) of approved cellular or lightweight concrete is placed over the subfloor, or finish floor is $^3/_4$-inch (19 mm) wood strip.

[2]Floor panels conforming with this table shall be deemed to meet the design criteria of Section 2312.

[3]Applicable to all grades of sanded exterior-type plywood. See UBC Standard 23-2 for plywood species groups.

[4]Applicable to underlayment grade and C-C (plugged) plywood, and single floor grade wood structural panels.

TABLE 23-II-F-2—ALLOWABLE SPANS FOR PARTICLEBOARD SUBFLOOR AND COMBINED SUBFLOOR-UNDERLAYMENT[1,2]

GRADE	THICKNESS (inches)	MAXIMUM SPACING OF SUPPORTS (inches)[3]	
	× 25.4 for mm	× 25.4 for mm	
		Subfloor	Combined Subfloor-Underlayment[4,5]
2-M-W	$^1/_2$	16	—
	$^5/_8$	20	16
	$^3/_4$	24	24
2-M-3	$^3/_4$	20	20

[1]All panels are continuous over two or more spans.

[2]Floor sheathing conforming with this table shall be deemed to meet the design criteria of Section 2312.

[3]Uniform deflection limitation: $^1/_{360}$ of the span under 100 pounds per square foot (4.79 kN/m^2) minimum load.

[4]Edges shall have tongue-and-groove joints or shall be supported with blocking. The tongue-and-groove panels are installed with the long dimension perpendicular to supports.

[5]A finish wearing surface is to be applied to the top of the panel.

TABLE 23-II-G—MAXIMUM DIAPHRAGM DIMENSION RATIOS

MATERIAL	HORIZONTAL DIAPHRAGMS	VERTICAL DIAPHRAGMS
	Maximum Span-Width Ratios	Maximum Height-Width Ratios
1. Diagonal sheathing, conventional	3:1	1:1[1]
2. Diagonal sheathing, special	4:1	2:1[2]
3. Wood structural panels and particleboard, nailed all edges	4:1	2:1[2]
4. Wood structural panels and particleboard, blocking omitted at intermediate joints.	4:1	[3]

[1]In Seismic Zones 0, 1 and 2, the maximum ratio may be 2:1.

[2]In Seismic Zones 0, 1 and 2, the maximum ratio may be $3^1/_2$:1.

[3]Not permitted.

TABLE 23-II-K—WOOD SHINGLE AND SHAKE SIDE WALL EXPOSURES

SHINGLE OR SHAKE	MAXIMUM WEATHER EXPOSURES (inches)			
	× 25.4 for mm			
	Single-Coursing		Double-Coursing	
Length and Type	No. 1	No. 2	No. 1	No. 2
16-inch (405 mm) shingles	$7^1/_2$	$7^1/_2$	12	10
18-inch (455 mm) shingles	$8^1/_2$	$8^1/_2$	14	11
24-inch (610 mm) shingles	$11^1/_2$	$11^1/_2$	16	14
18-inch (455 mm) resawn shakes	$8^1/_2$	—	14	—
18-inch (455 mm) straight-split shakes	$8^1/_2$	—	16	—
24-inch (610 mm) resawn shakes	$11^1/_2$	—	20	—

TABLE 23-IV-B—SIZE, HEIGHT AND SPACING OF WOOD STUDS

STUD SIZE (inches)	BEARING WALLS				NONBEARING WALLS	
	Laterally Unsupported Stud Height[1] (feet)	Supporting Roof and Ceiling Only	Supporting One Floor, Roof and Ceiling	Supporting Two Floors, Roof and Ceiling	Laterally Unsupported Stud Height[1] (feet)	Spacing (inches)
		Spacing (inches)				
× 25.4 for mm	× 304.8 for mm	× 25.4 for mm			× 304.8 for mm	× 25.4 for mm
1. 2 × 3[2]	—	—	—	—	10	16
2. 2 × 4	10	24	16	—	14	24
3. 3 × 4	10	24	24	16	14	24
4. 2 × 5	10	24	24	—	16	24
5. 2 × 6	10	24	24	16	20	24

[1]Listed heights are distances between points of lateral support placed perpendicular to the plane of the wall. Increases in unsupported height are permitted where justified by an analysis.
[2]Shall not be used in exterior walls.

TABLE 23-IV-D-2—ALLOWABLE SPANS FOR PARTICLEBOARD WALL SHEATHING[1]
(Not exposed to the weather, long dimension of the panel parallel or perpendicular to studs)

GRADE	THICKNESS (Inch)	STUD SPACING (inches)	
		× 25.4 for mm	
		Siding Nailed to Studs	Sheathing under Coverings Specified in Section 2320.11.3 Parallel or Perpendicular to Studs
		× 25.4 for mm	
M-1	$^3/_8$	16	16
M-S M-2 "Exterior Glue"	$^1/_2$	16	16

[1]In reference to Section 2320.11.3, blocking of horizontal joints is not required.

TABLE 23-IV-J-1—FLOOR JOISTS WITH *L*/360 DEFLECTION LIMITS
The allowable bending stress (F_b) and modulus of elasticity *(E)* used in this table shall be from Tables 23-IV-V-1 and 23-IV-V-2 only.

DESIGN CRITERIA:
Deflection — For 40 psf (1.92 kN/m^2) live load.
Limited to span in inches (mm) divided by 360.
Strength — Live load of 40 psf (1.92 kN/m^2) plus dead load of 10 psf (0.48 kN/m^2) determines the required bending design value.

Joist Size (in) × 25.4 for mm	Spacing (in)	Modulus of Elasticity, *E*, in 1,000,000 psi × 0.00689 for N/mm^2																
		0.8	0.9	1.0	1.1	1.2	1.3	1.4	1.5	1.6	1.7	1.8	1.9	2.0	2.1	2.2	2.3	2.4
2 × 6	12.0	8-6	8-10	9-2	9-6	9-9	10-0	10-3	10-6	10-9	10-11	11-2	11-4	11-7	11-9	11-11	12-1	12-3
	16.0	7-9	8-0	8-4	8-7	8-10	9-1	9-4	9-6	9-9	9-11	10-2	10-4	10-6	10-8	10-10	11-0	11-2
	19.2	7-3	7-7	7-10	8-1	8-4	8-7	8-9	9-0	9-2	9-4	9-6	9-8	9-10	10-0	10-2	10-4	10-6
	24.0	6-9	7-0	7-3	7-6	7-9	7-11	8-2	8-4	8-6	8-8	8-10	9-0	9-2	9-4	9-6	9-7	9-9
2 × 8	12.0	11-3	11-8	12-1	12-6	12-10	13-2	13-6	13-10	14-2	14-5	14-8	15-0	15-3	15-6	15-9	15-11	16-2
	16.0	10-2	10-7	11-0	11-4	11-8	12-0	12-3	12-7	12-10	13-1	13-4	13-7	13-10	14-1	14-3	14-6	14-8
	19.2	9-7	10-0	10-4	10-8	11-0	11-3	11-7	11-10	12-1	12-4	12-7	12-10	13-0	13-3	13-5	13-8	13-10
	24.0	8-11	9-3	9-7	9-11	10-2	10-6	10-9	11-0	11-3	11-5	11-8	11-11	12-1	12-3	12-6	12-8	12-10
2 × 10	12.0	14-4	14-11	15-5	15-11	16-5	16-10	17-3	17-8	18-0	18-5	18-9	19-1	19-5	19-9	20-1	20-4	20-8
	16.0	13-0	13-6	14-0	14-6	14-11	15-3	15-8	16-0	16-5	16-9	17-0	17-4	17-8	17-11	18-3	18-6	18-9
	19.2	12-3	12-9	13-2	13-7	14-0	14-5	14-9	15-1	15-5	15-9	16-0	16-4	16-7	16-11	17-2	17-5	17-8
	24.0	11-4	11-10	12-3	12-8	13-0	13-4	13-8	14-0	14-4	14-7	14-11	15-2	15-5	15-8	15-11	16-2	16-5
2 × 12	12.0	17-5	18-1	18-9	19-4	19-11	20-6	21-0	21-6	21-11	22-5	22-10	23-3	23-7	24-0	24-5	24-9	25-1
	16.0	15-10	16-5	17-0	17-7	18-1	18-7	19-1	19-6	19-11	20-4	20-9	21-1	21-6	21-10	22-2	22-6	22-10
	19.2	14-11	15-6	16-0	16-7	17-0	17-6	17-11	18-4	18-9	19-2	19-6	19-10	20-2	20-6	20-10	21-2	21-6
	24.0	13-10	14-4	14-11	15-4	15-10	16-3	16-8	17-0	17-5	17-9	18-1	18-5	18-9	19-1	19-4	19-8	19-11
F_b	12.0	718	777	833	888	941	993	1,043	1,092	1,140	1,187	1,233	1,278	1,323	1,367	1,410	1,452	1,494
	16.0	790	855	917	977	1,036	1,093	1,148	1,202	1,255	1,306	1,357	1,407	1,456	1,504	1,551	1,598	1,644
	19.2	840	909	975	1,039	1,101	1,161	1,220	1,277	1,333	1,388	1,442	1,495	1,547	1,598	1,649	1,698	1,747
	24.0	905	979	1,050	1,119	1,186	1,251	1,314	1,376	1,436	1,496	1,554	1,611	1,667	1,722	1,776	1,829	1,882

NOTE: The required bending design value, F_b, in pounds per square inch (× 0.00689 for N/mm^2) is shown at the bottom of this table and is applicable to all lumber sizes shown. Spans are shown in feet-inches (1 foot = 304.8 mm, 1 inch = 25.4 mm) and are limited to 26 feet (7925 mm) and less.

TABLE 23-IV-J-2—FLOOR JOISTS WITH *L*/360 DEFLECTION LIMITS
The allowable bending stress (F_b) and modulus of elasticity *(E)* used in this table shall be from Tables 23-IV-V-1 and 23-IV-V-2 only.

DESIGN CRITERIA:
Deflection — For 40 psf (1.92 kN/m^2) live load.
Limited to span in inches (mm) divided by 360.
Strength — Live load of 40 psf (1.92 kN/m^2) plus dead load of 20 psf (0.96 kN/m^2) determines the required bending design value.

Joist Size (in) × 25.4 for mm	Spacing (in)	Modulus of Elasticity, *E*, in 1,000,000 psi × 0.00689 for N/mm^2																
		0.8	0.9	1.0	1.1	1.2	1.3	1.4	1.5	1.6	1.7	1.8	1.9	2.0	2.1	2.2	2.3	2.4
2 × 6	12.0	8-6	8-10	9-2	9-6	9-9	10-0	10-3	10-6	10-9	10-11	11-2	11-4	11-7	11-9	11-11	12-1	12-3
	16.0	7-9	8-0	8-4	8-7	8-10	9-1	9-4	9-6	9-9	9-11	10-2	10-4	10-6	10-8	10-10	11-0	11-2
	19.2	7-3	7-7	7-10	8-1	8-4	8-7	8-9	9-0	9-2	9-4	9-6	9-8	9-10	10-0	10-2	10-4	10-6
	24.0	6-9	7-0	7-3	7-6	7-9	7-11	8-2	8-4	8-6	8-8	8-10	9-0	9-2	9-4	9-6	9-7	9-9
2 × 8	12.0	11-3	11-8	12-1	12-6	12-10	13-2	13-6	13-10	14-2	14-5	14-8	15-0	15-3	15-6	15-9	15-11	16-2
	16.0	10-2	10-7	11-0	11-4	11-8	12-0	12-3	12-7	12-10	13-1	13-4	13-7	13-10	14-1	14-3	14-6	14-8
	19.2	9-7	10-0	10-4	10-8	11-0	11-3	11-7	11-10	12-1	12-4	12-7	12-10	13-0	13-3	13-5	13-8	13-10
	24.0	8-11	9-3	9-7	9-11	10-2	10-6	10-9	11-0	11-3	11-5	11-8	11-11	12-1	12-3	12-6	12-8	12-10
2 × 10	12.0	14-4	14-11	15-5	15-11	16-5	16-10	17-3	17-8	18-0	18-5	18-9	19-1	19-5	19-9	20-1	20-4	20-8
	16.0	13-0	13-6	14-0	14-6	14-11	15-3	15-8	16-0	16-5	16-9	17-0	17-4	17-8	17-11	18-3	18-6	18-9
	19.2	12-3	12-9	13-2	13-7	14-0	14-5	14-9	15-1	15-5	15-9	16-0	16-4	16-7	16-11	17-2	17-5	17-8
	24.0	11-4	11-10	12-3	12-8	13-0	13-4	13-8	14-0	14-4	14-7	14-11	15-2	15-5	15-8	15-11	16-2	16-5
2 × 12	12.0	17-5	18-1	18-9	19-4	19-11	20-6	21-0	21-6	21-11	22-5	22-10	23-3	23-7	24-0	24-5	24-9	25-1
	16.0	15-10	16-5	17-0	17-7	18-1	18-7	19-1	19-6	19-11	20-4	20-9	21-1	21-6	21-10	22-2	22-6	22-10
	19.2	14-11	15-6	16-0	16-7	17-0	17-6	17-11	18-4	18-9	19-2	19-6	19-10	20-2	20-6	20-10	21-2	21-6
	24.0	13-10	14-4	14-11	15-4	15-10	16-3	16-8	17-0	17-5	17-9	18-1	18-5	18-9	19-1	19-4	19-8	19-11
F_b	12.0	862	932	1,000	1,066	1,129	1,191	1,251	1,310	1,368	1,424	1,480	1,534	1,587	1,640	1,692	1,742	1,793
	16.0	949	1,026	1,101	1,173	1,243	1,311	1,377	1,442	1,506	1,568	1,629	1,688	1,747	1,805	1,862	1,918	1,973
	19.2	1,008	1,090	1,170	1,246	1,321	1,393	1,464	1,533	1,600	1,666	1,731	1,794	1,857	1,918	1,978	2,038	2,097
	24.0	1,086	1,174	1,260	1,343	1,423	1,501	1,577	1,651	1,724	1,795	1,864	1,933	2,000	2,066	2,131	2,195	2,258

NOTE: The required bending design value, F_b, in pounds per square inch (× 0.00689 for N/mm^2) is shown at the bottom of this table and is applicable to all lumber sizes shown. Spans are shown in feet-inches (1 foot = 304.8 mm, 1 inch = 25.4 mm) and are limited to 26 feet (7925 mm) and less.

From the Uniform Building Code, ©1997, ICBO

TABLE 23-IV-J-3—CEILING JOISTS WITH *L*/240 DEFLECTION LIMITS
The allowable bending stress (F_b) and modulus of elasticity *(E)* used in this table shall be from Tables 23-IV-V-1 and 23-IV-V-2 only.

DESIGN CRITERIA:
Deflection — For 10 psf (0.48 kN/m²) live load.
Limited to span in inches (mm) divided by 240.
Strength — Live load of 10 psf (0.48 kN/mm²) plus dead load of 5 psf (0.24 kN/m²) determines the required fiber stress value.

Joist Size (in) ×25.4 for mm	Spacing (in)	Modulus of Elasticity, *E*, in 1,000,000 psi ×0.00689 for N/mm²																
		0.8	0.9	1.0	1.1	1.2	1.3	1.4	1.5	1.6	1.7	1.8	1.9	2.0	2.1	2.2	2.3	2.4
2×4	12.0	9-10	10-3	10-7	10-11	11-3	11-7	11-10	12-2	12-5	12-8	12-11	13-2	13-4	13-7	13-9	14-0	14-2
	16.0	8-11	9-4	9-8	9-11	10-3	10-6	10-9	11-0	11-3	11-6	11-9	11-11	12-2	12-4	12-6	12-9	12-11
	19.2	8-5	8-9	9-1	9-4	9-8	9-11	10-2	10-4	10-7	10-10	11-0	11-3	11-5	11-7	11-9	12-0	12-2
	24.0	7-10	8-1	8-5	8-8	8-11	9-2	9-5	9-8	9-10	10-0	10-3	10-5	10-7	10-9	10-11	11-1	11-3
2×6	12.0	15-6	16-1	16-8	17-2	17-8	18-2	18-8	19-1	19-6	19-11	20-3	20-8	21-0	21-4	21-8	22-0	22-4
	16.0	14-1	14-7	15-2	15-7	16-1	16-6	16-11	17-4	17-8	18-1	18-5	18-9	19-1	19-5	19-8	20-0	20-3
	19.2	13-3	13-9	14-3	14-8	15-2	15-7	15-11	16-4	16-8	17-0	17-4	17-8	17-11	18-3	18-6	18-10	19-1
	24.0	12-3	12-9	13-3	13-8	14-1	14-5	14-9	15-2	15-6	15-9	16-1	16-4	16-8	16-11	17-2	17-5	17-8
2×8	12.0	20-5	21-2	21-11	22-8	23-4	24-0	24-7	25-2	25-8								
	16.0	18-6	19-3	19-11	20-7	21-2	21-9	22-4	22-10	23-4	23-10	24-3	24-8	25-2	25-7	25-11		
	19.2	17-5	18-1	18-9	19-5	19-11	20-6	21-0	21-6	21-11	22-5	22-10	23-3	23-8	24-0	24-5	24-9	25-2
	24.0	16-2	16-10	17-5	18-0	18-6	19-0	19-6	19-11	20-5	20-10	21-2	21-7	21-11	22-4	22-8	23-0	23-4
2×10	12.0	26-0																
	16.0	23-8	24-7	25-5														
	19.2	22-3	23-1	23-11	24-9	25-5												
	24.0	20-8	21-6	22-3	22-11	23-8	24-3	24-10	25-5	26-0								
F_b	12.0	711	769	825	880	932	983	1,033	1,082	1,129	1,176	1,221	1,266	1,310	1,354	1,396	1,438	1,480
	16.0	783	847	909	968	1,026	1,082	1,137	1,191	1,243	1,294	1,344	1,394	1,442	1,490	1,537	1,583	1,629
	19.2	832	900	965	1,029	1,090	1,150	1,208	1,265	1,321	1,375	1,429	1,481	1,533	1,583	1,633	1,682	1,731
	24.0	896	969	1,040	1,108	1,174	1,239	1,302	1,363	1,423	1,481	1,539	1,595	1,651	1,706	1,759	1,812	1,864

NOTE: The required bending design value, F_b, in pounds per square inch (×0.00689 for N/mm²) is shown at the bottom of this table and is applicable to all lumber sizes shown. Spans are shown in feet-inches (1 foot = 304.8 mm, 1 inch = 25.4 mm) and are limited to 26 feet (7925 mm) and less.

From the Uniform Building Code, ©1997, ICBO

TABLE 23-IV-J-4—CEILING JOISTS WITH *L*/240 DEFLECTION LIMITS
The allowable bending stress (F_b) and modulus of elasticity (*E*) used in this table shall be from Tables 23-IV-V-1 and 23-IV-V-2 only.

DESIGN CRITERIA:
Deflection — For 20 psf (0.96 kN/m^2) live load.
Limited to span in inches (mm) divided by 240.
Strength — Live load of 20 psf (0.96 kN/m^2) plus dead load of 10 psf (0.48 kN/m^2) determines the required bending design value.

| Joist Size (in) | Spacing (in) | Modulus of Elasticity, *E*, in 1,000,000 psi | | | | | | | | | | | | | | | | |
| | | × 0.00689 for N/mm^2 | | | | | | | | | | | | | | | | |
× 25.4 for mm		0.8	0.9	1.0	1.1	1.2	1.3	1.4	1.5	1.6	1.7	1.8	1.9	2.0	2.1	2.2	2.3	2.4
2 × 4	12.0	7-10	8-1	8-5	8-8	8-11	9-2	9-5	9-8	9-10	10-0	10-3	10-5	10-7	10-9	10-11	11-1	11-3
	16.0	7-1	7-5	7-8	7-11	8-1	8-4	8-7	8-9	8-11	9-1	9-4	9-6	9-8	9-9	9-11	10-1	10-3
	19.2	6-8	6-11	7-2	7-5	7-8	7-10	8-1	8-3	8-5	8-7	8-9	8-11	9-1	9-3	9-4	9-6	9-8
	24.0	6-2	6-5	6-8	6-11	7-1	7-3	7-6	7-8	7-10	8-0	8-1	8-3	8-5	8-7	8-8	8-10	8-11
2 × 6	12.0	12-3	12-9	13-3	13-8	14-1	14-5	14-9	15-2	15-6	15-9	16-1	16-4	16-8	16-11	17-2	17-5	17-8
	16.0	11-2	11-7	12-0	12-5	12-9	13-1	13-5	13-9	14-1	14-4	14-7	14-11	15-2	15-5	15-7	15-10	16-1
	19.2	10-6	10-11	11-4	11-8	12-0	12-4	12-8	12-11	13-3	13-6	13-9	14-0	14-3	14-6	14-8	14-11	15-2
	24.0	9-9	10-2	10-6	10-10	11-2	11-5	11-9	12-0	12-3	12-6	12-9	13-0	13-3	13-5	13-8	13-10	14-1
2 × 8	12.0	16-2	16-10	17-5	18-0	18-6	19-0	19-6	19-11	20-5	20-10	21-2	21-7	21-11	22-4	22-8	23-0	23-4
	16.0	14-8	15-3	15-10	16-4	16-10	17-3	17-9	18-1	18-6	18-11	19-3	19-7	19-11	20-3	20-7	20-11	21-2
	19.2	13-10	14-5	14-11	15-5	15-10	16-3	16-8	17-1	17-5	17-9	18-1	18-5	18-9	19-1	19-5	19-8	19-11
	24.0	12-10	13-4	13-10	14-3	14-8	15-1	15-6	15-10	16-2	16-6	16-10	17-2	17-5	17-9	18-0	18-3	18-6
2 × 10	12.0	20-8	21-6	22-3	22-11	23-8	24-3	24-10	25-5	26-0								
	16.0	18-9	19-6	20-2	20-10	21-6	22-1	22-7	23-1	23-8	24-1	24-7	25-0	25-5	25-10			
	19.2	17-8	18-4	19-0	19-7	20-2	20-9	21-3	21-9	22-3	22-8	23-1	23-7	23-11	24-4	24-9	25-1	25-5
	24.0	16-5	17-0	17-8	18-3	18-9	19-3	19-9	20-2	20-8	21-1	21-6	21-10	22-3	22-7	22-11	23-4	23-8
F_b	12.0	896	969	1,040	1,108	1,174	1,239	1,302	1,363	1,423	1,481	1,539	1,595	1,651	1,706	1,759	1,812	1,864
	16.0	986	1,067	1,145	1,220	1,293	1,364	1,433	1,500	1,566	1,631	1,694	1,756	1,817	1,877	1,936	1,995	2,052
	19.2	1,048	1,134	1,216	1,296	1,374	1,449	1,522	1,594	1,664	1,733	1,800	1,866	1,931	1,995	2,058	2,120	2,181
	24.0	1,129	1,221	1,310	1,396	1,480	1,561	1,640	1,717	1,793	1,866	1,939	2,010	2,080	2,149	2,217	2,283	2,349

NOTE: The required bending design value, F_b, in pounds per square inch (× 0.00689 for N/mm^2) is shown at the bottom of this table and is applicable to all lumber sizes shown. Spans are shown in feet-inches (1 foot = 304.8 mm, 1 inch = 25.4 mm) and are limited to 26 feet (7925 mm) and less.

From the Uniform Building Code, ©1997, ICBO

TABLE 23-IV-R-1—RAFTERS WITH L/240 DEFLECTION LIMITATION
The allowable bending stress (F_b) and modulus of elasticity (E) used in this table shall be from Tables 23-IV-V-1 and 23-IV-V-2 only.

DESIGN CRITERIA:
Strength — Live load of 20 psf (0.96 kN/m²) plus dead load of 10 psf (0.48 kN/m²) determines the required bending design value.
Deflection — For 20 psf (0.96 kN/m²) live load.
Limited to span in inches (mm) divided by 240.

Rafter Size (in) × 25.4 for mm	Spacing (in)	Bending Design Value, F_b (psi) × 0.00689 for N/mm²										
		300	400	500	600	700	800	900	1000	1100	1200	1300
2×6	12.0	7-1	8-2	9-2	10-0	10-10	11-7	12-4	13-0	13-7	14-2	14-9
	16.0	6-2	7-1	7-11	8-8	9-5	10-0	10-8	11-3	11-9	12-4	12-10
	19.2	5-7	6-6	7-3	7-11	8-7	9-2	9-9	10-3	10-9	11-3	11-8
	24.0	5-0	5-10	6-6	7-1	7-8	8-2	8-8	9-2	9-7	10-0	10-5
2×8	12.0	9-4	10-10	12-1	13-3	14-4	15-3	16-3	17-1	17-11	18-9	19-6
	16.0	8-1	9-4	10-6	11-6	12-5	13-3	14-0	14-10	15-6	16-3	16-10
	19.2	7-5	8-7	9-7	10-6	11-4	12-1	12-10	13-6	14-2	14-10	15-5
	24.0	6-7	7-8	8-7	9-4	10-1	10-10	11-6	12-1	12-8	13-3	13-9
2×10	12.0	11-11	13-9	15-5	16-11	18-3	19-6	20-8	21-10	22-10	23-11	24-10
	16.0	10-4	11-11	13-4	14-8	15-10	16-11	17-11	18-11	19-10	20-8	21-6
	19.2	9-5	10-11	12-2	13-4	14-5	15-5	16-4	17-3	18-1	18-11	19-8
	24.0	8-5	9-9	10-11	11-11	12-11	13-9	14-8	15-5	16-2	16-11	17-7
2×12	12.0	14-6	16-9	18-9	20-6	22-2	23-9	25-2				
	16.0	12-7	14-6	16-3	17-9	19-3	20-6	21-9	23-0	24-1	25-2	
	19.2	11-6	13-3	14-10	16-3	17-6	18-9	19-11	21-0	22-0	23-0	23-11
	24.0	10-3	11-10	13-3	14-6	15-8	16-9	17-9	18-9	19-8	20-6	21-5
E	12.0	0.15	0.24	0.33	0.44	0.55	0.67	0.80	0.94	1.09	1.24	1.40
	16.0	0.13	0.21	0.29	0.38	0.48	0.58	0.70	0.82	0.94	1.07	1.21
	19.2	0.12	0.19	0.26	0.35	0.44	0.53	0.64	0.75	0.86	0.98	1.10
	24.0	0.11	0.17	0.24	0.31	0.39	0.48	0.57	0.67	0.77	0.88	0.99

Rafter Size (in) × 25.4 for mm	Spacing (in)	Bending Design Value, F_b (psi) × 0.00689 for N/mm²										
		1400	1500	1600	1700	1800	1900	2000	2100	2200	2300	2400
2×6	12.0	15-4	15-11	16-5	16-11	17-5	17-10					
	16.0	13-3	13-9	14-2	14-8	15-1	15-6	15-11	16-3			
	19.2	12-2	12-7	13-0	13-4	13-9	14-2	14-6	14-10	15-2	15-7	
	24.0	10-10	11-3	11-7	11-11	12-4	12-8	13-0	13-3	13-7	13-11	14-2
2×8	12.0	20-3	20-11	21-7	22-3	22-11	23-7					
	16.0	17-6	18-1	18-9	19-4	19-10	20-5	20-11	21-5			
	19.2	16-0	16-7	17-1	17-7	18-1	18-7	19-1	19-7	20-0	20-6	
	24.0	14-4	14-10	15-3	15-9	16-3	16-8	17-1	17-6	17-11	18-4	18-9
2×10	12.0	25-10										
	16.0	22-4	23-1	23-11	24-7	25-4	26-0					
	19.2	20-5	21-1	21-10	22-6	23-1	23-9	24-5	25-0	25-7		
	24.0	18-3	18-11	19-6	20-1	20-8	21-3	21-10	22-4	22-10	23-5	23-11
2×12	12.0											
	16.0											
	19.2	24-10	25-8									
	24.0	22-2	23-0	23-9	24-5	25-2	25-10					
E	12.0	1.56	1.73	1.91	2.09	2.28	2.47					
	16.0	1.35	1.50	1.65	1.81	1.97	2.14	2.31	2.48			
	19.2	1.23	1.37	1.51	1.65	1.80	1.95	2.11	2.27	2.43	2.60	
	24.0	1.10	1.22	1.35	1.48	1.61	1.75	1.89	2.03	2.18	2.33	2.48

NOTE: The required modulus of elasticity, E, in 1,000,000 pounds per square inch (psi) (× 0.00689 for N/mm²) is shown at the bottom of this table, is limited to 2.6 million psi (17 914 N/mm²) and less, and is applicable to all lumber sizes shown. Spans are shown in feet-inches (1 foot = 304.8 mm, 1 inch = 25.4 mm) and are limited to 26 feet (7925 mm) and less.

From the Uniform Building Code, ©1997, ICBO

TABLE 23-IV-R-2—RAFTERS WITH L/240 DEFLECTION LIMITATION
The allowable bending stress (F_b) and modulus of elasticity (E) used in this table shall be from Tables 23-IV-V-1 and 23-IV-V-2 only.

DESIGN CRITERIA:
Strength — Live load of 30 psf (1.44 kN/m²) plus dead load of 10 psf (0.48 kN/m²) determines the required bending design value.
Deflection — For 30 psf (1.44 kN/m²) live load.
Limited to span in inches (mm) divided by 240.

Rafter Size (in) × 25.4 for mm	Spacing (in)	Bending Design Value, F_b (psi) × 0.00689 for N/mm²										
		300	400	500	600	700	800	900	1000	1100	1200	1300
2 × 6	12.0	6-2	7-1	7-11	8-8	9-5	10-0	10-8	11-3	11-9	12-4	12-10
	16.0	5-4	6-2	6-10	7-6	8-2	8-8	9-3	9-9	10-2	10-8	11-1
	19.2	4-10	5-7	6-3	6-10	7-5	7-11	8-5	8-11	9-4	9-9	10-1
	24.0	4-4	5-0	5-7	6-2	6-8	7-1	7-6	7-11	8-4	8-8	9-1
2 × 8	12.0	8-1	9-4	10-6	11-6	12-5	13-3	14-0	14-10	15-6	16-3	16-10
	16.0	7-0	8-1	9-1	9-11	10-9	11-6	12-2	12-10	13-5	14-0	14-7
	19.2	6-5	7-5	8-3	9-1	9-9	10-6	11-1	11-8	12-3	12-10	13-4
	24.0	5-9	6-7	7-5	8-1	8-9	9-4	9-11	10-6	11-0	11-6	11-11
2 × 10	12.0	10-4	11-11	13-4	14-8	15-10	16-11	17-11	18-11	19-10	20-8	21-6
	16.0	8-11	10-4	11-7	12-8	13-8	14-8	15-6	16-4	17-2	17-11	18-8
	19.2	8-2	9-5	10-7	11-7	12-6	13-4	14-2	14-11	15-8	16-4	17-0
	24.0	7-4	8-5	9-5	10-4	11-2	11-11	12-8	13-4	14-0	14-8	15-3
2 × 12	12.0	12-7	14-6	16-3	17-9	19-3	20-6	21-9	23-0	24-1	25-2	
	16.0	10-11	12-7	14-1	15-5	16-8	17-9	18-10	19-11	20-10	21-9	22-8
	19.2	9-11	11-6	12-10	14-1	15-2	16-3	17-3	18-2	19-0	19-11	20-8
	24.0	8-11	10-3	11-6	12-7	13-7	14-6	15-5	16-3	17-0	17-9	18-6
E	12.0	0.15	0.23	0.32	0.43	0.54	0.66	0.78	0.92	1.06	1.21	1.36
	16.0	0.13	0.20	0.28	0.37	0.47	0.57	0.68	0.80	0.92	1.05	1.18
	19.2	0.12	0.18	0.26	0.34	0.43	0.52	0.62	0.73	0.84	0.95	1.08
	24.0	0.11	0.16	0.23	0.30	0.38	0.46	0.55	0.65	0.75	0.85	0.96

Rafter Size (in) × 25.4 for mm	Spacing (in)	Bending Design Value, F_b (psi) × 0.00689 for N/mm²										
		1400	1500	1600	1700	1800	1900	2000	2100	2200	2300	2400
2 × 6	12.0	13-3	13-9	14-2	14-8	15-1	15-6	15-11				
	16.0	11-6	11-11	12-4	12-8	13-1	13-5	13-9	14-1	14-5		
	19.2	10-6	10-10	11-3	11-7	11-11	12-3	12-7	12-10	13-2	13-6	
	24.0	9-5	9-9	10-0	10-4	10-8	10-11	11-3	11-6	11-9	12-0	12-4
2 × 8	12.0	17-6	18-1	18-9	19-4	19-10	20-5	20-11				
	16.0	15-2	15-8	16-3	16-9	17-2	17-8	18-1	18-7	19-0		
	19.2	13-10	14-4	14-10	15-3	15-8	16-2	16-7	16-11	17-4	17-9	
	24.0	12-5	12-10	13-3	13-8	14-0	14-5	14-10	15-2	15-6	15-10	16-3
2 × 10	12.0	22-4	23-1	23-11	24-7	25-4	26-0					
	16.0	19-4	20-0	20-8	21-4	21-11	22-6	23-1	23-8	24-3		
	19.2	17-8	18-3	18-11	19-6	20-0	20-7	21-1	21-8	22-2	22-8	
	24.0	15-10	16-4	16-11	17-5	17-11	18-5	18-11	19-4	19-10	20-3	20-8
2 × 12	12.0											
	16.0	23-6	24-4	25-2	25-11							
	19.2	21-6	22-3	23-0	23-8	24-4	25-0	25-8				
	24.0	19-3	19-11	20-6	21-2	21-9	22-5	23-0	23-6	24-1	24-8	25-2
E	12.0	1.52	1.69	1.86	2.04	2.22	2.41	2.60				
	16.0	1.32	1.46	1.61	1.76	1.92	2.08	2.25	2.42	2.60		
	19.2	1.20	1.33	1.47	1.61	1.75	1.90	2.05	2.21	2.37	2.53	
	24.0	1.08	1.19	1.31	1.44	1.57	1.70	1.84	1.98	2.12	2.27	2.41

NOTE: The required modulus of elasticity, E, in 1,000,000 pounds per square inch (psi) (× 0.00689 for N/mm²) is shown at the bottom of this table, is limited to 2.6 million psi (17 914 N/mm²) and less, and is applicable to all lumber sizes shown. Spans are shown in feet-inches (1 foot = 304.8 mm, 1 inch = 25.4 mm) and are limited to 26 feet (7925 mm) and less.

From the Uniform Building Code, ©1997, ICBO

TABLE 23-IV-R-3—RAFTERS WITH *L*/240 DEFLECTION LIMITATION
The allowable bending stress (F_b) and modulus of elasticity (*E*) used in this table shall be from Tables 23-IV-V-1 and 23-IV-V-2 only.

DESIGN CRITERIA:
Strength — Live load of 20 psf (0.96 kN/m^2) plus dead load of 15 psf (0.72 kN/m^2) determines the required bending design value.
Deflection — For 20 psf (0.96 kN/m^2) live load.
Limited to span in inches (mm) divided by 240.

Rafter Size (in)	Spacing (in)	Bending Design Value, F_b (psi)											
		× 0.00689 for N/mm^2											
× 25.4 for mm		300	400	500	600	700	800	900	1000	1100	1200	1300	1400	1500
2 × 6	12.0	6-7	7-7	8-6	9-4	10-0	10-9	11-5	12-0	12-7	13-2	13-8	14-2	14-8
	16.0	5-8	6-7	7-4	8-1	8-8	9-4	9-10	10-5	10-11	11-5	11-10	12-4	12-9
	19.2	5-2	6-0	6-9	7-4	7-11	8-6	9-0	9-6	9-11	10-5	10-10	11-3	11-7
	24.0	4-8	5-4	6-0	6-7	7-1	7-7	8-1	8-6	8-11	9-4	9-8	10-0	10-5
2 × 8	12.0	8-8	10-0	11-2	12-3	13-3	14-2	15-0	15-10	16-7	17-4	18-0	18-9	19-5
	16.0	7-6	8-8	9-8	10-7	11-6	12-3	13-0	13-8	14-4	15-0	15-7	16-3	16-9
	19.2	6-10	7-11	8-10	9-8	10-6	11-2	11-10	12-6	13-1	13-8	14-3	14-10	15-4
	24.0	6-2	7-1	7-11	8-8	9-4	10-0	10-7	11-2	11-9	12-3	12-9	13-3	13-8
2 × 10	12.0	11-1	12-9	14-3	15-8	16-11	18-1	19-2	20-2	21-2	22-1	23-0	23-11	24-9
	16.0	9-7	11-1	12-4	13-6	14-8	15-8	16-7	17-6	18-4	19-2	19-11	20-8	21-5
	19.2	8-9	10-1	11-3	12-4	13-4	14-3	15-2	15-11	16-9	17-6	18-2	18-11	19-7
	24.0	7-10	9-0	10-1	11-1	11-11	12-9	13-6	14-3	15-0	15-8	16-3	16-11	17-6
2 × 12	12.0	13-5	15-6	17-4	19-0	20-6	21-11	23-3	24-7	25-9				
	16.0	11-8	13-5	15-0	16-6	17-9	19-0	20-2	21-3	22-4	23-3	24-3	25-2	26-0
	19.2	10-8	12-3	13-9	15-0	16-3	17-4	18-5	19-5	20-4	21-3	22-2	23-0	23-9
	24.0	9-6	11-0	12-3	13-5	14-6	15-6	16-6	17-4	18-2	19-0	19-10	20-6	21-3
E	12.0	0.12	0.19	0.26	0.35	0.44	0.54	0.64	0.75	0.86	0.98	1.11	1.24	1.37
	16.0	0.11	0.16	0.23	0.30	0.38	0.46	0.55	0.65	0.75	0.85	0.96	1.07	1.19
	19.2	0.10	0.15	0.21	0.27	0.35	0.42	0.51	0.59	0.68	0.78	0.88	0.98	1.09
	24.0	0.09	0.13	0.19	0.25	0.31	0.38	0.45	0.53	0.61	0.70	0.78	0.88	0.97

Rafter Size (in)	Spacing (in)	Bending Design Value, F_b (psi)											
		× 0.00689 for N/mm^2											
× 25.4 for mm		1600	1700	1800	1900	2000	2100	2200	2300	2400	2500	2600	2700
2 × 6	12.0	15-2	15-8	16-1	16-7	17-0	17-5	17-10					
	16.0	13-2	13-7	13-11	14-4	14-8	15-1	15-5	15-9	16-1	16-5		
	19.2	12-0	12-4	12-9	13-1	13-5	13-9	14-1	14-5	14-8	15-0	15-4	
	24.0	10-9	11-1	11-5	11-8	12-0	12-4	12-7	12-10	13-2	13-5	13-8	13-11
2 × 8	12.0	20-0	20-8	21-3	21-10	22-4	22-11	23-6					
	16.0	17-4	17-10	18-5	18-11	19-5	19-10	20-4	20-9	21-3	21-8		
	19.2	15-10	16-4	16-9	17-3	17-8	18-1	18-7	19-0	19-5	19-9	20-2	
	24.0	14-2	14-7	15-0	15-5	15-10	16-3	16-7	17-0	17-4	17-8	18-0	18-5
2 × 10	12.0	25-6											
	16.0	22-1	22-10	23-5	24-1	24-9	25-4	25-11					
	19.2	20-2	20-10	21-5	22-0	22-7	23-1	23-8	24-2	24-9	25-3	25-9	
	24.0	18-1	18-7	19-2	19-8	20-2	20-8	21-2	21-8	22-1	22-7	23-0	23-5
2 × 12	12.0												
	16.0												
	19.2	24-7	25-4	26-0									
	24.0	21-11	22-8	23-3	23-11	24-7	25-2	25-9					
E	12.0	1.51	1.66	1.81	1.96	2.12	2.28	2.44					
	16.0	1.31	1.44	1.56	1.70	1.83	1.97	2.11	2.26	2.41	2.56		
	19.2	1.20	1.31	1.43	1.55	1.67	1.80	1.93	2.06	2.20	2.34	2.48	
	24.0	1.07	1.17	1.28	1.39	1.50	1.61	1.73	1.85	1.97	2.09	2.22	2.35

NOTE: The required modulus of elasticity, *E*, in 1,000,000 pounds per square inch (psi) (× 0.00689 for N/mm^2) is shown at the bottom of this table, is limited to 2.6 million psi (17 914 N/mm^2) and less, and is applicable to all lumber sizes shown. Spans are shown in feet-inches (1 foot = 304.8 mm, 1 inch = 25.4 mm) and are limited to 26 feet (7925 mm) and less.

TABLE 23-IV-R-4—RAFTERS WITH *L*/240 DEFLECTION LIMITATION
The allowable bending stress (*F*$_b$) and modulus of elasticity *(E)* used in this table shall be from Tables 23-IV-V-1 and 23-IV-V-2 only.

DESIGN CRITERIA:
Strength — Live load of 30 psf (1.44 kN/m^2) plus dead load of 15 psf (0.72 kN/m^2) determines the required bending design value.
Deflection — For 30 psf (1.44 kN/m^2) live load.
Limited to span in inches (mm) divided by 240.

Rafter Size (in) × 25.4 for mm	Spacing (in)	Bending Design Value, F_b (psi) × 0.00689 for N/mm^2												
		300	400	500	600	700	800	900	1000	1100	1200	1300	1400	1500
2 × 6	12.0	5-10	6-8	7-6	8-2	8-10	9-6	10-0	10-7	11-1	11-7	12-1	12-6	13-0
	16.0	5-0	5-10	6-6	7-1	7-8	8-2	8-8	9-2	9-7	10-0	10-5	10-10	11-3
	19.2	4-7	5-4	5-11	6-6	7-0	7-6	7-11	8-4	8-9	9-2	9-6	9-11	10-3
	24.0	4-1	4-9	5-4	5-10	6-3	6-8	7-1	7-6	7-10	8-2	8-6	8-10	9-2
2 × 8	12.0	7-8	8-10	9-10	10-10	11-8	12-6	13-3	13-11	14-8	15-3	15-11	16-6	17-1
	16.0	6-7	7-8	8-7	9-4	10-1	10-10	11-6	12-1	12-8	13-3	13-9	14-4	14-10
	19.2	6-0	7-0	7-10	8-7	9-3	9-10	10-6	11-0	11-7	12-1	12-7	13-1	13-6
	24.0	5-5	6-3	7-0	7-8	8-3	8-10	9-4	9-10	10-4	10-10	11-3	11-8	12-1
2 × 10	12.0	9-9	11-3	12-7	13-9	14-11	15-11	16-11	17-10	18-8	19-6	20-4	21-1	21-10
	16.0	8-5	9-9	10-11	11-11	12-11	13-9	14-8	15-5	16-2	16-11	17-7	18-3	18-11
	19.2	7-8	8-11	9-11	10-11	11-9	12-7	13-4	14-1	14-9	15-5	16-1	16-8	17-3
	24.0	6-11	8-0	8-11	9-9	10-6	11-3	11-11	12-7	13-2	13-9	14-4	14-11	15-5
2 × 12	12.0	11-10	13-8	15-4	16-9	18-1	19-4	20-6	21-8	22-8	23-9	24-8	25-7	
	16.0	10-3	11-10	13-3	14-6	15-8	16-9	17-9	18-9	19-8	20-6	21-5	22-2	23-0
	19.2	9-4	10-10	12-1	13-3	14-4	15-4	16-3	17-1	17-11	18-9	19-6	20-3	21-0
	24.0	8-5	9-8	10-10	11-10	12-10	13-8	14-6	15-4	16-1	16-9	17-5	18-1	18-9
E	12.0	0.13	0.19	0.27	0.36	0.45	0.55	0.66	0.77	0.89	1.01	1.14	1.28	1.41
	16.0	0.11	0.17	0.24	0.31	0.39	0.48	0.57	0.67	0.77	0.88	0.99	1.10	1.22
	19.2	0.10	0.15	0.22	0.28	0.36	0.44	0.52	0.61	0.70	0.80	0.90	1.01	1.12
	24.0	0.09	0.14	0.19	0.25	0.32	0.39	0.46	0.54	0.63	0.72	0.81	0.90	1.00

Rafter Size (in) × 25.4 for mm	Spacing (in)	Bending Design Value, F_b (psi) × 0.00689 for N/mm^2											
		1600	1700	1800	1900	2000	2100	2200	2300	2400	2500	2600	2700
2 × 6	12.0	13-5	13-10	14-2	14-7	15-0	15-4	15-8					
	16.0	11-7	11-11	12-4	12-8	13-0	13-3	13-7	13-11	14-2			
	19.2	10-7	10-11	11-3	11-6	11-10	12-2	12-5	12-8	13-0	13-3	13-6	
	24.0	9-6	9-9	10-0	10-4	10-7	10-10	11-1	11-4	11-7	11-10	12-1	12-4
2 × 8	12.0	17-8	18-2	18-9	19-3	19-9	20-3	20-8					
	16.0	15-3	15-9	16-3	16-8	17-1	17-6	17-11	18-4	18-9			
	19.2	13-11	14-5	14-10	15-2	15-7	16-0	16-4	16-9	17-1	17-5	17-9	
	24.0	12-6	12-10	13-3	13-7	13-11	14-4	14-8	15-0	15-3	15-7	15-11	16-3
2 × 10	12.0	22-6	23-3	23-11	24-6	25-2	25-10						
	16.0	19-6	20-1	20-8	21-3	21-10	22-4	22-10	23-5	23-11			
	19.2	17-10	18-4	18-11	19-5	19-11	20-5	20-10	21-4	21-10	22-3	22-8	
	24.0	15-11	16-5	16-11	17-4	17-10	18-3	18-8	19-1	19-6	19-11	20-4	20-8
2 × 12	12.0												
	16.0	23-9	24-5	25-2	25-10								
	19.2	21-8	22-4	23-0	23-7	24-2	24-10	25-5	25-11				
	24.0	19-4	20-0	20-6	21-1	21-8	22-2	22-8	23-3	23-9	24-2	24-8	25-2
E	12.0	1.56	1.71	1.86	2.02	2.18	2.34	2.51					
	16.0	1.35	1.48	1.61	1.75	1.89	2.03	2.18	2.33	2.48			
	19.2	1.23	1.35	1.47	1.59	1.72	1.85	1.99	2.12	2.26	2.41	2.55	
	24.0	1.10	1.21	1.31	1.43	1.54	1.66	1.78	1.90	2.02	2.15	2.28	2.41

NOTE: The required modulus of elasticity, *E*, in 1,000,000 pounds per square inch (psi) (× 0.00689 for N/mm^2) is shown at the bottom of this table, is limited to 2.6 million psi (17 914 N/mm^2) and less, and is applicable to all lumber sizes shown. Spans are shown in feet-inches (1 foot = 304.8 mm, 1 inch = 25.4 mm) and are limited to 26 feet (7925 mm) and less.

From the Uniform Building Code, ©1997, ICBO

TABLE 23-IV-R-5—RAFTERS WITH *L*/240 DEFLECTION LIMITATION
The allowable bending stress (F_b) and modulus of elasticity *(E)* used in this table shall be from Tables 23-IV-V-1 and 23-IV-V-2 only.

DESIGN CRITERIA:
Strength — Live load of 20 psf (0.96 kN/m²) plus dead load of 20 psf (0.96 kN/m²) determines the required bending design value.
Deflection — For 20 psf (0.96 kN/m²) live load.
Limited to span in inches (mm) divided by 240.

Rafter Size (in)	Spacing (in)	Bending Design Value, F_b (psi) $\times$ 0.00689 for N/mm²												
$\times$ 25.4 for mm		300	400	500	600	700	800	900	1000	1100	1200	1300	1400	1500
2 × 6	12.0	6-2	7-1	7-11	8-8	9-5	10-0	10-8	11-3	11-9	12-4	12-10	13-3	13-9
	16.0	5-4	6-2	6-10	7-6	8-2	8-8	9-3	9-9	10-2	10-8	11-1	11-6	11-11
	19.2	4-10	5-7	6-3	6-10	7-5	7-11	8-5	8-11	9-4	9-9	10-1	10-6	10-10
	24.0	4-4	5-0	5-7	6-2	6-8	7-1	7-6	7-11	8-4	8-8	9-1	9-5	9-9
2 × 8	12.0	8-1	9-4	10-6	11-6	12-5	13-3	14-0	14-10	15-6	16-3	16-10	17-6	18-1
	16.0	7-0	8-1	9-1	9-11	10-9	11-6	12-2	12-10	13-5	14-0	14-7	15-2	15-8
	19.2	6-5	7-5	8-3	9-1	9-9	10-6	11-1	11-8	12-3	12-10	13-4	13-10	14-4
	24.0	5-9	6-7	7-5	8-1	8-9	9-4	9-11	10-6	11-0	11-6	11-11	12-5	12-10
2 × 10	12.0	10-4	11-11	13-4	14-8	15-10	16-11	17-11	18-11	19-10	20-8	21-6	22-4	23-1
	16.0	8-11	10-4	11-7	12-8	13-8	14-8	15-6	16-4	17-2	17-11	18-8	19-4	20-0
	19.2	8-2	9-5	10-7	11-7	12-6	13-4	14-2	14-11	15-8	16-4	17-0	17-8	18-3
	24.0	7-4	8-5	9-5	10-4	11-2	11-11	12-8	13-4	14-0	14-8	15-3	15-10	16-4
2 × 12	12.0	12-7	14-6	16-3	17-9	19-3	20-6	21-9	23-0	24-1	25-2			
	16.0	10-11	12-7	14-1	15-5	16-8	17-9	18-10	19-11	20-10	21-9	22-8	23-6	24-4
	19.2	9-11	11-6	12-10	14-1	15-2	16-3	17-3	18-2	19-0	19-11	20-8	21-6	22-3
	24.0	8-11	10-3	11-6	12-7	13-7	14-6	15-5	16-3	17-0	17-9	18-6	19-3	19-11
E	12.0	0.10	0.15	0.22	0.28	0.36	0.44	0.52	0.61	0.71	0.80	0.91	1.01	1.13
	16.0	0.09	0.13	0.19	0.25	0.31	0.38	0.45	0.53	0.61	0.70	0.79	0.88	0.97
	19.2	0.08	0.12	0.17	0.23	0.28	0.35	0.41	0.48	0.56	0.64	0.72	0.80	0.89
	24.0	0.07	0.11	0.15	0.20	0.25	0.31	0.37	0.43	0.50	0.57	0.64	0.72	0.80

Rafter Size (in)	Spacing (in)	Bending Design Value, F_b (psi) $\times$ 0.00689 for N/mm²											
$\times$ 25.4 for mm		1600	1700	1800	1900	2000	2100	2200	2300	2400	2500	2600	2700
2 × 6	12.0	14-2	14-8	15-1	15-6	15-11	16-3	16-8	17-0	17-5	17-9	18-1	
	16.0	12-4	12-8	13-1	13-5	13-9	14-1	14-5	14-9	15-1	15-4	15-8	16-0
	19.2	11-3	11-7	11-11	12-3	12-7	12-10	13-2	13-6	13-9	14-0	14-4	14-7
	24.0	10-0	10-4	10-8	10-11	11-3	11-6	11-9	12-0	12-4	12-7	12-10	13-1
2 × 8	12.0	18-9	19-4	19-10	20-5	20-11	21-5	21-11	22-5	22-11	23-5	23-10	
	16.0	16-3	16-9	17-2	17-8	18-1	18-7	19-0	19-5	19-10	20-3	20-8	21-1
	19.2	14-10	15-3	15-8	16-2	16-7	16-11	17-4	17-9	18-1	18-6	18-10	19-3
	24.0	13-3	13-8	14-0	14-5	14-10	15-2	15-6	15-10	16-3	16-7	16-10	17-2
2 × 10	12.0	23-11	24-7	25-4	26-0								
	16.0	20-8	21-4	21-11	22-6	23-1	23-8	24-3	24-10	25-4	25-10		
	19.2	18-11	19-6	20-0	20-7	21-1	21-8	22-2	22-8	23-1	23-7	24-1	24-6
	24.0	16-11	17-5	17-11	18-5	18-11	19-4	19-10	20-3	20-8	21-1	21-6	21-11
2 × 12	12.0												
	16.0	25-2	25-11										
	19.2	23-0	23-8	24-4	25-0	25-8							
	24.0	20-6	21-2	21-9	22-5	23-0	23-6	24-1	24-8	25-2	25-8		
E	12.0	1.24	1.36	1.48	1.60	1.73	1.86	2.00	2.14	2.28	2.42	2.57	
	16.0	1.07	1.18	1.28	1.39	1.50	1.61	1.73	1.85	1.97	2.10	2.22	2.35
	19.2	0.98	1.07	1.17	1.27	1.37	1.47	1.58	1.69	1.80	1.91	2.03	2.15
	24.0	0.88	0.96	1.05	1.13	1.22	1.32	1.41	1.51	1.61	1.71	1.82	1.92

NOTE: The required modulus of elasticity, *E*, in 1,000,000 pounds per square inch (psi) ($\times$ 0.00689 for N/mm²) is shown at the bottom of this table, is limited to 2.6 million psi (17 914 N/mm²) and less, and is applicable to all lumber sizes shown. Spans are shown in feet-inches (1 foot = 304.8 mm, 1 inch = 25.4 mm) and are limited to 26 feet (7925 mm) and less.

From the Uniform Building Code, ©1997, ICBO

TABLE 23-IV-R-7—RAFTERS WITH *L*/180 DEFLECTION LIMITATION
The allowable bending stress (*F$_b$*) and modulus of elasticity (*E*) used in this table shall be from Tables 23-IV-V-1 and 23-IV-V-2 only.

DESIGN CRITERIA:
Strength — Live load of 20 psf (0.96 kN/m²) plus dead load of 10 psf (0.48 kN/m²) determines the required bending design value.
Deflection — For 20 psf (0.96 kN/m²) live load.
Limited to span in inches (mm) divided by 180.

Rafter Size (in) × 25.4 for mm	Spacing (in)	Bending Design Value, F_b (psi) × 0.00689 for N/mm²														
		200	300	400	500	600	700	800	900	1000	1100	1200	1300	1400	1500	1600
2 × 4	12.0	3-8	4-6	5-3	5-10	6-5	6-11	7-5	7-10	8-3	8-8	9-0	9-5	9-9	10-1	10-5
	16.0	3-2	3-11	4-6	5-1	5-6	6-0	6-5	6-9	7-2	7-6	7-10	8-2	8-5	8-9	9-0
	19.2	2-11	3-7	4-1	4-7	5-1	5-5	5-10	6-2	6-6	6-10	7-2	7-5	7-9	8-0	8-3
	24.0	2-7	3-2	3-8	4-1	4-6	4-11	5-3	5-6	5-10	6-1	6-5	6-8	6-11	7-2	7-5
2 × 6	12.0	5-10	7-1	8-2	9-2	10-0	10-10	11-7	12-4	13-0	13-7	14-2	14-9	15-4	15-11	16-5
	16.0	5-0	6-2	7-1	7-11	8-8	9-5	10-0	10-8	11-3	11-9	12-4	12-10	13-3	13-9	14-2
	19.2	4-7	5-7	6-6	7-3	7-11	8-7	9-2	9-9	10-3	10-9	11-3	11-8	12-2	12-7	13-0
	24.0	4-1	5-0	5-10	6-6	7-1	7-8	8-2	8-8	9-2	9-7	10-0	10-5	10-10	11-3	11-7
2 × 8	12.0	7-8	9-4	10-10	12-1	13-3	14-4	15-3	16-3	17-1	17-11	18-9	19-6	20-3	20-11	21-7
	16.0	6-7	8-1	9-4	10-6	11-6	12-5	13-3	14-0	14-10	15-6	16-3	16-10	17-6	18-1	18-9
	19.2	6-0	7-5	8-7	9-7	10-6	11-4	12-1	12-10	13-6	14-2	14-10	15-5	16-0	16-7	17-1
	24.0	5-5	6-7	7-8	8-7	9-4	10-1	10-10	11-6	12-1	12-8	13-3	13-9	14-4	14-10	15-3
2 × 10	12.0	9-9	11-11	13-9	15-5	16-11	18-3	19-6	20-8	21-10	22-10	23-11	24-10	25-10		
	16.0	8-5	10-4	11-11	13-4	14-8	15-10	16-11	17-11	18-11	19-10	20-8	21-6	22-4	23-1	23-11
	19.2	7-8	9-5	10-11	12-2	13-4	14-5	15-5	16-4	17-3	18-1	18-11	19-8	20-5	21-1	21-10
	24.0	6-11	8-5	9-9	10-11	11-11	12-11	13-9	14-8	15-5	16-2	16-11	17-7	18-3	18-11	19-6
E	12.0	0.06	0.12	0.18	0.25	0.33	0.41	0.51	0.60	0.71	0.82	0.93	1.05	1.17	1.30	1.43
	16.0	0.05	0.10	0.15	0.22	0.28	0.36	0.44	0.52	0.61	0.71	0.80	0.91	1.01	1.13	1.24
	19.2	0.05	0.09	0.14	0.20	0.26	0.33	0.40	0.48	0.56	0.64	0.73	0.83	0.93	1.03	1.13
	24.0	0.04	0.08	0.13	0.18	0.23	0.29	0.36	0.43	0.50	0.58	0.66	0.74	0.83	0.92	1.01

Rafter Size (in) × 25.4 for mm	Spacing (in)	Bending Design Value, F_b (psi) × 0.00689 for N/mm²													
		1700	1800	1900	2000	2100	2200	2300	2400	2500	2600	2700	2800	2900	3000
2 × 4	12.0	10-9	11-1	11-4	11-8	11-11	12-3	12-6							
	16.0	9-4	9-7	9-10	10-1	10-4	10-7	10-10	11-1	11-4	11-6				
	19.2	8-6	8-9	9-0	9-3	9-5	9-8	9-11	10-1	10-4	10-6	10-9			
	24.0	7-7	7-10	8-0	8-3	8-5	8-8	8-10	9-0	9-3	9-5	9-7	9-9	9-11	10-1
2 × 6	12.0	16-11	17-5	17-10	18-4	18-9	19-3	19-8							
	16.0	14-8	15-1	15-6	15-11	16-3	16-8	17-0	17-5	17-9	18-1				
	19.2	13-4	13-9	14-2	14-6	14-10	15-2	15-7	15-11	16-2	16-6	16-10			
	24.0	11-11	12-4	12-8	13-0	13-3	13-7	13-11	14-2	14-6	14-9	15-1	15-4	15-7	15-11
2 × 8	12.0	22-3	22-11	23-7	24-2	24-9	25-4	25-11							
	16.0	19-4	19-10	20-5	20-11	21-5	21-11	22-5	22-11	23-5	23-10				
	19.2	17-7	18-1	18-7	19-1	19-7	20-0	20-6	20-11	21-4	21-9	22-2			
	24.0	15-9	16-3	16-8	17-1	17-6	17-11	18-4	18-9	19-1	19-6	19-10	20-3	20-7	20-11
2 × 10	12.0														
	16.0	24-7	25-4	26-0											
	19.2	22-6	23-1	23-9	24-5	25-0	25-7								
	24.0	20-1	20-8	21-3	21-10	22-4	22-10	23-5	23-11	24-5	24-10	25-4	25-10		
E	12.0	1.57	1.71	1.85	2.00	2.15	2.31	2.47							
	16.0	1.36	1.48	1.60	1.73	1.86	2.00	2.14	2.28	2.42	2.57				
	19.2	1.24	1.35	1.46	1.58	1.70	1.82	1.95	2.08	2.21	2.34	2.48			
	24.0	1.11	1.21	1.31	1.41	1.52	1.63	1.74	1.86	1.98	2.10	2.22	2.34	2.47	2.60

NOTE: The required modulus of elasticity, *E*, in 1,000,000 pounds per square inch (psi) (× 0.00689 for N/mm²) is shown at the bottom of this table, is limited to 2.6 million psi (17 914 N/mm²) and less, and is applicable to all lumber sizes shown. Spans are shown in feet-inches (1 foot = 304.8 mm, 1 inch = 25.4 mm) and are limited to 26 feet (7925 mm) and less.

From the Uniform Building Code, ©1997, ICBO

TABLE 23-IV-R-8—RAFTERS WITH *L*/180 DEFLECTION LIMITATION
The allowable bending stress (F_b) and modulus of elasticity (*E*) used in this table shall be from Tables 23-IV-V-1 and 23-IV-V-2 only.

DESIGN CRITERIA:
Strength — Live load of 30 psf (1.44 kN/m^2) plus dead load of 10 psf (0.48 kN/m^2) determines the required bending design value.
Deflection — For 30 psf (1.44 kN/m^2) live load.
Limited to span in inches (mm) divided by 180.

Rafter Size (in) × 25.4 for mm	Spacing (in)	Bending Design Value, F_b (psi) × 0.00689 for N/mm^2														
		200	300	400	500	600	700	800	900	1000	1100	1200	1300	1400	1500	1600
2 × 4	12.0	3-2	3-11	4-6	5-1	5-6	6-0	6-5	6-9	7-2	7-6	7-10	8-2	8-5	8-9	9-0
	16.0	2-9	3-5	3-11	4-4	4-10	5-2	5-6	5-10	6-2	6-6	6-9	7-1	7-4	7-7	7-10
	19.2	2-6	3-1	3-7	4-0	4-4	4-9	5-1	5-4	5-8	5-11	6-2	6-5	6-8	6-11	7-2
	24.0	2-3	2-9	3-2	3-7	3-11	4-3	4-6	4-10	5-1	5-4	5-6	5-9	6-0	6-2	6-5
2 × 6	12.0	5-0	6-2	7-1	7-11	8-8	9-5	10-0	10-8	11-3	11-9	12-4	12-10	13-3	13-9	14-2
	16.0	4-4	5-4	6-2	6-10	7-6	8-2	8-8	9-3	9-9	10-2	10-8	11-1	11-6	11-11	12-4
	19.2	4-0	4-10	5-7	6-3	6-10	7-5	7-11	8-5	8-11	9-4	9-9	10-1	10-6	10-10	11-3
	24.0	3-7	4-4	5-0	5-7	6-2	6-8	7-1	7-6	7-11	8-4	8-8	9-1	9-5	9-9	10-0
2 × 8	12.0	6-7	8-1	9-4	10-6	11-6	12-5	13-3	14-0	14-10	15-6	16-3	16-10	17-6	18-1	18-9
	16.0	5-9	7-0	8-1	9-1	9-11	10-9	11-6	12-2	12-10	13-5	14-0	14-7	15-2	15-8	16-3
	19.2	5-3	6-5	7-5	8-3	9-1	9-9	10-6	11-1	11-8	12-3	12-10	13-4	13-10	14-4	14-10
	24.0	4-8	5-9	6-7	7-5	8-1	8-9	9-4	9-11	10-6	11-0	11-6	11-11	12-5	12-10	13-3
2 × 10	12.0	8-5	10-4	11-11	13-4	14-8	15-10	16-11	17-11	18-11	19-10	20-8	21-6	22-4	23-1	23-11
	16.0	7-4	8-11	10-4	11-7	12-8	13-8	14-8	15-6	16-4	17-2	17-11	18-8	19-4	20-0	20-8
	19.2	6-8	8-2	9-5	10-7	11-7	12-6	13-4	14-2	14-11	15-8	16-4	17-0	17-8	18-3	18-11
	24.0	6-0	7-4	8-5	9-5	10-4	11-2	11-11	12-8	13-4	14-0	14-8	15-3	15-10	16-4	16-11
E	12.0	0.06	0.11	0.17	0.24	0.32	0.40	0.49	0.59	0.69	0.79	0.91	1.02	1.14	1.27	1.39
	16.0	0.05	0.10	0.15	0.21	0.28	0.35	0.43	0.51	0.60	0.69	0.78	0.88	0.99	1.10	1.21
	19.2	0.05	0.09	0.14	0.19	0.25	0.32	0.39	0.47	0.54	0.63	0.72	0.81	0.90	1.00	1.10
	24.0	0.04	0.08	0.12	0.17	0.23	0.29	0.35	0.42	0.49	0.56	0.64	0.72	0.81	0.89	0.99

Rafter Size (in) × 25.4 for mm	Spacing (in)	Bending Design Value, F_b (psi) × 0.00689 for N/mm^2													
		1700	1800	1900	2000	2100	2200	2300	2400	2500	2600	2700	2800	2900	3000
2 × 4	12.0	9-4	9-7	9-10	10-1	10-4	10-7	10-10	11-1						
	16.0	8-1	8-4	8-6	8-9	9-0	9-2	9-5	9-7	9-9	10-0				
	19.2	7-4	7-7	7-9	8-0	8-2	8-5	8-7	8-9	8-11	9-1	9-3	9-5		
	24.0	6-7	6-9	7-0	7-2	7-4	7-6	7-8	7-10	8-0	8-2	8-4	8-5	8-7	8-9
2 × 6	12.0	14-8	15-1	15-6	15-11	16-3	16-8	17-0	17-5						
	16.0	12-8	13-1	13-5	13-9	14-1	14-5	14-9	15-1	15-4	15-8				
	19.2	11-7	11-11	12-3	12-7	12-10	13-2	13-6	13-9	14-0	14-4	14-7	14-10		
	24.0	10-4	10-8	10-11	11-3	11-6	11-9	12-0	12-4	12-7	12-10	13-1	13-3	13-6	13-9
2 × 8	12.0	19-4	19-10	20-5	20-11	21-5	21-11	22-5	22-11						
	16.0	16-9	17-2	17-8	18-1	18-7	19-0	19-5	19-10	20-3	20-8				
	19.2	15-3	15-8	16-2	16-7	16-11	17-4	17-9	18-1	18-6	18-10	19-3	19-7		
	24.0	13-8	14-0	14-5	14-10	15-2	15-6	15-10	16-3	16-7	16-10	17-2	17-6	17-10	18-1
2 × 10	12.0	24-7	25-4	26-0											
	16.0	21-4	21-11	22-6	23-1	23-8	24-3	24-10	25-4	25-10					
	19.2	19-6	20-0	20-7	21-1	21-8	22-2	22-8	23-1	23-7	24-1	24-6	25-0		
	24.0	17-5	17-11	18-5	18-11	19-4	19-10	20-3	20-8	21-1	21-6	21-11	22-4	22-9	23-1
E	12.0	1.53	1.66	1.80	1.95	2.10	2.25	2.40	2.56						
	16.0	1.32	1.44	1.56	1.69	1.82	1.95	2.08	2.22	2.36	2.50				
	19.2	1.21	1.32	1.43	1.54	1.66	1.78	1.90	2.03	2.15	2.28	2.42	2.55		
	24.0	1.08	1.18	1.28	1.38	1.48	1.59	1.70	1.81	1.93	2.04	2.16	2.28	2.41	2.53

NOTE: The required modulus of elasticity, *E*, in 1,000,000 pounds per square inch (psi) (× 0.00689 for N/mm^2) is shown at the bottom of this table, is limited to 2.6 million psi (17 914 N/mm^2) and less, and is applicable to all lumber sizes shown. Spans are shown in feet-inches (1 foot = 304.8 mm, 1 inch = 25.4 mm) and are limited to 26 feet (7925 mm) and less.

From the Uniform Building Code, ©1997, ICBO

TABLE 23-IV-R-9—RAFTERS WITH *L*/180 DEFLECTION LIMITATION
The allowable bending stress (*F$_b$*) and modulus of elasticity (*E*) used in this table shall be from Tables 23-IV-V-1 and 23-IV-V-2 only.

DESIGN CRITERIA:
Strength — Live load of 20 psf (0.96 kN/m²) plus dead load of 15 psf (0.72 kN/m²) determines the required bending design value.
Deflection — For 20 psf (0.96 kN/m²) live load.
Limited to span in inches (mm) divided by 180.

Rafter Size (in) × 25.4 for mm	Spacing (in)	Bending Design Value, F$_b$ (psi) × 0.00689 for N/mm²													
		200	300	400	500	600	700	800	900	1000	1100	1200	1300	1400	1500	1600
2×4	12.0	3-5	4-2	4-10	5-5	5-11	6-5	6-10	7-3	7-8	8-0	8-4	8-8	9-0	9-4	9-8
	16.0	2-11	3-7	4-2	4-8	5-1	5-6	5-11	6-3	6-7	6-11	7-3	7-6	7-10	8-1	8-4
	19.2	2-8	3-4	3-10	4-3	4-8	5-1	5-5	5-9	6-0	6-4	6-7	6-11	7-2	7-5	7-8
	24.0	2-5	2-11	3-5	3-10	4-2	4-6	4-10	5-1	5-5	5-8	5-11	6-2	6-5	6-7	6-10
2×6	12.0	5-4	6-7	7-7	8-6	9-4	10-0	10-9	11-5	12-0	12-7	13-2	13-8	14-2	14-8	15-2
	16.0	4-8	5-8	6-7	7-4	8-1	8-8	9-4	9-10	10-5	10-11	11-5	11-10	12-4	12-9	13-2
	19.2	4-3	5-2	6-0	6-9	7-4	7-11	8-6	9-0	9-6	9-11	10-5	10-10	11-3	11-7	12-0
	24.0	3-10	4-8	5-4	6-0	6-7	7-1	7-7	8-1	8-6	8-11	9-4	9-8	10-0	10-5	10-9
2×8	12.0	7-1	8-8	10-0	11-2	12-3	13-3	14-2	15-0	15-10	16-7	17-4	18-0	18-9	19-5	20-0
	16.0	6-2	7-6	8-8	9-8	10-7	11-6	12-3	13-0	13-8	14-4	15-0	15-7	16-3	16-9	17-4
	19.2	5-7	6-10	7-11	8-10	9-8	10-6	11-2	11-10	12-6	13-1	13-8	14-3	14-10	15-4	15-10
	24.0	5-0	6-2	7-1	7-11	8-8	9-4	10-0	10-7	11-2	11-9	12-3	12-9	13-3	13-8	14-2
2×10	12.0	9-0	11-1	12-9	14-3	15-8	16-11	18-1	19-2	20-2	21-2	22-1	23-0	23-11	24-9	25-6
	16.0	7-10	9-7	11-1	12-4	13-6	14-8	15-8	16-7	17-6	18-4	19-2	19-11	20-8	21-5	22-1
	19.2	7-2	8-9	10-1	11-3	12-4	13-4	14-3	15-2	15-11	16-9	17-6	18-2	18-11	19-7	20-2
	24.0	6-5	7-10	9-0	10-1	11-1	11-11	12-9	13-6	14-3	15-0	15-8	16-3	16-11	17-6	18-1
E	12.0	0.05	0.09	0.14	0.20	0.26	0.33	0.40	0.48	0.56	0.65	0.74	0.83	0.93	1.03	1.14
	16.0	0.04	0.08	0.12	0.17	0.23	0.28	0.35	0.41	0.49	0.56	0.64	0.72	0.80	0.89	0.98
	19.2	0.04	0.07	0.11	0.16	0.21	0.26	0.32	0.38	0.44	0.51	0.58	0.66	0.73	0.81	0.90
	24.0	0.04	0.07	0.10	0.14	0.18	0.23	0.28	0.34	0.40	0.46	0.52	0.59	0.66	0.73	0.80

Rafter Size (in) × 25.4 for mm	Spacing (in)	Bending Design Value, F$_b$ (psi) × 0.00689 for N/mm²													
		1700	1800	1900	2000	2100	2200	2300	2400	2500	2600	2700	2800	2900	3000
2×4	12.0	9-11	10-3	10-6	10-10	11-1	11-4	11-7	11-10	12-1	12-4	12-7			
	16.0	8-7	8-10	9-1	9-4	9-7	9-10	10-0	10-3	10-5	10-8	10-10	11-1	11-3	11-5
	19.2	7-10	8-1	8-4	8-6	8-9	8-11	9-2	9-4	9-7	9-9	9-11	10-1	10-3	10-5
	24.0	7-0	7-3	7-5	7-8	7-10	8-0	8-2	8-4	8-6	8-8	8-10	9-0	9-2	9-4
2×6	12.0	15-8	16-1	16-7	17-0	17-5	17-10	18-2	18-7	19-0	19-4	19-9			
	16.0	13-7	13-11	14-4	14-8	15-1	15-5	15-9	16-1	16-5	16-9	17-1	17-5	17-8	18-0
	19.2	12-4	12-9	13-1	13-5	13-9	14-1	14-5	14-8	15-0	15-4	15-7	15-11	16-2	16-5
	24.0	11-1	11-5	11-8	12-0	12-4	12-7	12-10	13-2	13-5	13-8	13-11	14-2	14-5	14-8
2×8	12.0	20-8	21-3	21-10	22-4	22-11	23-6	24-0	24-6	25-0	25-6	26-0			
	16.0	17-10	18-5	18-11	19-5	19-10	20-4	20-9	21-3	21-8	22-1	22-6	22-11	23-4	23-9
	19.2	16-4	16-9	17-3	17-8	18-1	18-7	19-0	19-5	19-9	20-2	20-7	20-11	21-4	21-8
	24.0	14-7	15-0	15-5	15-10	16-3	16-7	17-0	17-4	17-8	18-0	18-5	18-9	19-1	19-5
2×10	12.0														
	16.0	22-10	23-5	24-1	24-9	25-4	25-11								
	19.2	20-10	21-5	22-0	22-7	23-1	23-8	24-2	24-9	25-3	25-9				
	24.0	18-7	19-2	19-8	20-2	20-8	21-2	21-8	22-1	22-7	23-0	23-5	23-11	24-4	24-9
E	12.0	1.24	1.36	1.47	1.59	1.71	1.83	1.96	2.09	2.22	2.35	2.49			
	16.0	1.08	1.17	1.27	1.37	1.48	1.59	1.70	1.81	1.92	2.04	2.16	2.28	2.40	2.53
	19.2	0.98	1.07	1.16	1.25	1.35	1.45	1.55	1.65	1.75	1.86	1.97	2.08	2.19	2.31
	24.0	0.88	0.96	1.04	1.12	1.21	1.29	1.38	1.48	1.57	1.66	1.76	1.86	1.96	2.06

NOTE: The required modulus of elasticity, *E*, in 1,000,000 pounds per square inch (psi) (× 0.00689 for N/mm²) is shown at the bottom of this table, is limited to 2.6 million psi (17 914 N/mm²) and less, and is applicable to all lumber sizes shown. Spans are shown in feet-inches (1 foot = 304.8 mm, 1 inch = 25.4 mm) and are limited to 26 feet (7925 mm) and less.

From the Uniform Building Code, ©1997, ICBO

TABLE 23-IV-R-10—RAFTERS WITH *L*/180 DEFLECTION LIMITATION
The allowable bending stress (*F$_b$*) and modulus of elasticity (*E*) used in this table shall be from Tables 23-IV-V-1 and 23-IV-V-2 only.

DESIGN CRITERIA:
Strength — Live load of 30 psf (1.44 kN/m^2) plus dead load of 15 psf (0.72 kN/m^2) determines the required bending design value.
Deflection — For 30 psf (1.44 kN/m^2) live load.
Limited to span in inches (mm) divided by 180.

Rafter Size (in) × 25.4 for mm	Spacing (in)	Bending Design Value, *F$_b$* (psi) × 0.00689 for N/mm^2														
		200	300	400	500	600	700	800	900	1000	1100	1200	1300	1400	1500	1600
2×4	12.0	3-0	3-8	4-3	4-9	5-3	5-8	6-0	6-5	6-9	7-1	7-5	7-8	8-0	8-3	8-6
	16.0	2-7	3-2	3-8	4-1	4-6	4-11	5-3	5-6	5-10	6-1	6-5	6-8	6-11	7-2	7-5
	19.2	2-5	2-11	3-4	3-9	4-1	4-5	4-9	5-1	5-4	5-7	5-10	6-1	6-4	6-6	6-9
	24.0	2-2	2-7	3-0	3-4	3-8	4-0	4-3	4-6	4-9	5-0	5-3	5-5	5-8	5-10	6-0
2×6	12.0	4-9	5-10	6-8	7-6	8-2	8-10	9-6	10-0	10-7	11-1	11-7	12-1	12-6	13-0	13-5
	16.0	4-1	5-0	5-10	6-6	7-1	7-8	8-2	8-8	9-2	9-7	10-0	10-5	10-10	11-3	11-7
	19.2	3-9	4-7	5-4	5-11	6-6	7-0	7-6	7-11	8-4	8-9	9-2	9-6	9-11	10-3	10-7
	24.0	3-4	4-1	4-9	5-4	5-10	6-3	6-8	7-1	7-6	7-10	8-2	8-6	8-10	9-2	9-6
2×8	12.0	6-3	7-8	8-10	9-10	10-10	11-8	12-6	13-3	13-11	14-8	15-3	15-11	16-6	17-1	17-8
	16.0	5-5	6-7	7-8	8-7	9-4	10-1	10-10	11-6	12-1	12-8	13-3	13-9	14-4	14-10	15-3
	19.2	4-11	6-0	7-0	7-10	8-7	9-3	9-10	10-6	11-0	11-7	12-1	12-7	13-1	13-6	13-11
	24.0	4-5	5-5	6-3	7-0	7-8	8-3	8-10	9-4	9-10	10-4	10-10	11-3	11-8	12-1	12-6
2×10	12.0	8-0	9-9	11-3	12-7	13-9	14-11	15-11	16-11	17-10	18-8	19-6	20-4	21-1	21-10	22-6
	16.0	6-11	8-5	9-9	10-11	11-11	12-11	13-9	14-8	15-5	16-2	16-11	17-7	18-3	18-11	19-6
	19.2	6-4	7-8	8-11	9-11	10-11	11-9	12-7	13-4	14-1	14-9	15-5	16-1	16-8	17-3	17-10
	24.0	5-8	6-11	8-0	8-11	9-9	10-6	11-3	11-11	12-7	13-2	13-9	14-4	14-11	15-5	15-11
E	12.0	0.05	0.09	0.15	0.20	0.27	0.34	0.41	0.49	0.58	0.67	0.76	0.86	0.96	1.06	1.17
	16.0	0.04	0.08	0.13	0.18	0.23	0.29	0.36	0.43	0.50	0.58	0.66	0.74	0.83	0.92	1.01
	19.2	0.04	0.08	0.12	0.16	0.21	0.27	0.33	0.39	0.46	0.53	0.60	0.68	0.76	0.84	0.92
	24.0	0.04	0.07	0.10	0.14	0.19	0.24	0.29	0.35	0.41	0.47	0.54	0.61	0.68	0.75	0.83

Rafter Size (in) × 25.4 for mm	Spacing (in)	Bending Design Value, *F$_b$* (psi) × 0.00689 for N/mm^2													
		1700	1800	1900	2000	2100	2200	2300	2400	2500	2600	2700	2800	2900	3000
2×4	12.0	8-9	9-0	9-3	9-6	9-9	10-0	10-3	10-5	10-8	10-10	11-1			
	16.0	7-7	7-10	8-0	8-3	8-5	8-8	8-10	9-0	9-3	9-5	9-7	9-9	9-11	10-1
	19.2	6-11	7-2	7-4	7-6	7-9	7-11	8-1	8-3	8-5	8-7	8-9	8-11	9-1	9-3
	24.0	6-3	6-5	6-7	6-9	6-11	7-1	7-3	7-5	7-6	7-8	7-10	8-0	8-1	8-3
2×6	12.0	13-10	14-2	14-7	15-0	15-4	15-8	16-1	16-5	16-9	17-1	17-5			
	16.0	11-11	12-4	12-8	13-0	13-3	13-7	13-11	14-2	14-6	14-9	15-1	15-4	15-7	15-11
	19.2	10-11	11-3	11-6	11-10	12-2	12-5	12-8	13-0	13-3	13-6	13-9	14-0	14-3	14-6
	24.0	9-9	10-0	10-4	10-7	10-10	11-1	11-4	11-7	11-10	12-1	12-4	12-6	12-9	13-0
2×8	12.0	18-2	18-9	19-3	19-9	20-3	20-8	21-2	21-7	22-1	22-6	22-11			
	16.0	15-9	16-3	16-8	17-1	17-6	17-11	18-4	18-9	19-1	19-6	19-10	20-3	20-7	20-11
	19.2	14-5	14-10	15-2	15-7	16-0	16-4	16-9	17-1	17-5	17-9	18-1	18-5	18-9	19-1
	24.0	12-10	13-3	13-7	13-11	14-4	14-8	15-0	15-3	15-7	15-11	16-3	16-6	16-10	17-1
2×10	12.0	23-3	23-11	24-6	25-2	25-10									
	16.0	20-1	20-8	21-3	21-10	22-4	22-10	23-5	23-11	24-5	24-10	25-4	25-10		
	19.2	18-4	18-11	19-5	19-11	20-5	20-10	21-4	21-10	22-3	22-8	23-1	23-7	24-0	24-5
	24.0	16-5	16-11	17-4	17-10	18-3	18-8	19-1	19-6	19-11	20-4	20-8	21-1	21-5	21-10
E	12.0	1.28	1.39	1.51	1.63	1.76	1.88	2.01	2.15	2.28	2.42	2.56			
	16.0	1.11	1.21	1.31	1.41	1.52	1.63	1.74	1.86	1.98	2.10	2.22	2.34	2.47	2.60
	19.2	1.01	1.10	1.20	1.29	1.39	1.49	1.59	1.70	1.80	1.91	2.03	2.14	2.25	2.37
	24.0	0.90	0.99	1.07	1.15	1.24	1.33	1.42	1.52	1.61	1.71	1.81	1.91	2.02	2.12

NOTE: The required modulus of elasticity, *E*, in 1,000,000 pounds per square inch (psi) (× 0.00689 for N/mm^2) is shown at the bottom of this table, is limited to 2.6 million psi (17 914 N/mm^2) and less, and is applicable to all lumber sizes shown. Spans are shown in feet-inches (1 foot = 304.8 mm, 1 inch = 25.4 mm) and are limited to 26 feet (7925 mm) and less.

From the Uniform Building Code, ©1997, ICBO

TABLE 23-IV-R-11—RAFTERS WITH *L*/180 DEFLECTION LIMITATION
The allowable bending stress (F_b) and modulus of elasticity (*E*) used in this table shall be from Tables 23-IV-V-1 and 23-IV-V-2 only.

DESIGN CRITERIA:
Strength — Live load of 20 psf (0.96 kN/m²) plus dead load of 20 psf (0.96 kN/m²) determines the required bending design value.
Deflection — For 20 psf (0.96 kN/m²) live load.
Limited to span in inches (mm) divided by 180.

Rafter Size (in) × 25.4 for mm	Spacing (in)	Bending Design Value, F_b (psi) × 0.00689 for N/mm²														
		200	300	400	500	600	700	800	900	1000	1100	1200	1300	1400	1500	1600
2×4	12.0	3-2	3-11	4-6	5-1	5-6	6-0	6-5	6-9	7-2	7-6	7-10	8-2	8-5	8-9	9-0
	16.0	2-9	3-5	3-11	4-4	4-10	5-2	5-6	5-10	6-2	6-6	6-9	7-1	7-4	7-7	7-10
	19.2	2-6	3-1	3-7	4-0	4-4	4-9	5-1	5-4	5-8	5-11	6-2	6-5	6-8	6-11	7-2
	24.0	2-3	2-9	3-2	3-7	3-11	4-3	4-6	4-10	5-1	5-4	5-6	5-9	6-0	6-2	6-5
2×6	12.0	5-0	6-2	7-1	7-11	8-8	9-5	10-0	10-8	11-3	11-9	12-4	12-10	13-3	13-9	14-2
	16.0	4-4	5-4	6-2	6-10	7-6	8-2	8-8	9-3	9-9	10-2	10-8	11-1	11-6	11-11	12-4
	19.2	4-0	4-10	5-7	6-3	6-10	7-5	7-11	8-5	8-11	9-4	9-9	10-1	10-6	10-10	11-3
	24.0	3-7	4-4	5-0	5-7	6-2	6-8	7-1	7-6	7-11	8-4	8-8	9-1	9-5	9-9	10-0
2×8	12.0	6-7	8-1	9-4	10-6	11-6	12-5	13-3	14-0	14-10	15-6	16-3	16-10	17-6	18-1	18-9
	16.0	5-9	7-0	8-1	9-1	9-11	10-9	11-6	12-2	12-10	13-5	14-0	14-7	15-2	15-8	16-3
	19.2	5-3	6-5	7-5	8-3	9-1	9-9	10-6	11-1	11-8	12-3	12-10	13-4	13-10	14-4	14-10
	24.0	4-8	5-9	6-7	7-5	8-1	8-9	9-4	9-11	10-6	11-0	11-6	11-11	12-5	12-10	13-3
2×10	12.0	8-5	10-4	11-11	13-4	14-8	15-10	16-11	17-11	18-11	19-10	20-8	21-6	22-4	23-1	23-11
	16.0	7-4	8-11	10-4	11-7	12-8	13-8	14-8	15-6	16-4	17-2	17-11	18-8	19-4	20-0	20-8
	19.2	6-8	8-2	9-5	10-7	11-7	12-6	13-4	14-2	14-11	15-8	16-4	17-0	17-8	18-3	18-11
	24.0	6-0	7-4	8-5	9-5	10-4	11-2	11-11	12-8	13-4	14-0	14-8	15-3	15-10	16-4	16-11
E	12.0	0.04	0.08	0.12	0.16	0.21	0.27	0.33	0.39	0.46	0.53	0.60	0.68	0.76	0.84	0.93
	16.0	0.04	0.07	0.10	0.14	0.18	0.23	0.28	0.34	0.40	0.46	0.52	0.59	0.66	0.73	0.80
	19.2	0.03	0.06	0.09	0.13	0.17	0.21	0.26	0.31	0.36	0.42	0.48	0.54	0.60	0.67	0.73
	24.0	0.03	0.05	0.08	0.11	0.15	0.19	0.23	0.28	0.32	0.37	0.43	0.48	0.54	0.60	0.66

Rafter Size (in) × 25.4 for mm	Spacing (in)	Bending Design Value, F_b (psi) × 0.00689 for N/mm²														
		1700	1800	1900	2000	2100	2200	2300	2400	2500	2600	2700	2800	2900	3000	
2×4	12.0	9-4	9-7	9-10	10-1	10-4	10-7	10-10	11-1	11-4	11-6	11-9	11-11	12-2	12-4	
	16.0	8-1	8-4	8-6	8-9	9-0	9-2	9-5	9-7	9-9	10-0	10-2	10-4	10-6	10-9	
	19.2	7-4	7-7	7-9	8-0	8-2	8-5	8-7	8-9	8-11	9-1	9-3	9-5	9-7	9-9	
	24.0	6-7	6-9	7-0	7-2	7-4	7-6	7-8	7-10	8-0	8-2	8-4	8-5	8-7	8-9	
2×6	12.0	14-8	15-1	15-6	15-11	16-3	16-8	17-0	17-5	17-9	18-1	18-5	18-9	19-1	19-5	
	16.0	12-8	13-1	13-5	13-9	14-1	14-5	14-9	15-1	15-4	15-8	16-0	16-3	16-7	16-10	
	19.2	11-7	11-11	12-3	12-7	12-10	13-2	13-6	13-9	14-0	14-4	14-7	14-10	15-1	15-4	
	24.0	10-4	10-8	10-11	11-3	11-6	11-9	12-0	12-4	12-7	12-10	13-1	13-3	13-6	13-9	
2×8	12.0	19-4	19-10	20-5	20-11	21-5	21-11	22-5	22-11	23-5	23-10	24-4	24-9	25-2	25-8	
	16.0	16-9	17-2	17-8	18-1	18-7	19-0	19-5	19-10	20-3	20-8	21-1	21-5	21-10	22-2	
	19.2	15-3	15-8	16-2	16-7	16-11	17-4	17-9	18-1	18-6	18-10	19-3	19-7	19-11	20-3	
	24.0	13-8	14-0	14-5	14-10	15-2	15-6	15-10	16-3	16-7	16-10	17-2	17-6	17-10	18-1	
2×10	12.0	24-7	25-4	26-0												
	16.0	21-4	21-11	22-6	23-1	23-8	24-3	24-10	25-4	25-10						
	19.2	19-6	20-0	20-7	21-1	21-8	22-2	22-8	23-1	23-7	24-1	24-6	25-0	25-5	25-10	
	24.0	17-5	17-11	18-5	18-11	19-4	19-10	20-3	20-8	21-1	21-6	21-11	22-4	22-9	23-1	
E	12.0	1.02	1.11	1.20	1.30	1.40	1.50	1.60	1.71	1.82	1.93	2.04	2.15	2.27	2.39	
	16.0	0.88	0.96	1.04	1.13	1.21	1.30	1.39	1.48	1.57	1.67	1.76	1.86	1.96	2.07	
	19.2	0.80	0.88	0.95	1.03	1.10	1.18	1.27	1.35	1.44	1.52	1.61	1.70	1.79	1.89	
	24.0	0.72	0.78	0.85	0.92	0.99	1.06	1.13	1.21	1.28	1.36	1.44	1.52	1.60	1.69	

NOTE: The required modulus of elasticity, *E*, in 1,000,000 pounds per square inch (psi) (× 0.00689 for N/mm²) is shown at the bottom of this table, is limited to 2.6 million psi (17 914 N/mm²) and less, and is applicable to all lumber sizes shown. Spans are shown in feet-inches (1 foot = 304.8 mm, 1 inch = 25.4 mm) and are limited to 26 feet (7925 mm) and less.

From the Uniform Building Code, ©1997, ICBO

TABLE 23-IV-V-1—VALUES FOR JOISTS AND RAFTERS—VISUALLY GRADED LUMBER
For Use in Tables 23-IV-J-1 through 23-IV-R-12 and Chapter 23, Division V only.

These "F_b" values are for use where repetitive members are spaced not more than 24 inches (457 mm). For wider spacing, the "F_b" values shall be reduced 13 percent.

Values for surfaced dry or surfaced green lumber apply at 19 percent maximum moisture content in use.

SPECIES AND GRADE	SIZE (Inches) × 25.4 for mm	DESIGN VALUE IN BENDING "F_b" psi			MODULUS OF ELASTICITY "E" psi	GRADING RULES AGENCY
		Normal Duration	Snow Loading	7-day Loading		
		× 0.00689 for N/mm²				
ASPEN						
Select Structural	2 × 4	1,510	1,735	1,885	1,100,000	
No. 1		1,080	1,240	1,350	1,100,000	
No. 2		1,035	1,190	1,295	1,000,000	
No. 3		605	695	755	900,000	
Stud		600	690	750	900,000	
Construction		805	925	1,005	900,000	
Standard		430	495	540	900,000	
Utility		200	230	250	800,000	
Select Structural	2 × 6	1,310	1,505	1,635	1,100,000	
No. 1		935	1,075	1,170	1,100,000	
No. 2		895	1,030	1,120	1,000,000	
No. 3		525	600	655	900,000	
Stud		545	630	685	900,000	NELMA
Select Structural	2 × 8	1,210	1,390	1,510	1,100,000	NSLB
No. 1		865	990	1,080	1,100,000	WWPA
No. 2		830	950	1,035	1,000,000	
No. 3		485	555	605	900,000	
Select Structural	2 × 10	1,105	1,275	1,385	1,100,000	
No. 1		790	910	990	1,100,000	
No. 2		760	875	950	1,000,000	
No. 3		445	510	555	900,000	
Select Structural	2 × 12	1,005	1,155	1,260	1,100,000	
No. 1		720	825	900	1,100,000	
No. 2		690	795	865	1,000,000	
No. 3		405	465	505	900,000	
BEECH-BIRCH-HICKORY						
Select Structural	2 × 4	2,500	2,875	3,125	1,700,000	
No. 1		1,810	2,085	2,265	1,600,000	
No. 2		1,725	1,985	2,155	1,500,000	
No. 3		990	1,140	1,240	1,300,000	
Stud		980	1,125	1,225	1,300,000	
Construction		1,325	1,520	1,655	1,400,000	
Standard		750	860	935	1,300,000	
Utility		345	395	430	1,200,000	
Select Structural	2 × 6	2,170	2,495	2,710	1,700,000	
No. 1		1,570	1,805	1,960	1,600,000	
No. 2		1,495	1,720	1,870	1,500,000	
No. 3		860	990	1,075	1,300,000	
Stud		890	1,025	1,115	1,300,000	NELMA
Select Structural	2 × 8	2,000	2,300	2,500	1,700,000	
No. 1		1,450	1,665	1,810	1,600,000	
No. 2		1,380	1,585	1,725	1,500,000	
No. 3		795	915	990	1,300,000	
Select Structural	2 × 10	1,835	2,110	2,295	1,700,000	
No. 1		1,330	1,525	1,660	1,600,000	
No. 2		1,265	1,455	1,580	1,500,000	
No. 3		725	835	910	1,300,000	
Select Structural	2 × 12	1,670	1,920	2,085	1,700,000	
No. 1		1,210	1,390	1,510	1,600,000	
No. 2		1,150	1,325	1,440	1,500,000	
No. 3		660	760	825	1,300,000	

(Continued)

TABLE 23-IV-V-1—VALUES FOR JOISTS AND RAFTERS—VISUALLY GRADED LUMBER—(Continued)

SPECIES AND GRADE	SIZE (Inches) × 25.4 for mm	DESIGN VALUE IN BENDING "F_b" psi			MODULUS OF ELASTICITY "E" psi	GRADING RULES AGENCY
		Normal Duration	Snow Loading	7-day Loading		
		× 0.00689 for N/mm²				
COTTONWOOD						
Select Structural	2 × 4	1,510	1,735	1,885	1,200,000	
No. 1		1,080	1,240	1,350	1,200,000	
No. 2		1,080	1,240	1,350	1,100,000	
No. 3		605	695	755	1,000,000	
Stud		600	690	750	1,000,000	
Construction		805	925	1,005	1,000,000	
Standard		460	530	575	900,000	
Utility		200	230	250	900,000	
Select Structural	2 × 6	1,310	1,505	1,635	1,200,000	
No. 1		935	1,075	1,170	1,200,000	
No. 2		935	1,075	1,170	1,100,000	
No. 3		525	600	655	1,000,000	
Stud		545	630	685	1,000,000	NSLB
Select Structural	2 × 8	1,210	1,390	1,510	1,200,000	
No. 1		865	990	1,080	1,200,000	
No. 2		865	990	1,080	1,100,000	
No. 3		485	555	605	1,000,000	
Select Structural	2 × 10	1,105	1,275	1,385	1,200,000	
No. 1		790	910	990	1,200,000	
No. 2		790	910	990	1,100,000	
No. 3		445	510	555	1,000,000	
Select Structural	2 × 12	1,005	1,155	1,260	1,200,000	
No. 1		720	825	900	1,200,000	
No. 2		720	825	900	1,100,000	
No. 3		405	465	505	1,000,000	
DOUGLAS FIR-LARCH						
Select Structural	2 × 4	2,500	2,875	3,125	1,900,000	
No. 1 and better		1,985	2,280	2,480	1,800,000	
No. 1		1,725	1,985	2,155	1,700,000	
No. 2		1,510	1,735	1,885	1,600,000	
No. 3		865	990	1,080	1,400,000	
Stud		855	980	1,065	1,400,000	
Construction		1,150	1,325	1,440	1,500,000	
Standard		635	725	790	1,400,000	
Utility		315	365	395	1,300,000	
Select Structural	2 × 6	2,170	2,495	2,710	1,900,000	
No. 1 and better		1,720	1,975	2,150	1,800,000	
No. 1		1,495	1,720	1,870	1,700,000	
No. 2		1,310	1,505	1,635	1,600,000	
No. 3		750	860	935	1,400,000	
Stud		775	895	970	1,400,000	WCLIB WWPA
Select Structural	2 × 8	2,000	2,300	2,500	1,900,000	
No. 1 and better		1,585	1,825	1,985	1,800,000	
No. 1		1,380	1,585	1,725	1,700,000	
No. 2		1,210	1,390	1,510	1,600,000	
No. 3		690	795	865	1,400,000	
Select Structural	2 × 10	1,835	2,110	2,295	1,900,000	
No. 1 and better		1,455	1,675	1,820	1,800,000	
No. 1		1,265	1,455	1,580	1,700,000	
No. 2		1,105	1,275	1,385	1,600,000	
No. 3		635	725	790	1,400,000	
Select Structural	2 × 12	1,670	1,920	2,085	1,900,000	
No. 1 and better		1,325	1,520	1,655	1,800,000	
No. 1		1,150	1,325	1,440	1,700,000	
No. 2		1,005	1,155	1,260	1,600,000	
No. 3		575	660	720	1,400,000	

(Continued)

TABLE 23-IV-V-1—VALUES FOR JOISTS AND RAFTERS—VISUALLY GRADED LUMBER—(Continued)

SPECIES AND GRADE	SIZE (inches) × 25.4 for mm	DESIGN VALUE IN BENDING "F_b" psi			MODULUS OF ELASTICITY "E" psi	GRADING RULES AGENCY
		Normal Duration	Snow Loading	7-day Loading		
		× 0.00689 for N/mm²				
DOUGLAS FIR-LARCH (North)						
Select Structural		2,245	2,580	2,805	1,900,000	
No. 1/No. 2		1,425	1,635	1,780	1,600,000	
No. 3		820	940	1,025	1,400,000	
Stud	2 × 4	820	945	1,030	1,400,000	
Construction		1,095	1,255	1,365	1,500,000	
Standard		605	695	755	1,400,000	
Utility		290	330	360	1,300,000	
Select Structural		1,945	2,235	2,430	1,900,000	
No. 1/No. 2	2 × 6	1,235	1,420	1,540	1,600,000	
No. 3		710	815	890	1,400,000	
Stud		750	860	935	1,400,000	NLGA
Select Structural		1,795	2,065	2,245	1,900,000	
No. 1/No. 2	2 × 8	1,140	1,310	1,425	1,600,000	
No. 3		655	755	820	1,400,000	
Select Structural		1,645	1,890	2,055	1,900,000	
No. 1/No. 2	2 × 10	1,045	1,200	1,305	1,600,000	
No. 3		600	690	750	1,400,000	
Select Structural		1,495	1,720	1,870	1,900,000	
No. 1/No. 2	2 × 12	950	1,090	1,185	1,600,000	
No. 3		545	630	685	1,400,000	
DOUGLAS FIR (South)						
Select Structural		2,245	2,580	2,805	1,400,000	
No. 1		1,555	1,785	1,940	1,300,000	
No. 2		1,425	1,635	1,780	1,200,000	
No. 3		820	940	1,025	1,100,000	
Stud	2 × 4	820	945	1,030	1,100,000	
Construction		1,065	1,225	1,330	1,200,000	
Standard		605	695	755	1,100,000	
Utility		290	330	360	1,000,000	
Select Structural		1,945	2,235	2,430	1,400,000	
No. 1		1,345	1,545	1,680	1,300,000	
No. 2	2 × 6	1,235	1,420	1,540	1,200,000	
No. 3		710	815	890	1,100,000	
Stud		750	860	935	1,100,000	WWPA
Select Structural		1,795	2,065	2,245	1,400,000	
No. 1	2 × 8	1,240	1,430	1,555	1,300,000	
No. 2		1,140	1,310	1,425	1,200,000	
No. 3		655	755	820	1,100,000	
Select Structural		1,645	1,890	2,055	1,400,000	
No. 1	2 × 10	1,140	1,310	1,425	1,300,000	
No. 2		1,045	1,200	1,305	1,200,000	
No. 3		600	690	750	1,100,000	
Select Structural		1,495	1,720	1,870	1,400,000	
No. 1	2 × 12	1,035	1,190	1,295	1,300,000	
No. 2		950	1,090	1,185	1,200,000	
No. 3		545	630	685	1,100,000	

(Continued)

TABLE 23-IV-V-1—VALUES FOR JOISTS AND RAFTERS—VISUALLY GRADED LUMBER—(Continued)

SPECIES AND GRADE	SIZE (Inches) × 25.4 for mm	Normal Duration	Snow Loading	7-day Loading	MODULUS OF ELASTICITY "E" psi	GRADING RULES AGENCY
		× 0.00689 for N/mm²				
EASTERN HEMLOCK—TAMARACK						
Select Structural	2 × 4	2,155	2,480	2,695	1,200,000	
No. 1		1,335	1,535	1,670	1,100,000	
No. 2		990	1,140	1,240	1,100,000	
No. 3		605	695	755	900,000	
Stud		570	655	710	900,000	
Construction		775	895	970	1,000,000	
Standard		430	495	540	900,000	
Utility		200	230	250	800,000	
Select Structural	2 × 6	1,870	2,150	2,335	1,200,000	
No. 1		1,160	1,330	1,450	1,100,000	
No. 2		860	990	1,075	1,100,000	
No. 3		525	600	655	900,000	
Stud		520	595	645	900,000	
Select Structural	2 × 8	1,725	1,985	2,155	1,200,000	NELMA NSLB
No. 1		1,070	1,230	1,335	1,100,000	
No. 2		795	915	990	1,100,000	
No. 3		485	555	605	900,000	
Select Structural	2 × 10	1,580	1,820	1,975	1,200,000	
No. 1		980	1,125	1,225	1,100,000	
No. 2		725	835	910	1,100,000	
No. 3		445	510	555	900,000	
Select Structural	2 × 12	1,440	1,655	1,795	1,200,000	
No. 1		890	1,025	1,115	1,100,000	
No. 2		660	760	825	1,100,000	
No. 3		405	465	505	900,000	
EASTERN SOFTWOODS						
Select Structural	2 × 4	2,155	2,480	2,695	1,200,000	
No. 1		1,335	1,535	1,670	1,100,000	
No. 2		990	1,140	1,240	1,100,000	
No. 3		605	695	755	900,000	
Stud		570	655	710	900,000	
Construction		775	895	970	1,000,000	
Standard		430	495	540	900,000	
Utility		200	230	250	800,000	
Select Structural	2 × 6	1,870	2,150	2,335	1,200,000	
No. 1		1,160	1,330	1,450	1,100,000	
No. 2		860	990	1,075	1,100,000	
No. 3		525	600	655	900,000	
Stud		520	595	645	900,000	
Select Structural	2 × 8	1,725	1,985	2,155	1,200,000	NELMA NSLB
No. 1		1,070	1,230	1,335	1,100,000	
No. 2		795	915	990	1,100,000	
No. 3		485	555	605	900,000	
Select Structural	2 × 10	1,580	1,820	1,975	1,200,000	
No. 1		980	1,125	1,225	1,100,000	
No. 2		725	835	910	1,100,000	
No. 3		445	510	555	900,000	
Select Structural	2 × 12	1,440	1,655	1,795	1,200,000	
No. 1		890	1,025	1,115	1,100,000	
No. 2		660	760	825	1,100,000	
No. 3		405	465	505	900,000	

(Continued)

TABLE 23-IV-V-1—VALUES FOR JOISTS AND RAFTERS—VISUALLY GRADED LUMBER—(Continued)

SPECIES AND GRADE	SIZE (inches) × 25.4 for mm	DESIGN VALUE IN BENDING "F_b" psi			MODULUS OF ELASTICITY "E" psi	GRADING RULES AGENCY
		Normal Duration	Snow Loading	7-day Loading		
		× 0.00689 for N/mm²				
EASTERN WHITE PINE						
Select Structural	2 × 4	2,155	2,480	2,695	1,200,000	
No. 1		1,335	1,535	1,670	1,100,000	
No. 2		990	1,140	1,240	1,100,000	
No. 3		605	695	755	900,000	
Stud		570	655	710	900,000	
Construction		775	895	970	1,000,000	
Standard		430	495	540	900,000	
Utility		200	230	250	800,000	
Select Structural	2 × 6	1,870	2,150	2,335	1,200,000	
No. 1		1,160	1,330	1,450	1,100,000	
No. 2		860	990	1,075	1,100,000	
No. 3		525	600	655	900,000	
Stud		520	595	645	900,000	NELMA NSLB
Select Structural	2 × 8	1,725	1,985	2,155	1,200,000	
No. 1		1,070	1,230	1,335	1,100,000	
No. 2		795	915	990	1,100,000	
No. 3		485	555	605	900,000	
Select Structural	2 × 10	1,580	1,820	1,975	1,200,000	
No. 1		980	1,125	1,225	1,100,000	
No. 2		725	835	910	1,100,000	
No. 3		445	510	555	900,000	
Select Structural	2 × 12	1,440	1,655	1,795	1,200,000	
No. 1		890	1,025	1,115	1,100,000	
No. 2		660	760	825	1,100,000	
No. 3		405	465	505	900,000	
HEM-FIR						
Select Structural	2 × 4	2,415	2,775	3,020	1,600,000	
No. 1 and better		1,810	2,085	2,265	1,500,000	
No. 1		1,640	1,885	2,050	1,500,000	
No. 2		1,465	1,685	1,835	1,300,000	
No. 3		865	990	1,080	1,200,000	
Stud		855	980	1,065	1,200,000	
Construction		1,120	1,290	1,400	1,300,000	
Standard		635	725	790	1,200,000	
Utility		290	330	360	1,100,000	
Select Structural	2 × 6	2,095	2,405	2,615	1,600,000	
No. 1 and better		1,570	1,805	1,960	1,500,000	
No. 1		1,420	1,635	1,775	1,500,000	
No. 2		1,270	1,460	1,590	1,300,000	
No. 3		750	860	935	1,200,000	
Stud		775	895	970	1,200,000	WCLIB WWPA
Select Structural	2 × 8	1,930	2,220	2,415	1,600,000	
No. 1 and better		1,450	1,665	1,810	1,500,000	
No. 1		1,310	1,510	1,640	1,500,000	
No. 2		1,175	1,350	1,465	1,300,000	
No. 3		690	795	865	1,200,000	
Select Structural	2 × 10	1,770	2,035	2,215	1,600,000	
No. 1 and better		1,330	1,525	1,660	1,500,000	
No. 1		1,200	1,380	1,500	1,500,000	
No. 2		1,075	1,235	1,345	1,300,000	
No. 3		635	725	790	1,200,000	
Select Structural	2 × 12	1,610	1,850	2,015	1,600,000	
No. 1 and better		1,210	1,390	1,510	1,500,000	
No. 1		1,095	1,255	1,365	1,500,000	
No. 2		980	1,125	1,220	1,300,000	
No. 3		575	660	720	1,200,000	

(Continued)

TABLE 23-IV-V-1—VALUES FOR JOISTS AND RAFTERS—VISUALLY GRADED LUMBER—(Continued)

SPECIES AND GRADE	SIZE (inches) × 25.4 for mm	DESIGN VALUE IN BENDING "F_b" psi			MODULUS OF ELASTICITY "E" psi	GRADING RULES AGENCY
		Normal Duration	Snow Loading	7-day Loading		
		× 0.00689 for N/mm²				
HEM-FIR (North)						
Select Structural		2,245	2,580	2,805	1,700,000	
No. 1/No. 2		1,725	1,985	2,155	1,600,000	
No. 3		990	1,140	1,240	1,400,000	
Stud	2 × 4	980	1,125	1,225	1,400,000	
Construction		1,325	1,520	1,655	1,500,000	
Standard		720	825	900	1,400,000	
Utility		345	395	430	1,300,000	
Select Structural		1,945	2,235	2,430	1,700,000	
No. 1/No. 2	2 × 6	1,495	1,720	1,870	1,600,000	
No. 3		860	990	1,075	1,400,000	
Stud		890	1,025	1,115	1,400,000	NLGA
Select Structural		1,795	2,065	2,245	1,700,000	
No. 1/No. 2	2 × 8	1,380	1,585	1,725	1,600,000	
No. 3		795	915	990	1,400,000	
Select Structural		1,645	1,890	2,055	1,700,000	
No. 1/No. 2	2 × 10	1,265	1,455	1,580	1,600,000	
No. 3		725	835	910	1,400,000	
Select Structural		1,495	1,720	1,870	1,700,000	
No. 1/No. 2	2 × 12	1,150	1,325	1,440	1,600,000	
No. 3		660	760	825	1,400,000	
MIXED MAPLE						
Select Structural		1,725	1,985	2,155	1,300,000	
No. 1		1,250	1,440	1,565	1,200,000	
No. 2		1,210	1,390	1,510	1,100,000	
No. 3		690	795	865	1,000,000	
Stud	2 × 4	695	800	870	1,000,000	
Construction		920	1,060	1,150	1,100,000	
Standard		520	595	645	1,000,000	
Utility		260	300	325	900,000	
Select Structural		1,495	1,720	1,870	1,300,000	
No. 1		1,085	1,245	1,355	1,200,000	
No. 2	2 × 6	1,045	1,205	1,310	1,100,000	
No. 3		600	690	750	1,000,000	
Stud		635	725	790	1,000,000	NELMA
Select Structural		1,380	1,585	1,725	1,300,000	
No. 1	2 × 8	1,000	1,150	1,250	1,200,000	
No. 2		965	1,110	1,210	1,100,000	
No. 3		550	635	690	1,000,000	
Select Structural		1,265	1,455	1,580	1,300,000	
No. 1	2 × 10	915	1,055	1,145	1,200,000	
No. 2		885	1,020	1,105	1,100,000	
No. 3		505	580	635	1,000,000	
Select Structural		1,150	1,325	1,440	1,300,000	
No. 1	2 × 12	835	960	1,040	1,200,000	
No. 2		805	925	1,005	1,100,000	
No. 3		460	530	575	1,000,000	
MIXED OAK						
Select Structural		1,985	2,280	2,480	1,100,000	
No. 1		1,425	1,635	1,780	1,000,000	
No. 2		1,380	1,585	1,725	900,000	
No. 3		820	940	1,025	800,000	
Stud	2 × 4	790	910	990	800,000	NELMA
Construction		1,065	1,225	1,330	900,000	
Standard		605	695	755	800,000	
Utility		290	330	360	800,000	

(Continued)

TABLE 23-IV-V-1—VALUES FOR JOISTS AND RAFTERS—VISUALLY GRADED LUMBER—(Continued)

SPECIES AND GRADE	SIZE (Inches) × 25.4 for mm	DESIGN VALUE IN BENDING "F_b" psi			MODULUS OF ELASTICITY "E" psi	GRADING RULES AGENCY
		Normal Duration	Snow Loading	7-day Loading		
			× 0.00689 for N/mm²			
MIXED OAK—(continued)						
Select Structural		1,720	1,975	2,150	1,100,000	
No. 1		1,235	1,420	1,540	1,000,000	
No. 2	2 × 6	1,195	1,375	1,495	900,000	
No. 3		710	815	890	800,000	
Stud		720	825	900	800,000	
Select Structural		1,585	1,825	1,985	1,100,000	
No. 1		1,140	1,310	1,425	1,000,000	
No. 2	2 × 8	1,105	1,270	1,380	900,000	
No. 3		655	755	820	800,000	NELMA
Select Structural		1,455	1,675	1,820	1,100,000	
No. 1		1,045	1,200	1,305	1,000,000	
No. 2	2 × 10	1,010	1,165	1,265	900,000	
No. 3		600	690	750	800,000	
Select Structural		1,325	1,520	1,655	1,100,000	
No. 1		950	1,090	1,185	1,000,000	
No. 2	2 × 12	920	1,060	1,150	900,000	
No. 3		545	630	685	800,000	
MIXED SOUTHERN PINE						
Select Structural		2,360	2,710	2,950	1,600,000	
No. 1		1,670	1,920	2,080	1,500,000	
No. 2		1,500	1,720	1,870	1,400,000	
No. 3		865	990	1,080	1,200,000	
Stud	2 × 4	890	1,020	1,110	1,200,000	
Construction		1,150	1,320	1,440	1,300,000	
Standard		635	725	790	1,200,000	
Utility		315	365	395	1,100,000	
Select Structural		2,130	2,450	2,660	1,600,000	
No. 1		1,490	1,720	1,870	1,500,000	
No. 2	2 × 6	1,320	1,520	1,650	1,400,000	
No. 3		775	895	970	1,200,000	
Stud		775	895	970	1,200,000	SPIB
Select Structural		2,010	2,310	2,520	1,600,000	
No. 1		1,380	1,590	1,720	1,500,000	
No. 2	2 × 8	1,210	1,390	1,510	1,400,000	
No. 3		720	825	900	1,200,000	
Select Structural		1,730	1,980	2,160	1,600,000	
No. 1		1,210	1,390	1,510	1,500,000	
No. 2	2 × 10	1,060	1,220	1,330	1,400,000	
No. 3		605	695	755	1,200,000	
Select Structural		1,610	1,850	2,010	1,600,000	
No. 1		1,120	1,290	1,400	1,500,000	
No. 2	2 × 12	1,010	1,160	1,260	1,400,000	
No. 3		575	660	720	1,200,000	

(Continued)

TABLE 23-IV-V-1—VALUES FOR JOISTS AND RAFTERS—VISUALLY GRADED LUMBER—(Continued)

SPECIES AND GRADE	SIZE (Inches) × 25.4 for mm	DESIGN VALUE IN BENDING "F_b" psi			MODULUS OF ELASTICITY "E" psi	GRADING RULES AGENCY
		Normal Duration	Snow Loading	7-day Loading		
		× 0.00689 for N/mm²				
NORTHERN RED OAK						
Select Structural	2 × 4	2,415	2,775	3,020	1,400,000	
No. 1		1,725	1,985	2,155	1,400,000	
No. 2		1,680	1,935	2,100	1,300,000	
No. 3		950	1,090	1,185	1,200,000	
Stud		950	1,090	1,185	1,200,000	
Construction		1,265	1,455	1,580	1,200,000	
Standard		720	825	900	1,100,000	
Utility		345	395	430	1,000,000	
Select Structural	2 × 6	2,095	2,405	2,615	1,400,000	
No. 1		1,495	1,720	1,870	1,400,000	
No. 2		1,460	1,675	1,820	1,300,000	
No. 3		820	945	1,030	1,200,000	
Stud		865	990	1,080	1,200,000	NELMA
Select Structural	2 × 8	1,930	2,220	2,415	1,400,000	
No. 1		1,380	1,585	1,725	1,400,000	
No. 2		1,345	1,545	1,680	1,300,000	
No. 3		760	875	950	1,200,000	
Select Structural	2 × 10	1,770	2,035	2,215	1,400,000	
No. 1		1,265	1,455	1,580	1,400,000	
No. 2		1,235	1,420	1,540	1,300,000	
No. 3		695	800	870	1,200,000	
Select Structural	2 × 12	1,610	1,850	2,015	1,400,000	
No. 1		1,150	1,325	1,440	1,400,000	
No. 2		1,120	1,290	1,400	1,300,000	
No. 3		635	725	790	1,200,000	
NORTHERN SPECIES						
Select Structural	2 × 4	1,640	1,885	2,050	1,100,000	
No. 1/No. 2		990	1,140	1,240	1,100,000	
No. 3		605	695	755	1,000,000	
Stud		570	655	710	1,000,000	
Construction		775	895	970	1,000,000	
Standard		430	495	540	900,000	
Utility		200	230	250	900,000	
Select Structural	2 × 6	1,420	1,635	1,775	1,100,000	
No. 1/No. 2		860	990	1,075	1,100,000	
No. 3		525	600	655	1,000,000	
Stud		520	595	645	1,000,000	NLGA
Select Structural	2 × 8	1,310	1,510	1,640	1,100,000	
No. 1/No. 2		795	915	990	1,100,000	
No. 3		485	555	605	1,000,000	
Select Structural	2 × 10	1,200	1,380	1,500	1,100,000	
No. 1/No. 2		725	835	910	1,100,000	
No. 3		445	510	555	1,000,000	
Select Structural	2 × 12	1,095	1,255	1,365	1,100,000	
No. 1/No. 2		660	760	825	1,100,000	
No. 3		405	465	505	1,000,000	

(Continued)

TABLE 23-IV-V-1—VALUES FOR JOISTS AND RAFTERS—VISUALLY GRADED LUMBER—(Continued)

SPECIES AND GRADE	SIZE (inches) × 25.4 for mm	DESIGN VALUE IN BENDING "F_b" psi			MODULUS OF ELASTICITY "E" psi	GRADING RULES AGENCY
		Normal Duration	Snow Loading	7-day Loading		
		× 0.00689 for N/mm²				
NORTHERN WHITE CEDAR						
Select Structural	2 × 4	1,335	1,535	1,670	800,000	
No. 1		990	1,140	1,240	700,000	
No. 2		950	1,090	1,185	700,000	
No. 3		560	645	700	600,000	
Stud		540	620	670	600,000	
Construction		720	825	900	700,000	
Standard		405	465	505	600,000	
Utility		200	230	250	600,000	
Select Structural	2 × 6	1,160	1,330	1,450	800,000	
No. 1		860	990	1,075	700,000	
No. 2		820	945	1,030	700,000	
No. 3		485	560	605	600,000	
Stud		490	560	610	600,000	NELMA
Select Structural	2 × 8	1,070	1,230	1,335	800,000	
No. 1		795	915	990	700,000	
No. 2		760	875	950	700,000	
No. 3		450	515	560	600,000	
Select Structural	2 × 10	980	1,125	1,225	800,000	
No. 1		725	835	910	700,000	
No. 2		695	800	870	700,000	
No. 3		410	475	515	600,000	
Select Structural	2 × 12	890	1,025	1,115	800,000	
No. 1		660	760	825	700,000	
No. 2		635	725	790	700,000	
No. 3		375	430	465	600,000	
RED MAPLE						
Select Structural	2 × 4	2,245	2,580	2,805	1,700,000	
No. 1		1,595	1,835	1,995	1,600,000	
No. 2		1,555	1,785	1,940	1,500,000	
No. 3		905	1,040	1,130	1,300,000	
Stud		885	1,020	1,105	1,300,000	
Construction		1,210	1,390	1,510	1,400,000	
Standard		660	760	825	1,300,000	
Utility		315	365	395	1,200,000	
Select Structural	2 × 6	1,945	2,235	2,430	1,700,000	
No. 1		1,385	1,590	1,730	1,600,000	
No. 2		1,345	1,545	1,680	1,500,000	
No. 3		785	905	980	1,300,000	
Stud		805	925	1,005	1,300,000	NELMA
Select Structural	2 × 8	1,795	2,065	2,245	1,700,000	
No. 1		1,275	1,470	1,595	1,600,000	
No. 2		1,240	1,430	1,555	1,500,000	
No. 3		725	835	905	1,300,000	
Select Structural	2 × 10	1,645	1,890	2,055	1,700,000	
No. 1		1,170	1,345	1,465	1,600,000	
No. 2		1,140	1,310	1,425	1,500,000	
No. 3		665	765	830	1,300,000	
Select Structural	2 × 12	1,495	1,720	1,870	1,700,000	
No. 1		1,065	1,225	1,330	1,600,000	
No. 2		1,035	1,190	1,295	1,500,000	
No. 3		605	695	755	1,300,000	

(Continued)

TABLE 23-IV-V-1—VALUES FOR JOISTS AND RAFTERS—VISUALLY GRADED LUMBER—(Continued)

SPECIES AND GRADE	SIZE (Inches) × 25.4 for mm	DESIGN VALUE IN BENDING "F_b" psi			MODULUS OF ELASTICITY "E" psi	GRADING RULES AGENCY
		Normal Duration	Snow Loading	7-day Loading		
		× 0.00689 for N/mm²				
RED OAK						
Select Structural	2 × 4	1,985	2,280	2,480	1,400,000	
No. 1		1,425	1,635	1,780	1,300,000	
No. 2		1,380	1,585	1,725	1,200,000	
No. 3		820	940	1,025	1,100,000	
Stud		790	910	990	1,100,006	
Construction		1,065	1,225	1,330	1,200,000	
Standard		605	695	755	1,100,000	
Utility		290	330	360	1,000,000	
Select Structural	2 × 6	1,720	1,975	2,150	1,400,000	
No. 1		1,235	1,420	1,540	1,300,000	
No. 2		1,195	1,375	1,495	1,200,000	
No. 3		710	815	890	1,100,000	
Stud		720	825	900	1,100,000	NELMA
Select Structural	2 × 8	1,585	1,825	1,985	1,400,000	
No. 1		1,140	1,310	1,425	1,300,000	
No. 2		1,105	1,270	1,380	1,200,000	
No. 3		655	755	820	1,100,000	
Select Structural	2 × 10	1,455	1,675	1,820	1,400,000	
No. 1		1,045	1,200	1,305	1,300,000	
No. 2		1,010	1,165	1,265	1,200,000	
No. 3		600	690	750	1,100,000	
Select Structural	2 × 12	1,325	1,520	1,655	1,400,000	
No. 1		950	1,090	1,185	1,300,000	
No. 2		920	1,060	1,150	1,200,000	
No. 3		545	630	685	1,100,000	
REDWOOD						
Clear Structural	2 × 4	3,020	3,470	3,775	1,400,000	
Select Structural		2,330	2,680	2,910	1,400,000	
Select Structural, open grain		1,900	2,180	2,370	1,100,000	
No. 1		1,680	1,935	2,100	1,300,000	
No. 1, open grain		1,335	1,535	1,670	1,100,000	
No. 2		1,595	1,835	1,995	1,200,000	
No. 2, open grain		1,250	1,440	1,565	1,000,000	
No. 3		905	1,040	1,130	1,100,000	
No. 3, open grain		735	845	915	900,000	
Stud		725	835	910	900,000	
Construction		950	1,090	1,185	900,000	
Standard		520	595	645	900,000	RIS
Utility		260	300	325	800,000	
Clear Structural	2 × 6	2,615	3,010	3,270	1,400,000	
Select Structural		2,020	2,320	2,525	1,400,000	
Select Structural, open grain		1,645	1,890	2,055	1,100,000	
No. 1		1,460	1,675	1,820	1,300,000	
No. 1, open grain		1,160	1,330	1,450	1,100,000	
No. 2		1,385	1,590	1,730	1,200,000	
No. 2, open grain		1,085	1,245	1,355	1,000,000	
No. 3		785	905	980	1,100,000	
No. 3, open grain		635	730	795	900,000	
Stud		660	760	825	900,000	

(Continued)

TABLE 23-IV-V-1—VALUES FOR JOISTS AND RAFTERS—VISUALLY GRADED LUMBER—(Continued)

SPECIES AND GRADE	SIZE (inches) × 25.4 for mm	DESIGN VALUE IN BENDING "F_b" psi			MODULUS OF ELASTICITY "E" psi	GRADING RULES AGENCY
		Normal Duration	Snow Loading	7-day Loading		
		× 0.00689 for N/mm²				
REDWOOD—(continued)						
Clear Structural	2 × 8	2,415	2,775	3,020	1,400,000	
Select Structural		1,865	2,140	2,330	1,400,000	
Select Structural, open grain		1,520	1,745	1,900	1,100,000	
No. 1		1,345	1,545	1,680	1,300,000	
No. 1, open grain		1,070	1,230	1,335	1,100,000	
No. 2		1,275	1,470	1,595	1,200,000	
No. 2, open grain		1,000	1,150	1,250	1,000,000	
No. 3		725	835	905	1,100,000	
No. 3, open grain		585	675	735	900,000	
Clear Structural	2 × 10	2,215	2,545	2,765	1,400,000	
Select Structural		1,710	1,965	2,135	1,400,000	
Select Structural, open grain		1,390	1,600	1,740	1,100,000	
No. 1		1,235	1,420	1,540	1,300,000	
No. 1, open grain		980	1,125	1,225	1,100,000	RIS
No. 2		1,170	1,345	1,465	1,200,000	
No. 2, open grain		915	1,055	1,145	1,000,000	
No. 3		665	765	830	1,100,000	
No. 3, open grain		540	620	670	900,000	
Clear Structural	2 × 12	2,015	2,315	2,515	1,400,000	
Select Structural		1,555	1,785	1,940	1,400,000	
Select Structural, open grain		1,265	1,455	1,580	1,100,000	
No. 1		1,120	1,290	1,400	1,300,000	
No. 1, open grain		890	1,025	1,115	1,100,000	
No. 2		1,065	1,225	1,330	1,200,000	
No. 2, open grain		835	960	1,040	1,000,000	
No. 3		605	695	755	1,100,000	
No. 3, open grain		490	560	610	900,000	
SOUTHERN PINE						
Dense Select Structural	2 × 4	3,510	4,030	4,380	1,900,000	
Select Structural		3,280	3,770	4,100	1,800,000	
Non-Dense Select Structural		3,050	3,500	3,810	1,700,000	
No. 1 Dense		2,300	2,650	2,880	1,800,000	
No. 1		2,130	2,450	2,660	1,700,000	
No. 1 Non-Dense		1,950	2,250	2,440	1,600,000	
No. 2 Dense		1,960	2,250	2,440	1,700,000	
No. 2		1,720	1,980	2,160	1,600,000	SPIB
No. 2 Non-Dense		1,550	1,790	1,940	1,400,000	
No. 3		980	1,120	1,220	1,400,000	
Stud		1,010	1,160	1,260	1,400,000	
Construction		1,270	1,450	1,580	1,500,000	
Standard		720	825	900	1,300,000	
Utility		345	395	430	1,300,000	

(Continued)

TABLE 23-IV-V-1—VALUES FOR JOISTS AND RAFTERS—VISUALLY GRADED LUMBER—(Continued)

SPECIES AND GRADE	SIZE (inches) × 25.4 for mm	DESIGN VALUE IN BENDING "F_b" psi × 0.00689 for N/mm²			MODULUS OF ELASTICITY "E" psi	GRADING RULES AGENCY
		Normal Duration	Snow Loading	7-day Loading		
SOUTHERN PINE—(continued)						
Dense Select Structural	2 × 6	3,100	3,570	3,880	1,900,000	
Select Structural		2,930	3,370	3,670	1,800,000	
Non-Dense Select Structural		2,700	3,110	3,380	1,700,000	
No. 1 Dense		2,010	2,310	2,520	1,800,000	
No. 1		1,900	2,180	2,370	1,700,000	
No. 1 Non-Dense		1,720	1,980	2,160	1,600,000	
No. 2 Dense		1,670	1,920	2,080	1,700,000	
No. 2		1,440	1,650	1,800	1,600,000	
No. 2 Non-Dense		1,320	1,520	1,650	1,400,000	
No. 3		865	990	1,080	1,400,000	
Stud		890	1,020	1,110	1,400,000	
Dense Select Structural	2 × 8	2,820	3,240	3,520	1,900,000	
Select Structural		2,650	3,040	3,310	1,800,000	
Non-Dense Select Structural		2,420	2,780	3,020	1,700,000	
No. 1 Dense		1,900	2,180	2,370	1,800,000	
No. 1		1,730	1,980	2,160	1,700,000	
No. 1 Non-Dense		1,550	1,790	1,940	1,600,000	
No. 2 Dense		1,610	1,850	2,010	1,700,000	
No. 2		1,380	1,590	1,720	1,600,000	
No. 2 Non-Dense		1,260	1,450	1,580	1,400,000	
No. 3		805	925	1,010	1,400,000	
Dense Select Structural	2 × 10	2,470	2,840	3,090	1,900,000	SPIB
Select Structural		2,360	2,710	2,950	1,800,000	
Non-Dense Select Structural		2,130	2,450	2,660	1,700,000	
No. 1 Dense		1,670	1,920	2,080	1,800,000	
No. 1		1,500	1,720	1,870	1,700,000	
No. 1 Non-Dense		1,380	1,590	1,730	1,600,000	
No. 2 Dense		1,380	1,590	1,730	1,700,000	
No. 2		1,210	1,390	1,510	1,600,000	
No. 2 Non-Dense		1,090	1,260	1,370	1,400,000	
No. 3		690	795	865	1,400,000	
Dense Select Structural	2 × 12	2,360	2,710	2,950	1,900,000	
Select Structural		2,190	2,510	2,730	1,800,000	
Non-Dense Select Structural		2,010	2,310	2,520	1,700,000	
No. 1 Dense		1,550	1,790	1,940	1,800,000	
No. 1		1,440	1,650	1,800	1,700,000	
No. 1 Non-Dense		1,320	1,520	1,650	1,600,000	
No. 2 Dense		1,320	1,520	1,650	1,700,000	
No. 2		1,120	1,290	1,400	1,600,000	
No. 2 Non-Dense		1,040	1,190	1,290	1,400,000	
No. 3		660	760	825	1,400,000	

(Continued)

TABLE 23-IV-V-1—VALUES FOR JOISTS AND RAFTERS—VISUALLY GRADED LUMBER—(Continued)

SPECIES AND GRADE	SIZE (inches) ×25.4 for mm	Normal Duration	Snow Loading	7-day Loading	MODULUS OF ELASTICITY "E" psi	GRADING RULES AGENCY
		DESIGN VALUE IN BENDING "F_b" psi				
		×0.00689 for N/mm²				
SPRUCE-PINE-FIR						
Select Structural		2,155	2,480	2,695	1,500,000	
No. 1/No. 2		1,510	1,735	1,885	1,400,000	
No. 3		865	990	1,080	1,200,000	
Stud	2 × 4	855	980	1,065	1,200,000	
Construction		1,120	1,290	1,400	1,300,000	
Standard		635	725	790	1,200,000	
Utility		290	330	360	1,100,000	
Select Structural		1,870	2,150	2,335	1,500,000	
No. 1/No. 2	2 × 6	1,310	1,505	1,635	1,400,000	
No. 3		750	860	935	1,200,000	
Stud		775	895	970	1,200,000	NLGA
Select Structural		1,725	1,985	2,155	1,500,000	
No. 1/No. 2	2 × 8	1,210	1,390	1,510	1,400,000	
No. 3		690	795	865	1,200,000	
Select Structural		1,580	1,820	1,975	1,500,000	
No. 1/No. 2	2 × 10	1,105	1,275	1,385	1,400,000	
No. 3		635	725	790	1,200,000	
Select Structural		1,440	1,655	1,795	1,500,000	
No. 1/No. 2	2 × 12	1,005	1,155	1,260	1,400,000	
No. 3		575	660	720	1,200,000	
SPRUCE-PINE-FIR (South)						
Select Structural		2,245	2,580	2,805	1,300,000	
No. 1		1,465	1,685	1,835	1,200,000	
No. 2		1,295	1,490	1,615	1,100,000	
No. 3		735	845	915	1,000,000	
Stud	2 × 4	725	835	910	1,000,000	
Construction		980	1,125	1,220	1,000,000	
Standard		545	630	685	900,000	
Utility		260	300	325	900,000	
Select Structural		1,945	2,235	2,430	1,300,000	
No. 1		1,270	1,460	1,590	1,200,000	
No. 2	2 × 6	1,120	1,290	1,400	1,100,000	
No. 3		635	730	795	1,000,000	
Stud		660	760	825	1,000,000	NELMA NSLB WCLIB WWPA
Select Structural		1,795	2,065	2,245	1,300,000	
No. 1		1,175	1,350	1,465	1,200,000	
No. 2	2 × 8	1,035	1,190	1,295	1,100,000	
No. 3		585	675	735	1,000,000	
Select Structural		1,645	1,890	2,055	1,300,000	
No. 1		1,075	1,235	1,345	1,200,000	
No. 2	2 × 10	950	1,090	1,185	1,100,000	
No. 3		540	620	670	1,000,000	
Select Structural		1,495	1,720	1,870	1,300,000	
No. 1		980	1,125	1,220	1,200,000	
No. 2	2 × 12	865	990	1,080	1,100,000	
No. 3		490	560	610	1,000,000	
WESTERN CEDARS						
Select Structural		1,725	1,985	2,155	1,100,000	
No. 1		1,250	1,440	1,565	1,000,000	
No. 2		1,210	1,390	1,510	1,000,000	
No. 3		690	795	865	900,000	
Stud	2 × 4	695	800	870	900,000	WCLIB WWPA
Construction		920	1,060	1,150	900,000	
Standard		520	595	645	800,000	
Utility		260	300	325	800,000	

(Continued)

TABLE 23-IV-V-1—VALUES FOR JOISTS AND RAFTERS—VISUALLY GRADED LUMBER—(Continued)

SPECIES AND GRADE	SIZE (Inches) × 25.4 for mm	DESIGN VALUE IN BENDING "F_b" psi			MODULUS OF ELASTICITY "E" psi	GRADING RULES AGENCY
		Normal Duration	Snow Loading	7-day Loading		
		× 0.00689 for N/mm²				
WESTERN CEDARS—(continued)						
Select Structural		1,495	1,720	1,870	1,100,000	
No. 1		1,085	1,245	1,355	1,000,000	
No. 2	2 × 6	1,045	1,205	1,310	1,000,000	
No. 3		600	690	750	900,000	
Stud		635	725	790	900,000	
Select Structural		1,380	1,585	1,725	1,100,000	
No. 1	2 × 8	1,000	1,150	1,250	1,000,000	
No. 2		965	1,110	1,210	1,000,000	
No. 3		550	635	690	900,000	WCLIB WWPA
Select Structural		1,265	1,455	1,580	1,100,000	
No. 1	2 × 10	915	1,055	1,145	1,000,000	
No. 2		885	1,020	1,105	1,000,000	
No. 3		505	580	635	900,000	
Select Structural		1,150	1,325	1,440	1,100,000	
No. 1	2 × 12	835	960	1,040	1,000,000	
No. 2		805	925	1,005	1,000,000	
No. 3		460	530	575	900,000	
WESTERN WOODS						
Select Structural		1,510	1,735	1,885	1,200,000	
No. 1		1,120	1,290	1,400	1,100,000	
No. 2		1,120	1,290	1,400	1,000,000	
No. 3		645	745	810	900,000	
Stud	2 × 4	635	725	790	900,000	
Construction		835	960	1,040	1,000,000	
Standard		460	530	575	900,000	
Utility		230	265	290	800,000	
Select Structural		1,310	1,505	1,635	1,200,000	
No. 1		970	1,120	1,215	1,100,000	
No. 2	2 × 6	970	1,120	1,215	1,000,000	
No. 3		560	645	700	900,000	
Stud		575	660	720	900,000	WCLIB WWPA
Select Structural		1,210	1,390	1,510	1,200,000	
No. 1	2 × 8	895	1,030	1,120	1,100,000	
No. 2		895	1,030	1,120	1,000,000	
No. 3		520	595	645	900,000	
Select Structural		1,105	1,275	1,385	1,200,000	
No. 1	2 × 10	820	945	1,030	1,100,000	
No. 2		820	945	1,030	1,000,000	
No. 3		475	545	595	900,000	
Select Structural		1,005	1,155	1,260	1,200,000	
No. 1	2 × 12	750	860	935	1,100,000	
No. 2		750	860	935	1,000,000	
No. 3		430	495	540	900,000	
WHITE OAK						
Select Structural		2,070	2,380	2,590	1,100,000	
No. 1		1,510	1,735	1,885	1,000,000	
No. 2		1,465	1,685	1,835	900,000	
No. 3		820	940	1,025	800,000	
Stud	2 × 4	820	945	1,030	800,000	NELMA
Construction		1,095	1,255	1,365	900,000	
Standard		605	695	755	800,000	
Utility		290	330	360	800,000	

(Continued)

TABLE 23-IV-V-1—VALUES FOR JOISTS AND RAFTERS—VISUALLY GRADED LUMBER—(Continued)

SPECIES AND GRADE	SIZE (inches) × 25.4 for mm	DESIGN VALUE IN BENDING "F_b" psi			MODULUS OF ELASTICITY "E" psi	GRADING RULES AGENCY
		Normal Duration	Snow Loading	7-day Loading		
			× 0.00689 for N/mm²			
WHITE OAK—(continued)						
Select Structural	2 × 6	1,795	2,065	2,245	1,100,000	
No. 1		1,310	1,505	1,635	1,000,000	
No. 2		1,270	1,460	1,590	900,000	
No. 3		710	815	890	800,000	
Stud		750	860	935	800,000	
Select Structural	2 × 8	1,655	1,905	2,070	1,100,000	
No. 1		1,210	1,390	1,510	1,000,000	
No. 2		1,175	1,350	1,465	900,000	
No. 3		655	755	820	800,000	NELMA
Select Structural	2 × 10	1,520	1,745	1,900	1,100,000	
No. 1		1,105	1,275	1,385	1,000,000	
No. 2		1,075	1,235	1,345	900,000	
No. 3		600	690	750	800,000	
Select Structural	2 × 12	1,380	1,585	1,725	1,100,000	
No. 1		1,005	1,155	1,260	1,000,000	
No. 2		980	1,125	1,220	900,000	
No. 3		545	630	685	800,000	
YELLOW POPLAR						
Select Structural	2 × 4	1,725	1,985	2,155	1,500,000	
No. 1		1,250	1,440	1,565	1,400,000	
No. 2		1,210	1,390	1,510	1,300,000	
No. 3		690	795	865	1,200,000	
Stud		695	800	870	1,200,000	
Construction		920	1,060	1,150	1,300,000	
Standard		520	595	645	1,100,000	
Utility		230	265	290	1,100,000	
Select Structural	2 × 6	1,495	1,720	1,870	1,500,000	
No. 1		1,085	1,245	1,355	1,400,000	
No. 2		1,045	1,205	1,310	1,300,000	
No. 3		600	690	750	1,200,000	
Stud		635	725	790	1,200,000	NSLB
Select Structural	2 × 8	1,380	1,585	1,725	1,500,000	
No. 1		1,000	1,150	1,250	1,400,000	
No. 2		965	1,110	1,210	1,300,000	
No. 3		550	635	690	1,200,000	
Select Structural	2 × 10	1,265	1,455	1,580	1,500,000	
No. 1		915	1,055	1,145	1,400,000	
No. 2		885	1,020	1,105	1,300,000	
No. 3		505	580	635	1,200,000	
Select Structural	2 × 12	1,150	1,325	1,440	1,500,000	
No. 1		835	960	1,040	1,400,000	
No. 2		805	925	1,005	1,300,000	
No. 3		460	530	575	1,200,000	

TABLE 5-A—EXTERIOR WALL AND OPENING PROTECTION BASED ON LOCATION ON PROPERTY FOR ALL CONSTRUCTION TYPES[1,2,3]
For exceptions, see Section 503.4.

OCCUPANCY GROUP[4]	CONSTRUCTION TYPE	Bearing	Nonbearing	OPENINGS[5]
		EXTERIOR WALLS		
		Distances are measured to property lines (see Section 503).		
		× 304.8 for mm		
A-1	I-F.R. II-F.R.	Four-hour N/C	Four-hour N/C less than 5 feet Two-hour N/C less than 20 feet One-hour N/C less than 40 feet NR, N/C elsewhere	Not permitted less than 5 feet Protected less than 20 feet
A-1	II One-hour II-N III One-hour III-N IV-H.T. V One-hour V-N	Group A, Division 1 Occupancies are not allowed in these construction types.		
A-2 A-2.1 A-3 A-4	I-F.R. II-F.R. III One-hour IV-H.T.	Four-hour N/C	Four-hour N/C less than 5 feet Two-hour N/C less than 20 feet One-hour N/C less than 40 feet NR, N/C elsewhere	Not permitted less than 5 feet Protected less than 20 feet
A-2 A-2.1[2]	II One-hour	Two-hour N/C less than 10 feet One-hour N/C elsewhere	Same as bearing except NR, N/C 40 feet or greater	Not permitted less than 5 feet Protected less than 10 feet
A-2 A-2.1[2]	II-N III-N V-N	Group A, Divisions 2 and 2.1 Occupancies are not allowed in these construction types.		
A-2 A-2.1[2]	V One-hour	Two-hour less than 10 feet One-hour elsewhere	Same as bearing	Not permitted less than 5 feet Protected less than 10 feet
A-3	II One-hour	Two-hour N/C less than 5 feet One-hour N/C elsewhere	Same as bearing except NR, N/C 40 feet or greater	Not permitted less than 5 feet Protected less than 10 feet
A-3	II-N	Two-hour N/C less than 5 feet One-hour N/C less than 20 feet NR, N/C elsewhere	Same as bearing	Not permitted less than 5 feet Protected less than 10 feet
A-3	III-N	Four-hour N/C	Four-hour N/C less than 5 feet Two-hour N/C less than 20 feet One-hour N/C less than 40 feet NR, N/C elsewhere	Not permitted less than 5 feet Protected less than 20 feet
A-3	V One-hour	Two-hour less than 5 feet One-hour elsewhere	Same as bearing	Not permitted less than 5 feet Protected less than 10 feet
A-3	V-N	Two-hour less than 5 feet One-hour less than 20 feet NR elsewhere	Same as bearing	Not permitted less than 5 feet Protected less than 10 feet
A-4	II One-hour	One-hour N/C	Same as bearing except NR, N/C 40 feet or greater	Protected less than 10 feet
A-4	II-N	One-hour N/C less than 10 feet NR, N/C elsewhere	Same as bearing	Protected less than 10 feet
A-4	III-N	Four-hour N/C	Four-hour N/C less than 5 feet Two-hour N/C less than 20 feet One-hour N/C less than 40 feet NR, N/C elsewhere	Not permitted less than 5 feet Protected less than 10 feet
A-4	V One-hour	One-hour	Same as bearing	Protected less than 10 feet
A-4	V-N	One-hour less than 10 feet NR elsewhere	Same as bearing	Protected less than 10 feet
B, F-1, M, S-1, S-3	I-F.R. II-F.R. III One-hour III-N IV-H.T.	Four-hour N/C less than 5 feet Two-hour N/C elsewhere	Four-hour N/C less than 5 feet Two-hour N/C less than 20 feet One-hour N/C less than 40 feet NR, N/C elsewhere	Not permitted less than 5 feet Protected less than 20 feet
B F-1 M S-1, S-3	II One-hour	One-hour N/C	Same as bearing except NR, N/C 40 feet or greater	Not permitted less than 5 feet Protected less than 10 feet
B F-1 M S-1, S-3	II-N[3]	One-hour N/C less than 20 feet NR, N/C elsewhere	Same as bearing	Not permitted less than 5 feet Protected less than 10 feet
B F-1 M S-1, S-3	V One-hour	One-hour	Same as bearing	Not permitted less than 5 feet Protected less than 10 feet
B F-1 M S-1, S-3	V-N	One-hour less than 20 feet NR elsewhere	Same as bearing	Not permitted less than 5 feet Protected less than 10 feet

(Continued)

TABLE 5-A—EXTERIOR WALL AND OPENING PROTECTION BASED ON LOCATION ON PROPERTY FOR ALL CONSTRUCTION TYPES[1,2,3]—(Continued)

OCCUPANCY GROUP[4]	CONSTRUCTION TYPE	EXTERIOR WALLS Bearing	EXTERIOR WALLS Nonbearing	OPENINGS[5]
		Distances are measured to property lines (see Section 503).		
		× 304.8 for mm		
E-1 E-2[6] E-3[6]	I-F.R. II-F.R. III One-hour III-N IV-H.T.	Four-hour N/C	Four-hour N/C less than 5 feet Two-hour N/C less than 20 feet One-hour N/C less than 40 feet NR, N/C elsewhere	Not permitted less than 5 feet Protected less than 20 feet
	II One-hour	Two-hour N/C less than 5 feet One-hour N/C elsewhere	Same as bearing except NR, N/C 40 feet or greater	Not permitted less than 5 feet Protected less than 10 feet
	II-N	Two-hour N/C less than 5 feet One-hour N/C less than 10 feet NR, N/C elsewhere	Same as bearing	Not permitted less than 5 feet Protected less than 10 feet
	V One-hour	Two-hour less than 5 feet One-hour elsewhere	Same as bearing	Not permitted less than 5 feet Protected less than 10 feet
	V-N	Two-hour less than 5 feet One-hour less than 10 feet NR elsewhere	Same as bearing	Not permitted less than 5 feet Protected less than 10 feet
F-2 S-2	I-F.R. II-F.R. III One-hour III-N IV-H.T.	Four-hour N/C less than 5 feet Two-hour N/C elsewhere	Four-hour N/C less than 5 feet Two-hour N/C less than 20 feet One-hour N/C less than 40 feet NR, N/C elsewhere	Not permitted less than 3 feet Protected less than 20 feet
	II One-hour	One-hour N/C	Same as bearing NR, N/C 40 feet or greater	Not permitted less than 5 feet Protected less than 10 feet
	II-N[3]	One-hour N/C less than 5 feet NR, N/C elsewhere	Same as bearing	Not permitted less than 5 feet Protected less than 10 feet
	V One-hour	One-hour	Same as bearing	Not permitted less than 5 feet Protected less than 10 feet
	V-N	One-hour less than 5 feet NR elsewhere	Same as bearing	Not permitted less than 5 feet Protected less than 10 feet
H-1[2,3]	I-F.R. II-F.R.	Four-hour N/C	NR N/C	Not restricted[3]
	II One-hour	One-hour N/C	NR N/C	Not restricted[3]
	II-N	NR N/C	Same as bearing	Not restricted[3]
	III One-hour III-N IV-H.T. V One-hour V-N	Group H, Division 1 Occupancies are not allowed in buildings of these construction types.		
H-2[2,3] H-3[2,3] H-4[3] H-6 H-7	I-F.R. II-F.R. III One-hour III-N IV-H.T.	Four-hour N/C	Four-hour N/C less than 5 feet Two-hour N/C less than 10 feet One-hour N/C less than 40 feet NR, N/C elsewhere	Not permitted less than 5 feet Protected less than 20 feet
	II One-hour	Four-hour N/C less than 5 feet Two-hour N/C less than 10 feet One-hour N/C elsewhere	Four-hour N/C less than 5 feet Two-hour N/C less than 10 feet One-hour N/C less than 20 feet NR, N/C elsewhere	Not permitted less than 5 feet Protected less than 20 feet
	II-N	Four-hour N/C less than 5 feet Two-hour N/C less than 10 feet One-hour N/C less than 20 feet NR, N/C elsewhere	Same as bearing	Not permitted less than 5 feet Protected less than 20 feet
	V One-hour	Four-hour less than 5 feet Two-hour less than 10 feet One-hour elsewhere	Same as bearing	Not permitted less than 5 feet Protected less than 20 feet
	V-N	Four-hour less than 5 feet Two-hour less than 10 feet One-hour less than 20 feet NR elsewhere	Same as bearing	Not permitted less than 5 feet Protected less than 20 feet

(Continued)

From the Uniform Building Code, ©1997, ICBO

TABLE 5-A—EXTERIOR WALL AND OPENING PROTECTION BASED ON LOCATION ON PROPERTY FOR ALL CONSTRUCTION TYPES[1,2,3]—(Continued)

OCCUPANCY GROUP[4]	CONSTRUCTION TYPE	EXTERIOR WALLS		OPENINGS[5]
		Bearing	Nonbearing	
		Distances are measured to property lines (see Section 503).		
		× 304.8 for mm		
H-5[2]	I-F.R. II-F.R. III One-hour III-N IV-H.T.	Four-hour N/C	Four-hour N/C less than 40 feet One-hour N/C less than 60 feet NR, N/C elsewhere	Protected less than 60 feet
	II One-hour	One-hour N/C	Same as bearing, except NR, N/C 60 feet or greater	Protected less than 60 feet
	II-N	One-hour N/C less than 60 feet NR, N/C elsewhere	Same as bearing	Protected less than 60 feet
	V One-hour	One-hour	Same as bearing	Protected less than 60 feet
	V-N	One-hour less than 60 feet NR elsewhere	Same as bearing	Protected less than 60 feet
I-1.1 I-1.2 I-2 I-3	I-F.R. II-F.R.	Four-hour N/C	Four-hour N/C less than 5 feet Two-hour N/C less than 20 feet One-hour N/C less than 40 feet NR, N/C elsewhere	Not permitted less than 5 feet Protected less than 20 feet
I-1.1 I-1.2 I-3[2]	II One-hour	Two-hour N/C less than 5 feet One-hour N/C elsewhere	Same as bearing except NR, N/C 40 feet or greater	Not permitted less than 5 feet Protected less than 10 feet
	V One-hour	Two-hour less than 5 feet One-hour elsewhere	Same as bearing	Not permitted less than 5 feet Protected less than 10 feet
I-1.1 I-1.2 I-2 I-3	II-N III-N V-N	These occupancies are not allowed in buildings of these construction types.[7]		
I-3	IV-H.T.	Group I, Division 3 Occupancies are not allowed in buildings of this construction type.		
I-1.1 I-1.2 I-2 I-3	III One-hour	Four-hour N/C	Same as bearing except NR, N/C 40 feet or greater	Not permitted less than 5 feet Protected less than 20 feet
I-1.1 I-1.2 I-2	IV-H.T.	Four-hour N/C	Same as bearing except NR, N/C 40 feet or greater	Not permitted less than 5 feet Protected less than 20 feet
I-2	II One-hour	One-hour N/C	Same as bearing except NR, N/C 40 feet or greater	Not permitted less than 5 feet Protected less than 10 feet
	V One-hour	One-hour	Same as bearing	Not permitted less than 5 feet Protected less than 10 feet
R-1	I-F.R. II-F.R. III One-hour III-N IV-H.T.	Four-hour N/C less than 3 feet Two-hour N/C elsewhere	Four-hour N/C less than 3 feet Two-hour N/C less than 20 feet One-hour N/C less than 40 feet NR, N/C elsewhere	Not permitted less than 3 feet Protected less than 20 feet
	II One-hour	One-hour N/C	Same as bearing except NR, N/C 40 feet or greater	Not permitted less than 5 feet
	II-N	One-hour N/C less than 5 feet NR, N/C elsewhere	Same as bearing	Not permitted less than 5 feet
	V One-hour	One-hour	Same as bearing	Not permitted less than 5 feet
	V-N	One-hour less than 5 feet NR elsewhere	Same as bearing	Not permitted less than 5 feet
R-3	I-F.R. II-F.R. III One-hour III-N IV-H.T.	Four-hour N/C	Four-hour N/C less than 3 feet Two-hour N/C less than 20 feet One-hour N/C less than 40 feet NR, N/C elsewhere	Not permitted less than 3 feet Protected less than 20 feet
	II One-hour	One-hour N/C	Same as bearing except NR, N/C 40 feet or greater	Not permitted less than 3 feet
	II-N	One-hour N/C less than 3 feet NR, N/C elsewhere	Same as bearing	Not permitted less than 3 feet
	V One-hour	One-hour	Same as bearing	Not permitted less than 3 feet
	V-N	One-hour less than 3 feet NR elsewhere	Same as bearing	Not permitted less than 3 feet

(Continued)

From the Uniform Building Code, ©1997, ICBO

TABLE 5-A—EXTERIOR WALL AND OPENING PROTECTION BASED ON LOCATION ON PROPERTY FOR ALL CONSTRUCTION TYPES[1,2,3]—(Continued)

OCCUPANCY GROUP[4]	CONSTRUCTION TYPE	EXTERIOR WALLS		OPENINGS[5]
		Bearing	Nonbearing	
		Distances are measured to property lines (see Section 503).		
		× 304.8 for mm		
S-4	I-F.R. II-F.R. II One-hour II-N[3]	One-hour N/C less than 10 feet NR, N/C elsewhere	Same as bearing	Not permitted less than 5 feet Protected less than 10 feet
	III One-hour III-N IV-H.T. V One-hour V-N	Group S, Division 4 open parking garages are not permitted in these types of construction.		
S-5	I-F.R. II-F.R. III One-hour III-N IV-H.T.	Four-hour N/C less than 5 feet Two-hour N/C elsewhere	Four-hour N/C less than 5 feet Two-hour N/C less than 20 feet One-hour N/C less than 40 feet NR, N/C elsewhere	Not permitted less than 5 feet Protected less than 20 feet
	II One-hour	One-hour N/C	Same as bearing except NR, N/C 40 feet or greater	Not permitted less than 5 feet Protected less than 20 feet
	II-N[3]	One-hour N/C less than 20 feet NR, N/C elsewhere	Same as bearing	Not permitted less than 5 feet Protected less than 20 feet
	V One-hour	One-hour	Same as bearing	Not permitted less than 5 feet Protected less than 20 feet
	V-N[3]	One-hour less than 20 feet NR elsewhere	Same as bearing	Not permitted less than 5 feet Protected less than 20 feet
U-1[3]	I-F.R. II-F.R. III One-hour III-N IV-H.T.	Four-hour N/C	Four-hour N/C less than 3 feet Two-hour N/C less than 20 feet One-hour N/C less than 40 feet NR, N/C elsewhere	Not permitted less than 3 feet Protected less than 20 feet
	II One-hour	One-hour N/C	Same as bearing except NR, N/C 40 feet or greater	Not permitted less than 3 feet
	V One-hour	One-hour	Same as bearing	Not permitted less than 3 feet
	II-N[2]	One-hour N/C less than 3 feet[3] NR, N/C elsewhere	Same as bearing	Not permitted less than 3 feet
	V-N	One-hour less than 3 feet[3] NR elsewhere	Same as bearing	Not permitted less than 3 feet
U-2	All	Not regulated		

N/C — Noncombustible.
NR — Nonrated.
H.T. — Heavy timber.
F.R. — Fire resistive.

[1]See Section 503 for types of walls affected and requirements covering percentage of openings permitted in exterior walls. For walls facing streets, yards and public ways, see also Section 601.5.

[2]For additional restrictions, see Chapters 3 and 6.

[3]For special provisions and exceptions, see also Section 503.4.

[4]See Table 3-A for a description of each occupancy type.

[5]Openings requiring protection in exterior walls shall be protected by a fire assembly having at least a three-fourths-hour fire-protection rating.

[6]Group E, Divisions 2 and 3 Occupancies having an occupant load of not more than 20 may have exterior wall and opening protection as required for Group R, Division 3 Occupancies.

[7]See Section 308.2.1, Exception 3.

From the Uniform Building Code, ©1997, ICBO

Index

Essential Code Resources

. . . from ICB

1997 Fire and Life Safety Workbook

This study aid is an essential reference for understanding the fire- and life-safety provisions in Volume 1 of the 1997 *Uniform Building Code* (UBC). Completely revised and updated to the 1997 UBC, this comprehensive workbook contains numerous illustrations that clarify code provisions and is an excellent resource for classroom use or self-study.

Over 600 pages in length, the workbook contains 13 lessons which include numerous study questions at the end of each lesson to accurately measure the reader's level of knowledge.

Per copy $35.00
Item No. 221W97

UBC Field Inspection Workbook

Never before has there been such a comprehensive workbook published by ICBO for studying the provisions of the 1994 *Uniform Building Code* (UBC). Divided into 12 sessions, this workbook focuses on the UBC combustible construction requirements for the inspection of wood-framed construction.

All study sessions contain specific learning objectives, a list of statements and questions summarizing the key points for study, illustrations representing respective code provisions, and quizzes designed to assess your retention of technical knowledge. The *UBC Field Inspection Workbook* is designed for independent study to allow you to complete the study program at your own pace. *(506 pages)*

Per copy $37.95
Item No. 202W94

1997 UBC Workbook: A Code Companion

Completely revised with hundreds of new illustrations and points of study, this workbook is designed for independent study or use with instructor-led programs based on Volume 1 of the 1997 UBC. This extensive study guide contains 18 learning lessons, each with key objectives, illustrations and study questions. The *UBC Workbook: A Code Companion* is a valuable resource for anyone wanting to enhance their understanding and knowledge of the UBC.

Nearly 600 pages in length, this publication contains essential information helpful to architects, designers, contractors, plans examiners and inspectors.

Per copy $32.00
Item No. 215W97

Illustrated Guide to Conventional Construction Provisions of the UBC

This comprehensive guide and commentary provides detailed explanations of the conventional construction provisions contained in Chapter 23 of the 1994 UBC Code text, descriptive discussion and illustrated drawings are used to convey the prescriptive provisions related to wood-framed construction.

This publication has nearly 150 pages of essential information helpful to those involved in design, plan review or inspection of wood-framed structures. *(193 pages)*

Per copy $27.50
Item No. 210W94

Place Your Order Today!
Phone (800) 284-4406
Fax (562) 692-3853

International Conference of Building Officials
www.icbo.org

Practical References for Builders

Contractor's Guide to QuickBooks Pro

This user-friendly manual walks you through QuickBooks Pro's detailed setup procedure and explains step-by-step how to create a first-rate accounting system. You'll learn in days, rather than weeks, how to use QuickBooks Pro to get your contracting business organized, with simple, fast accounting procedures. On the CD included with the book you'll find a full version of QuickBooks Pro, good for 25 uses, with a QuickBooks Pro file preconfigured for a construction company (you drag it over onto your computer and plug in your own company's data). You'll also get a complete estimating program, including a database, and a job costing program that lets you export your estimates to QuickBooks Pro. It even includes many useful construction forms to use in your business. **320 pages, 8¹/₂ x 11, $39.75**

Contractor's Index to the 1997 *Uniform Building Code*

Finally, there's a common-sense index that helps you quickly and easily find the section you're looking for in the *UBC*. It lists topics under the names builders actually use in construction. Best of all, it gives the full section number and the actual page in the UBC where you'll find it. If you need to know the requirements for windows in exit access corridor walls, just look under *Windows*™. You'll find the requirements you need are in Section 1004.3.4.3.2.2 in the *UBC* — on page 115. This practical index was written by a former builder and building inspector who knows the *UBC* from both perspectives. If you hate to spend valuable time hunting through pages of fine print for the information you need, this is the book for you. **192 pages, 8¹/₂ x 11, paperback edition, $26.00**
192 pages, 8¹/₂ x 11, loose-leaf edition, $29.00

Uniform Building Code, Vol. 1

The official codebook you'll need for constant reference during 1999. Here you'll find the safety and structural provisions you need to pass inspection and build to code. Hundreds of charts, tables, and equations help you see what the code requires. Published by the International Conference of Building Officials, this is the code adopted by most western states.
464 pages, 8¹/₂ x 11, paperback edition, $61.25
464 pages, 8¹/₂ x 11, loose-leaf edition, $70.45

CD Estimator

If your computer has *Windows*™ and a CD-ROM drive, *CD Estimator* puts at your fingertips 85,000 construction costs for new construction, remodeling, renovation & insurance repair, electrical, plumbing, HVAC and painting. You'll also have the *National Estimator* program — a stand-alone estimating program for *Windows*™ that *Remodeling* magazine called a "computer wiz." Quarterly cost updates are available at no charge on the Internet. To help you create professional-looking estimates, the disk includes over 40 construction estimating and bidding forms in a format that's perfect for nearly any word processing or spreadsheet program for *Windows*™. And to top it off, a 70-minute interactive video teaches you how to use this CD-ROM to estimate construction costs. **CD Estimator is $68.50**

Markup & Profit: A Contractor's Guide

In order to succeed in a construction business, you have to be able to price your jobs to cover all labor, material and overhead expenses, and make a decent profit. The problem is knowing what markup to use. You don't want to lose jobs because you charge too much, and you don't want to work for free because you've charged too little. If you know how to calculate markup, you can apply it to your job costs to find the right sales price for your work. This book gives you tried and tested formulas, with step-by-step instructions and easy-to-follow examples, so you can easily figure the markup that's right for your business. Includes a CD-ROM with forms and checklists for your use. **320 pages, 8¹/₂ x 11, $32.50**

Basic Lumber Engineering for Builders

Beam and lumber requirements for many jobs aren't always clear, especially with changing building codes and lumber products. Most of the time you rely on your own "rules of thumb" when figuring spans or lumber engineering. This book can help you fill the gap between what you can find in the building code span tables and what you need to pay a certified engineer to do. With its large, clear illustrations and examples, this book shows you how to figure stresses for pre-engineered wood or wood structural members, how to calculate loads, and how to design your own girders, joists and beams. Included FREE with the book — an easy-to-use version of NorthBridge Software's *Wood Beam Sizing* program.
272 pages, 8¹/₂ x 11, $38.00

 Craftsman Book Company
6058 Corte del Cedro
P.O. Box 6500
Carlsbad, CA 92018

☎ 24 hour order line
1-800-829-8123
Fax (760) 438-0398

Name _____

Company _____

Address _____

City/State/Zip _____
◯ This is a residence

Total enclosed_____(In California add 7.25% tax)
We pay shipping when your check covers your order in full.

In A Hurry?
We accept phone orders charged to your
◯ Visa, ◯ MasterCard, ◯ Discover or ◯ American Express

Card#_____

Exp. date_____Initials_____

Tax Deductible: Treasury regulations make these references tax deductible when used in your work. Save the canceled check or charge card statement as your receipt.

10-Day Money Back Guarantee

◯ 38.00 Basic Lumber Engineering for Builders
◯ 68.50 CD Estimator
◯ 39.75 Contractor's Guide to QuickBooks Pro
◯ 26.00 Contractor's Index to the *UBC* — *Paperback*
◯ 29.00 Contractor's Index to the *UBC* — *Loose-leaf*
◯ 32.50 Markup & Profit: A Contractor's Guide
◯ 61.25 *1997 Uniform Building Code*, Vol 1 — *Paperback*
◯ 70.45 *1997 Uniform Building Code*, Vol 1 — *Loose-leaf*
◯ 39.00 Contractor's Guide to the Building Code Revised
◯ FREE Full Color Catalog

Prices subject to change without notice

Order online http://www.craftsman-book.com

Free on the Internet! Download any of Craftsman's estimating costbooks for a 30-day free trial! http://costbook.com

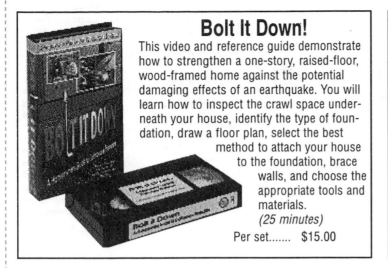

Bolt It Down!

This video and reference guide demonstrate how to strengthen a one-story, raised-floor, wood-framed home against the potential damaging effects of an earthquake. You will learn how to inspect the crawl space underneath your house, identify the type of foundation, draw a floor plan, select the best method to attach your house to the foundation, brace walls, and choose the appropriate tools and materials.
(25 minutes)
Per set....... $15.00

Analysis of Revisions to the 1997 Uniform Codes™

The *Analysis of Revisions to the 1997 Uniform Codes*™ discusses the changes included in the 1997 editions of the *Uniform Building Code*™, Volumes 1, 2 and 3; *Uniform Mechanical Code*™; *Uniform Fire Code*™; *Uniform Administrative Code*™; *Uniform Code for Building Conservation*™; and *Uniform Housing Code*™.

	Members	Nonmembers
Per copy	$12.25	$16.50
Item No. 109S97		

Craftsman Book Company
6058 Corte del Cedro
P.O. Box 6500
Carlsbad, CA 92018

☎ 24 hour order line
1-800-829-8123
Fax (760) 438-0398

Name

Company

Address

City/State/Zip
○ This is a residence

Total enclosed_____(In California add 7.25% tax)

We pay shipping when your check covers your order in full.

In A Hurry?
We accept phone orders charged to your
○ Visa, ○ MasterCard, ○ Discover or ○ American Express

Card#_____

Exp. date_____Initials_____

Tax Deductible: Treasury regulations make these references tax deductible when used in your work. Save the canceled check or charge card statement as your receipt.

10-Day Money Back Guarantee

○ 38.00 Basic Lumber Engineering for Builders
○ 68.50 CD Estimator
○ 39.75 Contractor's Guide to QuickBooks Pro
○ 26.00 Contractor's Index to the *UBC — Paperback*
○ 29.00 Contractor's Index to the *UBC — Loose-leaf*
○ 32.50 Markup & Profit: A Contractor's Guide
○ 61.25 *1997 Uniform Building Code,* Vol 1 — *Paperback*
○ 70.45 *1997 Uniform Building Code,* Vol 1 — *Loose-leaf*
○ 39.00 Contractor's Guide to the Building Code Revised
○ FREE Full Color Catalog
Prices subject to change without notice

Order online http://www.craftsman-book.com
Free on the Internet! Download any of Craftsman's estimating costbooks for a 30-day free trial! http://costbook.com

---

Mail This Card Today
For a Free Full Color Catalog

Over 100 books, annual cost guides and estimating software packages at your fingertips with information that can save you time and money. Here you'll find information on carpentry, contracting, estimating, remodeling electrical work, and plumbing.

All items come with an unconditional 10-day money-back guarantee. If they don't save you money, mail them back for a full refund.

Name

Company

Address

City/State/Zip

Craftsman Book Company / 6058 Corte del Cedro / P.O. Box 6500 / Carlsbad, CA 92018

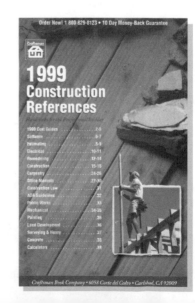

BUSINESS REPLY MAIL
FIRST-CLASS MAIL PERMIT NO. 81 WHITTIER, CA

POSTAGE WILL BE PAID BY THE ADDRESSEE

ATTN: ORDER DEPT
INTERNATIONAL CONFERENCE
OF BUILDING OFFICIALS
5360 WORKMAN MILL RD
WHITTIER CA 90601-9904

BUSINESS REPLY MAIL
FIRST CLASS MAIL PERMIT NO. 271 CARLSBAD, CA

POSTAGE WILL BE PAID BY ADDRESSEE

 Craftsman Book Company
6058 Corte del Cedro
P.O. Box 6500
Carlsbad, CA 92018-9974

BUSINESS REPLY MAIL
FIRST CLASS MAIL PERMIT NO. 271 CARLSBAD, CA

POSTAGE WILL BE PAID BY ADDRESSEE

 Craftsman Book Company
6058 Corte del Cedro
P.O. Box 6500
Carlsbad, CA 92018-9974